MW01484656

Engines of Redemption

R. SCOTT HUFFARD JR.

Engines of Redemption

Railroads and the Reconstruction of
Capitalism in the New South

The University of North Carolina Press *Chapel Hill*

This book was published with the assistance of the Authors Fund of the University of North Carolina Press.

© 2019 The University of North Carolina Press
All rights reserved
Set in Arno Pro by Westchester Publishing Services
Manufactured in the United States of America

The University of North Carolina Press has been a member of the Green Press Initiative since 2003.

Library of Congress Cataloging-in-Publication Data
Names: Huffard, R. Scott, Jr., author.
Title: Engines of redemption : railroads and the reconstruction of
    capitalism in the New South / R. Scott Huffard Jr.
Description: Chapel Hill : University of North Carolina Press, [2019] |
    Includes bibliographical references and index.
Identifiers: LCCN 2019004397 | ISBN 9781469652801 (cloth : alk. paper) |
    ISBN 9781469652818 (pbk : alk. paper) | ISBN 9781469652825 (ebook)
Subjects: LCSH: Railroads—Southern States—History—19th century. |
    Capitalism—Southern States—History—19th century. | Southern States—
    Economic conditions—19th century. | Southern States—Race relations—
    History—19th century.
Classification: LCC HE2761 .H84 2019 | DDC 385.0976/09034—dc23
    LC record available at https://lccn.loc.gov/2019004397

Cover illustrations: (Front) Thomas Nast, *Our Standard (Gauge)
Adopted All Over the Union* (courtesy of the Library of Congress Prints and
Photographs Division, LC-USZ62-102101); (back) William Jasper Stimson,
Train Wreck of Bostian Bridge, Iredell County, N.C., 27 August 1891
(courtesy of the State Archives of North Carolina, N.88.9.12).

Portions of this book were previously published in a different form. Chapter 4
appeared as "Infected Rails: Yellow Fever and Southern Railroads," *Journal of
Southern History* 79, no. 1 (February 2013): 79–113. Portions of chapter 5 appeared
in "Ghosts, Wreckers, and Rotten Ties: The 1891 Train Wreck at Bostian's Bridge,"
Southern Cultures 20, no. 2 (Summer 2014): 25–39. All material is used here
with permission.

For my parents

Contents

Figures and Graph

Acknowledgments

Like a rambling rail car, this book has been moving down main lines and unwanted sidetrack diversions for almost a decade now. When I was an undergrad, the outstanding history faculty at Penn State first stoked my interest in the nineteenth century, and this book had its origins in a number of graduate seminars at the University of Florida. I am grateful to my many wonderful professors I found in Gainesville. My advisor Sean Adams encouraged me as my interests shifted from coal mining to railroads and capitalism, and I am grateful for how he always pushed me to aim high with my research. I was lucky to find a committee that both sustained my project's grounding in the U.S. South and prodded me to look at the bigger picture. It is probably Bill Link's fault that I ended up as a southern historian, and the first piece of this project was born in one of his southern history research seminars. His friendship and the robust southern history cohort he built at Florida (and his weekly racquetball matches) served as excellent motivators as I found my way in this profession. Paul Ortiz always pushed me to consider labor history and first pointed me toward the fascinating story of Railroad Bill. Sheryl Kroen was enthusiastic about the project from the start, and she helped pull the project in interesting directions and to draw comparisons between the South's experience with capitalism and that of France and Europe. Pamela Gilbert's feedback similarly reminded me of the importance of the railroad in Victorian England.

I consider myself lucky to have worked with such a strong cohort at the University of Florida. When I arrived in Gainesville as a fresh-faced young graduate student, older students quickly took me under their wings, and I would like to think this spirit of collegiality and cooperation continued throughout my time there. Formal and informal conversations with graduate students in seminars and in less distinguished venues like the Salty Dog and the Top were also invaluable. Gainesville was an exciting place to spend my grad school years, and I am grateful for the camaraderie from friends like Mike Brandon, Angela Diaz, Jim Broomall, Ben Miller, Jessica Taylor, Matt Hall, Tim Fritz, Clay Cooper, Scott McPherson, Allison Fredette, and more, as we cheered on the high-flying Gator football team (and drew inspiration from Tim Tebow's 2008 "Promise Speech"), explored scuzzy punk shows downtown, biked on old rail trails, and sampled offerings from the city's burgeoning craft beer scene.

I would also like to thank my current institution, Lees-McRae College, both for providing me with a rewarding and exciting position in the Blue Ridge Mountains and for the professional development support to help get this book over the finish line. Teaching a wide range of courses here has certainly improved the manuscript, and though students in my classes are probably all tired of hearing me talk about railroads, they have influenced this final product more than they know. As I worked to adjust to my new role as an assistant professor, my division chair, Ken Craig, and colleague Michael Joslin were excellent mentors and guides. Working with colleagues like Robert Turpin, Kevin Keck, and Matthew Wimberley, who all have been active in writing and publishing works of their own, has also provided a fertile atmosphere for my research activities.

Institutional support from a wide range of venues has been critical. Research grants from the Newberry Library, North Caroliniana Society, Filson Historical Society, University of Florida History Graduate Society, and University of Florida History Department all helped provide the financial support to complete the necessary archival research for this project. Though time in the archives is, by its nature, a solitary endeavor, I would like to thank companions on the road and those who have given me a place to crash while researching, or who at least served as helpful local guides for when the archive closed. In particular, Blake Renfro, Melissa Houle, Mike Brandon, and Jim Broomall helped provide housing during trips. Of course, this project would not be complete without the often-invisible labors of many others. The staff at countless libraries and archives have been welcoming and helpful, and baristas at the coffee shops I have haunted—from Volta in Gainesville to Espresso News and Mountain Grounds in western North Carolina—witnessed the writing and revision of much of this manuscript, and I am grateful for the writing space and caffeine their shops have provided.

This work is much stronger due to the engagement with my work from a wide range of scholars, and I am appreciative of the input from many sources. The University of North Carolina Press has been a welcoming home for this project. My editor, Chuck Grench, has been excited about this project from the start. He and his staff have been outstanding in showing this first-time author the ropes. The revision process has produced a much stronger manuscript, and I am thankful for the substantive critiques and feedback from the two anonymous readers. Feedback from the audience at meetings of organizations like the Business History Conference, Southern Historical Association, Southern Industrialization Project, and Harvard Conference on the History of Capitalism helped sharpen my analysis at critical points in my writing. Perhaps even more invaluable are the friendships and informal connections I have made across the historical profession. I am thankful for conference friends like Matt Stanley, Judkin Browning, Bob Hutton, Angela Riotto, and countless others. People who have read and commented on various parts of the project in either formal or informal venues helped guide and shape the final product. Many have seen parts or portions of this book, but I would especially like to thank Scott Reynolds Nelson, Paul M. Renfro, Kate Jewell, Matthew Wimberley, Robert Turpin, and the scholars who volunteered their time and energies for the Business History Dissertation Colloquium.

Finally, none of this would have been possible without the backing my family has provided me. My parents encouraged me to follow my interests and to pursue graduate school and this career in the first place, and their support has been invaluable.

Abbreviations

A&F	Atlanta & Florida Railroad
A&NC	Atlantic & North Carolina Railroad
C&O	Chesapeake & Ohio Railroad
CF&YV	Cape Fear & Yadkin Valley Railroad
GS&F	Georgia Southern & Florida Railroad
IC	Illinois Central Railroad
L&N	Louisville & Nashville Railroad
NOStL&C	New Orleans, St. Louis and Chicago Railroad
NC RR	North Carolina Railroad
PRR	Pennsylvania Railroad
R&D	Richmond & Danville Railroad
SRSC	Southern Railway Security Company
V&M	Vicksburg & Meridian Railroad

Engines of Redemption

Introduction

A System Grand and Harmonious

Type of the modern—emblem of motion and power—pulse of the continent.
—Walt Whitman, "To a Locomotive in Winter"

The train lurched forward. Bells clanged, and the engine gained momentum, roaring out of the station into the dark and dreary Louisiana night. The passengers slumbering in the trailing cars could only dream of what transpired in the cab of the engine, where Hunt McCaleb, a journalist and self-described amateur, had climbed aboard for a brief glimpse of the life of an engineer. The midnight mail train was soon flying along the 200-mile route between Meridian and New Orleans. The speed of the train hit sixty miles per hour, and conversation between the three men in the cab died. Out the window, McCaleb could see dense forests, interspersed with water tanks, lonely way stations, red and white signal lights, and the other usual landmarks of a rail corridor fly by. Struck by the sublimity of the moment, McCaleb lost control of his emotions and later wrote that he was enchanted with "the magic spell that overcomes the uninitiated." "No one who has not had the experience can ever realize or appreciate the sensations produced by riding on an engine," he argued. His thrills quickly turned to horrors, though. In his entranced state he had "visions of train wreckers galore"—criminals who deliberately wrecked trains to exact a grudge—and he recalled "the hundred wrecks he has read of caused by the negligence of a sleepy brakeman." With the train hurtling through the dark at such speeds, McCaleb knew there would be no time to brake for obstacles, and he gained new appreciation for the bravery of the nation's railroad engineers. Finally, the train slowed, and pulled into Meridian ahead of schedule, and as the travel companions departed the cab, the proud engineer patted engine no. 415 "with the affection a mother would have for her child."[1]

McCaleb's trip embodied the many processes that helped make the New South simultaneously exhilarating and horrifying. But at the time of this journey in 1892, there was nothing unique about the route on which he rode. Every night, trains rumbled down this track, carrying mail from New Orleans to Meridian, and their travels were the culmination of a number of extraordinary historical processes: from the organization of the Queen & Crescent Railroad Company, which joined the financial might of investors from England, New York, and New Orleans, to the careful plotting of the route by surveyors trekking through isolated bayous and swamps, to the backbreaking labor of work crews toiling to grade the road and lay down rails and ties, and finally to the engineering and construction work behind the steam-powered engine that could hit unrivaled speeds. The line was but one link in a network of iron rails that connected the Crescent City to Cincinnati and to northern cities far beyond. McCaleb dashed through the night thanks to pooled investments of capital, the managerial structures of the modern corporation, the labor of workers, coal-powered energy, and industrialized production. McCaleb's journey was more than just a train ride—it was the most direct contact imaginable with late-nineteenth-century capitalism.[2]

In the form of the railroad, the forces of capitalism that generated McCaleb's thrills transformed the entire South in the decades after the Civil War. The railroad was by no means new at this point. The technology arrived early in the region when South Carolina completed one of the nation's first lines in the 1820s, and a burst of construction in the 1850s integrated the region on the eve of secession.[3] But the slave economy had placed limits on the transformative power of the railroad in this era. Railroads built in the antebellum era were typically harnessed to local economic goals, and they lacked the systemic vision of later companies. State governments, and not private corporations, directly funded many of these lines. Gauges varied wildly from state to state, vast pockets of the South lacked any rail connections, and the region lagged behind the mileage of the North.[4] After Civil War and Reconstruction came a railroad revival, and from 1880 to 1890, the mileage of southern railroads almost doubled from 14,778 to 29,263, as the network grew at a rate that outpaced the rest of the nation's lines. By 1890, nine out of every ten southerners lived in a county with a railroad. These lines plugged the substantial gaps in the antebellum network, connecting once-isolated corners of the South to the world of the railroad. Along with adding new mileage, work crews improved already existing lines by speeding up service, matching gauges to northern standards, and fully integrating southern railroads to large national systems backed by northern and global capital. Consolidation inevitably followed expansion, and by the turn of the century, large corporations like the Illinois Central, Southern Railway, and Louisville & Nashville controlled the bulk of southern rail lines.[5] In 1880, Henry Grady was well on his way to becoming the unofficial spokesman for the New South when he marveled that a "system grand and harmonious" was coming into form, and indeed, few aspects of southern life would remain untouched by the growing rail network.[6]

The story of this railroad boom and the New South's transformation has often been told in sheer economic terms, by historians who tabulate numbers of railroad mileage, figures of economic growth, wage levels, freight rate fluctuations, and other numerical metrics. The new connections encouraged the growth of a southern manufacturing sector, based largely on textiles and steel, and encouraged extractive industries like coal and timber. The expanded network reoriented the geography of trade, dispersing business to country stores, channeling commerce away from ports to interior rail centers like Atlanta, and supplanting the primacy of rivers and steamboats. As Yankee capital and expertise fostered extractive industries that exploited southern raw materials, railroads bound the South to the North in a semicolonial relationship, and they tied southern farmers' fates even more closely to the whims of global markets. Railroads brought the modern corporation to the South—the new conglomerates like the Southern Railway were the largest companies the region had ever seen.[7]

Southern railroads also have played a starring role in histories of New South race relations and the onset of Jim Crow. Most famously, *Plessy v. Ferguson*, the Supreme Court case that enshrined the "separate but equal" doctrine that underpinned decades of segregation, was based on a legal challenge on a New Orleans rail line. Rail travel jumbled together southerners of different races and classes in intimate quarters, and these new railroads became critical sites of contestation. To codify the emerging customs of segregation on the ground, white southerners moved to segregate rail cars in a wave of new legislation in the 1880s and '90s. Scholars tracing the advance of segregation as a culture, as custom, and as a legal reality, and those following black resistance and protest against these laws, thus place heavy focus on the shifting developments in southern rail cars, which were the leading edge of the region-wide push for Jim Crow.[8] At least in the 1890s, this is typically a story of declension, ending in de jure segregation and the nadir of American race relations, but the railroad also played a key role in African American resistance and racial uplift. For black southerners, railroads were more than just sites of oppression and protest. They were also means of escape and empowering mobility, conduits for the Great Migration, providers of secure middle-class jobs, and inspirations for music and other forms of expression.[9]

These two approaches to the New South railroad—as a revolutionary agent of economic change and the prime battleground for racial conflict and segregation—provide points of departure for the two new tracks we explore in *Engines of Redemption*. First of all, *Engines of Redemption* moves beyond the rail car to analyze the New South's railroads as a cohesive network—Grady's "grand and harmonious system"—that integrated and connected the South through a capitalist means. Passenger travel was important, but southerners also experienced the railroad as a system, an interconnected network of rapid circulation that was something new and distinct from what came before it. This network was more than just a means of travel; it was a conveyor of disease, a target of violent robbers, a force of dramatic change in the countryside, a powerful and monopolistic corporation, and a builder and destroyer of towns. Moreover, a heavy focus on interactions within rail cars obscures larger historical forces at work, the infusion of the energies and motives of capitalism into the region via this railroad network. Decisions that brought railroads to certain areas or towns, policies about freight rates and quarantines, and purchases that could seal a corporation's fate were made in corporate boardrooms, in newspaper offices, and on Wall Street, and in the prominence of the rail car we have lost sight of the bigger picture and of who pulled the strings that directed the network. Simply put, I interrogate the railroad as a corporate entity and as a structure that directed, constrained, and revolutionized people's lives, and as way for white and black southerners to directly interact with the forces of capitalism rapidly altering the South and the nation.[10]

Second, I examine the railroad as an idea, a symbol, and a narrative device that described the advance of capitalism during a critical turning point for the South and the nation. The railroad's transformations always meant more than just the cold reckoning of an account book's ledger, or the staid tally of statistics in a trade journal. When explaining the dominance and persistence of capitalism, one must move beyond economics and turn to the mentalities, mores, and stories told about the system. And as a symbolic harbinger of the forces of industrial capital remaking nineteenth-century life, the railroad was without peer.[11] Few moments could match the exuberance of a town welcoming its first locomotive or the adventure of the first rail excursion through what once was wilderness. From the vantage point of a lonely depot, the arrival of a train could symbolize escape, a new beginning, a narrative break, or the glamour of cities and destinations far down the line. Songs romanticizing train travel and the hardships of railroad labor echoed from work camps to recording studios to airwaves far beyond. And in its idealized form, the experience of rail travel—seeing stunning panoramic views, traversing new landscapes, and moving at rapid speeds—fired the imaginations of travelers like few other experiences.[12] As the southern railroad system took shape in the

1880s and '90s, and as southerners rode the rails, invested capital in new railroad companies, shipped products to far-off destinations, and labored to build rail lines, the railroad came to represent capitalism itself in a way the Iron Horse had not before the Civil War.

Viewing the railroad as a force for connection and as a narrative of capitalist expansion helps us reassess the New South in light of the new, more critical histories of capitalism that have emerged in the past decade. Historians like Sven Beckert, Edward Baptist, Joshua Rothman, and Walter Johnson present the antebellum South as a land alive with the energy and turbulence of capitalism. Freewheeling land speculators, riverboat gamblers, and planters on the cotton frontier pushed the region into a central role in global capitalism. After the expropriation of Native peoples and rapid expansion of slavery, plantations in states like Louisiana and Alabama produced cotton that powered mills from Lowell to Lancashire. Developments on capitalism's periphery of cotton plantations had direct connection to events in the financial and industrial core. Vicious booms and busts, borne of reckless banks and out-of-control speculation in the Old Southwest, roiled the national economy, and the race to produce more cotton on plantations inspired many of industrial capitalism's innovations in labor management.[13] As scholars make renewed arguments for the capitalist nature of the Old South, an obvious question that follows is how we are to treat the New South. Do we present the New South as a warped form of capitalist development, a region traveling down a deviant path? Or is it a mere colony, serving up raw materials to the industrial North? And how do we square the various horrors of the New South with the allegedly empowering and democratic nature of capitalism?[14]

Many of these arguments about the capitalist nature of the New South economy hinge on definitions of capitalism, or differentiations between various forms of capitalism, but a focus on the railroad allows us to examine the impacts of key elements of capitalism, such as connections, circulation, standardization, rationalization, corporate consolidation, and movement directed by the profit motive. The railroad constitutes "capitalism in action," and tracing train stories and interactions with the railroad network allows us to examine capitalism as both an economic system *and a culture*, and to trace how southerners accommodated to, contested, adopted, and assimilated into the system.[15] Implicit in the denial of capitalism in the Old South was the Cold War–era assumption connecting capitalism to progress, democracy, and equality. If we are to take a more critical view of capitalism, and see the Old South as a site of capitalist disaster, it makes sense to see the New South not as an aberration, but as a function of untrammeled capitalism. Just as the calamities of the Old South can be blamed on global capitalism, the New South was a society pulsating with the powerful and dangerous forces of capitalism via the railroad, and a society in the process of completing a reconstruction of capitalism's values.[16]

The reconstruction of capitalism in the South was necessary, as it is clear that the upheavals of the Civil War and its aftermath decisively recast the region's role in global capitalism. The violence of war rendered the region's physical landscape an unruly ruin marked with the charred remnants of factories, fallow farms, twisted and warped iron ties, and plundered plantations. Emancipation wiped out the wealth stored in over four million slaves and ended the slave labor system that had proven so profitable to planters, traders, and industrialists. Observers ranging from Yankee troops to journalists to embittered ex-Confederates recognized that capitalism clearly was not operating the way it had before the war.[17] In the face of brutal resistance, freedmen and freedwomen sought to assert their political rights and secure an economic future for their families and communities, but the transition from enslaved to free wage labor was rocky, and many became mired in sharecropping arrangements that more resembled feudalism. Economic uncertainty dragged into the 1870s, as northern and European investors balked at the region's political turmoil, and the calamitous Panic of 1873 undid many of the gains of the immediate postwar period. Moreover, the wealth and confidence of the white elite that had once, and would soon again, run the region was in tatters. White men haunted by their crushed dreams of military glory and the ghosts of fallen comrades carried physical scars and bitter resentments toward Yankee occupiers and the newly empowered freedmen. White southerners wrote of a malaise, perpetual stagnation, or gloom that settled over the region. Political "redemption" of the region by violent white paramilitary groups may have heartened white elites, but it did little to resolve the question of how to rekindle the magic of capitalism in the South.[18]

For the self-styled "Redeemers" who took power after Reconstruction, the path out of this quagmire was along the gleaming steel track of the railroad. The men at the helms of the South's dozens of new railroads, "Bourbon" (pro-business redeemer) politicians, small-town boosters, and businessmen aggressively pushing for new connections recognized the power of the Iron Horse. The railroad, the nineteenth century's quintessential symbol of progress, helped these elites consolidate their power in a region in flux. At regional expositions and local railroad celebrations, and in their travel narratives and rhetoric in pamphlets and newspapers, boosters harnessed this symbolic power of the railroad to support their claims that a New South had risen. In an 1887 pamphlet, booster M. B. Hillyard articulated this link between rail-roads, capitalism, and regional redemption, arguing that the 14,000 new miles of railroad built since 1880 were "proof of development and of the confidence of the capitalists of the civilized world." "The logic of confidence in the South's progress is enunciated in the golden argument of capital, and is voiced in the fierce rhetoric of thunderous and clattering railroad trains," boasted the *Manufacturers' Record* in 1890.[19] In hitching their rule to the improved railroad network, these elites also linked the New South to the forces of capitalism. Their narrative was simple: railroads and capital would save the region and complete its recovery from the Civil War.

On the surface, and despite the fact that it came from a minority of the population, this story seemed to hold up, and like other narratives of capital-ism, the New South story held real power. It gave legitimacy to the Bourbon conservative white Democratic leadership of the region, and the message of progress beat back systemic critiques from the Populists, the Knights of Labor, and African Americans contesting new segregation regimes.[20] It se-duced northern politicians and investors, who invested economically in the region but abruptly pulled back from the efforts at social change witnessed during Reconstruction and subsequently left southern politicians to their own devices.[21] Sectional reconciliation thus took place on terms dictated by the white South, and the New South era saw the rise of new legends about the southern past, from the notion of an Old South filled with moonlight, mag-nolias, and happy slaves to the interpretation of Reconstruction as an era of corrupt black rule and military occupation.[22] The New South story also sup-ported the project of reestablishing white supremacy and of rebuilding the racial order challenged by emancipation and Reconstruction. The railroad revival therefore moved in tandem with horrific racial violence, a surge in lynchings, and legal efforts to institute Jim Crow segregation. Finally, the myth gave outsized power to the ascendant railroad corporations by forestalling seri-ous attempts at regulation or improving conditions for workers.[23]

The New South boosters and their northern allies told a compelling story about the railroad, capitalism, and progress, but the inevitable moments of crisis and doubt, like McCaleb's visions of disaster, raised serious questions and threatened to shatter this nexus. What if the train flying sixty miles per hour through a dark forest was doomed to a fiery wreck? What if the railroad corporation was an agent of chaos, rather than a harbinger of order? And what if capitalism was not the regional savior its boosters made it out to be? Recent histories of capitalism have done more than just highlight the impor-tance of the American South. They have also showed a willingness to engage capitalism's disasters and more unsavory elements. Financial panics (whether in 1839, 1873, 1929, or 2008), labor exploitation, violent strikes, slave revolts, corporate scandals, corruption, and traumatic enclosures and expropriations mark the history of capitalism, and in a post–Cold War climate, this darker side of the story of American capitalism has come more into focus. Economists like Thomas Piketty suggest that the capitalist system itself is doomed to fail and generate inequalities that threaten to topple the system.[24] There is, of course, nothing *new* about arguments that capitalism is inherently flawed. Observing the exploitation of the working class in the nineteenth century, Karl Marx predicted ruin, revolution, and a progression to socialism, and he argued that the bourgeois society had "conjured up such gigantic means of production and exchange, like the sorcerer, who is no longer able to control the powers of the nether world whom he has called up by his spells." As the spells of the railroad began to unravel and sow chaos, how could the idea of the New South and capitalist progress survive?[25]

Defenders of capitalism tend to overlook and downplay these disasters, but a selective composition of the story of capitalist expansion was not an accident. Walter Benjamin called this disjuncture between booster visions and historical reality the "phantasmagoria of progress." As he argued, the rapid spread of capitalism and new technologies, prime among them the railroad, induced a "dream filled sleep," a collective hallucination that obscured the new forms of exploitation and misery produced by these advances of capital. The New South myth certainly constitutes a phantasmagoria, and the defeated white South was especially primed for such a myth, as white men who saw their delusions of military grandeur vanish at Gettysburg or Appomattox were more than ready to seek new glory in the railroading realm. The dream consciousness of capitalism can help explain the persistence of the system in spite of its challenges. The march of progress obliterates the past, as a society is blinded by the phantasmagoria, and society remembers the new rail line, and not its opponents; it honors the rail baron, and not the worker buried in a cave-in or the child hit by a train. In other words, capitalism's creative destruction did more than just wipe out physical manifestations of the past; it masked a history of contestation that matched its spread.[26]

Evidence of this phantasmagoria was all over the New South, and to peer behind this curtain, one must examine narratives, mentalities, and encounters with the symbols of progress that accompany capitalism's perpetual revolutions. Trains were the most prominent symbols of nineteenth-century modernity and a tangible manifestation of the spread of capitalism, so train stories like McCaleb's and the more cohesive tale of the New South boosters are narratives of Capitalism, the self-writing history of the age. In part I of this book, we construct this phantasmagoria and piece together the ways white and black southerners tried to harness the magic of the railroad. Chapter 1 addresses the genealogy of the link between railroads, capitalism and the South's salvation, beginning with this narrative's birth from the ashes of the Civil War and tracing it through its connection to the New South movement. For white boosters and Redeemers, the railroad was definitive proof that a New South had risen and the Civil War was in the past. Then chapter 2 begins with a microcosm of the railroad's transformations, the New Orleans Exposition of 1884, and follows the spread of the values this event promoted. From expositions to small towns across the South, white elites bought into the myth of this event and the untrammeled promise of the railroad, and they extended these railroad dreams into the southern hinterland. Chapter 3 details the struggle between white and black southerners over the empowering magic of the railroad. Black southerners had a railroad progress story of their own, but the story told by white elites was the story that endured thanks to a conscious effort to downplay and circumscribe the role of black southerners as laborers, consumers, and travelers.

This idea that railroad magic would redeem the region was a mirage promulgated by elites and boosters. Walter Benjamin argued that the dream-filled sleep of capitalism's phantasmagoria led to a "reactivation of mythic forces," and again and again, demons—like the imaginary train wreckers that stalked McCaleb—haunted southerners' encounters with the railroad in the 1880s and '90s. The appearance of monsters, or of unleashed powers from Marx's "nether world," in the historical record can serve as a convenient sign that something is awry, that a transformation has unleashed a deeper anxiety or a new form of resistance. The men plotting the colonization of the New World conjured up a many-headed hydra to express the multifarious foes, from unruly pirates to rebellious slaves, they marshaled toward their task. The antebellum South had as its bogeymen various forms of real and imagined slave insurrection, a fear that boiled over in a series of panics. The imposing octopus, with tentacles entangling all aspects of political and economic life, came to represent the domination of corporations like the Southern Pacific Railroad and Standard Oil in the development of the West. Even today, twenty-first-century journalists refer to Goldman Sachs and other institutions behind the Great Recession as "vampire squids," draining the lifeblood of the national economy.[27] Understanding these moments of crisis, when the language of monstrosity, terror, and dark magic appears, is critical if we are to recover the anxieties that accompanied capitalism's expansion.

While champions of capitalism will argue that these moments of disaster should be ignored in favor of larger metrics of progress and growth, it is in these crises that the inner workings of this complicated system are revealed. A farmer may not fully comprehend the vast web of institutions that hold his debt until the mortgage officer arrives, just as residents of a southern railroad town may only pause to take stock of the extent of their connections when disease or a wanted criminal appears in a town down the line. Moreover, these crises constitute potential turning points, where alternatives to capitalism come into view, and the ways in which capitalism overcomes these challenges and the ways in which the downsides and disasters of capitalism are written out of its history help explain the persistence and dominance of the system. There was nothing natural or preordained about the victory of capitalism, a fact that makes the revolutionary New South period, when the leaders of a defeated region aggressively adopted capitalism's values, of particular interest.[28]

Railroad boosters and previous generations of historians have lauded the railroad as a harbinger of order and stability, but the railroad corporation itself was an agent of bedlam. Alfred Chandler set the entire paradigm of the field of business history by arguing that the nature of the railroad corporation pioneered corporate organization and created the "invisible hand" of the modern corporation's managerial structures. The advance of the railroad corporation through history then spread rationality and helped structure the chaos of the nineteenth century. Other twentieth-century histories of the railroad portray them as essential "colonizers," and they connect rail corporations like the Burlington, Illinois Central, and more to the broader economic development of their regions. The implicit assumption behind these works was that railroads were responsible, even necessary, to build up large portions of the vast country.[29] Very often the railroad was a force for stability and positive growth, but the history of the railroad and the narratives in this book demonstrate that the logic of the corporation—to maximize profits, consolidate toward bigness, generate "creative destruction," and maximize efficiency—could just as soon lead to chaos. The railroad, heralded as the first big business in history, demonstrated that modernity could be quite disorderly.[30]

Tracing the tracks of the Iron Horse around the globe reveals a long history of contestation and resistance. Americans lamented the "machine in the garden" for ruining pastoral landscapes, worried about the role of women in this new public space, and assailed railroad companies for their corruption and grip on the political system. European travelers fretted about murder in compartments and invented new maladies like railway spine, and the imagery of the railroad entered politics in a place like Mexico, where both supporters and opponents of Porfirio Díaz invoked the symbolism of the country's new railroads. Travel narratives from the height of Japan's railroad boom spoke to tensions in changing gender roles, the perils of obsessive punctuality, and cultural predispositions to suicide. As apparatuses of imperial empires, railroads took on even darker meanings, increasing the exploitation of resources and Native peoples in Africa, and spreading cholera through India and beyond. If train stories helped to write the global narrative of capitalism's ascendancy in the late nineteenth century, critiques of railroads spoke to the anxieties of these transitions.[31]

Engines of Redemption extends this global story of railroad and capitalist carnage to the New South, and argues that the railroad was uniquely destructive and problematic in this region. While part I of the narrative creates the railroad phantasmagoria and discusses what this story obscures, in part II we descend to the netherworld, and in a series of case studies, we examine railroad crises that were distinctive to the New South. The very traits lauded by boosters as central to the railroad's power introduced new dangers and anxieties in southern life. As chapter 4 details, railroads spread yellow fever, a terrifying disease, into new corners of the region and provoked an angry extralegal backlash, the shotgun quarantine. The new southern railroads were built quickly and cheaply and thus crashed at a higher rate than those in the rest of the nation, and chapter 5 argues that this threat led southerners to fear conspiracies of train wrecking. Malicious gangs of criminals seemed to stalk southern rail lines as derailments and collisions surged in the 1890s. Chapter 6 discusses how the anonymity and predictability of the network abetted the crimes of two train robbers, Railroad Bill and Rube Burrow, and in chapter 7 we examine how capitalism's natural tendency toward consolidation allowed for the ascendance of monopolistic corporations and the arrival of the octopus in the South. Though its backers touted the company's arrival as further proof of New South progress, a wide range of political foes challenged this consolidation process, and the metaphor of this company as a grasping octopus became common. Though all of these counternarratives share elements of commonality with railroad disasters in other locations, as a whole, this a story that—due to environmental factors, the backdrop of recent war, racial tensions, and the regional position in the national political economy— could only take place in the specific time and place of the American South in the 1880s and '90s.

From this first thesis on the distinctly pernicious impacts of the railroad on the New South comes the more overarching argument of the book, that railroad companies and their white southern allies exploited the region's racial tensions to paper over the destructive aspects of capitalism and ensure the survival of the railroad phantasmagoria. The white South first of all circumscribed access to the railroad's power. For capitalism to be palatable to white southerners, the magical aspects of the system were denied to black southerners. This was an ideological effort, as seen in white accounts that downplayed black contributions, that marginalized black labor, and that divorced black mobility from the purposeful movement of capitalism. Confronted with middle-class black travelers, empowered workers, or respectable black women, whites tried to link these upwardly mobile black men and black women with Old South stereotypes—seeing the Pullman porter as a subservient slave, for example—and tried to harden the color line through Jim Crow legislation demarcating strict black and white divisions in rail travel. White travelers and authors applied the railroad's magic to African Americans and conjured up new terrifying archetypes and stock characters like the shiftless wanderer, anonymous crowd, or Railroad Bill, the shapeshifting, ubiquitous criminal. These exaggerated images disconnected black southerners from the railroad and portrayed them as precapitalist and mired in the past, or helplessly doomed or distorted by the forces of capitalism.

Along with these efforts to delineate access to the railroad, white southerners and railroad corporations used black southerners as scapegoats and distractions from the railroad's crises. In moments of contestation and in key turning points, the specter of black domination or empowerment proved more frightening to white southerners than the dark forces of capitalism. Division, racial scapegoating, and calls for genocidal extermination marked the yellow fever epidemics detailed in chapter 4. As seen in chapters 5 and 6, panics over train wrecks and robberies similarly were resolved by deflecting anger toward anonymous black men, imagined criminals, and grisly rituals of commodification and collective punishment. And in chapter 7, we look at how white supremacist appeals invoking a vampire of black rule crushed a powerful antimonopoly attack on the Southern Railway. The end result was that the rapid advance of an agent of connection, directed by capitalistic means and motives, contributed to the hardening of white supremacy and the onset of Jim Crow. It is certainly not new to assert that the New South era witnessed extreme racial hostility and violence, but often scholars overlook the role of new technology and of large corporations, many of which were backed by northern or foreign capital.[32]

Before we roll down these tracks, a word on methodology and sources. Because this book is a history of a grand narrative of capitalism's progress promulgated by southern elites and because it is a book that tries to reinsert political economy into the narrative of the New South, we place heavy emphasis on top-down sources like railroad archival collections, newspapers, and other publications that by their nature privilege the voices of white elites. To address the creation, contestation, and survival of the story of New South capitalist redemption by rail, it is essential to analyze structure, and start from the top, with the voices of those who created this story and gave it power. We approach these sources with a critical eye to and an awareness of their flaws and limitations. Corporate archives, especially those from corporate entities still in existence, can obscure the truth, as I discovered when I found a collection that was missing folders of correspondence dealing with train wrecks. Newspapers provide a selective viewpoint, as they were typically published by the booster or business-oriented class of the white population. Many newspapers of this era were even owned directly by railroad companies or railroad allies. Published accounts, railroad prospectuses, ephemera, and travel narratives also are valuable sources for this work. A critical read of these white, elite sources can reproduce booster arguments, which is essential to describe the railroad phantasmagoria, but it can also reveal anxieties and tensions. For example, it is significant that the same newspapers proclaiming the rise of the New South published sensational stories on train wrecking or panicky reports on the progress of yellow fever epidemics, and McCaleb's published travel narrative betrayed his deepest fears about rail travel.[33]

Where possible, this narrative incorporates accounts from black travelers and observations from prominent black figures like Ida B. Wells and James Weldon Johnson. The very absence of black voices in the historical record is noteworthy, and we are careful to note this absence when necessary, such as in expositions that marginalized black contributions or in railroad reports that downplayed dangerous work conditions. An emphasis on white voices does not detract from the strength of our conclusions on the composition of white supremacy and Jim Crow. The process of constructing white supremacy relied on interactions on the ground and in top-down messaging and political strategy.[34] To get into questions of memory, which are critical in a project addressing the persistence of a certain view of history, we turn at times to folklore and music. The train song constitutes an important source that gives voice to previously hidden narratives from both black and white southerners. Train wreck ballads, for example, provide an oral record of disasters that may have occurred decades before the song conquered the airwaves.

Through these sources, *Engines of Redemption* gives voice to the wonder and terror of this moment of the rapid expansion of capitalism in a region with a political economy torn asunder by war and its aftermath. Capitalism as spread by the southern railroad was a source of wonder, mystery, and terror, and it introduced new forms of enchantment into southern life.[35] The events described in this book often tug at the edges of reality. As the region fell under the spell of the railroad, shape-shifting train robbers, horrific diseases, monopolistic conspiracies, and ghostly train wreck victims haunted southerners, and grandiose schemes and fantastical visions of the future fired their imaginations. The thrills of McCaleb's nighttime ride to Meridian were replicated en masse as the South got on the rails.

Part I
Casting the Spell

CHAPTER ONE

Reunited with Bands of Iron

When the iron-horse sweeps over the Long Bridge down the Potomac
and across the Virginia plains to Richmond in three and a half hours
from Washington, there is progress in the South.
—A. K. McClure, 1886

As he flew south through Virginia and Tennessee on a private train in 1886,
northern journalist Henry Field could not get the Civil War out of his mind.
Invited to join the president of the Louisville & Nashville (L&N) Railroad
and a dozen other assorted capitalists, Field's goal was to write a report sum-
marizing the "new life, new industries, and new ambitions" for readers of his
New York newspaper. In this, he would be quite successful. His descriptions
of southern industrial progress proved so popular they were copied by southern
newspapers, and then published as a book. The overarching message of the
account was that North and South were now united, so it's no surprise that
his writings resonated with a wide audience in a decade where Americans
yearned for reconciliation. A swift rail journey, argued Field, was the ideal
way to experience southern progress, as it "enables one to traverse a wider
space; to sweep over more degrees of latitude and longitude; and thus to see
more lands and people."[1]

Reunion was the dominant theme of his writings, but the war haunted his
reports of the South and periodically disrupted his narrative. He paired a discussion of Atlanta's status as a "great railroad center" with a reminder that
"this valley among the hills was like the Valley of Gehenna into which shot
and shell were poured, as fire from heaven fell upon Sodom and Gomorrah."
He also passed by silent forts on the Potomac, viewed the Manassas battlefield, and noted how Lynchburg was the destination of General Lee's 1865 retreat from Richmond. In Tennessee, he reminded readers that the state was
the site of four of the war's most critical battles, and his time traveling reached
a fever pitch. As his train moved by the imposing ironworks at South Pitts-
burg, just west of Chattanooga's battlefields, he mused, "We are constantly
passing from one thing to another—from war to peace, and from peace to
war." The war threatened to overshadow his message, were it not for the
power of the railroad, which literally and symbolically carried his narrative
away from the horrors of the late conflict. After dwelling on the battle of

Franklin, Field used a vivid description of the Tennessee scenery to rest his mind. As he wrote, "After brooding over the horrors of a battlefield, it is a relief to get into the solemn stillness of the woods, among the murmuring pines." And at Chattanooga, he listened to details on the battle there just as the "train was flying away from the scene of this great struggle at the rate of forty miles per hour." Just in case the symbolism of his rail journey was lost on readers, he made his thoughts clear at the conclusion of his trip, noting that the nation was now "at last happily reunited, and bound together, not only with bands of iron, but by millions of loyal and loving hearts."[2]

Field's narrative highlighted the most basic function of a railroad, the ability to provide physical connections and passenger travel, and he imbued this tangible movement with a messianic message of sectional reunion. He translated one of the basic economic functions of a corporation into a narrative of great cultural importance to white southern conservatives and their northern allies. Rail travel was famously lauded for its ability to annihilate space and time, to destroy the distance between points, and to compress far-flung cities to mere points on a railroad map.[3] But for New South boosters, perhaps the most essential ideological function of the railroad journey was its annihilation of history and its support of a new narrative of southern history that both rehabilitated the forces of capitalism and wrote black southerners out of the story of war, Reconstruction, and rebirth.

The ruined South was a land primed for an infusion of myth and magic. Defeated nations have a tendency to lurch wildly from rage to fantastical rationalizations to desperate schemes for renewal. Wolfgang Schivelbusch argues a "state of unreality—or dreamland" descends on vanquished lands as the fever of war breaks. Four years of war left a ruined landscape across wide swaths of the South, and it shattered the cotton and slave-backed political economy of the antebellum era. Through Reconstruction, freedmen and freedwomen balanced the joy of Emancipation, heady rush of new political rights, and dream of a brighter future, with the tortuous task of day-to-day survival in a violent and hostile region. Confederate veterans staggered home with memories of wartime horror, and many forever carried war wounds and bitter resentments toward their former foes. Some found their renewal in the violent reassertion of white supremacy, donning the ghostly garb of the Ku Klux Klan and participating in the overt political warfare of Redemption.[4] But as this chapter relates, the irresistible track of the Iron Horse, and the railroad corporation—as a conveyor of passengers, area of investment, field of employment, and physical link—was another crucial way to channel white southern dreams and move beyond the trauma of war and Reconstruction.

CONSTANT REMINDERS of the recent struggle marked southern travel in the decade after the Civil War. This acknowledgment of the war's memory was aided by a historical truth, that railroads had played a central role in the military drama of the war. The very presence of railroads made possible stunning feats of generalship such as Stonewall Jackson's Valley Campaign, and the structure of the network allowed the Confederacy to efficiently shift resources to major battlefronts. The Confederate government also recognized the value of forging the fledgling nation's disparate rail lines into a cohesive system, chartering and subsidizing four lines to connect gaps between state-constructed rail systems.[5] Northern generals quickly learned that mastering the South's geography of iron ties was just as important as conquering its physical geography, and by 1864, Union generals were targeting railroads and either destroying them or using them to their advantage. This new strategy was epitomized by William Sherman's destructive march through Georgia and South Carolina, which laid waste to this section's rail lines, leaving behind the twisted wreckage of "Sherman's neckties."[6] Many of the war's greatest dramas—the daring mission to commandeer "the General" locomotive and destroy lines north of Atlanta, rapid troop movements saving armies in the nick of time at Bull Run and Shiloh, and Sherman's incineration of Atlanta—played out on Southern rail lines.

The disjointed nature of the region's railroads would end up harming the Confederacy's cause considerably during the Civil War, when Jefferson Davis and his lieutenants struggled to integrate a network that had been designed to serve specific states and localities. In his recounting of the Confederate war effort, Jefferson Davis lamented how Southern railroads were "insufficient in number," and furnished with rolling stock and manned by operatives largely from the North. And he recalled that one of the worst "embarrassments suffered in the last two years of the war was from the want of rolling-stock, with which to operate our railroads, as required for the transportation of troops and supplies." For Davis and other postwar Confederate apologists, blaming railroads for defeat helped sustain the Lost Cause myth by forming part of a broader argument about the overwhelming nature of the North's industrial advantage. Pinning the Confederate downfall on inadequate railroads supported boosters' largely false image of a precapitalist Old South. While the Old South may have fallen short of the level of industrial development in the antebellum North, the South in 1860 had a rail network that by many metrics matched the North's. One could even make the case that the Confederacy's skillful use of interior rail lines prolonged the war. And the Lost Cause notion of wartime railroad failure clearly held implications for the southern future. The logical conclusion to draw from the wartime failures was that a New South must include improved railroads.[7]

In addition to pointing out southern industrial deficiencies, railroads reminded many of the ruination of the postwar South. After Lee's surrender, travelers descended upon the South to experience the sights and sounds of the ruined region by rail. Many of these journeys had political goals—to either push for black suffrage or excoriate the alleged horrors of Reconstruction—but discussions of railroad conditions formed a backdrop to all of them.[8] These writers experienced the devastated railroad network firsthand as they made their way through the war-torn region. In 1865, Whitelaw Reid described "a train composed of a wheezy little locomotive and an old mail agent's car, with all the windows smashed out and the seats gone" in eastern North Carolina, and marveled that a trip over a junky line in Virginia did not end in disaster. He noted that on one road in Tennessee, officers estimated that out of a hundred-mile stretch, "not less than 16 miles ought to be removed without one day's delay," and near Knoxville his "train crept slowly over long lines of trestle-work which timid passengers fancied they could see swaying beneath us." Between Jackson, Mississippi, and Grand Junction, Tennessee, Reid could "only remember a dismal night of thumpings over broken rails, and lurchings and contortions of the cars, as if we were really trying in our motion to imitate the course of the rails the Yankee raiders had twisted."[9]

These accounts emphasized the slow speed, extreme discomfort, and interrupted connections of the southern railroad network. In 1866, Sidney Andrews noted how "sleeping cars are apparently an unknown thing on southern railways," and he called southerners "stupidly opposed to comfort." He complained that the "average rate of railway speed is about nine miles per hour in South Carolina and about eleven miles per hour in North Carolina."[10] While approaching Columbia, Andrews found the city walled in by desolation, circled by the endpoints of five different railroads destroyed during the course of the war. In some parts of South Carolina, the railroads were "all gone—not simply broken up, but gone," and "miles and miles of iron have actually disappeared, gone out of existence." He listed the principal attractions of Branchville, South Carolina, as "enormously large mosquitoes, ravenously hungry bedbugs, and smashed-up railroad engines."[11] In another postwar travel account, J. T. Trowbridge described how the Savannah and Charleston road "was struck and smashed by Sherman in his march from the sea" and reasoned there was no hope for its repair due to its financial trouble before the war. The Central of Georgia between Savannah and Macon was similarly "an impassable hiatus of bent rails and burnt bridges, at the time of my journey."[12]

John Kennaway made this link between wartime campaigning and his troubled travels clear by titling his journey "On Sherman's Track." He described the wreckage of the Savannah and Charleston Railroad's bridge as a "a wretched spectacle," an "unmistakable piece of Sherman's handiwork." Between these two cities, travelers had to ride in old military ambulances between a fifty-mile gap, which took twelve or thirteen hours. On another historic rail corridor visited by Sherman's forces, it took Kennaway fourteen hours to travel the 138 miles between Chattanooga and Atlanta in 1867, and he described a "weary" journey to Petersburg that included broken seats, worn rails, and shaky tracks.[13] In all of these accounts from the immediate postwar period, the authors replaced the typical language of capitalist activity of vibrancy, excitement, and magic—with stagnation, disruption, and ruination. The notion of a "New South" depended on a departure from the horror of a "prostrate South" laid low by war, and destroyed railroads vividly made the point that 1865 was indeed Year Zero for the southern economy.[14]

Between these vivid descriptions of ruined tracks and broken connections, and the memory of the Confederacy's logistical struggles, railroads became inextricably linked with Southern defeat in the minds of white southern elites and northern travelers. When these two groups took to the rails in the 1880s, this Civil War destruction was never far from their minds, and many made explicit comparisons to the condition of Southern railroads in the 1860s. William Kelley looked to the past to report on the progress of the South after a journey through Tennessee, Alabama, Georgia, and South Carolina in 1888. He noted that "in 1867 the South was a land of desolation" but "the changes wrought in the meantime have been marvelous, and may justly be regarded as the work of titans." And the centerpiece of these changes was the railroad network on which he rode. He noted, "The systems of railroad that now traverse the South are as perfect in the construction of roadbed, track, and bridges and in passenger cars and the means provided for the transportation of freight, as those of the north."[15] While traveling south over the stretch of war-torn Virginia land between Richmond and Potomac, A. K. McClure contrasted his swift travel with the "tedious day's journey" between the two cities he experienced after the war. By 1886, it was "merely a pleasant excursion from one city to the other and back between breakfast and dinner." Railroad connections between Washington, D.C., and Richmond both expunged the memory of the war and pointed toward the recovery of postwar Virginia.[16]

The condition of the lines themselves spoke to advancement, as outside experts on rail travel provided testimony about the southern rail network that gave some legitimacy to the New South boosters' breathless claims. Nationwide rail publications like the *Railway Gazette* provided one venue for travelers to comment on the South's progress. One traveler on southern roads, writing in 1887, marveled at how far the region's network had come since his last journey south in 1868. As he argued, "fifteen miles an hour was a common passenger speed then; trains were rarely on time, run-offs were innumerable, and the roughness of the roads were terrible." But in 1887, "they ride very smoothly now, have handsome passenger cars, and speeds of 25–30 miles per hour are common."[17] A civil engineer writing to the *Railway Gazette* in 1888 wrote, "On my recent trips South, I also noticed a great improvement in the general condition of the track and the alignment." Noting improvements on lines carrying through traffic like the L&N, he concluded, "No section of the United States can show greater comparative improvement within the last three years in their railroads than the Southern states."[18] Lady Duffus Hardy, a British traveler, was worried going into her trip south in 1883, fretting about rumors of bad eating houses, long waits in isolated rural stations, and "jolting cars and rough roads." But she was pleasantly surprised with "the energy with which the South is throwing itself into the work of restoration" and the development of the network.[19]

The ghosts of the Civil War also stalked Ernest Ingersoll's pleas for outside investment in the South. In 1885, Ingersoll journeyed from Harrisburg, Pennsylvania, down the spine of the Appalachian Mountains to Tennessee, and he described the changes the railroad brought to the mountain region. As his train plunged down the valley, he blended descriptions of the fast-moving scenery with an account of Stonewall Jackson's Valley Campaign. While traveling over the Virginia Central, he remarked that the destruction of this vital artery was the objective of every federal force in the valley. His train later passed just underneath the site of the Battle of the Crater outside Petersburg, where a "terrific charge ensued which marked that farm-slope as one of the bloodiest fields of the Civil War," and at Salem he noted the smooth and solid track that replaced the destruction of war and the old iron rails, "out of which Hunter's men curled such fantastic neckties around the oaks." Like other narratives, he blended enticements for investors with war history. Jackson's Valley Campaign only served to provide context for the "umber, ochre, copper, manganese, marble, kaolin, fire-clay and various other useful metals and earths" beneath this once-contested ground. He was also sure to emphasize the speed of the new rail network, marveling at the pace of the fast mail train leaving Harrisburg. This train gathered up the mail from Memphis, New Orleans, and Atlanta and sped north up the Shenandoah Valley, in "the quickest time ever made on southern railroads." And as further proof of the improved rail network, the account closed with a detailed description of the many different routes travelers could take to head south.[20] Ingersoll's travel narrative used the movement of his train as a guide through both the South's varied physical spaces and its imagined economic pasts and futures.

It was not just the scenery and experience of rail travel that supported the arguments of the New South boosters. The passengers on these journeys also attested to the railroad's destruction of the past. In 1881, veterans with New York's Seventy-First Infantry embarked on a tour of the South by rail, a self-proclaimed "New Invasion of the South," and they published their account in the hope that it would be a "forerunner of that era of national fraternity on which so much of the future of our great country depends." Their destination was New Orleans, where they were to meet up with "Louisiana regiments which had plunged into the fire and smoke of Bull Run." The train was decorated with banners reading "Seventy-First regiment, *en route* New York and New Orleans," and "Seventy-First New York, Louisiana Tigers—1861–1881," which was a "source of amusement" and probably confusion to observers along the road. As the train headed south, the passengers noticed a marked difference, and commented on the black firemen and "the sparseness of its settlement, and a certain air of lack of capital." Later the train traveled along the Mississippi River, and passengers marveled at Old South ruins, noting how the "cabins and houses had a ruinous look," and "the train whirled by the ruins of a cotton press, at one time no doubt, the busy centre of a great plantation." The common theme that ran through this tour of the dilapidated South was a need for northern investment. At one stop, former Confederate general Winfield Scott Featherston addressed the party, saying, "We welcome you here. We want you to see our people and our fertile soil. All we need now is capital."[21]

The constant desire for investment was one consistent refrain of this travel narrative, but the overriding message was one of sectional reconciliation. In perhaps the most dramatic moment in the regiment's journey, a Union and a Confederate veteran met in Hammond, Louisiana. Both discovered that they still carried bullets from war wounds, and one man declared "with tears in his eyes" that he would give a thousand dollars to get both bullets out so they could exchange them. The two men went off to get a drink together and "everybody within hearing wished that they had a bullet in some portion of their body." In New Orleans the regiment listened to a speech given by the king of the Mardi Gras carnival, in which the king lauded the shift in the meaning of the rail lines connecting North and South. He argued, "Long ago the steel rail connecting North and South has ceased to be a military road for the transportation of troops." The rail "to us now only is a ribbon of steel, along which flows the electric current of friendship."[22] As the cultural project of sectional reconciliation picked up steam, the tearful reunion of Northern and Southern soldiers became a common trope appearing again and again in both real-life events and literature. But the memories these reunions created were selective, prioritizing vague paeans to military glory and sacrifice over the political meaning of the war's horrific violence. The absence of black soldiers in this and many other narratives further divorced emancipation and the struggle for black freedom from the meaning of the war.[23] In this case, the railroad tour helped foster this simplified, and investment-focused, reunion of New York and Louisiana veterans.

Fictional accounts also used the trope of the railway journey as a venue for reconciliation and commemoration of the Southern past. Rebecca Harding published a serialized account of southern rail travel in *Harpers New Monthly Magazine* in 1887, following a group of curious northerners, "explorers into an unknown country," on a trip from Cincinnati to New Orleans. The party was stunned at the hustle and bustle of the South. The most skeptical member expected to find a "mouldering aristocracy, passively wasting away in their ruined homes." But they still found lingering elements of the past in their journey. In the most dramatic moment in the trip, the train paused at the foot of a hill somewhere outside Montgomery. The travelers saw a windswept and "picturesque old mansion," framed by a brilliant sunset, bedecked in shingles "mossed with age" and with a "thin wisp of smoke drifting from its chimney." The stunning scene seemed to "embody all the tragedy of the departed South." At the same time, a man entered the car, with a "haughty reserve in the high-featured face, better befitting a cavalier than a ploughman." Overcome with the emotion of the moment, the traveler proclaimed this man "the typical southerner at last!" But of course, this moment of acknowledgment of the romanticized Southern past was ephemeral. The train soon chugged onward toward the New Orleans Exposition and other sites of progress, carrying away the imagined cavalier and leaving the decrepit old mansion behind.[24]

The Louisville & Nashville Railroad similarly used a fictional travel account to recognize the company's advancement from wartime destruction in a company-produced promotional pamphlet entitled *The Dream of "Ellen N."* The account followed a group on a "ramble over the South" on the L&N's

tracks from Louisville to New Orleans. Due to its connection between Louisville and Tennessee, the rail line was critical during the war, "marched over by the contending armies of the blue and gray." At the height of its decrepitude, with "bad rails, crowded tracks and few switches," it took over a week for supplies to go from Cincinnati to Nashville. But as the travelers moved south en route to New Orleans, they found "no reminiscence of that fierce and bloody time." Even if one asked an employee of the road, one would receive "only the vaguest and most indefinite of answers" regarding the history of the line; these are "dead issues that are forever at rest."[25]

Just as Field flew away from old battlefields in Tennessee, these travelers' narratives were propelled beyond these sites by the movement of the railroad. When the Southern past showed up in these accounts, it was fleeting and ephemeral, acknowledged but quickly forgotten in the face of the unceasing circulation of the rail network. When these accounts did pause, it was to linger at New South boomtowns, where the authors typically linked the railroad to the growth of industry and the region's bright future. After he arrived in Birmingham, A. K. McClure noted in 1886 how "twelve years ago the solitude of Birmingham was arrested by a single ordinary farmhouse: but two railways finally crossed each other there, and this invited capitalists to investigate" the area's resources. When "railways began to traverse the New South," capitalists arrived and Birmingham became the "Magic City."[26] A description of the development of Virginia's Shenandoah Valley noted the Norfolk and Western Railroad had a "talismanic effect" on the area, and described how the intersection of two rail lines led to the rapid growth of Roanoke, another "magic place."[27] One could even take a planned rail excursion to visit the sights of New South industrial progress. Raymond's Vacation Excursions, a travel company, planned an excursion in 1890, "with a view to giving northern people—capitalists, investors and others—an opportunity to visit the chief centres of southern development." The advertisement noted that thanks to northern capital, "energies which have lain dormant" in the South "have suddenly been brought into action. The tour promised to show investors the "true state of things," and on elegant Pullman sleeping cars, the party would visit romantic scenes of the Old South, learn the history of the war, and scout out potential investments. The tour organizers were explicit in their focus on economic development, taking the travelers to New South boomtowns like Bristol and Roanoke in Virginia, Middlesboro in Kentucky, Birmingham, and Chattanooga.[28]

This focus on the future was also a key function of railroad trips taken by investors scouting out the South. A group of capitalists traveled south in 1889 to "spy out the land" and wrote a series of letters for the *Manufacturers' Record*. One excited traveler wrote that they "traveled through a continuous and unbroken strain of what has been aptly termed the music of progress—the whirr of the spindle, the buzz of the saw, the roar of the furnace and the throb of the locomotive."[29] Sylvester Cary, who led the development of a series of towns along the Southern Pacific line in southwest Louisiana, used descriptions of rail travel to spur larger development projects. Writing for a northern audience in a series called "Going South as Seen from a Car Window," he described a trip that started in Dubuque, Iowa, in the middle of a snowstorm. As the party went south the snow and winter weather faded away, and the sunny South's climatic advantages were easy to see. At Cairo, Illinois, they "left old snow; the dreary snow," and in New Orleans he marveled at the Spanish moss, saw oranges on trees, and looked at "huge piles of cotton."[30] He later told a tale of another mythic journey west from New Orleans. Cary had traveled to visit New Orleans during Mardi Gras in 1882, and he met a friend who told him rumors of great and readily available land in southwest Louisiana. Cary traveled west on the Southern Pacific line, got off the train, looked around, and immediately decided to buy the land and start the town of Jennings.[31]

The New South myth, from its inception, was grounded in the image of the preindustrial Old South and a narrative of rebirth from wartime destruction. Railroad journeys provided the perfect venue to acknowledge both these facets of the myth, as from the vantage point of white travelers in the 1880s, the South's past, present, and future were on display. Rail travel on the improved railroads of the New South literally and symbolically carried boosters from the Civil War to the New South, and boosters harnessed the imaginative power of the railroad to demonstrate southern progress. The New South boosters built their arguments on an ideological edifice that contained a specific view of the Civil War. Lost Cause myths explaining Confederate defeat fixated on railroad and industrial deficiencies, Yankee depredations like Sherman's neckties, and acts of Southern valor, while ignoring the central role of slavery and emancipation in the conflict. The war was to be forgotten. It was instead explicitly acknowledged as a starting point for the railroad's magical transformations. But the experience of travel was not the only way railroads moved the region from war to redemption.

TO SAY E. D. FROST had a hard job would be putting it mildly. The year was 1875, and he was stationed in Water Valley, Mississippi, along a line that bisected the state in a north-to-south direction. Frost was the chief lieutenant to Henry McComb, head of the New Orleans, St. Louis and Chicago Railroad, and McComb had high hopes for this well-placed route. In theory one could use this line to get from New Orleans to Chicago after a quick connection with the Illinois Central (IC), and McComb won control of the line after a bitter struggle for control with former Confederate general P. G. T. Beauregard. But heavy debt, a by-product of a region short on capital, and an uncertain economic environment plagued McComb's lines and filled the pages of Frost's letters to McComb with angst.[32]

The physical condition of a railroad has a direct correlation to the financial well-being of the corporation that operates it, and McComb's company was starved for capital. On McComb's road, day-to-day maintenance issues like upgrading steel ties and improving rolling stock were compounded by the deliberate destruction of Yankee raiders, and by the heavy strain that wartime traffic had placed on Confederate rails and rolling stock. Frost's dispatches to his superiors capture his increasingly desperate struggles to operate the line. By 1875 the line was too broke to even pay employees with regularity, and the road was marked with "petty accidents" that Frost argued were the result of "the demoralization that exists among our employees on account of long delays in receiving wages."[33] Frost directed that the road's "trains run at a speed commensurate with the condition of our track," which meant the speed of freight trains was cut to ten miles per hour and he ordered passenger trains to not try to make up any time.[34] Frost was desperate to attract passengers to the line, but travelers were unwilling to risk their lives on the slow and dangerous road. By 1876, conditions got so bad that ticket sellers in Chicago were warning travelers that the road is "very dangerous" and its "trains are all the time in the ditch."[35] Later that month, the road experienced two separate accidents and delays on the same day, and Frost rued the fact that "passengers will not ride over this road more than once."[36] Henry V. Poor's *Manual of the Railroads of the United States*, perhaps the definitive judge of a rail line's condition, simply labeled the road "unsatisfactory."[37]

Like many southern lines in this period, this route through Mississippi would be salvaged by northern capital. In 1876, McComb's company fell into receivership, and the Chicago-based Illinois Central snatched up the indebted fragments. One would be hard pressed to find a line more northern in its origins than the IC. Originally the brainchild of Stephen Douglas, it stretched south to Cairo before the war, building up Illinois farmland with a generous policy of land grants. As further proof of this corporation's Yankee heritage, both Abraham Lincoln and George McClellan were on the company payrolls in the 1850s as lawyers. In the 1870s, leadership of the Illinois

Central looked south, to expand beyond Cairo. The road's president, William Ackerman, first scouted out port facilities in New Orleans while on the way back from a vacation in Cuba in 1871–72.[38] Letters from the road's president in early 1878, asking contacts for information on Mississippi's economy, offering suggestions for building up the territory, and asking about the potential for a continuous line of steamers linking New Orleans and South America demonstrate that the IC saw the southern line as a key piece in a corporate strategy of expansion, a means to build up Mississippi, connect the road to the Gulf of Mexico's trade, and respond to the system-building efforts of other southern railroads like the L&N.[39]

After absorption of the southern corridor to New Orleans, infusions of capital translated quickly into physical rejuvenation on the ground in Mississippi. Annual reports to the company's stockholders celebrated how workmen repaired shattered bridges and structures, replaced broken-down rails with over 16,000 tons' worth of steel rails, and began work on extensions tapping undeveloped corners of Mississippi. By 1879, these improvements had shaved five hours off the time between New Orleans and East Cairo, and trains were running "with regularity and safety." On August 1, 1881, workers shifted the gauge of the road to match the northern standard gauge of 4 feet 8½ inches, eliminating the need for time-consuming hoists at Cairo. These efforts culminated in the completion of a four-mile bridge over the Ohio River at Cairo in 1889. When the first train ran over the bridge at Cairo, the symbolism was not lost on the company. A historian of the company compared this bridge's completion to the driving of the Golden Spike that finalized the first transcontinental railroad at Promontory Point, as the IC similarly united the country, and a passenger could finally take a direct train from Chicago to New Orleans. After the bridge's completion, the Illinois Central's report to stockholders noted, "the exchange of commodities between the North and South is steadily increasing," and it crowed that the railroad was "assured of a continually increasing flow of commerce North and South."[40]

The Illinois Central's southern expansion demonstrated how the railroad corporation itself, as a container for northern investment that translated directly into southern improvements, could aid the process of reconciliation. "No better indication of the progress towards an effective reunion can be desired than is furnished in the rapid railroad development now taking place in many of the Southern States," crowed a piece in *DeBow's Review* in 1867 that spoke to the mission of Reconstruction by rail.[41] However, not every southern railroad had a narrative of rebirth as neat or tidy as the Mississippi Central, and the process of reconstruction was highly uneven. While Frost's lines in Mississippi struggled, other lines rebounded quickly. The L&N took heavy damage during the war due to its location in highly contested Tennessee, but it made out handsomely after the war. Like other rail lines under federal occupation, the L&N received generous government subsidies for carrying troops and equipment, as well as ample support to rebuild bridges and broken-down track sections after the war. Because of these subsidies, the company was able to accumulate stockpiles of capital that would aid in the system's growth after the war.[42] By 1866, most railroads in the South were providing at least rudimentary service thanks mainly to northern assistance. But as the postwar travel accounts demonstrated, this service usually left much to be desired.[43]

Republican-controlled state governments also assisted in the process of railroad reconstruction and undertook many new projects in this era. In contrast with the far more controversial goals of Reconstruction, such as extending citizenship to freedmen and transitioning from slavery to free labor, legislating new aid for railroads provided an issue that in theory would attract a broad base of support and secure a lasting power base for these tenuous new regimes. After all, few could argue against the notion that the South needed more railroads and economic progress. Southern Republicans saw railroad aid as the cement that could bind together their precarious coalition of freedmen, northern "carpetbaggers," and southern white "scalawags." But with the political and financial uncertainty of these years, the numerical results of new construction were mediocre. The mileage of the southern railroad network only improved from 9,135 to 13,322 between 1865 and 1875, a 46 percent jump that paled in comparison with the dynamic growth witnessed elsewhere in the nation.[44]

Even worse for the Republicans, white southerners locked out of political power assailed the new railroads as the cause of excessive waste and fraud. For the Redeemers, any project built by "carpetbag" or "black Republican" governments was tainted with the stench of corruption. These intimations of scandal helped fuel the political backlash that doomed southern Republicans. Some of the hue and cry over corrupt railroads was imagined and motivated by racist assumptions about the incapacity and inherently crooked nature of black legislators, and much of it was unfair. In the freewheeling atmosphere of Gilded Age economic development, it would be hard to find any railroad project, from the transcontinental lines on down, that was free of shady dealings, but some of this abuse was rightly deserved.[45]

In North Carolina, for example, the ill-fated and ambitious Western North Carolina Railroad, designed to pierce the Blue Ridge Mountains, became a focal point of anticorruption attacks. North Carolina first chartered the road in 1855 to run from Salisbury to Asheville, but construction proceeded slowly due to the treacherous terrain involved and the disruptions of the Civil War. North Carolina's Reconstruction government threw half of all its railroad aid to the road in 1868 and 1869, but with little success, as the two men in charge of building the road, George Swepson and Milton Littlefield, ended up using $3 million worth of North Carolina bonds to invest in what one historian termed "railroad adventures" in Florida. This scandal even helped bring down a Republican governor, contributing to the impeachment of Governor W. W. Holden. Construction was tied up in litigation until the end of the decade, and the road remained incomplete in 1875, when a traveler through the mountain region described "the unfinished embankments, the half-built culverts and arches of the Western North Carolina Railroad," which he wrote were "monuments to the rapacity and meanness of a few men in whom those counties placed confidence."[46]

More than just rhetorical attacks echoed down southern rail lines in the turbulent atmosphere of Reconstruction. As natural centers of power in the occupied South, rail corridors were the focus of violence. When occupying Northern troops fanned out across the South, they often centered operations on junctions or important railroad towns. Just as the Civil War was shaped by the geography of the network, the projection of federal power into the countryside during Reconstruction relied heavily on the southern railroad system.[47] On the flip side of the conflict, organizers with terrorist groups like the Ku Klux Klan used railroad hubs to spread their message and to focus violence. Many of the Klan's actions targeted newly empowered black railway workers along revitalized rail lines. Klan organizers linked the railroad's corruption of state governments with black empowerment, rehabilitated Confederacy imagery and symbolism, and cast themselves as defenders of the South against the Yankee interlopers working to dominate the region's rail lines.[48]

For those who did take steps to systematize southern railroads during Reconstruction, sectional tensions hamstrung the process of consolidation. The Pennsylvania Railroad's (PRR) attempts to build a southern system reflected the challenges for outside capital during Reconstruction. Tom Scott, head of the PRR, looked south after the war in an attempt to build traffic for his system and was met with hostility and economic challenges. Virginians attempted to sabotage and wreck the company's trains after the PRR bought the Alexandria & Fredericksburg Railway in 1870, and when Scott attempted to stitch together a few southern lines into a corridor from Atlanta to Richmond, he had to do so in the shadows. An outright consolidation would have been a political disaster, so he created the Southern Railway Security Company (SRSC), a holding company to buy the separate pieces of his system. At its peak, the company controlled thirteen railroads with 2,131 miles of track, and it had come close to forging three separate southern trunk lines. This impressive achievement came undone in the aftermath of the Panic of 1873. The Pennsylvania sold many of its key assets in 1874, and by 1880 the SRSC was history. As we will see, this corridor would form the core of the Southern Railway in 1894, but in the politically tense atmosphere of Reconstruction, the project was a failure.[49]

The Panic of 1873 also doomed many of the precarious new projects undertaken by Republican state governments, and only added to the Democrats' cries of corruption. Struggles over rail lines thus formed the backdrop to the more overt battles to restore white supremacy and "redeem" southern states from the rule of biracial Republican governments. As northern railway capitalists turned on the Republican governments that controlled many of the state-owned railroads, they found eager allies in the rising Redeemers. In state after state in the South, northern capitalists and outside holding companies snatched up southern railroads, many of which had been state-owned enterprises, while at the same time, Redeemers wrested control of states from Republican control. Political redemption by the Democrats went in tandem with the sale of state-owned railroad properties to northern business interests, and southern states like North Carolina, Georgia, and South Carolina were in effect "redeemed by railway."[50]

The Compromise of 1877, which settled the disputed presidential election of 1876 and led to the withdrawal of Northern troops, also spoke to this new spirit of development. The most immediate consequences of this agreement were the end of Northern occupation and final demise of Republican state governments, but railroad machinations motivated much of this settlement. Just as the Electoral Commission met to decide the election, Congress voted on the Texas and Pacific Railroad subsidy bill, which a congressman argued was "one of the simplest and yet surest means of reconciling the interests and harmonizing the sentiment of the whole country." Aid for this long-promised route across the country would constitute another olive branch to the South, and for conservative white southerners, the agreement finished the rehabilitation of the railroad's image.[51]

The post-Compromise economic terrain suited the aims of both sides of the New South alliance. By 1880, conservative southerners who had lambasted support for Republican-backed railroad projects were eagerly promoting new schemes of their own. The narrative of Republican corruption attached new significance to the lines built after 1880s, as these roads were planned and built by Redeemers, and allegedly free of the Reconstruction-era abuses. Without a blink of irony, the Bourbon Democrats endorsed internal improvements with the same, if not more, zeal as their Republican predecessors. In perhaps the most extreme example of the aggressive stance of the new state governments, one has to turn to Florida. In 1881, the state set up an Internal Improvement Fund, which handed out land to railroad companies and capitalists at bargain prices. By 1884, the state's Democratic legislature had given out 22,360,000 acres to railroad companies, despite the fact that only 14,831,739 of these acres were considered to be in the public domain.[52] On the other side of the Mason-Dixon Line, and across the Atlantic in England, investors welcomed the apparent stability of the new Bourbon regimes. Between allegations of corruption, extralegal assassinations, broken-down rails, and terroristic violence, the environment of Reconstruction hardly inspired confidence. Further impetus for new railroad development came from the national economic recovery that gained steam after 1877. In 1879, for example, more than twice as many rails were laid in the United States than in any year since 1873, and 180 new corporations were born.[53]

The alliance of northern capitalists and southern Redeemers thus was forged via the northern capital coursing south into railroad corporations such as the IC, the L&N, the SRSC, and other new projects. Yankee investment, through both the federal government and corporations, literally repaired broken rails along with a more secretive and often contested process of corporate realignment. The end result, improved southern railroad facilities, was clear to see. In contrast with many of the South's more intractable problems, such as finding a new labor source for cotton or establishing rights for freedmen, rebuilding transportation was rather straightforward, and the project was a prime example of the wonders that could come with an embrace of capitalism. But black and white Republican involvement, whether via pro-railroad state governments or as empowered workers, had to be purged from the narrative, and southern railroads had to be firmly on the side of white supremacy before white southerners could again praise the railroad. As further proof of the rehabilitation of the railroad and the values of capitalism, one only has to look at the new class of men in charge of the railroads and the South after 1877.

HENRY GRADY COULD HARDLY contain himself. Ebullient from his travels with Victor Newcomb, vice president of the L&N, over the winter of 1880,

Henry Grady proclaimed to his thousands of readers that the "War of the Rail" had begun in the South. "There is no more interesting subject" than railroading, declared Grady, and "the history of wars does not tell of grander results, more thrilling crises and more massive assaults than is furnished in the history of the railroad combinations of the past few months." He continued, "Giants have been fighting giants—millions have been put against millions, dollars have been placed into battalions and phalanxes as men, and bonds have been broken like bones." Railroad presidents were scoping out maps like "Old Van Moltke" of the Prussian army, and over the course of the next decade "the forces here and there in clumps" were "being swiftly marshaled for a struggle that is grander in scopes and result than the South ever saw fought."[54]

It was a marriage made in heaven, or at least conjured up in the fevered dreams of businessmen and reconciliation-minded partisans on both sides of the Mason-Dixon Line. Grady, young Atlanta newspaperman and prophet of the New South revival, and Victor Newcomb, the thirty-six-year-old whiz-kid vice president of the L&N, who had saved the road from certain ruin in the aftermath of the Panic of 1873, joined forces for a whirlwind tour of Atlanta, Nashville, Louisville, and other southern railroad centers in January 1880. The immediate cause of this union was a series of developments that threatened to recast Atlanta's role in the southern rail network. Newcomb's company had been planning to construct the Georgia Western (later the Georgia Pacific) railway line from Atlanta to the West, a project that would tap Alabama's growing coalfields and send the fifth major rail line into the city. Grady's updates from the road quickly took on more urgency as he uncovered an even grander railroad scheme. The L&N was about to purchase a major competitor, the St. Louis, Nashville & Chattanooga, and take steps toward forming a system that spanned the South.[55]

Grady was beginning to step into his role as head spokesman for the South's story that defined this decade, the New South movement, and his travels with a railroad magnate were a perfect way to demonstrate the existence of a "New" South and celebrate the end of Reconstruction. Railroads formed the literal, financial, and ideological connections between Old and New South, linking Grady's selective version of the past and the future. As he traveled with Henry Newcomb, Grady related his version of southern railroad history, painting the Reconstruction years as characterized by malaise. After the war, he argued, southern railroads were "so short, and so seriously entangled and embarrassed that no northern operator cared to take hold of enough of them to make a trunk line." For the ten years before 1880, "the

South has therefore for ten years sat patient and resigned, seeing the whitening drift." Grady lamented how any attempt to consolidate the patchwork of lines was met with "a cry of monopoly."[56]

The "War of the Rail," and the struggle to form cohesive southern railroad systems, was so critical to Grady that he spent weeks on the road with Newcomb, in a personal alliance that symbolized the new regional political economy. The feeling between these two men was mutual, and Newcomb even offered Grady $250 a month to travel as his personal secretary. Not willing to give up his beloved work with the *Constitution*, Grady continued to travel with Newcomb and report on the machinations of "Newcomb's Octopus." Grady declined the offer of employment, but ended up with an even better prize when Newcomb persuaded a friend to loan Grady $20,000 to purchase a share of the *Constitution*. Grady may not have joined the railroad business explicitly, but with a financial stake and prime editorial position at the *Constitution*, his status as spokesman for the "New South" was only enhanced.[57] In a fitting coda to his journey, Grady took in the sights and sounds of New York City, even attending a play with his city's wartime tormentor, General William Tecumseh Sherman, in a Fifth Avenue theater and allowing the general to defend his wartime record in an interview at his hotel.[58] But perhaps the most important lessons from Grady's missives home regarded the wild forces of speculation that northern capitalists were poised to unleash on the South. His trip ended on a Wall Street trading floor, where Grady marveled at the machinations behind the South's "war of the rail." Here Grady described "brokers and operators run[ning] to and fro in a perfect frenzy, with railroads as the cards and millions for stakes—putting fortune, future, home and other honor itself on the turn of a single chance."[59]

Just as capital coursed through railroad corporations and travelers sojourned south by rail, personal trajectories also followed the irresistible track of the railroad, as a new class of leadership took the helm of southern railroads. These new men were critical in moving the railroad network from serving local to regional and national goals. Antebellum southern railroads were meant to develop the resources or the economic base of the towns that built it, or serve the needs of specific states. Presidents or directors of these old roads would be from the towns along the line, and the interests of the company typically matched the interests of these local figures. A new group of leaders emerged in the 1880s, who saw their roads not as distinct entities, but as pieces of a larger puzzle. Their vision was decisive in forging the locally or state-oriented southern roads into a fully integrated national network and in shifting corporate strategies from developmental railroading to territorial. Instead of building railroads to build up a locality, the new railroad barons built lines to carve out territory and gain a competitive advantage over rivals.[60]

Victor Newcomb's L&N serves as an excellent example of the new strategy of railroading. As we have seen, the Civil War had actually proven profitable for the L&N, thanks to federal assistance.[61] But it was only after the ascendancy of Victor Newcomb that the railroad took steps to construct a regional system. Newcomb, a former financial wizard and son of another railroad titan, epitomized the new speculative outlook in the boardrooms of southern railways. At the age of thirty, Newcomb saved the L&N from ruin in 1874 when he induced a London banking house, Baring & Brothers, to take the company's bonds at a favorable price. Upon the death of his father, Newcomb ascended to a position on the L&N board, and then became vice president in 1876. As vice president, and later president, he oversaw a period of aggressive expansion in 1878, and the railroad burst from its original trackage in Kentucky and Tennessee to gain entry into Atlanta and plotting out lines south through Alabama to the Gulf.[62]

The 1880 purchase of the rival St. Louis, Nashville, and Chattanooga system was a perfect capstone. This type of leadership dazzled Henry Grady, who called Newcomb the "youngest of the great gamesters," who was "dazzling the older heads with the rapidity and vastness of his operations." Grady praised how Newcomb was "striking with the rapidity of lightning," and noted how "the apparent disorder of his movements is clearing away and a system grand and harmonious beyond what any one had conceived is taking shape and definiteness." In his moves to consolidate southern railroads, Newcomb had "changed the map of the South, in a half dozen rapid strokes, quickened sluggish currents of commerce and opened new highways." For Grady, more than just personal admiration and friendship was at stake; the entire region's economic future was bound up with Newcomb and the new class of "gamesters" at the helm of southern railroads. Grady praised Cole, the head of the bought-out system, as the "first man that ever gave to the South what it must have before it can win stature or independence—a grand through line from the west to the ocean."[63]

Across the South, similarly ambitious presidents took charge of lines during the 1870s, transforming local and state-based lines to attract traffic from across the region and nation. Examples of these new systems included the Chicago-based Illinois Central, which plotted a route to New Orleans that tapped Mississippi's products, and the Richmond & Danville (R&D), a railroad that once simply connected its namesake cities. Under the leadership of

A. S. Buford, a southerner who one historian argued "personified the southern country gentleman," and capital of northern rail magnate Tom Scott, the R&D linked up with the North Carolina Railroad (NC RR) and grew to dominate the crucial rail corridor between Atlanta and Richmond. The East Tennessee, Virginia & Georgia also made moves to expand from eastern Tennessee to the rest of the state by leasing the Memphis and Charleston in 1877.[64]

The presence of ex-Confederates as either token figureheads or actual leaders was key in solidifying political support for these projects, as evidenced by the career of John Brown Gordon, who played a pivotal role in Grady's Atlanta railroad schemes in 1880. Gordon's career path perfectly exemplified how railroad management could bridge the gap between Old and New South for former Confederates. Eighteen years before this convergence, Gordon was clinging to life on a patch of Maryland farmland, grievously wounded from five Yankee bullets at the Battle of Antietam. In the course of this ferocious battle, Gordon was shot in the calf, leg, shoulder, and arm and most threateningly in the cheek. As he lay unconscious on the field of battle, he nearly drowned to death in his own blood, except that a bullet hole in his cap, placed there as he recalled by "the act of some Yankee . . . as if to save my life," drained the blood. He recovered from these wounds and rose through the Confederate ranks, commanding a brigade in the invasion of Pennsylvania, and excelling during the defense of Richmond in 1864.[65]

Gordon spent the Reconstruction years floundering in a few business interests before launching his political career, rising to the head of the Georgia Ku Klux Klan, and gaining election to the Senate in 1872. In the Senate he served as a personal embodiment of reconciliation, acting as a regional spokesman, defending the South from attacks and urging his northern countrymen to move past the war. When he abruptly resigned this plum position in 1880 to take a railroad job with the Georgia Western, Georgia was roiled by the news. Why would this war hero and highly successful southern partisan suddenly step aside? The answer lay in Grady's machinations with the Georgia Western Railroad. To secure the vital route west of Atlanta, Grady needed to curry favor with Joe Brown, head of a rival western line linking Atlanta to Chattanooga. After complex negotiations, Gordon ended up in charge of the Georgia Western, and Joe Brown gained appointment to Gordon's old Senate seat. Despite "widespread circulation of charges that he had sold his office," Gordon entered the high-stakes world of railroad construction, and an unreconstructed rebel clasped hands with northern capital.[66]

Gordon's wartime experience, as relayed in his 1904 memoir, helps shed light on how Gordon framed his conversion. The new position brought prestige and a financial windfall, but tracing his personal history, one can see how Gordon's past would add extra inspiration to the Georgia Pacific's goal to improve southern rail connections. Describing southern industrial shortcomings and reinforcing the myth of a pre-capitalist Old South, he noted, "We were an agricultural people," which "induced a large majority of our population to cling to rural life and its delightful occupations." Consequently, the South's "railroads were constructed through cotton belts rather than through coal- and iron-fields." His account of Appomattox discussed how the South's future "seemed to them shrouded in gloom," emphasizing the economic disaster the section faced, with "every dollar of our circulating medium rendered worthless," commodities and credit destroyed, slaves emancipated, and "the railroads torn up or the tracks worn out." Fittingly, his journey back home from Appomattox was made "over broken railroads and in such dilapidated conveyances as had been left in the track of the armies." In this retelling of Appomattox, economic redemption would be the South's main challenge, the next battleground in his lifelong career of fighting for the region, so his move from sectional political partisan to railroad tycoon was not a radical ideological departure.[67]

Gordon was not the only one to make such a move from Confederate military service to railroading. In 1861, William Mahone was using railroad chicanery to foil Northern generals. As Union troops were massed in Portsmouth and preparing to move on the Confederate capital, he ran a single train into Norfolk repeatedly, blowing the whistle as many times as possible to trick the Northern troops into thinking his force was much larger than it was. When Robert E. Lee contemplated resigning in the aftermath of the Gettysburg disaster, he recommended Mahone as his replacement. Mahone never rose to these heights, but as general his troops were crucial in saving the Confederate line during the Battle of the Crater. When the war ended, Mahone quickly moved into railroading in this same terrain, becoming head of the Norfolk and Petersburg Railroad. From here he worked to consolidate Virginia's lines during Reconstruction. As a biographer noted, he loved a fight, whether it was against federal troops, voracious northern capitalists, or the Bourbon democratic establishment.[68] Plans for the Texas and Pacific Railway, which culminated in a federal aid package distributed as part of the Compromise of 1877, gained a huge boost after the backing of Jefferson Davis, Alexander Stephens, Beauregard, and R. M. T. Hunter. Samuel Spencer, who would become head of the Southern Railway, spent his war years in the Confederate cavalry.[69]

Men like Henry Grady, William Mahone, and John Gordon epitomized how railroad ventures could spark a mental shift in the white South from war to Reconstruction to New South. White Southern elites went from fighting literal battles with blue-coated Yankees, to the political and more covert resistance of Reconstruction, to the full-throated embrace of the powers of capital in the form of the railroad. New ambitious corporate leaders, old Confederates, and business-minded boosters all found their careers hitched to the railroad boom of the 1880s.

A VISITOR TO ATLANTA on May 31, 1886 would have noticed a stunning sight. In this typically bustling railroad hub not a single train was running. Engines sat idle in roundhouses, and the tangle of lines that converged on the "terminus city" was silent. The only sound emanating from Atlanta rail yards came from within shops, where one could hear the clang and clatter of work crews performing the painstaking work of changing the gauge, or width between the two rails, of these lines from 5 feet to the northern "standard gauge" of 4 feet 8 inches. It was, as the *Atlanta Constitution* cleverly noted, the second time in the history of Atlanta that none of its trains were running. And it did not take much thought to recall the first moment—General Sherman's burning of the city in 1864.[70] In contrast with Sherman's pyrotechnics, southerners eager to fully integrate their rail lines with northern systems welcomed this stoppage. But like the 1864 campaign, this day was a clear victory for the North. Southern railroads were matching the northern gauge, and the symbolism was hardly lost on observers—this shift would constitute yet another way in which the railroad reunited the warring sections, and in this case the connection was literal.

May 31, 1886 was, by any reckoning, a remarkable day in southern railroading. All across the South, traffic ground to a halt as major systems like the L&N, Central of Georgia, and East Tennessee, Virginia & Georgia shifted to the standard gauge. The standardization of southern railroad gauges was at its most basic level an economic process, inspired by the demand to increase efficiencies and eliminate delays and costs at the transfer points between gauges. But like all aspects of southern railroading, the gauge held powerful cultural meaning. The gauge of a railroad is one of the best examples of how a decision that seemed strictly economic in nature could be influenced by culture. Idiosyncratic choices by individual engineers and officials could have a lasting impact, and the history of a line, a corporation, or an entire region mattered in determining the gauge of a road and its connections. Virginia adopted the Stephenson gauge of 4 feet 8½ inches, which would become the standard gauge only due to the personal whims of Moncure Robinson, who had examined British railways before building four Virginia railroads in the 1830s. Gauges could also serve to mark out territory. A road would choose a distinct gauge to delineate the boundaries of its system and clearly demonstrate the area it served, or a state could mandate that all railroads within its boundaries match a certain gauge. For example, in the 1850s, North Carolina's state government tried to channel commerce to the state's coastal ports by requiring that all the state's railroads match a 4-foot-8½-inch gauge.[71]

Southern railroads adopted a wide variety of gauges in the antebellum era, but Virginia and North Carolina's standard-gauge roads would prove the exception to the rule. The 5-foot gauge took off in the region in the 1850s, becoming established as the "southern" gauge, and farther to the west, in the trans-Mississippi South, a 5-foot-6-inch gauge came to dominate. The high point in terms of gauge diversity for North America was in 1863, a fact that bedeviled Confederate railroad managers. The North Carolina Railroad in particular stood out as a chokepoint. The road's standard-gauge territory was situated in the center of the Confederacy's network but surrounded by 5-foot gauges. The Confederate government hoped to change the gauge of the NC RR between Charlotte and Danville to 5 feet, but the work did not begin until April 1865, just as the war ended. Just as crews began to shift the gauge of this line, rolling stock from South Carolina was sent up the line to flee Sherman's advancing army. Immediately after the war, the NC RR shifted back to the standard gauge, but when the R&D system leased the road in 1871, the lease allowed it to modify the gauge back to 5 feet. A lengthy legislative and court battle ensued between legislators seeking to preserve the state's old gauge and the system looking to match that of its Virginia lines. An 1875 court ruling allowed the R&D to change the gauge to 5 feet, but when the rest of the southern lines adjusted to match standard gauge in 1886, the NC RR was changed back to the gauge it originally had held, giving the road a record of four different shifts in gauge in the two decades after the war.[72]

As traffic between the North and South picked up after the war, the expense of managing the gauge breaks began to outweigh the cost of shifting to standard gauge. These breaks between the northern standard gauge and 5-foot southern gauge became literal dividing points between the regions. While on a trip south, Henry Field's train had to stop at Danville, where "we had another proof that we were getting South in a change of gauge." Here the train was run into a framework of timbers, and the entire Pullman car was lifted by hydraulic machinery. The wheels were then swapped to match the southern gauge, and after five minutes the shift was complete. Field noted this would be a major inconvenience if the train was longer. Danville was not the only such point, as elaborate machinery also shifted cars at intergauge junctions like Cairo and Louisville.[73]

The same economic climate of increased traffic and heightened competition that drove corporate consolidation and territorial expansion also motivated southern railroads to match the standard gauge. More traffic meant more work for the hoists, which meant more costs and more delays. After the IC took control of lines in Mississippi in 1878, it soon became apparent to management that the arrangement of hoists at Cairo was not working well. In 1880, the line's president, William Ackerman, wrote to complain about a car that had to wait two days to cross into the North from the South. He wrote that "consigners complain very much on account of this delay" and he argued that "if any further evidence was necessary to show the need of a change of gauge of the southern line you have it in this statement."[74] For the IC, shifting the gauge was part of a general effort to smooth over the connections between Chicago and New Orleans. The company also bought cars for the southern division of the line and went to great expense to replace old ties and iron rails in the South. Several times in 1880 the road had to temporarily suspend the shipment of freight at Cairo, and the road's annual report to stockholders argued that on the southern line "a change of gauge to correspond with that of the Illinois Central is imperative and will be made this year."[75]

As one of the first northern systems to launch a southern expansion, the IC was also one of the first to shift its southern lines' gauge, doing so in 1881. The company's experience in shifting the gauge of its line proved invaluable to other southern lines considering changes. J. F. White, a master mechanic at the IC shops in Water Valley, Mississippi, wrote to fellow southern mechanics about the problems he faced in the gauge transition. In a letter to an engineer with the Charleston & Savannah Railroad, he noted the average cost of the transition, and went over engineering details of how to alter wheels and the bottoms of cars. He also warned that after the change "your cars will be sent to all parts of the country where the standard gauge of railroads" exists, and that southern companies could face more liability for derailments that occurred due to wheels not matching the new gauge perfectly. He suggested carefully labeling every wheel to avoid problems in this department. Copies of this letter were also sent to mechanics with the Central Railroad of Georgia at Augusta, Savannah, and Macon, which further proves the important role of the IC in leading the way in the change of gauge.[76]

Once large systems resolved to change gauge, the rest of the South's railroads had little choice but to follow. As lines switched, they increased the value of conversion for connecting lines, and they would have to also switch. In 1881, the *Railway Gazette* argued the "5 ft. gauge seems doomed to disappear," and as with the change of some roads in Kentucky and the shift of the Illinois Central, "the territory of the 5 ft. gauge will be invaded on all except the ocean sides."[77] Southern railroads competing for northern traffic could ill afford the expense and delay of the hoist system, and stood to lose ground to roads like the IC that shifted first. In an 1883 special report to the president, an official with the L&N argued that the system needed to consider changing to standard gauge because "competition and the exacting demands of commerce" required the company to move products with fewer transfers, and he estimated annual savings of $100,000 and predicted that all the other southern lines would change within a year of the L&N's change.[78] The Georgia Railroad's 1886 report to stockholders claimed the road could "ill afford to incur the expense" of changing the road's gauge, but lamented there was no alternative.[79] Even though the Central of Georgia Railroad's manager thought the 5-foot gauge was a more practical option, "too great a majority of the railroad mileage of the country has been constructed to the four feet nine gauge to consider for a moment the possibility of a change from that standard."[80]

The date of the change itself was set for May 31, 1886, at a time of the year with relatively light traffic. The shift involved a massive mobilization of labor both in rail shops and out along rail lines. Within shops, men like J. F. White worked quickly to ready their cars. Working along the L&N, machinist John Flynn recalled how his force was split into gangs, each with their own assignment. First they used jacks to lift the engines so they cleared the rails. Then they removed the trucks and disassembled the pieces. After removing old rods and driver brakes, they heated the tires, then hammered them into the trucks to match the new gauge. Finally they reassembled the trucks and attached them back onto cars, and they were ready to go.[81] As much of the South's rolling stock was held up in shops or waiting for the new gauge, manufacturers and coal operators were unable to ship their wares even before the suspension of traffic on the 31st.[82]

With every delay costly, the gauge shift itself was understandably rushed. On the L&N's line, in Aspen Hill, Tennessee, section foreman Leon Cox gathered his men at daybreak of May 31, and gave a rousing speech to inspire his men. Eight thousand men poised in similar positions throughout the South as the sun came up, ready with claw bars, spike mauls, and track gauges.

The L&N offered a reward of $100 to the foreman who changed his section in the shortest time, and Cox declared his intention to win this prize. He stated that if there was a "man in that crowd that couldn't run, rain or shine," he should get out and quit, and with an added incentive of postwork beer, whiskey, and barbecue, the men set to work. On the track, the men set to work on the arduous task of lifting up the rails on one side, and placing them back at the proper gauge width. Cox and his crew managed to finish their task by 10:25 A.M. Cox won not only the $100, which he used to buy the promised barbecue and whiskey for his ebullient men, but also a $25 bet with a track supervisor.[83]

For those not working on the tracks or toiling in shops, the day was a moment of both celebration and reflection, with the whole of the South focused on railroads for a day. Crowds gathered in cities like Louisville, where "quite a number of curiously disposed people gathered in the Louisville & Nashville yards and along the track yesterday to witness the change of gauge."[84] Other reporters lauded the technological feat of the shift. On the Waycross Short Line, the Savannah, Florida & Western Road hoped to complete the change so fast that the fast mail could travel from Savannah to Jacksonville on the old gauge, and return three hours later on the new gauge. The Constitution argued, "If they succeed it will be a wonderful feat of railroad enterprise, and will serve as an illustration of the rapidity of the age in which we live."[85] Even if one had no interest in the technological details of the gauge change, the interruption of rail service meant everyone in towns along the lines changing gauge had to be aware of the process. But for some, the interruption of service exposed anxieties and an overreliance on technology. In Atlanta, "many people were made aware of their dependence upon the railroads yesterday. Those that wanted to leave the city could not do so and those that were anxious for their mails could not get them. Today the dependence will be more noticeable"[86] Some towns at intersections of roads changing gauge, like Chattanooga, were totally cut off from rail communication for a day.[87]

But through all these logistical concerns, the reconciliationist meaning of this shift, and the symbolism of connecting the railroads of the formerly warring sections of the country, was certainly not lost on observers. A *Harpers Weekly* cartoon depicting female representations of North and South grasping an American flag in front of a locomotive, with a caption declaring "The Last Spike in Commercial Union," perfectly epitomized the way in which the gauge change exorcised war demons for northerners.[88] Southerners were a little more jovial about what the gauge change meant for sectional relations. A jokester with the *Savannah Morning News* noted that "a good many northern papers think the narrowing of the gauge of the southern railroads makes the union additionally secure, and the possibility of disunion more remote." This is undoubtedly true, as the writer argued, "If any of the northern states try to secede we will whip them back into the union in short order."[89] As he contemplated the gauge transition at Danville, Henry Field celebrated the moment, describing it as "a happy symbol of other changes by which the course of things North and South is hereafter to be run on the same track to the end of a common prosperity?"[90]

Not everything went as smoothly as it did for Cox and his crew in Tennessee. For one, the complicated process of changing wheels and tracks led to some mishaps. On June 10, the *Atlanta Constitution* counted "at least a dozen accidents" on southern railroads since the change of gauge. A railroad man called the accidents "a matter of course" and argued "it would have been a feat without parallel could the changes have been made without being followed by accidents." He defended the ultimate results of the day, arguing there would have been less surprise about these accidents had "the magnitude of the change been fully appreciated."[91] An interview with a railroad man in the *Atlanta Constitution* hinted at the broader significance of the gauge change. He argued "the change of gauge will naturally make railroad combinations easier and will result in such consolidations of railroad interests as will make it more convenient to restrict the number of railroad centers." Railroad combinations like that of the Georgia Central, which "has made Macon a way station," would be even more common, as "all the little roads must tie on to some of the big combinations or be driven to the wall." The man predicted the "growling about railroad combinations in times past" was nothing compared with what would happen after gauge standardization.[92]

These grumblings notwithstanding, one did not have to be a traffic manager to recognize that people flowing back and forth on North–South rail routes was a harbinger of sectional reconciliation. Reunion between the North and South is often located in veterans' reunions, disputes over monuments, and other direct manifestations of Civil War memory, or it is found by tracking the resolution of the political battles that consumed legislators during Reconstruction.[93] But for white southern Redeemers and northern businessmen, the symbol and reality of the railroad, as a method of travel, container for northern investment, and physical network, came to symbolize the New South project and the region's moves past the Civil War. The improved facilities and speed made a direct testament to the region's advancement. Statistics and numbers were certainly important to boosters, but a railroad journey provided tangible evidence of progress. Northern capital flowed south to rejuvenate lines as northern names slowly infiltrated lists of boards of directors. More ominously, these railroad dreams also helped white southerners write the struggles of black southerners out of the history of the War and Reconstruction. Compared with the more intractable problems in the South after the Civil War—such as the rights and the future of freedmen, political terrorism from white supremacists, economic malaise, and the tumultuous transition from slave to free labor in the countryside—railroad progress was much easier to measure. Railroads put the war in the past, and as a new system took shape in the 1880s, the new rail lines and the powerful forces they brought to the South would unleash magical thinking in both white and black southerners.

CHAPTER TWO

The Phantasmagoria of the Rail

The greatest enterprise of the nineteenth century . . . is now in full glory . . .
the most complete, most comprehensive, most exhaustive, most instructive
and beautiful gathering of the products of the world and its peoples, that has
ever been organized.

—*Official Catalogue of the World's Industrial and Cotton Centennial Exposition*, 1884

When describing southern scenery, travel writers in the 1880s never failed to
pour on the hyperbole, but even taking into account their usual exuberance,
they all agreed that the approach to New Orleans by rail was a sight to behold.
As a prospective traveler, you had a number of options. On the Louisville &
Nashville route along the Gulf Coast, the water views of Biloxi and Gulfport
gave way to Louisiana swamps that evoked all the horrors of the gothic South.
Trains on this line cut through grim forests, flew past lazy alligators, and
ducked under Spanish moss draped from ancient live oaks. As British travel
writer George Sala described his experience, "the dark trees tortured into a
thousand phantasmagoric forms" as the pale sun rose amidst the "ghostly
gloom." But this nightmare ended as the line tracked over a wide-open stretch
of land skirting the edge of Lake Pontchartrain. An especially adventurous
conductor would use this opportunity to fire the engines and pick up speed.
"The pulsating breath of the great iron horse," exclaimed one traveler, "kept
time to the increased beating of our own hearts," as his group anticipated the
excitement of the city.[1]

Or one could hop aboard the Richmond & Danville, later to become the
Southern Railway, which traversed "the storied soil" of Virginia battlefields,
traced the Blue Ridge down the Shenandoah Valley to Atlanta, passed the
"Magic City" of Birmingham and its burgeoning coalfields, and then headed
southwest to the Crescent City. Reminders of the southern past and hints of
the region's future coexisted along this tour.[2] Lastly, a tourist could take the
most direct route from the north, a straight shot from Chicago to New Orleans, and watch the scenery transition from the homes and growing factories
of the burgeoning metropolis to well-ordered Illinois farms to ramshackle
plantation ruins. After crossing the Mississippi River and the North-South
divide at Cairo, the line traversed tracks once torn to shreds by Yankee invaders

in a Mississippi version of Sherman's neckties. Periodically, travelers could see broken-down cotton presses and other ruins of the antebellum economy. Dwelling on the past may have appealed to some, but speed was likely the most attractive feature of this route. "Thursday evening you may take supper in Chicago, on Saturday dine in New Orleans," promised one promotional pamphlet.[3]

The travel guides describing routes to New Orleans presented diverse panoramas that unfolded like a dream, and in this idealized state of travel, passengers viewed a variety of landscapes and scenes from multiple eras of southern history. In the illusory world of these guides, the downsides of southern rail travel—racial division enforced with violence, economic exploitation, and various inconveniences and discomforts of spending days on the rails—were totally absent. But if one was to take these routes to New Orleans over the winter of 1884 and 1885, the dreamworld could continue with a short streetcar ride to the Garden District and the grounds of the New Orleans Exposition. After paying a fifty-cent admission fee, you could find, as one piece of enthusiastic ephemera promised, "the most complete, most comprehensive, most exhaustive, most instructive and beautiful gathering of the products of the world and its peoples, that has even been organized."[4] In nine buildings, exhibits displayed every product imaginable, from 115 varieties of "famous Tennessee marble," to 164 types of wood from Louisiana, to "fruits in profusion" from Mississippi, phosphates "in all shapes manufactures and uses" from South Carolina, forty-five Florida ferns, and 1,100 card photographs of Kentucky scenery.[5] One could also stroll to the Machinery Hall and witness an "endless array of machines, adapted to nearly every known want," or check out the Horticultural Hall, a "fairyland" in which one experienced the "splendors of the electric light, with the playing fountains, the vistas of lights and shade; the intoxications of its perfumes."[6] One guide boasted that the 1,650,030 square feet in the main building alone outdid the size of all the other prominent expositions of the age, from Crystal Palace in 1851, Paris in 1855 and 1868, Vienna in 1873, and Atlanta in 1881.[7]

"What does this exposition mean?" pondered a journalist overwhelmed by the magnitude of the affair. The man called the event an "inexhaustible mine—an unknowable study," but the message of this event was by no means inscrutable.[8] Since the first exposition of this format at London's Crystal Palace, these events had become well-known markers of progress for the societies that hosted them, or as Walter Benjamin argued, they constituted "training schools" for the masses, indoctrinating visitors into the rules of the capitalist system. In gathering and displaying every imaginable object, expositions allowed guests and observers to view everything as a commodity and a potentially consumable item. Overstimulated visitors on a whirlwind tour of these events saw rapidly dancing visions of products to buy, technologies to admire, and futuristic architecture to ponder, and they encountered swarms of faceless crowds. The experience at the fairs is what Benjamin called the phantasmagoria, a condensed metaphor for the "dream-like sleep" that descended on the West as modern capitalism took command. The ephemera, travel guides, newspaper reports, and firsthand accounts associated with the New Orleans Exposition attempted to situate the South within this global network of dreamworlds, and they announced the region's arrival to this new age of capitalism. The ebullient accounts of the event made one fact clear: the phantasmagoria of nineteenth-century capitalism had come to Dixie.[9]

Or at least that was what the organizers hoped. A phantasmagoria, by its nature, has limited powers. It is a flickering mirage, not easily seen, and the harsh truths the dreamworld's imagery obscures can easily come to light. This magic also may be visible to a select few. In this case, the phantasmagoria of the exposition had a specific audience of white southerners and northern investors. A black traveler who attempted to partake in an idyllic journey to the exposition would have encountered at best a degrading move to a dirty, smoky Jim Crow car, and at worst outright violence or expulsion. And as we will see, exposition organizers shunted black contributions, and a distinctive African American presentation of modernity, to a segregated corner of the fairgrounds, ignoring the centrality of black labor to the production of the event's displays.

However, the false nature of this story does not lessen the power of the myth the event perpetuated. For the organizers of this event and the New South boosters, northern investors, curious tourists, and more who eagerly attended this gathering, the exposition presented a cohesive grand narrative for southern redemption via the railroad and the magical powers of capitalism. This chapter begins with the event and its condensed metaphor for the railroad's magic transformations, and we will follow the spread of this meta-narrative through a select but powerful subset of the southern populace. The spirit of the exposition and the phantasmagoria of the railroad seduced both southern Redeemers and northern investors as the railroad boom descended on the South in the decade after the end of Reconstruction.

IN A BROAD SENSE, all of the nineteenth-century world's fairs shared the same educational purpose: to inculcate the multitudes to the ways of the new capitalist order. But each fair had a slightly distinct ideological agenda that reflected the host country or region. For the New Orleans Exposition, the southern recovery from war lurked in the backdrop of the proceedings. Charles Dudley Warner, northern author and exposition guest, wrote that the event proved that "the war is over in spirit as well as in deed. The thoughts of the people are not upon the war, not much upon the past at all . . . but upon the future, upon business, a revival of trade."[10] The *New York World Democrat* agreed with these sentiments, noting the event "will convincingly show how completely the South accepted the result of the war, and, so soon as the carpet-bag robbing regime was removed from the region, turned its attention to the development of its wonderful resources."[11] The event's southern flavor could also be seen in its name. Organizers dubbed the exposition the "World Cotton Centennial Exposition," commemorating the hundredth anniversary of the first shipment of raw cotton to England and honoring the crop that powered the economic growth of New Orleans and the American South in the first half of the nineteenth century. Along with the commodified black bodies that harvested this crop, cotton had been integral to the explosive spread of capitalism in both the South and abroad.[12]

The centrality of cotton in the event surely reminded guests of the nexus of enslaved black men and black women, cotton plantations, and global trade that had so enriched planters and northern industrialists before the Civil War, but it also suggested that the exposition could address some as-yet-unresolved questions for the present and future of the region and its place in the global capitalist economy. As boosters and promoters of the New South kept saying, the war and the cotton-based economy that came before it were in the past. So as its talisman, the 1884 exposition took on a new symbol, the railroad. The scenes in New Orleans would not have been possible without the recent revolutions in southern railroading. Pamphlets for the exposition never failed to highlight the improved railroad network the "six grand trunk lines of railway" that connected the city with the rest of the continent.[13] One guide succinctly summarized the link between the encyclopedic displays of products and New Orleans's newfound status as a rail hub, noting the city had "a perfect network of iron ties over which can be gathered the cotton and sugar of the South, the corn, wheat and meats of the West, and the Wines of the Pacific slope."[14] On a more tangible level, railroad corporations provided heavy financial assistance to the event, by giving direct contributions and by reducing passenger and freight rates to allow guests and exhibitors to reach the Crescent City.[15]

Displays, guides, and accounts of the event all spoke to this same message, that the railroad was the essential symbol and the driving force behind this new magical phase in the history of capitalism. The travel guides for the event placed New Orleans at the center of a sprawling and interconnected network, and overwhelming displays of carefully categorized products demonstrated the commodification of the southern countryside. The exploitation of Kentucky coal, North Carolina amethysts, or Georgia lumber, for example, was impossible without rail links and the circulation that moved these products from their origins to market. The exposition took this new southern railroad network's annihilation of space and time to its logical conclusion, gathering the resources, capital, and people of the region under one roof, and placing them on display as commodities for potential consumption.

It was this last function, the commodification of products, that performed a crucial sleight-of-hand on visitors. The commodity was key to the emergence of modern capitalism. When something became commodified, that is, reduced solely to its exchange value, as determined by the whims of the market, the origins of the object were obscured. The labor that went into harvesting, extracting, producing, or transporting the object would then melt away as a potential consumer considers just a numerical price. The value of exposition displays like a slab of Alabama slate or a board of Georgia pine bore little relation to the labor that went into such a product. The exhibits showed all of the South on display, and on sale, thanks to the magical circulation of the New South railroad network. The guides imploring guests to take careful time for study and lauding the event as an "inexhaustible mine" further spoke to the comprehensive and overwhelming magnitude of the event.[16]

Within the halls, the Iron Horse also reigned supreme. Railroad companies set up displays of products from their respective territories, and maps adorned exhibit walls to commemorate railroad growth and to aid those plotting future construction. The Richmond & Danville set up a 6,000-square-foot exhibit, a "wonderful display of mineral and woods, gathered from the country contiguous to its lines," and the Georgia Pacific Railroad brought a fourteen-ton block of coal from a mine near its track.[17] Nebraska displayed a map of the state "aristocratically ornamented with cut corn" that showed all the state's rail lines, as well as the position of each train at 10:00 every morning.[18] The U.S. General Land Office and the office of the Commissioner of Railroads set up an exhibit that displayed a collection of "large maps and diagrams, specially designed to show graphically the growth and mileage of the railroads of this county at different periods." And of course, one could simply look at trains at the exposition. The Cincinnati, New Orleans and Texas railroad built a full-size sample of a section of its track, and though it promised to show a locomotive made entirely of materials from along its line, this engine apparently never made it to the exposition. The Pullman Palace Car Company brought a "fine model of its works" and the company town that produced these cars. The *Railway Gazette* described the exhibition of locomotives as "most of the usual types," with "engines of widely different weights and sizes" from a diverse range of companies from Pittsburgh, Roanoke, Rhode Island, and more.[19] The Baltimore & Ohio Railroad exhibit connected the railroading present to its storied past, showing the first steam locomotive ever used on an American road.[20]

Exhibits displaying an abundance of commodities were not the only part of the fair that served as a microcosm for the dramatic changes introduced by the railroad network. To circulate visitors through the various buildings, organizers set up a mini–electric railroad system that mirrored the development of the network at large. One pamphlet argued, "This plan of rapid general tours and inspection of the entire grounds and buildings . . . will be found preferable to the common plan of an objectless loitering tour which will result in the visitor having no well-settled idea of what he has seen."[21] Other guidebooks offered dire warnings to those who failed to adopt "a systematic course" in viewing the exhibits, the implication being that one would miss important sites, waste time, or become overwhelmed and lost. For example, when entering the U.S. Building, the visitor "should commence with Iowa," then "follow the Guide-Book strictly." Proper order was of utmost importance. When entering the Florida exhibit showing the woods of northern Florida, one must "commence with end next to house in center with magnolia" to have "a proper understanding of them." Though the Machinery Hall may look intimidating, "there are easy and safe steps on and over the platform upon which great engines rest, and by following Guide, no difficulty will be experienced."[22]

The obsession with traveling a fixed route marked a significant transition. Urban travelers prior to this point would take in a cityscape by acting as what Walter Benjamin called a flâneur. A flâneur experienced the city through aimless wandering and witnessed various sights at the pace and direction of their own choosing. But in this new phase of capitalism, ushered in by the railroad, the traveler and consumer's experience was guided not by individual whims, but by corporations and their marketers, promoters, and boosters. This was most apparent within the bounds of the exposition, where guidance was necessary to navigate the overwhelming amount of exhibits, but these transformations also spilled out into the southern railroad network at large in the guides that directed travelers to New Orleans. Railroad companies created carefully curated travel routes that would demonstrate the best attributes of the South, and like the exhibition, distract from more unsavory sites. Deviation from the fixed track of the railroad was impossible, so a rail traveler saw only the country that the railroad traverses, and furthermore, the readers of these accounts, on an imagined journey of their own, experienced only what the author wanted them to. As the accounts of travel to New Orleans demonstrated, the phantasmagoric aspect of the exhibition was easily extended to the southern countryside.[23]

While some visitors surely had perfectly enjoyable times at the exposition, the image presented by pamphlets and ephemera deviated greatly from conditions on the ground. If one looked a little closer at the exposition, cracks appeared in this façade. For one, the exposition itself was not nearly the success its boosters made it out to be. It ended up $470,000 in debt and attracted only 1.1 million visitors, far short of the four million predicted by organizers. It created hardly any noticeable increase in economic development in New Orleans, and a prominent figure in its organization fled to Honduras after being indicted for embezzlement and forgery.[24] A postmortem editorial regretted that "it was impossible to have the exhibits in order at the opening day," a fact that led to negative press.[25] Claims of the city's healthful character could not dissuade some from fears of yellow fever, a disease that, as we will see, periodically stalked the city. More observant visitors may have noticed decreased activity and an eerie calm on the once-bustling levees, evidence that the very railroad network that aided the exposition was slowly draining trade away from the Mississippi River and shattering New Orleans's stranglehold on the cotton trade.[26]

Beyond the structural issues with New Orleans's post–Civil War economy, the phantasmagoria of the event was a creation for a white audience that provided an incomplete definition of capitalist progress. For one, the informal and formal segregation regimes emerging in this decade severely constrained the movement of black visitors and guests. While southern travel was usually not as transcendent as pamphlets made it out to be, smooth travel experiences were even harder to come by for African Americans. Within the exposition halls, black visitors could freely browse exhibits, and the organizers devoted a space for African American contributions. Crammed in the far northeast corner of the U.S. Building, organizers set up a "Colored People's Department." The displays were organized by state, and the exhibits contained inventions, artwork, and other examples to demonstrate African American progress. It was not a complete collection—unfortunately, a train wreck obliterated Iowa's African American exhibit en route to New Orleans—but an author of a guidebook still found the display's inventions to be "very ingenious and useful" and the display of art to be "very commendable."[27]

The earnest efforts of these black artisans and inventors should not be downplayed, as African Americans typically took advantage of events like this to display racial progress and advancement. But at this and other southern fairs, the realities of the Jim Crow South usually undermined most aspects of the black community's presentations. For example, in Atlanta's 1895 exposition, an exhibit of black progress was undercut by a mockup of an Old South Plantation and a re-creation of a West African village, complete with black natives in loincloths.[28] Even more insidiously, highlighting one small corner of the event as a "Colored People's Department" ignored African American contributions in other areas. Just as black men and black women picked the cotton crop that the event honored, they also laid much of the track of the railroad network, and they mined, harvested, or extracted the bulk of the items on display. The organizers thus rendered invisible the black labor crucial to building both Old and New South capitalism, and the exposition reports that focused solely on descriptions of exhibits only perpetuated this illusion.

The exposition was but one ephemeral moment, and the event fell short of its lofty expectations, but the message it conveyed about the importance of the railroad went far beyond New Orleans. Newspapers and trade journals disseminated rosy reports to a receptive national audience, and the imagined exposition created in these accounts in many ways held more significance than what actually happened in New Orleans. The exposition, or at least this romanticized version of the gathering, translated the economic transitions of the South's recent railroad growth into a cultural narrative that told a clear story about the progress of the region, and the role of the railroad and capitalism in bringing about this progress. It distilled the railroad network's functions into a single event, and it presented the idealized dream of what railroads and capitalism could do for the South. Overwhelming displays of commodities, signs of progress in the countryside, and the experience of rapid rail travel combined to form the New South's railroad phantasmagoria.

This railroad dreamworld was in its most condensed form at the exposition, but the idea could be seen in smaller communities across the region as the railroad boom picked up steam in the 1880s. In their descriptions of new rail lines, celebrations of the railroad, and accounts of construction, elites continued to promote the same mythology that emerged from the exposition. They touted connectivity and boasted of the network's many new links;

they celebrated circulation, the rapid movement of peoples and commodities through the network; and they welcomed the commodification of the southern environment that the railroad fostered. This message came from a distinct minority of urban, business-oriented southern white men, and it presented a warped view of capitalism that prioritized what they saw as magical and natural growth over labor and the contributions of black southerners. But the top-down origins of this story did not dull its impact. These were the men at the helm of the regional political economy, and their message about burying sectional hostility and welcoming investment resonated well beyond the South.

ON AN APRIL AFTERNOON in 1886, W. W. Collins saw an old acquaintance, Jeff Lane, strolling down Second Street in Macon, Georgia, and was struck with divine inspiration. Like that of so many ambitious men of the New South, Collins's mind was lost in railroad reverie. He dreamt of a new rail line that would reach Florida, and the fortuitous appearance of Lane reminded Collins that Lane's father, Col. A. J. Lane, just so happened to hold a charter for such a road. After this rendezvous, Collins and Lane began to scheme to make the dream come to fruition. A third man, W. B. Sparks, was relaxing on his farm, with a desire to "supply the missing link between the snow and the sunshine." Hearing of Collins's efforts, Sparks joined the plot, and from these humble origins the Georgia Southern & Florida Railroad (GS&F) was born.[29] So goes the apocryphal story of the birth of the GS&F as told by a journalist with the *Macon Telegraph* on the date of one of the line's first excursions. A chance encounter between prominent Macon men was all it took for the construction of the 285-mile line linking Macon with Palatka, Florida. The truth of this legend is unknown, but for readers of the *Telegraph*, an exaggerated story like this served to personify and localize the larger forces and flows of capital that allowed the road to be built. A tortuous process involving outside investment, Wall Street financing, and a lengthy construction process with a massive mobilization of labor was reduced to a meeting of three Macon businessmen. The careful crafting of this tale spoke to a critical point about a new railroad: every railroad had a story, and the way that local elites crafted these corporate narratives mattered. The narrative of a road, as told through promotional pamphlets, local newspapers, and railroad leadership, inspired investment, motivated locals, and linked these areas into the broader New South story of progress.

These local railroad stories spoke to how the spirit of the New Orleans Exposition was seen in statehouses, town squares, and corporate offices across the South in the 1880s. When explaining why a railroad arrived in an area, structural economic factors like the availability of investment, strength of the national economy, or stability of the region were key, but new rail projects would be impossible without the inspiration and support from local elites.[30] Here we examine three southern towns, Macon, Georgia; Troy, Alabama; and Greensboro, North Carolina, that all hitched their fortunes to new railroad projects in the 1880s. Macon boosters built the Georgia Southern & Florida; Troy welcomed the Alabama Midland Railroad that linked Montgomery, Troy, and Bainbridge, Georgia; and Greensboro was a crucial point along the Cape Fear and Yadkin Valley Railroad (CF&YV), which eventually stretched from Mt. Airy to Wilmington and the sea. These three towns certainly do not encompass all of southern railroad development in this decade, but their experiences are emblematic of a broader trend. Out of the fifty-eight southern railroads operating in 1890 with more than 100 miles of track, eighteen of these lines had been constructed since 1880, so the southern railroad boom was more than just the expansion of large systems.[31]

The southern railroads built in the 1880s had a distinct message when compared with the railroad stories told in other parts of the nation. For one, these lines were hitched to a regional message of rebirth that framed new economic development as a response to war and Reconstruction. A promotional pamphlet for the CF&YV line reminded readers that the state's general assembly first chartered the road in 1879, just as "the political rehabilitation and reconstruction of the seceded states had been accomplished." The message here was clear: the project would not be tainted with Reconstruction-era corruption, since the right men—Redeemers—were in charge now.[32] The *Troy Messenger* similarly recalled how Troy was "but a small village" after the Civil War, and with the arrival of the town's first railroad, the Mobile & Girard, an "era of growth commenced, which only a railroad could have brought." The line gathered trade from surrounding areas, cotton receipts grew, and "the modest quiet country town" had taken on "city airs." But in the years since, "the world moves, and railroad owners, as a class, are no respecters of towns." Competing projects crisscrossed the region, threatening to leave Troy "high and dry—a mere way station on a trunk line." Fortunately Troy had "some businessmen who had brains to conceive, and pluck to carry out" a scheme to build the Alabama Midland.[33] This line would save the town from certain ruin, and place it back on a trajectory of growth launched in the aftermath of the war.

Local control, or the fact that businessmen from the town played a role in the road, was hugely important to the narratives behind these lines, as evidenced by the random encounter that led to the creation of the GS&F. When Colonel Lane first applied for the original charter of the road in 1883, twenty-five of Macon's "most prominent citizens," as well as a few representatives from counties that the proposed line would go through, drew up an application.[34] In a letter to the local paper, Colonel Lane expressed desire that the road should be a "people's road," and that Macon and the counties through which the road ran should own it.[35] As construction proceeded, the *Macon Telegraph* crowed that the road was "a Macon institution. Her capitalists and citizens have paid out $600,000 in hard cash to inaugurate and fairly start the undertaking" and "the people of Macon own a large majority of the stock."[36] Promoters of the CF&YV similarly touted the Tarheel origins of their project. The *Greensboro Patriot* lauded the fact that every man in the company was "a native North Carolinian," and the *Fayetteville Observer* bragged that "the gentlemen who control this enterprise are all North Carolinians fully imbued with the spirit of progress which now pervades the whole South."[37] In the road's 1883 annual report, the president wrote to stockholders that "the management and affairs of the Company will to-day go into the hands of gentlemen of ample means and the highest character—native North Carolinians—and thoroughly identified with her interests."[38]

Along with being manifestations of local control that echoed the regional cries for development from New South boosters, all three of these lines were in some measure assertions of independence from the larger rail systems coalescing around the region. Greensboro merchants, who hoped to avoid monopoly control of their town's transportation, first conceived the CF&YV as a cudgel against outside domination. By the 1880s, North Carolina's railroads increasingly were falling under the sway of large systems, specifically the Richmond & Danville, which recently leased the North Carolina Railroad, a move that threatened to render Greensboro economically irrelevant.[39] More than just a demonstration of independence from outside corporations, the road would also be free from the restraints of state interference. A letter from "JUSTICE" praised Mr. Gray, the road's president, for his hard work and noted that if not for his devotion the road "would long since have gone, like the State's other railroads, upon the public shambles, a humiliating spectacle to her citizens."[40] At both ends of the GS&F, businessmen seized on the new line as a way to become more independent in the midst of a wave of consolidation in both Georgia and Florida. In Palatka, Florida, editorialists complained about the growing monopoly power of the Plant System, which seemed poised to buy the rival Florida Railway Navigation Company in 1888. Prior to 1888, the *Palatka Daily News* explained, Florida had "enjoyed the benefits of the competition for her business." Florida's towns, the paper argued, "could only preserve their independence by defeating the purpose of the monopolists." The GS&F would be independent of the Plant system, yet the paper worried that the monopoly would eventually strangle the new railroad from both sides and cut off its business.[41] A letter to the *Macon Telegraph* echoed this sentiment, attacking the monopolistic actions of the Plant System. Florida, the author wrote, "is not asleep, neither it bound by the chains of steel, welded together by the hands of monopoly." The arrival of a new independent road was a "bright light approaching from the North and we hail the coming of the locomotive over the rails of the Georgia Southern and Florida Railroad."[42]

The president of the Alabama Midland road framed his attempt to build the line as a battle against the Central of Georgia, "that giant corporation," which was the "implacable and insatiable enemy" of the Alabama Midland. The Central had recently been expanding into southeast Alabama, and with the dearth of railroads in the region, the road enjoyed what amounted to monopoly power. The Alabama Midland, an independent road that had the potential to link up with competing systems, posed such a threat to the Georgia Central that the Central tried to legally and physically block the construction of the new road. In a lengthy letter to area newspapers, the Alabama Midland's president listed a series of grievances against the Central of Georgia, which was allegedly trying to block the construction of his new road in 1889. The Georgia Central first tried to foil the road in the early negotiating phase, then stole rolling stock that had to pass over its line, and constructed a line to a crucial ridge just to prevent the Alabama Midland from building there. He closed by claiming the line would be open in the next ninety days, "in spite of the opposition of this grasping and oppressive monopoly."[43]

The discourses surrounding the development of these three lines framed them as locally controlled, independent businesses, but these arguments masked the connections to outside sources of capital that were crucial to building these roads. For all Troy residents' bluster about funding the road and the antimonopoly sentiments of Captain Woolfork, the success of the Alabama Midland depended on the magnanimity of another system, Henry Plant's Savannah Florida & Western Railway, which saw the road as a lever to gain access to this growing part of Alabama and beat back the influence of the Central of Georgia. Final construction of the line was guaranteed only after Plant signed a contract for many of the road's bonds.[44] The CF&YV road was ostensibly a state-chartered project to help North Carolinians, but in 1883, the state sold its share to a group of New York capitalists. Only after this point could the road reach completion. Frustrated with long delays, the *Greensboro Patriot* eventually welcomed this inconsistency, arguing simply, "We want the road completed. The interests of the whole State demand its speedy construction."[45] W. B. Sparks, president of the GS&F, made constant trips to New York to sell bonds of the road. After a trip in February 1888, the *Telegraph* bragged that Sparks found "many warm friends of the road in the North," who eagerly awaited the road's completion.[46]

These small-town boosters held a deep faith in competition as a salve for local economic woes, and in their minds, a bright future with lower rates and rapid business growth was only one new railroad away. Theoretically, the more railroads a town had, the more competition the town could expect for the shipment of its products, and the lower rates the town would have. Rates were often based on whether a location was a competitive point, with multiple railroads, or a noncompetitive point, where one railroad or system controlled all rail transportation. The desire of every town to become a competitive point fed into a dynamic of overconstruction, and the building of lines that seemed inefficient from the perspective of the incipient large rail systems. For rail managers trying to set stable rates, the proliferation of new railroads to spur competition was a nightmare, leading to rate wars and wild swings in rates. Overcompetition is most often linked with railroads in the west, where the seemingly random fluctuations of rates inspired outrage and confusion, but southern towns subscribed to the same theories. From the perspective of communities like Macon, or Greensboro, which had rail transportation but had higher rates than larger neighbors like Atlanta or Raleigh, they could never have enough railroads.[47]

The importance of new railroads to small southern towns may be best illustrated by the desperate pleadings of towns that missed out on new connections. Alabama rail projects like the Alabama Midland and various extensions of the Central of Georgia continuously bypassed the small town of Andalusia, and the town had to wait until 1899 to get a railroad. Pathos dripped from the editorial pages of the *Covington Times*, which spent the bulk of the preceding decade publishing periodic editorials dubbed "railroad rumbles," in an attempt to attract the attention of one of the major rail corporations building in the area. In one such article, the paper exhorted its citizens to "slip off the worn-out clothes of inactivity and don't-care and pull on the modern paraphernalia of progress," and work with the Central of Georgia to ensure the town could "hear the shrill yell of the iron horse."[48] Another editorial claimed that town had all the necessary amenities to be the foremost metropolis of southeast Alabama, but the only element the town lacked was a railroad.[49] A railroad would "press the button" and Andalusia would "spring up as if touched by magic, and her sister towns would soon fade completely into insignificance."[50]

The bleary-eyed rhetoric of railroad boosters in towns like Macon, Greensboro, Troy, and even tiny Andalusia provided localized versions of the regional narrative of New South railroad progress, and it tied the far corners of the South into a global story of the phantasmagorical spread of capitalism. Places with railroads were magical, vibrant, and energetic, while places without rail connections were stagnant, inactive, lethargic, and at risk of decay. Without railroads, a town would fade into irrelevancy and wither away, but with railroads, the magic of capitalism's development could spring a town into life. The narratives crafted to support these new railroads promised physical connections to the southern railroad network, guaranteed a measure of independence and local control, and touted the benefits of connections to the magical forces of capitalism, and they assured ideological links to the New South project. But as all of these boosters would soon find out, it was one thing to plan a railroad—building one was a whole other matter entirely.

FROM HIS CAMPSITE in the Mississippi Delta in 1882, Charles Iverson Graves could hardly care less about these far-off forces shaping southern railroad development, or the many wonderful things boosters were writing about railroads. Graves simply missed his wife. A whirlwind of a life had brought Graves to the profession of building railroads, and his services were in high demand by 1882. Before this job, Graves had served in the Civil War as a Confederate naval officer; operated a farm near Rome, Georgia; and trained men as an officer in the Egyptian army. Graves got into the railroad business with a job on the Georgia Pacific, and the railroad boom of the 1880s kept him on the move and gainfully employed, which is how he ended up in the swampy swath of land between Memphis and Vicksburg in August 1882, where his task was to both locate a route and construct 100 miles of railroad.[51] He set up his headquarters in Memphis, but life in the railroad's world was lonely. He wrote his wife and begged, "Perhaps some of these days when we are working on the road you will come down and see me!"[52] Men like Graves, the white elites directing construction of the South's new railroads, were on the leading edge of the advancement of the exposition's values into the southern countryside. From the perspective of planners, railroad officials, and local newspapers, the phantasmagoria appeared again, imbuing their actions with magic and obscuring the arduous and often deadly labor involve in railroad building and the ever-present financial struggles of running a railroad company.

On a systemic level, New South boosters liked to speak of the naturalness of the railroad network's spread, so metaphors comparing railroad expansion to the plant or animal world were common. One post-exposition editorial boasted, "Slowly, toilfully, surely the great spider of progress—the railway—spins the web that is destined to catch the flies of a new prosperity for the South!" As these "busy railway spiders go on spinning," the editorial continued, the "movement, born of the Expositions, goes steadily on!"[53] A British traveler on southern roads similarly celebrated how railroad companies "have laid down branch lines in all directions, running out like the arms of an octopus, grasping at distant towns and villages and halting in the most beautiful secluded spots in the inmost quarters of the land."[54] These comparisons made railroad growth seem inevitable and a foregone conclusion, and they placed the exposition at the center of this magical expansion.

On the ground, the process of railroad building was not nearly as smooth, and accounts from the front lines revealed a language far less graceful than the elegant spinning of spiders—that of contestation and of hypermasculine visions of conquest and warfare. The neat, orderly displays of products at the New Orleans Exposition belied the fact that the commodification of the southern hinterlands was not an easy process, but the men overseeing new railroads were still able to twist the magic of the railroad into personal glories. The martial nature of railroad building, referred to by Henry Grady as the "war of the rail," began from the top down, with the men who directed these projects.[55] The men behind southern railroad projects were dreamers, schemers, and self-styled masters of men. Many, like Graves, were ex-Confederates who perhaps still suffered from the lingering traumas of defeat. Captains, colonels, and generals, keeping the military honors they earned during the Civil War, littered the rolls of southern railroad management. Examples include Captain Woolfork with the Alabama Midland; Colonel Lane, the original patron of the GS&F; and General Gordon, who funded the Georgia Pacific. A well-placed Confederate war hero could work wonders for a corporation looking to establish itself in the New South. General P. G. T. Beauregard, hero of the early Confederate war effort, helped piece together the fragments of the Mississippi Central immediately after the war. Indeed, in 1870, the roster of the officers and directors of this line contained three generals, six colonels, a major, a captain, two doctors, and one judge.[56]

Whether they were actual or self-styled generals, many of these men portrayed railroad construction as a form of warfare between rival corporations. As the Alabama Midland neared completion, the rival Central of Georgia system got a judge to issue an injunction to prevent the construction crews from building to the small town of Ozark, where the Alabama Midland crews were storing thirteen cars of steel, rails, and other construction material. The injunction effectively locked the Midland out of its equipment, and as soon as a Montgomery judge overturned the injunction, building crews raced to reach Ozark before the Central could respond. Employees even stood watch at the Ozark telegraph station to prevent Central employees from alerting their superiors. As soon as the line was completed to Ozark, the train with the aptly martial name "R. E. Lee" picked up the material and brought it back to the Alabama Midland line.[57] The claiming of new territory also seemed like an army's conquest. As the GS&F advanced through south Georgia, the company got involved in such a fight, with "three railroads in the field, all fighting over the rich, but unused territory" between other lines.[58] In the minds of the press, rival companies in the mad scramble for southern territory constituted warring armies, waiting to claim land and its resources for the company.

Railroad presidents similarly saw themselves as engaged in fierce combat. While he was building bridges north of Vicksburg, Graves was on the front lines of a clash between the IC and its rivals. In 1880, the Mississippi Delta constituted virgin territory, as far as railroads were concerned. For long, few had thought it was feasible, let alone profitable, to build railroads through the flood-ravaged plains and primeval forests between the Mississippi and Yazoo Rivers.[59] In 1878, the IC gained control of a rail corridor through Mississippi, an integral part of its main line linking New Orleans and Chicago, and company officials began charting plans for new construction. In 1885, J. C. Clarke, a vice president with the IC, journeyed through the area, and though he noted the physical difficulties of building a line through the Delta region, he also found the lands rich, describing "the largest timber I have ever seen," and the "corn, cotton, and oats, and can grow hay, German millet, sweet and Irish potatoes" that locals grew there.[60] But all the German millet in the Delta could not singlehandedly inspire construction there. The real reason the IC began to plot extensions was to foil competitors. Clarke argued the IC needed to quickly move into the area north of Yazoo City "rather than leave open a territory that is sure to be occupied sooner or later by some interest that may possibly prove to be rival to the best interest" of his company.[61] After hearing a report that a narrow-gauge line between Jackson and Natchez was seeking to extend, Clarke declared, "The theory of invasion of territory of our competitors of such territory as they claim as theirs, is a thing of the past" and rued how the company's competitors no longer hesitated to impinge on their territory.[62] The real force behind this narrow-gauge incursion turned out to be railroad titan Collis Huntington, and in response to this rumor, an IC official argued that the system "must extend from Yazoo City northward at once and occupy this territory, otherwise our Yazoo division will be a failure."[63] As large swaths of the South were parceled out for development, claiming land for a rail line was akin to the rivalries between warring nations for these railroad men.

Like actual armies in the field, the crews building southern railroads had to rely on supply lines, in this case infusions of capital from investors, that kept open the flow of steel rails and workers' pay. Men like Graves were acutely aware of the connections to networks of global capital that determined their progress. Before his stop in the Memphis area, Graves worked on the Georgia Pacific between Atlanta and Birmingham, when work suddenly stopped as the precariously funded company teetered on the brink of insolvency. In May 1882, Graves wrote, "It seems that the tightness of the money market has prevented them from getting money on reasonable terms and so it has been necessary to 'hold up' on the work." General Gordon, an officer with the road, traveled to Europe with the hope of floating the road's bonds, and his success would lead to "a boom" with the road.[64] Two weeks later, construction still was at a standstill, and though prospects were brightening, Graves fretted that "much will depend upon the result of Gen Gordon's visit to Europe and the money Market."[65]

Looking at the men behind these railroads certainly helps explain why they applied language of war to the project of capitalist expansion, but more than just the egos of railroad presidents and embittered former Rebels justifies this militaristic tone. Examining the impact of these new railroads on the environment points to another form of railroad warfare. In excursions and pamphlets, boosters touted how new railroads would impose the logic of capitalism on the countryside and bring order out of the supposed chaos of undeveloped areas. The GS&F actively encouraged both turpentine production and lumbering. Before the road was even completed, the *Telegraph* reported that "sites have been located and there will soon be established sixteen saw mills and four large turpentine stills, the freight from which alone will be sufficient to pay the interest on the company's bonds."[66] In Wenona, a correspondent reported that the forest was so thick that sawmills were being placed every five miles along the line.[67] Along the CF&YV, a promotional pamphlet argued that the road would "render accessible a vast area of virgin timber land" and give an impetus to the production of naval stores and a well-ordered arrangement of industries, as "the puffing engines of the mills erect one at every station, and the forests resound, as the train speeds along, with the axe of the woodman."[68] And a series of prospectuses in the *Montgomery*

Advertiser laid out the potential products along the line of the Alabama Midland. They detailed Southeast Alabama's "vast forests of yellow pine," and gave a county-by-county survey of the agricultural practices of obscure Alabama counties from the iron ore deposits in Butler County to the yellow pine of Covington County.[69]

These accounts all speak to how the railroad network compelled structure, standardization, and commodification. Trains required flat surfaces, manageable grades of elevation, and a clear path, and the accouterments of a railroad—watering stations, depots, loading docks, and more—similarly needed to fit a certain form. As railroad systems grew larger and larger, sprawling interstate companies could hardly tolerate local idiosyncrasies. For the sake of simplicity, and for more efficient construction, many companies applied a standardized design for passenger depots. This geography created by the railroad took a familiar form no matter where it went. Even today, a driver in the rural South can easily spot a town built by the railroad by a distinctive cluster of older buildings, usually a depot and other businesses, along a faded rail corridor.[70] As the railroad prospectuses demonstrate, the harvesting of resources also took on a predictable configuration. Camps for producing turpentine or for logging had to be marked off by corporate territories and spaced out in an efficient manner.

As work progressed on new lines, the battle to impose this structure on nature certainly evoked military metaphors. Graves next moved to the Delta to work on a line between Vicksburg and Memphis, where he and his fellow workers quite literally were at war with the environment. Major Wilson, the man in charge, later recalled the enormous difficulties his construction crews faced. The country north of Vicksburg was "almost a wilderness in 1882," subject to the whims of the Mississippi River. Yearly floods and levee breaks periodically cut off progress, and Wilson noted "over many miles it seemed as if the foot of man had never trod. It was nothing in the world but a canebrake and a wilderness."[71] Conditions along the GS&F, and the wide-open Georgia Wiregrass, were not nearly as formidable, but building crews did encounter some difficulty. Thirty-two miles south of Macon, the line passed through a deep cut of soft limestone, and a force of hands labored "night and day" for fifteen days to dig through the rock.[72] Even once the line opened, this spot was trouble, as every time it rained heavily the embankment caved in and covered the track.[73] The Blue Ridge Mountains, which stretch from Maryland to Georgia, formed perhaps the most prominent natural barrier in the region. The Western North Carolina Railroad finally succeeded in crossing this impediment in the 1880s, and promotional material touted both the "cu-

rious curves, embankments, cuttings and tunnels" in the picturesque mountain region, and the "boldest strokes of engineering in this country" that
allowed it to be built.[74]

Even after these railroads were completed, the imposition of capitalism's
geography on the surrounding territory also was a struggle. Deep into the
nineteenth century, large portions of the southern countryside remained an
open range. Wild hogs, the descendants of pigs that escaped from Spanish
conquistadors, roamed wild, and a vast forest of longleaf pine stretched up
the Atlantic coast from Florida to Virginia. The South lagged behind the
Northeast in closing off these areas, much to the chagrin of antebellum agricultural reformers and antebellum travelers who constantly complained
about the ramshackle nature of the landscape, but to the delight of poor
whites and blacks, who could use these common areas to supplement their
meager farm production. Roaming hogs made excellent meals, as evidenced
by the spread of pork barbecue traditions, and open-range forests gave nearby
residents access to hunting, fishing, and gathering. The Civil War also helped
render disarray in the countryside. Livestock died by the millions from disease or combat, and marching armies trampled fences or harvested them to
build breastworks or build fires.[75]

The rapid advance of the railroad was, along with the war, a turning point
in the battle between order and chaos in the southern landscape. States gifted
vast tracts of land to railroad companies to help encourage development, and
these companies naturally sought profitable development on the land along
their lines. Moreover, a newly built railroad inevitably carried a lot of debt
and held the hopes of investors for profit, and the best way to make up this
debt was to haul commodities from the area around the line. So if an area had
good soil, a familiar agricultural landscape emerged. The amount of cotton
cultivation in the South increased dramatically when railroads penetrated
new areas. Other areas were locked into the production of certain cash crops,
such as melons in parts of south Georgia or oranges in Florida.[76] Railroads
through the South's longleaf pine forests usually led directly to a proliferation
of turpentine camps and lumbering operations.[77] The Richmond & Danville
Railroad's exhibit at the exposition was sure to remind visitors that "four-
fifths of the lines traversed by these roads is still in forests, and these include
all the best woods common to the section."[78] If there is any common denom-
inator to these various forms of economic activity, they all inspired fencing
and the marking off of land.

Though the results varied by landscape and environment, a new railroad
invariably led to a more capitalistic use of space in the area in which it moved,

and the open range of the South came to an end thanks to railroad expansion. In some cases this meant the killing of entire animal populations. As the GS&F neared completion, a traveler spotted thousands of doves thirty miles south of the line's terminus in Macon, and the local paper noted that a "party will be made up to slay the birds" and a "special car will be obtained." While southern rail lines could not match the magnitude of the buffalo slaughter on transcontinental lines, many new lines like GS&F did penetrate territory with significant populations of animals.[79] Fences inevitably followed the taming of wild landscapes, both to stake a claim to territory and to keep wandering livestock off of tracks. Fences controlled humans as well, as they barred people from certain areas and gave boundaries to the crime of trespassing. The rationality of numbers and statistics supported the fencing off of southern land. In 1905, the L&N calculated the amount of money the company paid for killing livestock and compared this with the cost of fencing. The money expended for fencing jumped from $68,068 to $440,798 between 1890 and 1904, and the amount of money paid for stock declined from $.01361 to $.00785. The conclusions were clear: fencing along company roads saved the company 29 percent of the money invested in fencing, and the continued use of fences made economic sense to the company.[80]

The privatization of these commons areas was nothing less than a southern version of the enclosure movement. The sharecroppers, squatters, and other landless poor folk of the South lost access to commons resources with the closure of the southern range. The lords and landowners who fenced off the British commons in the seventeenth and eighteenth centuries did so with the aid of a whole series of new laws criminalizing offenses like vagrancy and trespassing. State violence, in the form of brutal executions, forced expropriation to the New World, and imprisonments, was critical to the expansion of capitalist economic relations. This certainly was also true for the growth of the New South railroad network. State coercion supported this privatization of space and expropriation of squatters, and as we will see, the system of convict leasing was critical in the construction of these railroads.[81]

The vantage point of the southern environment, landless squatter, or worker casts the intrusion of the railroad in a violent light, as an invader, conqueror, or harbinger of calamity. So perhaps the notion of railroad building as war gives a hint at the deeper violence at work in these transformations. When it comes to the Janus-faced mind of the South toward railroads and the environment, William Faulkner's short story *The Bear* is most neatly poised on this divide. Faulkner's protagonist Isaac McCaslin had spent years stalking Old Ben, a large black bear lurking in the woods of Yoknapatawpha County,

Faulkner's fictional county based loosely on his Mississippi home. Old Ben, the representative of the fading wilderness, eventually is slain by the hunters, and Isaac later returns to the site of the hunt, but the clamor of a passing train disrupted his peaceful reflections. "It had been harmless then," reflected the narrator as he recalled past hunts near the track, and they would hear the train pass "for one petty moment" before it was "absorbed by the brooding and inattentive wilderness without even an echo." But after the ultimate killing of Old Ben, Isaac's coming of age, and the growth of the railroad and the nearby sawmill, the train took on a different and darker meaning. It "had brought with it into the doomed wilderness even before the actual axe the shadow and portent of the new mill not ever finished yet and the rails and ties which were not even laid."[82]

As Faulkner reminds us, railroad construction thrust its participants into a broader American saga, the quintessential struggle between civilization and wilderness. The notion that the new southern railroads penetrated virgin wilderness was, of course, a myth. Native American cultures altered and transformed many of these areas long before Europeans even set foot on New World soil.[83] Southern railroad construction also was more a process of infilling than expansion. These lines connected already existing towns, like Macon and Palatka, instead of plowing into unoccupied spaces like in the West. But from the perspective of the railroad crews, areas without railroads, and without the structuring power of capitalism, were savage and untamed. Boosters sometimes made this contrast explicitly. The "throb of the locomotive is the heart-beat of civilization. Intelligence, wealth, Christianity, follow it everywhere," proclaimed a speaker at an 1890 Atlanta chamber of commerce meeting.[84] Framing the pine forest waiting to be harvested as a wilderness only heightened the urgency of their projects, and it placed boosters at the forefront of a battle to tame and order the American wilderness that drew a line from the Puritans to Manifest Destiny and to the ultimate closing of the frontier in 1890.[85]

As crews began to translate railroad dreams into tangible reality, railroad construction lent itself readily to comparisons with war. The unfulfilled desires of victory from ex-Confederates, the adventure of the life in a work camp, the struggle against natural vagaries, and the process of imposing order on chaos fueled this martial mentality. For the men behind these projects, the militarization of railroad building invested in the process of translating investment into concrete action with even more importance and it would also render the ultimate victory, the completion of the line, that much sweeter for the men behind these projects. While this front-line perspective may not have been as smooth as boosters' metaphors of animal growth, like the exposition spiders spinning their webs of progress, it performed a similar feat of obfuscation. At both the big-picture and the ground level, white southerners used railroad magic to foreground narratives of white heroism, whether these tales be of economic wizardry, martial glory, skillful mastery of men, or the imposition of order on a chaotic environment. This phantasmagoria obscured the unsavory aspects of railroad construction and the process of commodifying the southern countryside, writing the labor of African Americans and other common workers out of the story, and reducing the southern environment to a field of conquest.

WELL BEFORE THE DEATH of Old Ben in the Yoknapatawpha County woods, epochs of southern history collided in William Faulkner's fictional town of Jefferson on the day the town's first railroad opened. When Jefferson welcomed its first train, it rolled into town decorated with flowers. Colonel Sartoris, community leader since before the war and driving force behind the new railroad, stood at the helm blowing blasts on the whistle. When the train stopped, "there were speeches at the station, with more flowers and a Confederate flag and girls in white dresses and red sashes and a band."[86] The Civil War past and its railroading future united around Sartoris and the flower-bedecked locomotive. Though fictional, Faulkner certainly was familiar with the veneration of new railroad connections thanks to his father's career building a line through northern Mississippi, and this scene could have occurred in any small town welcoming a new rail line.[87] The opening of a new rail line formed one of the most significant moments in many towns' histories, the capstone to a lengthy construction effort, a harbinger of future growth, and an announcement that the locale had joined the railroading world. As new railroads opened up in town after town across the South, the railroad phantasmagoria again appeared in these localized celebrations.

Just before New Year's Day in 1890, the elite of Troy and the greater area of southeast Alabama gathered for a similar scene. The occasion was the completion of the Alabama Midland, a project that, as the *Troy Messenger* argued, would "set in motion the wheels of progress and develop southeast Alabama in to what God destined her to be—the garden spot of this entire sunny Southland." A special train left the line's terminus in Bainbridge, Georgia, and arrived in Troy in the afternoon after picking up guests from points all along the brand new route. At 8 o'clock the guests gathered for the "grand banquet" for the road's stockholders, where they were welcomed with an "outburst of music" and a dinner menu that included oysters, Kansas City beef, and mince pie. During the lengthy dinner, the "Toastmaster" gave a series of salutes to investors, railroad officials, local religious leaders, town authorities, engineers, and the press. At the emotional peak of the event, a man stood up and delivered a seventeen-stanza ode to the road's builders. The song began, "Now, some think building railroads the softest kind of snap," and then detailed the many steps involved in railroad construction, from raising money, acquiring right-of-way, purchasing engines and cars, setting up the telegraph lines, and hiring superintendents. The song closed by noting, "Of all the enterprises, that are underneath the sky, there's none that beat the A.T.I. and A.M. Ry."[88] Troy's boosters presumably slept well that night, full of whiskey, oysters, and good spirits due to their hope that their town had just experienced economic salvation.

In town after town, ritualized railroad celebrations solidified the phantasmagoria of the railroad—uniting town elites, outside investors, and corporate officials behind a veneration of the awe-inspiring power of the Iron Horse. Though the exact date would vary wildly due to lags in construction, celebrations also marked the arrival of the CF&YV all up and down the line. The ultimate completion of the road to Greensboro in 1884 led to a celebration that included speeches by at least six prominent men, music from the Greensboro Concert Band, a fireworks display, and a banquet with dancing.[89] And in June 1888, the road reached Mt. Airy, and "excursion trains carried thousands of people from every point along the line" of the road to mark "Mt Airy's railroad connection with the great outer world." For a town like Mt. Airy, receiving a railroad for the first time, the opening of the line was understandably a major milestone in the history of the town.[90] When a branch of the GS&F reached the small town of Culloden, excursionists on the first train enjoyed the drilling of the Quitman Guards, and heard a speech from Judge Emory Speer, a native of the town who had risen fast through the federal judiciary.[91] Railroad building was an exercise in town building, and the completion ceremonies served to cement this link.

The process of construction of the South's new connections was arduous, messy, and costly in terms of blood and treasure, but the railroad celebration distilled this process to the arrival of a train and all its glorious symbolism. On the pages of the local press, a new railroad brought forth dramatic imagery from the pens of editorialists. Many used language that conveyed loud sounds and blasts to signify progress, and they framed the railroad as a dream for the surrounding countryside. As the GS&F pushed its way south, the *Telegraph* reported, "The locomotives will soon be nosing around in a country that never dreamed before of having a railroad."[92] The new trains "must appear like a vision to the people in sections through which a railroad never traversed before, as it sped along like a streak of gold and ebony."[93] Hearing the whistle for the first time was a common metaphorical device to display the hope of new towns that were about to receive a rail connection for the first time. A correspondent in the small town of Gordon wrote that the Alabama Midland was "one of the assured successes of the present age," noting, "it is now probable that the Iron Horse will roll up to Gordon within the next 60 days for our citizens to hear its whistle."[94]

The railroad celebration did more than just unite townspeople; it cemented the link between a town and its hinterlands. Typically, a new railroad would run excursion trains to let people survey the line, and to demonstrate the town's newfound mastery over the surrounded countryside. The excitement of rail travel heightened the power of these opening ceremonies, and the printed accounts of these new journeys disseminated this message to an audience beyond those who attended the ceremonies. After the GS&F opened in 1888, a journalist with the *Macon Telegraph* traveled down the new line to describe the road and the country through which it ran. The author lauded how the trip from Macon to Valdosta was "strictly upon schedule time over as smooth a road bed as can be found in Georgia," and on the return trip north he stopped off at various towns on the line. At Valdosta, a town "drawing in closest affiliation the citizens of Macon," he found active business, heavy rail traffic, and a robust trade in cotton. Heading back north, he noticed "vast and primeval forests of pine" ready to supply both lumber and turpentine. By the time he reached Adele, a town "which the new railroad has called into existence," he could barely contain himself. Only a few months before, this town was "one unbroken pine forest with not a stick amiss." "Behold the talismanic effect of the railroad!" he proclaimed. The rest of his journey back to Macon continued in the same vein. At Cordele, "everything continues on a boom," and in Vienna, "the wheels of progress continue more freely."[95]

Two years later, the opening of a GS&F branch line to Culloden was marked with an excursion with several hundred local residents. A reporter described how the "train moved swiftly on past many factories in operation and other structures in course of completion," offering tangible evidence of the real and ever-growing prosperity of Macon." After leaving Macon, the line went "through gardens and farms, showing what kind of traffic is germane to the road." The reporter commented on melons, pine trees, corn, and cotton, and "as the train sped on groups of whites and blacks gathered along the track, waved welcome to the road which brings such better changes and such greater prosperity to their future."[96] These narratives read the exact same way as accounts of the exposition's exhibits, as they detailed exhaustive lists of resources, and they spread a similar lesson about the ease with which everything in the South could be commodified. Every product seen out of the window on these trips constituted a potential windfall, every rail junction served as a potential boomtown, and every panoramic view was full of resources waiting to be harvested.

Even after the initial trip down a new line, newspapers continued to follow the progress of the countryside with periodic reports from the towns farther on down the line that extolled the remarkable impact of the railroad. For Macon reporters, the exciting growth in the territory tributary to the GS&F was a much-celebrated focus of travel accounts in the years after the road's opening. One man riding along the line argued, "The rapid development of the country through which the road passes forms one of the most striking chapters in the history of Georgia's growth."[97] As the road began to run, reporters marveled at the changes in the countryside. In the newly formed railroad town Cordele, a writer went back to the Civil War to form a broader narrative of progress for the area, noting, "the slaves have been emancipated, the cotton and corn furrows leveled, and the steam whistles of two great arteries of commerce now resound through a neat and thrifty town increasing every day in population and importance."[98] On an excursion to Cordele, one "is reminded of the towns up West which the papers tell us 'grow up like magic.'"[99] Any evidence of growth or progress was attributed to the magic powers of capital, channeled into a new area by the railroad. The fate of Fayetteville, along the CF&YV, "seemed to hang upon a thread" until the completion of the road.[100] Another editorial noted the town was "stirred now with the life of great expectations, its waste places building up, its warehouses and its homes in demand at any price, its streets trod again by traders from afar."[101] After the Alabama Midland's ultimate completion at Bainbridge, the *Troy Messenger* reported, "The entire region of Southeast Alabama is feeling the impulse of a renewed energy. All along the road new towns are springing up, new farms are being opened, mills are erected in many places, and the march of improvement keeps steadily on."[102]

When the CF&YV reached its long-awaited outlet on the North Carolina coast at Wilmington in 1890, the *Wilmington Messenger* released a special "Cape Fear and Yadkin Valley Edition" of the paper, complete with prominent depictions of the road's management, and detailed descriptions of the towns along the line. The issue let Wilmington residents take stock of their new connections, pay homage to the corporation's leaders, and learn about the new areas opened up to rapid trade and travel. Another article detailed the potential commodities on the line, like coal, timber, and farming products, while another listed improvements like sawmills, churches, and new towns that were springing up along the line. In one fell swoop, Wilmington gained connections with all these potentially productive areas, and the paper framed the road's arrival as a turning point in the history of the town. With the port's natural advantages, and newly completed connection, the city could compete with other Atlantic ports like Norfolk, and the *Messenger* concluded, "The Die of Destiny favors the metropolis of N.C."[103]

From the initial celebration, the first expedition down the line, to the resulting narrative in local papers, the opening of a new rail line took on a common sequence of events. As town after town opened up more and more rail lines, this progression was repeated across the South, and it would be readily familiar to business-oriented "New South" white men. The white elite who performed this ritual consciously celebrated some aspects of rail construction—finding and securing sources of capital, engineering marvels, and economic impacts—while ignoring the contestation, exploitation, and violence inherent in railroad construction.

OF COURSE, WE HAVE seen that the transition from hinterland to profit was not that simple. And like the troubled financial fortunes of the exposition, railroad dreams of so many southern towns failed to live up to the lofty futures promised in these events. The gleaming new rail lines often became abandoned, rusted-out shells as companies fell into financial distress, or outside systems seized control of these independent lines. Macon, as anyone who has been to Georgia knows, did not supplant Atlanta and become the railroad center of the South. But the railroad celebration, both the actual gathering and the attendant press coverage, brought the railroad phantasmagoria and the myths of the exposition to small towns across the South. As railroads spread throughout the South in the 1880s, a cohesive narrative took shape: the railroad and its unbridled connection, circulation, and commodification would save the region. The elites in charge of the region's political economy hitched these economic transformations to the powerful symbolism of the railroad to support this story. This also was a story with national resonance. Northerners, whether they be investors, railroad officials, politicians, or consumers, embraced this story as a way to reintegrate a troubled region into the national economy. And just like the phantasmagoria distracted from the many issues with southern railroading, the New South story let the nation conveniently sidestep messy issues like the economic and political rights of African Americans and the intractability of southern poverty.

Despite its power, a minority of the southern population created and sustained the exposition story, and it coexisted among a wide range of counternarratives. Gleaming exposition organizers woke up from their dream with a financial (and perhaps literal) hangover, the investors behind the GS&F saw their railroad victory turn to horror when their company fell into financial ruin, and all the railroad glories in the world could not bring Charles Iverson Graves solace when he ended up forlorn and alone in a dismal patch of land deep in the Mississippi Delta. So it is with all dreams. The dreamer may awake to a sober reality, or a pleasant reverie could quickly turn into a hellish nightmare. Was the exposition the greatest fair ever held or an unabashed failure? Were new railroads a peaceful force of nature or an engine of violent warfare? Did the rail line through Yoknapatawpha County deserve Jefferson's revelry or Isaac McCaslin's mourning? What else did the dreamland of the exposition render invisible? Though we can already see the tensions lurking beneath the surface of the dream, the New South story, and the notion that capitalism would redeem the South, maintained its power. To discover why, one must examine how this story fended off other challenges to its primacy, and we will next turn to a series of narratives that white boosters deliberately wrote out of the broader New South story: the experiences of African Americans.

CHAPTER THREE

Conjure the Railroad

There is not in the world a more disgraceful denial of human brotherhood
than the Jim Crow car of the southern United States.
—W. E. B. Du Bois

The black men swung their picks and hammers in unison, chanting in tune as
they toiled away at a nameless and obscure work site. Their labors were intense, as the process of grading and laying track for a railroad was, to say the
least, a grueling, monotonous, and repetitive job. After the corporation secured
the necessary funding, surveyors plotted out a route, and lawyers acquired
the necessary rights to the land, crews went to work moving soil, rock, and
clay to grade the track and provide a smooth surface to satiate the demands
of the Iron Horse. Once the grade was set, workers pierced the flattened
earth, driving iron ties and steel rails into wooden ties and the soil below.
This work took on a steady rhythm—a highly coordinated effort would allow a gang of workers to efficiently drive in a section and then move on
down the line at a rapid clip. This beat often inspired singing among the work
crews, giving the men a way to pass the time and keep up morale on a grueling job.[1] As the men at this site sang, their lyrics spoke of many topics—the
hardship of the work at hand, tales of the legendary "bad men" of their race,
and sorrows of their life on the road—but they all circled back to a common
theme: the railroad. Songs mentioned southern railroad companies like the
Seaboard Air Line and the Southern Railway, and they yearned for "that ole
railroad train" which could someday take the men away from this distant
camp and back to their homes. One of their songs spoke to the process of
crafting these narratives. As the lyrics related, their songs would "conjure the
buildings up out of black earth, conjure the railroads into steel-blue snakes
with singing."[2]

   This exact scene was fictional, appearing in one of sociologist Howard
Odum's "Black Ulysses" novels, but it was inspired by Odum's extensive field-
work with black southerners. In these works, Odum took readers on a journey with his invented character Black Ulysses, a rambling African American
man who drifted from work site to work site. Ulysses was a uniquely New
South creation, as he was a freely mobile black man whose life was inextricably linked to the railroad network and the forces of capitalism that pulsed

through it. Not only did he work at railroad construction sites, the railroad carried him from job to job, and the railroad infused the folklore, songs, and legends of Black Ulysses and the other black men and black women he encountered. Sometimes he settled down long enough to find a lover, but the lure of the road always returned and he would inevitably leave for a new adventure.[3]

Odum's portrayal of this character leads to two conclusions that frame the investigations to follow in this chapter. For one, the saga of Black Ulysses reveals the ways in which white southerners used the lens of the railroad to stereotype and marginalize black southerners. The alienated black worker was a gross exaggeration of the damage industrialization waged on black families and a racist stereotype to boot. Many black men held on to industrial work in railroads, lumber camps, and more, as a means of supporting a stable family, and the extensive descriptions of Ulysses's criminality and wayward ways reinforced white perceptions of the inherent nature of black criminality. Odum's writings suggested precisely the opposite, that black labor, particularly the type of mobile work fostered by the expanding railroad network, served only to degrade, not to uplift, the black race, and this perspective placed black labor, like the displays at the New Orleans Exposition, outside of the enervating powers of capitalism.[4]

But Black Ulysses's invitation to "conjure the railroad" can also provide a valuable entry point into an aspect of southern railroading that white southern elites liked to ignore: the ways in which black southerners were able, like the New South boosters, to invoke the railroad's magic. In his swaggering boasts of work site triumphs, his cross-country rambles and adventures, and his invocation of black folk heroes like John Henry, Odum's Black Ulysses demonstrated some of the ways that black southerners could appropriate the railroad and construct counternarratives to the New South booster story. To "conjure the railroad" could mean a wide range of things. It was a powerful metaphor. It imbued the railroads with magic, transmuting them into dancing snakes. The danger of the snake adds an element of menace that speaks to how the railroad created new spaces for black men and black women to fight back against white supremacy's advances. Finally, the rest of the song reveals how this metaphor was connected to a long history of struggle. The following lyrics invite singers to "conjure the cotton, conjure the shovel, conjure the mule teams, conjure all the scrapers," citing the labors of slavery.[5]

We have seen how white boosters, politicians, and travelers invoked the magic of the railroad to heal the trauma of war, signify a brighter future, justify their political rule, and unite their local communities behind outside corporations. But as the forces of capitalism spread through the South via the railroad, black southerners also sought to harness this power. In work camps, rail cars, courtrooms, churches, and dance halls, black men and black women tried to "conjure the railroad" and reinsert themselves into the history of capitalism. In doing so, they met with efforts by white southerners to tame this railroad magic. In the white mind, the railroad network introduced bewildering and often-menacing new archetypes of black southerners and white elites, and the southern mass media deployed these stereotypes to devastating effect. In this chapter we trace how black southerners seized the opportunities provided by the new era of railroad-fueled capitalism, namely, labor, mobility, and consumption, and we examine the pains the white South took to deny these powers to black southerners and ensure they remained outside the grand narrative of the New South's rise.

THE WORK SITE where Black Ulysses was able to "conjure the railroad" could have been any railroad camp in this era. As work crews laid tens of thousands of miles of track in the South in the decades after the Civil War, a metronomic clang of metal and mournful vocal accompaniment reverberated throughout the region.[6] Singing during railroad work drew on a long musical tradition for the crews, who were mostly African American by virtue of the New South's heavily racialized convict labor system. Decades before the railroad boom, on sweltering plantations in Louisiana, Mississippi, and other states of the Old Southwest, planters and their overseers pushed gangs of enslaved people to faster and faster rates of picking and processing through a brutal speed-up known as the pushing system. Physical torture—a cavalcade of calibrated whippings and beatings—and the increased cadence of the gang system unleashed productivity gains in the fields that in turn fed a ready supply of cheap cotton to mills around the world.[7] In the face of this early form of industrial time discipline, slaves sang songs of sorrow, defiance, and deliverance. Odum argued that the movement seen in black folk songs at the turn of the twentieth century evoked "the swaying bodies, the soothing rhythm, and swelling harmony of the old spirituals." So while the railroad would become the quintessential symbol of the great nineteenth-century capitalist speedup, it had an antecedent in southern cotton fields.[8]

Returning to the sparse camps after a day of punishing labor on the rail lines, men continued to share stories and tales from their work sites. Perhaps a worker accomplished feats of unimaginable strength in the day's task, or perhaps the crew had encountered a particularly imposing physical obstacle. For a population that largely lacked access to the written word, this oral form of news was the best way to keep up with events and learn about the wider world. These snippets of information would then make their way into the songs sung on the track. From here, these stories took on a whole new life. They traveled and evolved, taking advantage of the mobile nature of railroad work. When a line was finished, crews scattered to new jobs, bringing legends and tales from previous work sites and spreading songs through the railroad network. At new camps, old stories could be shared, and certain verses could be updated and changed. This rapidly moving infrastructure of camps constituted a new means of cultural expression and resistance. Decisions made in a New York office building, a Richmond statehouse, or a London trading house set in motion these work crews and generated these new shifting narratives from the ground up.[9] Like the synchronized speedup of the gang system, this subversive communication network also had precursors in slavery. Though masters liked to assume their slaves were totally compliant worker drones, slaves clearly talked to other slaves and shared stories, folklore, and plots of resistance and rebellion. The mobility and connection of capitalist exchange only aided in these clandestine interactions. For example, subversive ideas spread via the ships, port cities, and plantations of the interconnected Atlantic world of the 1700s, and touched off a series of rebellions from New York City to Jamaica to South Carolina.[10]

The significance of these songs and snippets of narrative that emerged from railroad work camps was heightened by the fact that black railroad workers were not a group particularly well represented in standard historical sources. A man working an entire day in a convict labor camp had no time or ability to write a diary or compose a series of letters to loved ones, and after his departure or death he would likely have left behind nothing but a tally or ledger in an overseer's log book. The difficulty of recording the day-to-day livelihoods of common laborers was compounded by the willful ignorance of top-down sources. Companies and prison officials listed crews as numbers and calculated their existence in the harsh accounting of profit and loss. Railroad celebrations like those in Troy and Macon honored the men who planned the line or marveled at resources found in the newly untapped countryside, but ignored those who actually built the new railroad. Similarly, local newspapers cheered the progress of a line, but hardly devoted attention to life in work camps. The New South project, as we have seen in the New Orleans Exposition, was largely predicated on ignoring or marginalizing the crucial labor of black men and black women.

In the early twentieth century, folklore specialists and sociologists like Odum descended on Appalachia and other corners of the rural South, and they collected hundreds of examples of folk songs. Their efforts were to some extent a race against the modernizing advance of the Iron Horse. As one professor feared, "the rattle of the locomotive" would overwhelm "the thin tones of the dulcimer and quavering voice of the Last Minstrel of the Cumberlands."[11] For white academics seeking out lingering vestiges of the past and reminders of the "Old South," isolated mountain whites and African Americans, many of whom were still ensnared in sharecropping arrangements that seemed to be out of time, were an intriguing prospect to study. Though their collections are often tainted by the racial biases of the day and by the collectors' notions that they were studying uncivilized and backward groups of people, their collected songs, tales, and legends of the railroad camp—these counternarratives of resistance from below—speak to the experiences of the black men and black women who toiled in railroad construction camps.

One such story from below emerged from the mountains of western North Carolina after a particularly nightmarish construction process. Boosters celebrated the completion of the Western North Carolina Railroad, which stretched from Salisbury to Asheville and beyond, as the opening of an awe-inspiring route to the "Land of the Sky," but from the start this project was plagued with issues. The Civil War and a series of corrupt deals during Reconstruction long delayed the progress of this line, but once funding was secured, political pressure to complete this route was immense, and the work progressed at a brutal pace. The foremost challenge in building this line was one of geography. To get from Old Fort to Black Mountain, the line had to ascend over 1,000 feet in three and a half miles, while maintaining a suitably low grade. The only way to solve this engineering riddle was for the route to snake along a creek and ascend higher and higher in a series of loops. Mountains proved even more formidable barriers, and workers had to blast six separate tunnels through the rocky peaks to connect these loops.[12] The state sent 500 convict laborers to build this road, and at least 125 died over the course of the grueling drive to connect Asheville to the rest of the South. The company allotted a mere thirty cents a day to care for and feed workers, and the crews had to contend with a breakneck pace of work, the vagaries of the mountain climate, and bosses who were largely indifferent to the loss of life and suffering. Tunnel construction brought its own hazards. Workers deep inside a mountain could contract "the bends" and die slowly, or perish quickly in one of the many cave-ins that plagued the project.[13]

This was a story that did not make it into the rosy pamphlets promoting the route to prospective mountain tourists. One advertisement noted the "grand connection" the road made and how it was "another line of transport to the productions of the great West to the seaboard." "For mountain scenery the road is unequaled, and commends itself to the sight-seeing tourist," the pamphlet further bragged.[14] When the song collectors reached the mountain communities near Asheville, they found a grim song called "Swannanoa Tunnel." "All caved in," repeats this song's lament, sharing the tragedy of the Western North Carolina Railroad. The song is a ballad with a beat that matched the rhythm of a railroad grading gang. It is a simple tune, and its genius is in the ease in which singers could modify or add in new verses. One can easily see how the song could grow and change as it moved from singer to singer. Further verses reference the cold wind of December, the hooting of an owl (an Appalachian death omen), a boast about hammer-swinging prowess, and the death of John Henry. It unveils a series of tragic stories from below, and reveals a world of unjust convict labor and extreme danger—a railroad nightmare, to be precise. Most significantly, it humanizes the black men and black women who toiled on this road, giving voice to their sufferings.[15]

The ballad of Swannanoa Tunnel does more than just relate the news of this specific disaster. It serves as an introduction into the nightmarish convict labor system that built most of the South's railroads. The men and women who worked and died on this road were ensnared in the pernicious convict labor system, a peculiarly New South form of labor exploitation. Convict labor took off in the region after the Civil War, as it fulfilled elites'—both planters' and industrialists'—goals of industrial advancement and labor control, and it turned the alleged criminality of the convicts into profit for state governments that were desperately short on funds. In some ways the system was worse than slavery, as industrialists had little incentive to treat their hired workers well. Men, and some women could be swept up into the system after receiving hefty sentences for trivial offenses like vagrancy or failing to pay off minor debts. In coal mines, turpentine and lumber camps, railroads, and other industrial sites, these convicts performed labor crucial to the modernization of the South. Without the heavily discounted labor costs provided by convict labor, much of the southern railroad network would not have been built. For example, for nearly every new railroad in Georgia constructed between the end of the Civil War through the 1880s, the grueling task of grading the route was done entirely by convict labor.[16]

Convict leasing also functioned as a system of racial control that helped sustain white supremacy. The vast majority of the convicts were black, so the system meshed with white assumptions about black criminality, and it supported the rise of Jim Crow segregation in law and practice. After emancipation, a whole body of pseudo-scientific literature emerged using racist explanations for what whites saw as the predilection of African Americans for crime. The roots of these arguments lay in antebellum justifications for slavery. Slavery was essential, slaveowners had maintained, because it controlled an otherwise violent, lazy, and dangerous black population. In the New South era, white scientists argued that freeing slaves only awakened latent tendencies toward criminality in black men and black women. The notion that the black men and black women in the convict system were unredeemable only bolstered the cruelty of the system and expendability of the convicts.[17]

The use of convicts did more than just cheapen construction of southern railroads. For many southern whites it served to ameliorate concerns over the human cost of rail construction. Convict labor labeled these workers as criminal, so the white press covering new rail lines held few qualms about the morality of this system. As the CF&YV line neared Greensboro, the local press breathlessly updated the progress of the line, and cheered the continuous arrival of new convicts, as more men meant speedier construction. In December 1882, the sheriff delivered a "colored convict" to the road and reported that things were lively, with 114 hands grading the line. "Hasten the day," concluded the reporter.[18] Papers even lauded the road for its good treatment of laborers. Only seven "broken down, worked down hands" had to be returned to the penitentiary, and rates of sickness had never gone above 2 percent.[19] Few white readers bothered to worry about the fate of the crews of black men working in strange and dangerous pockets of the South, as they had seemingly deserved their fates. As the *Greensboro Patriot* argued concerning a fifteen-year-old black boy arrested for stealing a pistol, the boy was "a fit subject for the C.F.& Y RR."[20] Reporters covering the progress of new lines also downplayed the horrors of convict labor by describing the workers as faceless massed armies. A Macon reporter described a force of men "as thick as bees" at work on the GS&F line and expressed hope that once the tracklayers "strike the Wiregrass they will have clean sailing and the steel rails will cover the long distances in a hurry."[21] Another news piece describing the Macon Construction Company's 800 men at work on the line held a more important message to readers: that "no line of road promises more for Macon than does this."[22] The accounts reckoned the labor of these men as a pure commodity stripped of its humanity, just as the exhibition displays—of Alabama pine, Florida phosphates, or Arkansas cotton—were seen solely in terms of their monetary worth.[23]

The invisibility of railroad labor and the convict system was further compounded by the fact that the construction of the southern railroad network occurred in distant corners of the South, a fact that not only made life miserable (and deadly) for workers but also obscured these labors from the eyes of observers. Charles Graves was a free white man, a former Confederate veteran who embarked on a life of railroad construction after the war, and his letters constantly complained about his distant workplaces. By 1883, Charles Graves was deep in the Yazoo Delta, and a fellow engineer expressed sorrow "to learn that you are broken down in that abominable place." As he argued, "no white man has any business to live in the valley of the Yazoo River," and he hoped Graves "may be quartered on your new divisions in a much healthier and more pleasant location."[24] Another itinerant New South railroad worker, H. A. Grady, traveled from one obscure locale to another as he worked on railroad construction projects in Alabama, Georgia, Louisiana, and Texas. Grady's lowest point came in Louisiana, where he sent one letter from a location simply named "Louisiana Swamp." Near Girard, he described how "everything is covered with long gray moss," and "it is all very unhealthy and having chills is the chief employment of the leisure hours of all."[25] In this later stage of railroad development, the swaths of land that lacked railroads were typically far-off hinterlands with challenging terrain, such as deep forests, swamps, or treacherous mountains.

Though this work was mostly unseen or it was rationalized or unrecorded by white observers, the human cost of southern railroad construction was considerable. In Florida, J. C. Powell dubbed the state's network of camps an "American Siberia," and he wrote of a band of convicts sent "into the tropical marshes and palmetto jungles" of the Lake Eustace area to build a new railroad line. These men "went to certain death," as the camps lacked provisions for shelter and "the commissary department dwindled into nothing." Men ate the tops of palmetto trees to survive, overseers tortured dissidents, and diseases quickly spread through the ranks. Similar horrors awaited the men building the Waycross Short Line between Jacksonville and Savannah. Crews experienced great difficulty as construction proceeded through Fox Swamp, a "wide and dangerous quagmire." After the camp moved to Camp Hillyard, thirty-two miles north of Jacksonville, spinal meningitis broke out among the convicts and the camp became "human shambles," and even the guards asked to be discharged. The "treatment" for this disease was to hose the workers down with cold water.[26]

It would be unfair to blame these disasters solely on the harsh Florida climate, as conditions were little better farther north in Georgia. During construction of the Selma, Rome and Dalton Railroad, sixteen out of the 211 convicts employed by the road died in a six-month period in 1868. Contractors pushed their crews to their physical and mental limit, keeping them at the work site as long as possible. Drivers enforced discipline with whippings and beatings as convicts toiled to move earth by shovel, pick, and in the most extreme cases, dynamite. In all, an estimated 400 convicts died during the twelve years the state leased them out, a rate that far outpaced both the mortality in antebellum prisons and the deaths on free labor railroad projects. Men could be swept into this system easily—one man from Augusta was convicted of a misdemeanor and toiled at four different railroads in different corners of the state. As in the rest of the South, the cruelties of Georgia's convict leasing fell mostly on the state's black residents. The percentage of convicts who were black hovered around 90 percent for much of the system's existence. Despite what the typical gendered division of labor of the time would seem to suggest, women also played a role in the forced construction of southern railroads, and in Georgia's earliest experiments with convict labor on rail lines, they performed many of the same duties as men. The labor may have been the same, but female convict laborers' traumas were compounded by sexualized punishments, rape and sexual exploitation, and callous attitudes toward childbirth.[27]

Due to the lack of capital endemic to southern railroad projects, the use of convicts was essential in pushing underfunded projects to completion, as seen in the case of the Virginia and North Carolina Construction Company. Investors formed this company at a meeting in Danville in April 1888 to build the Roanoke Southern Railroad from Roanoke to North Carolina. The project was chronically short on funds from the start, so the investors tried multiple strategies to raise money. As road surveyors plotted their path to the South, they waited to set the final route, hedging their bets in an effort to get towns like Rocky Mount and Salem to compete to raise bonds for the road. When this money came up short, the company sent officials north to induce outside investment. With such uncertain financing, the road had to save money on labor, so to cut costs of construction, the road paid both North Carolina and Virginia for convict laborers, who cost the company less than a dollar a day per worker. From April to October, their work camp swelled from twelve to forty-seven convicts, but corporate leaders had to continually wrangle with state governments and competing industrial interests for access to more convicts. As construction hit its peak on both sides of the state line, 100 from Virginia were at work in Henry County, and 120 from North Carolina worked near Walnut Cove, along with a number of free laborers. But even this was not enough for the men behind this road. In 1890, a new law in Virginia opened up more convict labor, and the road's president personally went to Richmond and Raleigh to plead his case with officials from both states.[28]

The ultimate human toll exacted on this project, and on countless other rail lines, will probably never be known. Official reports and advertisements rendered the vast majority of convicts faceless, and most workers were seen only as numbers that could save money for a company and rush a line to completion. The bulk of the Roanoke Southern line's story that survived in print concerned, as one surveyor argued, the "imperfectly developed" mineral resources, heretofore unappreciated by locals, that the line could tap.[29] The *Manufacturers' Record*'s mused that once completed, the line "would be a powerful competitor for the profitable traffic which is now held by the Richmond & Danville," and the paper hoped the road would "carry the products of Virginia's coal mines, its furnaces and its grain fields" and "furnish the tobacco regions of North Carolina with a new outlet to the markets of the country."[30]

Some may see the prevalence of convict labor as an example of a New South deviation from capitalist development, just as the Old South was an allegedly pre-capitalist aberration in an aggressively capitalistic United States. Without free labor, how could there be capitalism? But it makes more sense to see convict labor as capitalism taken to its extreme. If we are to see the Old South, as many newer histories do, as central to global capitalist development, convict labor forms a crucial continuity between two eras of southern history. The labor of commodified black bodies was essential in both, and slavery and convict labor both sustained the racial order of white supremacy.[31] From the perspective of record books and account books like that of the Roanoke Southern, convict labor took the logic of capitalist labor exploitation to its extreme, extracting as much profit and wealth from workers as possible. The phantasmagoria's obscuration of labor, far from being a flaw in New South capitalism, was the point. By cleaving free labor from the railroad network's growth, the white South and railroad corporations denied black southerners the potentially empowering nature of railroad work.

The danger this free labor represented to the New South racial order can be seen in the ways white Americans aggressively circumscribed the black railroad labor that was outside the convict system. For all of the black men and black women ensnared in convict labor, plenty of black southerners worked in jobs that paid some kind of wage. Between 1890 and 1910, the number of black workers in railroad companies rose from 145,717 to 334,433, an increase thanks mainly to the better pay of these jobs, the growing railroad systems, and the desire of black men to move to more urban areas. About four-fifths of these men were common laborers, and these black men moved cargo, inspected and repaired track, toiled in locomotive shops, worked on construction crews, and performed the other manual labor tasks required by the vast railroad network. Though much of this work was unskilled, and thus not very well compensated, black men were able to rise to higher positions—like fireman or brakeman—on some southern lines.[32]

Unlike convict labor, this was a potential challenge to the leadership of the white South and their emerging postwar regime of white supremacy. Under the employment of the growing railroad companies, black workers could earn steady, middle-class wages, and escape the trap of rural poverty and sharecropping. Recognizing the empowering nature of railroad work, white workers often mobilized against black employment on railroads. During Reconstruction, Ku Klux Klan violence targeted black workers empowered by railroad jobs along expanding rail corridors in North and South Carolina. White union workers with the Georgia Railroad struck multiple times, in 1898, 1907, and 1909, to deny black men the right to work these jobs. During the 1907 strike, sympathetic whites in towns along the line got out rifles and took potshots at trains manned by black workers. While some union leaders, notably Eugene Debs of the American Railway Union, recognized that racial solidarity would be a boon for the working class, most railroad brotherhoods were all white. For many white union men, black railroad workers were seen as strikebreakers and scabs, a threat to their positions.[33]

Beyond using violence, whites also rationalized using black labor by emphasizing how these roles meshed with white stereotypes. This is mainly true when it comes to black firemen and brakemen. These were dangerous jobs, as in a train wreck, these men in the front cab would typically be the first casualties. In addition to the threat of a wreck, the day-to-day tasks of these jobs—like loading wood into fires, decoupling machinery at high speeds, and operating heavy equipment—had a high margin for error. Many white conductors preferred black men in these roles not out of a sense of interracial solidarity but because of what they thought was the subservient nature of black men. A good fireman or brakeman had to be ready at all times to follow the conductor's orders, so obedience was a desired trait for these jobs. These stereotypes carried on into popular culture, as black men appear in the cabs of many of the train wreck ballads that came out of the South. For example, the legend of Casey Jones gained wide purchase partially due to a song composed by his black fireman, and the engineer of the doomed Old 97 told his "black, greasy fireman" to shovel more coal onto the car. These black men functioned as mere sidekicks to the ballads' foregrounded narratives of white heroism, bravery, and sacrifice.[34]

A similar form of typecasting could be seen with the many black men who found jobs working as porters for the Pullman Palace Car Company. This company touted its Pullman cars as the height of luxury, a comfortable way for passengers of means to travel the country via rail, and a key part of this comfort was the service of their legion of porters who catered to passengers' every needs. By 1914 the Pullman Company employed over 6,000 men, making it the largest employer of black men in the country. This was a mixed victory for these men. On the one hand, these porter jobs afforded black men a measure of financial security and status that many in their communities lacked. Porters helped form the backbone of a rising black middle class, and in the twentieth century, the influential Brotherhood of Sleeping Car Porters union played a role in launching the civil rights movement. But these were hard jobs, with long hours on the road—porters typically spent all but four days of every month on the road—and meager pay, and they were degrading jobs. To address a porter, travelers just used "George," stripping the workers of their names. Indeed, whites accepted the widespread use of black men as Pullman porters because of stereotypes about black servility. In the obedient porter figure that followed travelers' whims and desires, whites could see the reassuring Old South image of the old faithful slave.[35]

Railroads were notable in that they did actually allow black employment, unlike other industrial work like the southern textile industry, which was almost entirely closed off to blacks.[36] But all of these jobs had to, on some level, conform to white stereotypes about black men. Track laying and grading fit the white image of black men as better suited for manual labor, convict labor meshed with white assumptions of black criminality, and porter jobs reinforced notions of black servility. So whether through these stereotypes, the willful erasure of labor at the exposition, or the use of convicts, white boosters were able to obscure the critical nature of black labor in sustaining their railroad dreams.

Beyond sustaining white supremacy, the invisibility of black railroad labor also supported a key assertion of the New South boosters, the notion that the South had a particularly quiescent work force. In a nation riven by violent struggles between labor and capital, southern boosters promoted the idea that the region was a safe refuge from labor chaos. As their argument went, southern workers were docile, antiunion, and pliable.[37] It was a message that was designed to appeal to outside investors, and as with most myths, there was a kernel of truth to this notion. When put up against the exceptional violence in the North, which stood out even on a world stage, the South did seem calmer. The Great Railroad Strike of 1877, a spasm of labor violence that spread like a contagion through the national rail network, largely bypassed the South. Southern papers gleefully pointed this fact out. The *New Orleans*

Times bragged, "A genial climate and fertile soil makes the Southern man less exacting than his Northern neighbor."[38] But despite this notion, southern workers did indeed form unions, go on strike, and even cooperate across racial lines.[39] A series of strikes on Jay Gould's southwestern lines in 1886 touched the borders of the former Confederacy, spreading into Texas. The building of southern railroad systems—mileage had grown dramatically in the years since 1877—exposed the region to more and more of the labor upheaval that plagued northern lines.[40]

In the face of this willful amnesia when it comes to labor, narratives from below offer a bold challenge to the boosters' work of erasure. The most famous story of them all was the tale of John Henry, a man who took on legendary status by virtue of the railroad camps' ability to disseminate culture. As the folktale goes, John Henry died of exhaustion after beating a newfangled machine at the task of hammering rails. However, John Henry's real story was likely a little different from this. After John Henry served an unduly harsh ten-year prison sentence for minor theft, the Virginia convict labor system sent him to work on a Chesapeake & Ohio Railroad (C&O) line that drilled straight through West Virginia's mountains. Along with over 100 other workers, he likely died of silicosis, a by-product of the fine particles kicked up by the steam drills hammering into the mountains. He was buried in an unmarked grave near the Virginia penitentiary, and the company did its best to hide the horrors of this construction.[41]

This likely occurred in the early 1870s, just before a huge boom in railroad construction, and this timing was fortuitous. With this surge in railroad building, new camps sprung up across the region, and the story of John Henry quickly spread and took on a new life and many different meanings. He was the ultimate symbol of man's defeat against industrial capitalism, felled both by the increased demands of his boss—the push to rapidly complete this rail line, no matter the cost—and the new machinery that blasted the mountains into deadly small pieces. For black workers, his legendary feats, which grew and grew as his story spread, were a source of pride. As the epitome of manly black strength and power, he stands in stark contrast to the emasculated Pullman, "George." Moreover, it was an act of resistance that a man laid low by silicosis emerged as a mighty legend in work sites across the South. His visibility and the fact that he had a widely known name are significant in the face of a convict labor system that sought to reduce workers to a soulless commodity. In the face of these many tragedies of the rail, John Henry's many feats take on new resonance and power, as do the many other songs composed, edited, and disseminated by railroad workers. The official record of these new railroads may have omitted the travails of the laborers who built them, but in folklore the stories live on.[42]

IDA B. WELLS HANDED the conductor her ticket, the train lurched to a start, and she took a seat in the first-class car. The year was 1884, and Wells was only twenty-one—years away from the national fame she would receive for her antilynching activities. This mundane series of actions occurred millions of times on railroad cars across the nation, but this journey was destined for more drama. After she took her seat in the first-class car, the conductor immediately demanded she move to the forward car, a "smoking car" which was full of lower-class white travelers and other black men and black women. She refused, and the conductor opted to use force. As he grabbed her arm, she bit the back of his hand, but this victory was short-lived. As she later wrote, she "braced her feet against the seat in front," while multiple men tried to dislodge her from her seat. Other white passengers stood on their seats to watch and cheered while the railroad men dragged her into the smoking car. Rather than suffer the further indignity of riding in the smoking car, Wells got out at the next station and plotted her revenge.[43]

After she got back to Memphis, Wells filed suit against the railroad for denying her access to the first-class accommodations she paid for. She won the first court case, and the judge, a former Union soldier from Minnesota, awarded her $500 in damages. Not wanting this decision to set a precedent that applied to all black travelers, the C&O appealed this decision to the Supreme Court, and the company tried multiple times to get Wells to settle out of court. She declined their offers and eventually lost the case, as the Court found her suit "not in good faith to obtain a comfortable seat for her short ride." Reflecting on her defeat in her diary, Wells expressed disappointment and wrote that she had "hoped such great things from my suit for my people generally." The law was on her side, she thought, but the defeat demoralized her. She fantasized about how she would "gather my race in my arms and fly far away with them." Rail travel was, for Wells, about more than just the journey. Far from a gleaming beacon of southern revival, the railroad for Wells represented a zone of contestation, a proving ground of citizenship, and a symbol of the dashed promise of the New South.[44]

Ida Wells and her challenge spoke to the contradictory meanings of rail travel for African Americans in the decades after emancipation, but for African Americans rail travel had always held deep importance. Rail travel represented the pinnacle of mobility in the nineteenth century, and one of the central functions of slavery was to limit and control movement of enslaved people. If they were even allowed to travel, slaves had to adhere to a strict pass system in much of the South, and to run away constituted one of the highest forms of resistance. The rail lines spreading through the antebellum South may have been built with slave labor, and they largely hauled the cotton that slaves picked, but to many slaves, a train speeding by could represent freedom and escape. While it was not a literal railroad, the widespread use of the Underground Railroad metaphor to describe secret routes to freedom also speaks to the powerful connection between railroads and freedom. Very often, the escape from slavery occurred on actual trains, as in the case of Frederick Douglass, who famously boarded a train as part of his flight. Free blacks similarly saw rail travel, and the ability to move freely and unmolested through the country, as more than just a way to get from point A to point B. It was a key component of their citizenship and their belonging in the burgeoning Republic.[45]

After emancipation, mobility arguably took on even more importance for the freedmen and freedwomen of the South. In the immediate aftermath of the Civil War, freed slaves took to southern roads and railroads to find loved ones, reconstruct shattered families, escape the drudgery of the countryside, or search for a brighter economic future. As the promise of Reconstruction collapsed into racial violence and the malaise of sharecropping, many blacks found hope in the Exoduster movement, in which African Americans migrated to Kansas and other western areas or to the North.[46] As the most tangible symbol of movement in the New South, the railroad, in its idealized form, represented freedom and escape for black men and black women, much like the metaphor (and reality) of the underground railroad had provided escape from slavery. The rapidly expanding southern railroad network of the 1880s and '90s gave black activists and travelers a potential boon. For one, thousands of newly constructed rail depots, passenger cars, and roadside accommodations were brand new spaces in which to resist segregation. The network's connectivity and circulation gave black workers the ability to move freely from job to job at booming industrial sites and the means to escape the stagnant countryside. Middle-class black men and black women could, in theory, take advantage of improved accommodations and buy first-class tickets to travel for pleasure or business. Consolidation and systemization of the network further opened up space for challenges. Rail systems that crossed state lines could fall under federal jurisdiction, and litigants hoped that northern-owned companies would have more sympathy to the plight of southern blacks. Moreover, the African American generation that came of age in these decades after reconstruction held a renewed readiness to challenge segregation practices and secure equal travel accommodations.[47]

The railroad was a technology with the radical potential for racial liberation, but it very often fell short of these lofty goals. The idealized image of the railroad continued to hold power for black Americans, but on the ground, the experience ran into the harsh realities of the segregated Jim Crow car. In the 1830s, soon after the birth of the railroad, companies in the Northeast began to mandate that free black travelers, even those who paid the full first-class ticket price, sit in the special "Jim Crow" car, which took its name from a popular antiblack stage show. Black activists fought back against these restrictions, and the battlegrounds of this fight in the antebellum North were numerous. While in Massachusetts an early generation of activists protested the first Jim Crow car, black women led a later fight against segregation in 1854 in New York City. Despite these efforts, in much of the antebellum North, railroad companies excluded free blacks from rail cars, and victories, like that of the Massachusetts activists who got railroads to end the Jim Crow car in the 1840s, were fleeting and the exception to the rule.[48]

The rapidly shifting currents of Reconstruction's politics and the wildly divergent experiences of different areas of the South render it difficult to make any generalization about the continued use of the Jim Crow car after the war. The Black Codes of the immediate postwar period had a limited lifespan due to the arrival of military Reconstruction, but in three states, Mississippi, Florida, and Texas, these codes included a provision for railroad segregation. Of course, on the ground, southern whites did not need a law to forcibly exclude black passengers from first-class accommodations, and in many areas civil rights laws were straight up ignored. In other instances, especially after the passage of the 1875 federal Civil Rights Act, blacks successfully integrated rail cars. For example, one black traveler rode in an integrated car from Raleigh to Savannah and encountered no difficulties at all. Much of this flexibility continued after the end of Reconstruction. It took a decade after Yankee troops left for the first state to pass a Jim Crow law. Two different foreign observers traveling in 1879 noted with some surprise that black travelers had equal treatment in railroad accommodations. In 1883, the Supreme Court nullified the 1875 act, adding more confusion to the situation on the ground in southern rail cars.[49]

The era of the New South railroad boom thus presented both new opportunities and new challenges for black travelers. Beyond the expanding physical infrastructure of protest, efforts to achieve travel equality could find an ally in the need for railroad companies to keep costs down. It was expensive for companies to build extra depots, run an additional Jim Crow car, or hire the manpower to police and enforce racial segregation rules. In 1883 the Mobile and Ohio Railroad's vice president wrote the Alabama Railroad Commission to complain that "colored travel" was not large enough to fill an extra coach. The commission suggested dividing cars in half by race, a solution that would have introduced even more chaos for travelers.[50] Class distinctions between blacks, particularly the rise of a black middle class of professionals, ministers, and more, also gave new arguments against the Jim Crow car. Middle-class and upper-class black travelers, who had the means to ride in a first-class car, especially chafed at their exclusion from travel accommodations they could pay for. This exclusion of paying customers violated a basic rule of business, that buying a first-class ticket merited first-class accommodations. White travel writer Edward King encountered an "intelligent looking mulatto" in Virginia who "began a violent harangue against the railroad authorities saying it made his blood boil to be refused a first class ticket." King pointed out that this well-dressed man would have certainly had room to sit in a New York car, but southern prejudices denied him this right in Virginia.[51] Another white author, Henry Field, agreed that black travelers had grounds for complaint, noting that many "who are as decent and well-behaved as the common run of white passengers" were kicked out of cars that they had paid full fare for, "with a degree of roughness and violence" that even aroused indignation among southerners. He called it a "plain rule of justice" that "every man is entitled to what he pays for."[52] How could it be fair, these arguments went, to force respectable, ticket-holding first-class black travelers to ride with the often-rowdy and dirty lower-class travelers in the Jim Crow car?

Drawing on a long tradition of protest against railroad inequities, black activists in the 1880s and '90s pressed for access and appealed to companies and governments in a variety of ways. Simply riding on a railroad to assess accommodations or adherence to nondiscrimination laws was a common strategy. Ida Wells's violent encounter with a Tennessee railroad conductor was one of the most notable of these attempts, and the most enduring effort came when Homer Plessy tried to board a white car on the East Louisiana Railroad in New Orleans in 1892. His arrest and the ensuing legal battles were by design. Plessy and the city's African American community were hoping to test the state's Jim Crow laws in court. The court case *Plessy v. Ferguson* went all the way to the Supreme Court, which ruled that "separate but equal" segregated accommodations were legal. Though black accommodations in railroads were of course far from equal, this case enshrined Jim Crow segregation regimes in law in 1896. Even after the courts seemed to settle the matter, black men and black women in cities across the South from Richmond to Mobile to Savannah participated in streetcar boycotts as a way to fight back against spreading segregation laws.[53] Just as work songs and strikes sought to reclaim the humanity of black workers, these challenges sought to reassert African Americans' roles as consumers.

WHILE BATTLES OVER SEGREGATED rail travel took place all over the nation, in the New South, activists' efforts confronted a new and more virulent form of white supremacy and renewed efforts to strictly demarcate the boundaries of whiteness. After redemption, white men who had been dispossessed of power and privilege during Reconstruction aggressively moved to limit black access to public spaces and cut off black involvement in politics.[54] Just as the highly networked nature of the region could support protest, it also fed racial divisions. People on railway journeys encountered strangers, saw rapidly flickering images, and watched the world fly by at previously unimaginable speeds. We have seen how white boosters strengthened the power of their arguments when they filtered their accounts of New South progress, Civil War memory, and small-town growth through the magical lens of rail travel. But the railway journey could also disorient.[55] The same railroad magic that helped gather commodities and enliven boosters' narratives of southern history often produced confusion, hostility, and fear when white travelers encountered blacks.

In many of the New South travel narratives produced by white authors, narrators used a language of disorder, bewilderment, and terror to describe African Americans in depots, on trains, and in the surrounding countryside. As their trains pulled into or waited at depots, white observers typically described blacks as faceless mobs, loitering with unclear intent. Henry Field found "the Negroes are a source of infinite amusement, as they swarm around every railway station as if they had nothing to do but to enjoy this idleness." Julian Ralph similarly observed, "Whenever a boat lands or a train stops, one is sure to find half a dozen or even two dozen Negroes to each white person in the crowd that gathers on the levee or at the station."[56] On his trip through Georgia, Thomas Harley noted, "At every station, that is about every five miles, we mark the ubiquitous Negro."[57] An L&N publication complained about the "score or more of ragged, tattered colored boys" who swarmed travelers at the Montgomery depot.[58] Black men, women, and children were already present in large numbers in many of the South's depots, but rapidly moving trains traversing many areas and depots only heightened the sense of ubiquity felt by these white travelers.

Other accounts from white authors contrasted the alleged idleness of African Americans with the speed of the passing train, in effect placing blacks outside of the railroad's modernity. The travelers in Rebecca Harding's "Here and There in the South" passed an "appendage of dilapidated Negro quarters and neglected farm lands—a gray, hoary wreck of prosperous days" on their way to Montgomery, where they saw "Negroes in rags lounged against the worm-fence, too lazy to look up at the train." The train continued on to other sites of southern progress, but the message with regard to Alabama's rural black population was clear: they needed to "get on the train," or at least acknowledge its passing.[59] As the railroad and its speed came to define what was modern in the New South, all that was off the train and stagnant seemed to be behind the times.

When black men and black women did "get on the train," white chroniclers saw their movements as random or directionless. When Henry Field traveled through Georgia in 1890, he marveled at the crowds of African Americans that filled the trains, and he wrote, "It is a great mystery where they all come from and go to—there are many strangely marked faces of men whom it would be a pleasure to know."[60] George Sala vividly described what he called the average black man in the South. He could be "any age between 16 and 60," he donned a shredded shirt, and he did nothing but loaf around depots with an attitude of "complete and apathetic immobility." He is a "derelict—a fragment of flotsam and jetsam cast upon the not too hospitable shore of civilization."[61] Sala also critiqued the budding Exoduster movement, and he included a derogatory quote from a minister, who called the exodus "nothing but tramping instead of toiling by people who are drones of the colored race, who find more pleasure in wandering from place to place than in working from day to day." Field similarly argued that it "seemed a strange venture" for migrating blacks to "wander so far away from the place where they were born."[62]

These accounts show that just as white southerners rendered the labor of black southerners invisible, they sought to reduce the power of black southerners as consumers. There were any number of reasons why black travelers would ride southern railroads, but in their travel accounts, white observers typically failed to ascribe any motivation to these movements.[63] Rendering black southerners as idle or directionless let white travelers place limits on the transformative power of rail travel. If railroad speed defined the New South, descriptions of blacks as stagnant placed them behind the times. Similarly, seeing blacks as wayward cleaved their habits from the purposeful movement of capitalism. The same white passengers who complained about idleness and vagrancy saw normal participation in the railroad economy as an existential threat, a threat that inspired a whole series of laws that sought to curb black mobility around the turn of the century.[64] The movement, energy, and speed of rail travel excited white travelers when white boosters applied these traits to lists of commodities, or descriptions of Civil War battle sites, but the circulation of black travelers seemed threatening and confusing. The fact that these images were often contradictory did not make them less dangerous to white observers. Numerous troubling archetypes could coexist and still support the push for white supremacy.

These descriptions attempted to sever the actions of black southerners from the mobility of the railroad, but black men and black women clearly were traveling in large numbers. Within the highly charged space of the passenger car, another zone of contestation emerged. The experience of travel itself—the uneven speeds, unexpected delays, bumps in the road, isolation of the road, and awful food that invariably accompanied a long journey—could be disorienting and stressful. More seriously, the rail compartment brought strangers together into enclosed spaces for extended periods of time, which created a potentially combustible situation. When George Sala sought to escape the vagaries of southern travel in a standardized Pullman sleeping car, the crowded conditions and noisy passengers forced him to fall "mentally into a fretful fractious, nervous and irritable state." He contemplated killing a howling baby, struggled to wash and clean in cramped quarters, and quaffed a wide variety of pills in a hopeless attempt to get some sleep. By the end of his week in the car he began to imagine himself as part of a Gypsy or circus caravan.[65] Sala found dark humor in his plight, but often an absurd situation could quickly turn to horror. French railways were struck with a panic when a man was violently murdered in a compartment by an unknown assailant. Female travelers also agonized over the proper way to act in this new ambiguous space of the railroad car. Was the passenger compartment a public or private space? Rail travel could put women in the company of strange and unfamiliar men, leading to dangerous or uncomfortable situations.[66]

As Reconstruction, or at least its military and political component, wound down and the last Yankee troops left the South in 1877, attempts at a more racially just society were replaced with a regional effort to reassert white power, an effort stoked by mass media and race-baiting politicians like Ben Tillman and Redeemers who perpetuated false notions of black criminality and disposition to rape and murder. The rapidly growing railroad network introduced a volatile new element to this mix, and though black activists surely saw hope in new railroads, white southerners encountering strange black travelers saw visceral fear, danger, and a need for regulation. Faster rail travel and more connectivity increased interactions between white and black travelers, and it produced anonymity by allowing travelers to go far beyond where they were familiar, and by placing strangers from varied regions in close prox-imity. Confronted with unfamiliar black faces, white passengers resorted to stock characters or archetypes to interpret their fellow passengers. Viewed from a window, a crowd of loitering African Americans could seem amusing, but travelers inside a car shared a more intimate relationship with their fellow passengers. So if the railroad car was a contested space in the abstract, it held exceptional danger in the New South.[67]

The young working-class black man often coded as a criminal or rapist in fearful white eyes, and the assumptions of black criminality that sustained convict labor regimes could turn to panic if a white traveler encountered such a traveler in a train. These unfamiliar black faces became easy scapegoats for imagined rapes, leading to a surge in lynchings in the 1890s.[68] Whites also fell back on negative stereotypes, like the notion that black men and black women had a distinctive smell. Lady Duffus Hardy recoiled in horror as she saw a couple of black families about to enter her car near Savannah, until a porter assured her they would have to ride in a second-class car. Though she did not "object to the colour of God's image carved in ebony," she found that "their neighborhood is not odorous."[69] The myth that black men were especially predisposed to rape was especially threatening to whites in an enclosed space like a passenger car, so the need to protect white female travelers framed many of white travelers' complaints about black passengers. A petition from Hatchechubbee, Alabama, asked the Alabama Railroad Commission to re-quire the construction of new depot, as the present space became crowded in bad weather. In these conditions, the petitioners complained, "white and col-ored are crowded together which is annoying and disgusting," and they hoped the commission would step in so that "our wives and daughters be not made to suffer the indignities of the past season while waiting for trains."[70] One passenger wrote to the head of the Illinois Central's branch line in Lex-ington, Mississippi, "It is no pleasant idea to be, especially for a lady, seated by the average swamp negro."[71]

The formation of interstate systems and incorporation of new space into the network turned these local conflicts into disputes mandated at the state level. And faced with a wave of complaints and disputes on the ground, southern legislatures turned the de facto segregation practices of many rail-roads into law. In a wave of legislation, eight different southern states passed laws segregating railroads between 1887 and 1891, a period of time coinciding with the tail end of the region's meteoric growth in rail mileage. Georgia, North Carolina, South Carolina, and Virginia passed their segregation laws in another burst of lawmaking in 1898 and 1899. By 1900, every southern state had some kind of law on the books that officially segregated rail cars, and by this point the defeat of Homer Plessy's Supreme Court case ensured that these laws would remain legal in federal eyes.[72]

While white travelers, and those responsible for enforcing these laws, saw the new regulations as (literally) a black-and-white issue, the reality on the ground was far messier. The spell cast by railroad circulation and connectivity created ambiguous and challenging figures in the eyes of traveling whites. Faced with these bewildering rapid changes, white Americans looked to an imagined Old South, with its strict racial hierarchies, to solidify whiteness and unite the white North and white South. Mass culture and advertisements became littered with mammies, old faithful slaves, and a generally rosy view of the plantation South. Growing corporations fed into this nostalgia with advertisements and packaging, and railroads were no exception. In Pullman cars, white travelers encountered an updated version of the faithful slave in the emasculated and obedient porter. But these Old South archetypes of the faithful slave, the plantation mammy, or the premodern figure hopelessly left behind by the train coexisted and clashed with the more troubling archetypes created by railroad circulation, characters like the anonymous black face, the bad man or criminal, the rootless wanderer or Black Ulysses figure, the middle-class traveler, and the swaggering, upwardly mobile "New Negro," who may himself hold a railroad job.[73]

Beyond this disjuncture between whites' Old and New South images of African Americans, plenty of black travelers did not fit well into the stereotypes of danger and violence that underpinned the logic of these laws. What to do with the "respectable" black traveler, say, a preacher traveling to a different congregation, a mixed-race businessman from New Orleans, or a black merchant on the road to proffer his wares? Or what about the harmless elderly black man or woman? A reputable black woman posed another gendered challenge to segregation regimes. On a train ride in 1884, white journalist George Washington Cable recoiled against one of the implications of this rule when he saw "a most melancholy and revolting company," a linked chain of nine convicts form the penitentiary, barge into the same car as a young black mother and her child.[74] To deflect from scenes like this, white conductors and enforcers tried to de-emphasize the femininity of black women. Hence the conductor on Ida Wells's fateful trip emphasized the biting and scratching aspects of her resistance. Suggestions that black women were dirty or had a distinctive odor served a similar purpose.[75]

The ultimate aim of the railroad network was to standardize, as seen in the gauge width debates, to classify, like the exposition commodities, and to rationalize costs in order to turn a profit, and the state segregation laws of the 1880 and '90s attempted to apply this logic to passengers. Railroad companies liked the clarity this could provide, but on the ground, it was trickier to implement segregation. In response to Mississippi's segregation law, James Fentress, the head lawyer for the IC wrote a frustrated letter to the state's railroad commission asking for clarification. The law threatened heavy fines for noncompliance, but Fentress saw numerous loopholes and gray areas in the stark black-and-white law. He posited a number of scenarios: a "sick white person with negro nurse," a "colored maid in charge of white children," the presence of Asian and Indian travelers, and most confusingly, mixed-race "octaroons." Fentress asked if separation depended on color or race, and if on race, "what degree of negro blood will class white." He closed his letter with a complaint about the "ill-expressed and foolish statute" and hoped that his questions would prove the road had made a good effort to comply and reduce his road's liability.[76] Fentress may have just been trying to stave off lawsuits or further regulation with his letter, but he still exposed the contradictions embedded in the Jim Crow car.

Regulatory bodies like railroad commissions were a main goal of many anticorporate and antirailroad politicians in the 1880s and '90s. Faced with the concentrated corporate power of the railroads, southern reformers saw a government agency as the proper countervailing force, even in a region especially suspicious of state and federal power. But instead of checking the authority of railroads—via rate regulation, enforcing antimonopoly laws, or improving safety—many of these commissions spent their early years of existence implementing new segregation regimes. In 1888, a commissioner with the Mississippi Railroad Commission spent much of his job on the road, going from depot to depot on Mississippi's railroads to record how well the railroad companies were enforcing the state's new segregation laws. Armed with petitions of complaint from citizens across the state, he entered buildings and inspected each depot's accommodations for passengers. In his trip over the Vicksburg and Meridian Railroad, he deemed the passenger depots at Brandon, Clinton, Bolton, Covina, and Vicksburg "unsuitable and insufficient." At Brandon "passengers of every class, color and condition are crowded into the one reception room," and at Clinton there was only one sitting room for all. In cases where the depots were found to be too small, or not easy enough to segregate, the commission ordered the railroad company to construct a new depot or face a lawsuit.[77]

To respond to this type of regulation, railroad companies operating in the South came up with standardized designs for Jim Crow stations. As with all aspects of railroading, standardization translated to efficiency, so companies wanted to make this new system work as rationally as possible. In the Illinois Central's design, black passengers sitting in the segregated space were not even able to see the arriving trains, so in the company's depots across the South, the imaginative powers of a passing train were denied to black travelers.[78] From the railroad commissioner's record book, the process of segregation seemed easy enough to put into effect. A divider through a common waiting area or an extra room tacked on to the back of the building would surely fulfill the law's demands. But in reality Jim Crow legislation proved tricky to implement. Human races were harder to classify than the minerals, wood samples, and other commodities on display during the New Orleans Exposition. A slab of Tennessee granite, for example, could easily be classified by its type and grade, and set in its proper position, but this logic did not always work for human passengers.

Between rapidly changing laws, shifting corporate policies, and the widely varying implementation of these mandates on the ground, race relations on railroads in the 1880s and '90s were characterized by instability and flux.[79] With the rise of this complicated set of legal and cultural codes to navigate, African Americans riding on southern railroads could never be sure to get the transportation they paid for. Railroads touted their reliability to white travelers, but the experience of travel for African Americans was anything but predictable in the 1880s and '90s. Having to navigate these shifting boundaries, with the threat of violence always lurking in the background, constrained the experience of travel for African Americans. For young African Americans, train travel could form an important yet tragic milestone in a coming-of-age story. Many young black boys and girls experienced their first conflict with Jim Crow on a train, and they marked their travels as the moment where they became aware of the limitations imposed on their race.[80]

We have seen how critical the experience of riding the rails and the production of travel narratives were to the idea of the New South. In its ideal form for the white men behind this myth, rail travel was used to convey southern progress. It was structured, swift, and enjoyable, and these journeys displayed scenic views, sites of a mythologized southern past, and areas of progress and growth. While some black travelers surely saw their activism and their participation in the railroad economy as part of a New South, free of the racial hostility and exclusion of the Old South, their accounts in this era often emphasized the divisive and exclusionary aspects of their journeys. James Weldon Johnson boarded a train in Jacksonville bound for Atlanta in 1890, a year after Florida passed a law segregating rail cars. Unaware of the new law, Johnson and his friend sat in the first-class car they had paid for, only to be warned by the conductor that there would be trouble if they stayed there. After Johnson's friend spoke in Spanish, the conductor relented and let them remain in the car for the rest of their trip. The successful conclusion of this encounter notwithstanding, Johnson called the episode his "first impact against race prejudice as a concrete fact."[81]

On a later trip back to Jacksonville, Johnson and his traveling party had a much scarier encounter with Jim Crow. Georgia had not passed a segregation law yet, so Johnson and his friends took their seats in a first-class car. After they sat down, a "murmur started" in the car, and a white man warned them that someone had sent a telegram to Baxley, and a mob was waiting there to drag them out of the train when they arrived. The urgings of a black porter convinced Johnson that the threat was real, and they moved to the Jim Crow car. As Jim Crow legislation advanced unevenly through the South in the 1890s, black travelers passing through multiple states had to keep track of the various shifts in state laws. On a train from Charleston to Jacksonville in 1896, Johnson was forced to get up and move to a different car at the South Carolina and Georgia border. South Carolina had not passed a segregation law, but at this point Georgia had.[82]

Pullman cars, because they traversed state lines, were technically open to interstate black passengers, but as Johnson noted, there were "parts of the country where a Negro puts his life in jeopardy whenever he travels in a Pullman car."[83] Railroads often tried to exclude black passengers from Pullman cars by refusing to sell them tickets. After a 1904 editorial in the *Nashville American* demanded that southern railroads put black passengers in separate Pullman cars, officials with the L&N worriedly corresponded about ways to prevent legislative action that would force them to run extra Pullmans at increased expense to the railroad. The chairman of the company suggested instead that ticket agents simply inform black passengers that they could not buy tickets. This was illegal, so the chairman insisted that the denial of service must be done "in a quiet way."[84] Pullman cars became linked to African American culture in another way, as sites of black labor, due to the ubiquity of the African American Pullman porter.

So for African Americans, the sensory appeal of train travel—the majestic views of the South that entranced white boosters and fueled their evocative narratives—was often off limits. W. E. B. Du Bois best captured this dynamic in his essay "Of Beauty and Death," which contrasted the wonders of the environment—mountains, pine trees, shores, and oceans—with the exclusion of black travelers from the locomotive cars that visit such sights. The "very thought of a journey tended to depress" the black family he asked about travel. Indignities of southern rail travel included the crowded Jim Crow waiting room, watched over by a tired agent who "browbeats and contradicts you"; the Jim Crow car, covered in dirt, dust, and smoke from the engine; the rude conductor and smoking white passengers; and the lack of decent toilet facilities or food.[85] African American travel accounts describe not the scenery, but the poor conditions of the Jim Crow car, or the struggle to negotiate shifting laws and mores. Johnson called the usual Jim Crow arrangement "unkempt, unclean and ill smelling, with one toilet for the sexes." White men were not uncommon in the Jim Crow car, as it was "custom for white men to go into that car whenever they felt like doing things that would not be allowed in the 'white' car." This meant they smoked, gambled, and drank heavily.[86]

By the turn of the century, the battle over the magic of rail travel was thus, despite black protest and resistance, and the continued ambiguities and varying interpretations of new segregation laws largely resolved in favor of the white South. While companies constructed new segregated depots and tacked on extra Jim Crow cars, cases like *Plessy v. Ferguson* limited future legal challenges. In practice, in law, and in written accounts, white southerners circumscribed black access to the empowering mobility of the new railroad network. Just as official corporate pamphlets and records downplayed the critical role of black workers in the building of these railroads, white travel accounts saw black travelers as unable to participate in railroad circulation. When black southerners did try to ride the rails, they were met with violence and legal prohibitions. In a stark contrast with the delight and ebullience of white passengers and their travel narratives, confusion, despair, intimidation, and degradation all marked the stories of African American encounters with the railroad. But a counternarrative of resistance, from black travelers who rode the rails, resisted segregation, or reclaimed the magic of the railroad, survived.

THIS SAME DYNAMIC of black usage of the railroad and white denial of the railroad's potential empowerment continued into the twentieth century. White folklorist Howard Odum, who studied African American life in the South in the first few decades of the twentieth century, was neatly poised on the knife's edge between the creation and perpetuation of white stereotypes and the continued importance of the railroad in black culture. Odum was particularly concerned with the impact of modernization, namely, the railroad and industrial development, on black Americans. On issues of race, Odum was far more enlightened than most southerners of his time, but his writings provide a coda to the ambiguous, dangerous, and confusing descriptions of blacks seen in New South accounts. In his examinations of black life, he returned again and again to a rootless black man he called "the Wanderer." The Wanderer was a black man who rambled around the nation for work, pleasure, or an escape from various legal or romantic pursuers. According to Odum, he "has been to Memphis, Atlanta, Birmingham, New Orleans and all de big places. He has seldom worked a stroke since he left home, yet he has always had plenty to eat and a place to stay and has sometimes actually had money to spend." Closely related to this character was the "Bad Man," a rebellious ne'er-do-well beholden to no law (or woman). In the Black Ulysses novels, Odum presented readers with a character who was the apotheosis of these various archetypes.[87]

Odum's Wanderer character provides testament to how the railroad's spells continued to influence white perceptions of black Americans. The mobility of labor aided by the railroad became, in white eyes, evidence of the degradation and alienation of the black race. The Wanderer was an updated version of the white descriptions of black families in sharecropping shacks watching trains fly by, or of the faceless swarms of African Americans at depots. While Odum played a key role in cementing certain stereotypes about black southerners, reading through the lines of his work, one can see a more positive view of the ways in which black men and black women were able to "conjure the railroad" and in how railroad magic permeated black culture. Black Ulysses may have been rendered rootless and lonesome by the train, but as a creation of the railroad network, he did at least reclaim the mobility that whites so often denied black Americans. His saga was entirely rooted to the rails and the invisible forces of the market. At the age of twelve, Black Ulysses hopped his first train, and from there he continued to drift around the nation. The network of freight trains coursing through the country gave him a means to escape and a way to return home, though he reports having the "railroad blues" at a particularly low point. In his lowest moments, the Wanderer sometimes contemplated suicide, and the railroad could accommodate this dark desire as well—perhaps he could lay his head on some lonesome rail line as a final escape. Odum also connected Black Ulysses to other legendary bad men of the black race, men like the infamous murderer Stagolee or Railroad Bill, who, as we will see, was quite adept at using the railroad to aid his criminality.[88]

Beyond documenting the experience of the mobile laborer, Odum collected a wealth of African American folk songs, many of which spoke to the centrality of the rail network to the experience of black workers. These songs fixated on the railroad as a means of escape, a reminder of home, or the source of one's lonely struggles. As Odum noted, "from riding the rails to a long-desired trip back to his sweetheart, the Negro is the frequent patron of the train." The life of a man "wandering down that lonesome road" was troubled, and the traveler's songs often used the railroad as a means of escape or a reminder of home. The song "L&N," was a "song of the wanderer," sung by black workers hoping to one day again go home. "Thought I Heard that K.C. Whistle Blow" told the story of a group of black workers bamboozled by western business agents. Left stranded at a distant work site, the men hoped for a way home, and they kept thinking they heard "that K.C. Whistle blow." Other versions of this song substituted the names of any other railroad as the device to bring the lonesome traveler back home again. Another song, entitled "Frisco Ragtime," performed a similar act of flexibility, allowing the Wanderer to adapt the song to that person's particular railroad of woe.[89] Some of Odum's collected songs offered a direct challenge to the denial of mobility that came with Jim Crow segregation laws. "I'm Gonna Have Me a Red Ball All My Own" tells the story of a black man who attempted to catch the "Red Ball," a fast freight train, only to be told "No nigger can ride the Red Ball." So the prospective traveler instead decided to paint his face white, but he forgot to paint his neck and hands, and got turned away again. He resolved to "get me a mule an' name him Red Ball, an' I can ride just the same."[90]

A reclamation and celebration of mobility is at the heart of all of these narratives. On the one hand, this points to the continuities in the importance of the railroad to black Americans. Even though railroad magic was often off limits to African American travelers, the railroad still was inspirational to black southerners. Another way in which the imaginative power of the railroad spread into black cultural life was via the "train song," a distinct creation of African American musicians. In a "train song," performers did more than just sing about trains—they used instruments and vocals to emulate the sound of a traveling locomotive. As Odum wrote, "the negro has unusual powers for picturing the sound of the running train." Odum marveled at how the black singers would strike strings in different ways to simulate bells and whistles. Meanwhile, a man with a guitar announced the progress of the journey as the "train" left the station and picked up speed, and onlookers would add exclamations like "Lawd, God, she's a-runnin' now!" In these songs, black musicians translated railroad rhythm, speed, and grandeur into an entirely new and distinctively African American form of culture.[91]

The musical and lyrical invocation of trains went beyond just the train song, and it filtered into all kinds of black music and cultural life. In African

American gospel music from the early twentieth century, the metaphor of the train delivering black worshippers to heaven was common. The song "Well You Better Get Yo' Ticket" implored congregants to ensure they have a ticket for their trip to heaven. "I Cannot Stay Here by Myself" fretted about being left behind as this holy train departs. As the song went, "de train done whistled and de cars er gone." And "Gospel Train" implored sinners to get on the train before it was too late.[92] To further drive this point home, these trains of the afterlife could also go in the other direction. Black preachers warned their congregants about the "Black Diamond Express to Hell" or the "Hell Bound Express Train." The "Hell Bound Express Train," as described in a sermon from Atlanta preacher J. M. Gates, had "damnation bells," and it picked up liars, gamblers, and drunkards and stopped at Rampart Street in New Orleans, Beale Street in Memphis, 18th Street in Birmingham, and other neighborhoods of known vice. Preachers also portrayed death as a "little black train," and they warned listeners to get their business in order before it arrived.[93]

Black religious life also utilized the physical infrastructure of the railroad. Abandoned boxcars became sites of worship, depots were meeting spots, and the movement of rail cars certainly fostered gatherings of worshippers. Savvy preachers realized the increasing connectivity of the South would aid their evangelizing efforts, so they traveled by rail to expand their range and built churches near new junctions. Southern railroads explicitly targeted black travelers with all-black excursion trains. These special trains would take day trips to a revival meeting, to a larger town for weekend shopping, or to a fair or festival site. Segregation laws tried to deny and limit the power of black consumerism, but railroad companies clearly still welcomed black patronage.[94]

Perhaps the strongest counterargument to the exclusionary white narrative of capitalism's advance would occur during the Great Migration, when African Americans streamed north on southern rail lines. With the onset of World War I and the departure of millions of American soldiers for Europe, industrial jobs opened up in northern cities, and southern blacks jumped at the chance to escape Jim Crow oppression and the drudgery of sharecropping. The movement neatly tracked with the routes of southern railroads. For example, the Illinois Central brought blacks from Mississippi to Chicago, and the Southern and Seaboard Air Line carried them from the Carolinas to New York. As this movement picked up, southern whites again sought to limit the mobility of blacks, harassing labor agents and using violence to try to keep their labor force in place. With this migration, railroads took on a meaning that echoed the antebellum era: for black Americans they symbolized freedom and escape.[95]

The resonance of the railroad for blacks during the Great Migration can be best seen in a new genre of music that emerged around the same time, the blues. The blues borrowed from both the musical creation of the "train song" and the lyrical use of train metaphors seen in the collected folk songs. Bessie Smith's "Dixie Flyer Blues" started off with a train whistle, and the chugging of a train runs throughout the entire song. Meanwhile, Smith implored the conductor to hold the train so she could make it back home, "way down into Dixieland." In "The L&N Blues" by Walter Davis, the singer lamented that the L&N Blues is a fast train, and he begged the L&N to bring the singer's baby back. Companies that owned direct routes from South to North, like the IC and the Southern Railway, became names and subjects of blues songs such as the "Illinois Central" and "Dry Southern" blues. "O Illinois Central what can you spare? / Fo' my baby's is trouble an' I ain't dere," asked the singer of "Louisiana Blues." Blues artists linked railroads to the severing of relationships and family ties, as Sunnyland Slim warned listeners that the Illinois Central will "steal your woman, and blow back at you." Junctions like the spot where "the Southern crosses the Yellow Dog," the meeting point of the Southern Railway and Yazoo Delta Railroad in the Mississippi Delta, became legendary via the blues. The chug of the railroad lived on in black music well into the twentieth century. By the 1930s and '40s, black musicians would "play the train" and emulate railroad sounds in big band music. Indeed, many of the riffs used in swing music were directly derived from the sounds of the railroad.[96]

FROM WORK CAMPS to depots to passenger compartments to the image of the speeding train itself, the spreading railroad infrastructure of the New South was a contested space. White observers imbued railroads and capitalism with fantastical powers, and as they preached about the railroad's centrality to the regional revival, they took pains to mesh these powers with the cultural project of rebuilding white supremacy. If the progress of the railroad meant a weakening of white racial dominance, this would hardly be a success for the men in charge of the post-Reconstruction South. What ensued was an ideological effort that divorced the actions of blacks—as workers, travelers, and consumers—from their celebratory odes to capitalism and progress. This was matched with a legal push to codify these on the ground and intellectual efforts, as seen in Jim Crow legislation and other efforts to bar black mobility.

The battle to circumscribe the magic of the railroad helps explain the rapid spread of segregation laws in the 1880s and '90s. It was no coincidence that these efforts came at the tail end of the southern railroad boom.[97] But far from being stagnant and directionless, black southerners traveled with purpose and actively participated in the new railroad economy. The same railroad dreams that entranced white boosters brightened black cultural life just as well. White accounts tried to write the actions of black southerners out of the history of capitalism, but a powerful counternarrative emerged in courts, in confrontations in railroad cars, and in the folk songs and tales that emerged in work camps and black life.

The onset of Jim Crow segregation on southern railroads, a modern response to a new technology, is a well-worn story, but the railroad was more than just a mere battleground for Jim Crow segregation laws. In a region emerging from the racial turmoil of the Reconstruction era, the very experience of rail travel accentuated racial hostility as it fueled dangerous new stereotypes of black Americans. The forces of connectivity and circulation that rapidly reordered southern life fostered racial mingling and spread ambiguity and confusion. As much as black southerners wanted the figure of the respectable black middle-class traveler to define their experience with the railroad, white southerners experiencing the anonymity produced by rail travel saw troubling new railroad-linked archetypes—the black rapist, unredeemable convict laborer, unladylike woman, wayward worker, stagnant rural laborer, and more—and these figures, both in day-to-day encounters and when deployed by southern elites, supported and sustained the regional push toward white supremacy. White Americans yearned for the comforting faithful slave or the subservient Pullman porter, but in the railroad world, and in the bewildering experience of New South modernity, black Americans seemed to take new and threatening forms in white eyes. The danger and menace that haunted white southerners' everyday encounters with the railroad were matched, as we will see, by terrifying moments of crisis, disasters that threatened to untangle the link between railroads, capitalism, and progress that defined the New South. We turn next to these railroad nightmares and the ways in which the white South struggled to sever the railroad's demons from its glories.

Part II

To the Netherworld

CHAPTER FOUR

Flight of the Yellow-Winged Monster

From swamps morbific it doth now arise,
And with an awful golden touch of death
Can close in pain the light of laughing eyes,
And stain and spoil with its consuming breath.
Beware, ye cities, and all folk thereof;
Beware its advent, ye that hate or love . . .
Beware, beware, oh! People, kneel and pray
The yellow blight of hell now speeds your way

—"Yellow Fever—Poetry" by a *New York Sun* writer, Grenada, Mississippi, 1878

Residents of Grenada, Mississippi, had much to celebrate as another hot summer dawned in 1878. The growing town sat astride an increasingly critical rail junction, at the point where a busy line north from New Orleans split into two branches, one veering toward Memphis and the main line of the Illinois Central heading north on a path toward Cairo, Illinois, and on to Chicago. At a time when the national economy had just begun to pull out of a deep depression, even rumors of a yellow fever outbreak in New Orleans could do little to dampen the enthusiasm of town boosters. Every day, residents witnessed crews disinfecting the northbound freight so it could continue through the strict quarantine in Memphis, but Grenada's citizens saw little to fear. The disease had a long history of devastating outbreaks in New Orleans, but Grenada had never experienced an epidemic of the fearsome plague. Grenadans assumed yellow fever could not spread there, so officials only established a partial quarantine. Trains were allowed to stop, but not discharge passengers, and only essential commodities could be unloaded. Months later, the Mississippi Board of Health's report would accuse the town of being in a "state of apathy" regarding this quarantine, as hardly anyone obeyed these meager rules.[1]

Life in Grenada continued its normal patterns, and trains continued to stop and pass through town that summer, until August 25, a fateful day when a Mrs. Fields fell ill and died of a mysterious ailment. Shortly after her passing, neighbors and friends who had been visiting the ailing woman all began suffering similar symptoms, prime among them the "black vomit," an unpleasant discharge caused by blood in the stomach. Nine days after her death, physicians officially announced the news portended by this awful indicator, that yellow fever, which had "so mysteriously entered the town," was epidemic in the city, and panic overtook Grenada. Those who could, in the dramatic words of a postmortem investigation, "fled into the adjacent country and to distant cities, and carried the seeds of the pestilence with them to bear disastrous fruits." Residents who lingered in the stricken city, whether out of civic duty or poverty, suffered a dreadful toll. By the time frost killed off the last of the disease-bearing mosquitoes and the epidemic finally died out, almost 1,500 had fallen ill, and 367 were dead, including the town's leadership, a staggering toll in a town with a pre-epidemic population of about 2,500.[2]

How did yellow fever reach this town for the first time? Finger pointing began as soon as the outbreak subsided, and investigators had an easy lead to follow due to Fields's status as the epidemic's "Patient Zero." Her bodily movements both before and after death suggested a wide range of culprits. Some blamed a gruesome accident at her widely attended funeral, where a leak in her casket unleashed a nauseating stench on her mourners. New Orleans newspapers first blamed the sickness on foul vapors emanating from a disgusting sewer, full of decomposing animal corpses in the middle of town.[3] But an investigation into Mrs. Fields's activities just before falling ill suggested an unexpected villain, more surprising than the other theories linking the disease to these atmospheric—or to use the term of the day, miasmatic—causes. Investigators noted that she lived in a house that was in "good sanitary condition," only two blocks from the railroad depot. Before falling ill, she made the short walk to the depot to see her daughter off on a short trip to Okolona. She briefly entered the cars as the train made its twenty-minute stop for breakfast. She paced the cars just as crews labored to fumigate the interiors and the Mississippi Board of Health concluded that this was how yellow fever took root in Grenada. Another rumor fixated on an "infected" dress Fields had recently purchased from New Orleans. The report noted that this story was unconfirmed, but it was clear that connections to the outside world, specifically the town's treasured rail link with New Orleans, had caused the devastating outbreak in Grenada.[4]

Throughout the dreadful summer of 1878, yellow fever flowed along southern rail lines, moving far inland from its usual seaside haunts and devastating railroad towns like Grenada in the interior South. Upwards of 20,000 lost their lives to this virus that summer, and in town after town, investigators reached the same conclusions as those in Grenada. If the New Orleans Exposition constituted the ultimate dream of what the railroad could accomplish for the South, yellow fever provided the nightmare, a horror show that threatened to spread death and misery every summer. Though the South would never be menaced with an epidemic as severe as that in 1878, the outbreak ensured that the rapid advance of the railroad in the region was matched by an annual fear. A rumored appearance of yellow fever quickly inverted the meaning of southern railroads, leading southerners to contest circulation and the free movement of commerce on the rails. How did public health officials and southern economic boosters untangle this dangerous link? In this chapter we trace the origins of the New South's yellow fever dystopia, and follow the struggle to sever the link between railroads, capitalism, and disease, a fight waged by government officials, merchants, railroad companies, and medical experts.

EXCITABLE NEWSPAPER WRITERS GAVE yellow fever the curiously affectionate moniker "Yellow Jack," but its impact upon nineteenth-century Americans seemed anything but kind. Today we now know that yellow fever is transmitted solely through the bite of the *Aedes aegypti* mosquito. After a mosquito bites an infected person, it can then transmit the disease to anyone else it bites. A few days after contact with the disease, sufferers experience an acute fever, and in serious cases the infected's skin turns yellow, blood seeps from every orifice, and the victim expels the dreaded black vomit, which gets its color from blood digested in the stomach. To add to the horror of the ailment, newspapers eagerly supplied lurid descriptions of deathbed scenes, complete with these grim details, to readers. The capricious and violent methods Yellow Jack used to claim its victims made the disease one of the nineteenth century's most feared. The invention of a yellow fever vaccine has given modern health officials a means to prevent infection, but once the disease sets in, there is still no known cure.[5]

Historically, a number of geographic and climatic factors dictated where yellow fever could take hold. Because the disease only became epidemic in an area once a critical mass of mosquitoes and humans was present, yellow fever was typically the scourge of crowded urban areas with ample damp areas where mosquitoes could breed. The plague-bearing mosquitoes could only thrive in warm, humid climes, so the bulk of the American epidemics struck during sweltering summers in the South. When the first frost of the year killed off the mosquito vectors, an epidemic would end. While the disease lingered permanently in parts of the Caribbean and South American, in the United States, *Aedes aegypti* mosquitoes could survive year-round only in extreme southern parts of Florida, so it typically had to be imported from tropical areas to start an American epidemic. Therefore, most epidemics in the

United States started in southern port cities—like Savannah, Pensacola, Jacksonville, and Charleston—that had some kind of connection with the tropics.

Spreading the disease to new areas happened when either infected persons or mosquitoes traveled, and without fast transportation like the railroad, early epidemics rarely spread far from coastal urban centers or areas along rivers. Specifically, railroads carried the disease in one of two ways. Infected passengers fleeing an infected city could easily spread the disease to areas where the *Aedes aegypti* mosquito already was present. An incubation period of a few days meant infected people could travel long distances without realizing the threat they posed. Alternatively, the trains themselves could harbor the mosquitoes, as dirty, damp freight cars provided excellent breeding grounds. Once the train stopped in a town, these mosquitoes could exit the train, bite new victims, and start a new epidemic.

Yellow fever played an outsized role in the history of the Western Hemisphere since it first crossed the Atlantic Ocean. Taking root in the tropical climates of the Caribbean and South America, the disease bolstered Spanish defenses in the New World, laying waste to any European army foolish enough to wage a lengthy campaign. The disease also helped turn the tide in South America's independence campaigns, as acclimated armies of liberation parried back attacks from European legions.[6] But if anything, yellow fever's territory seemed to be shrinking over the course of the nineteenth century. The disease no longer menaced northern cities like Philadelphia, site of a 1793 epidemic, and seemed to be more a problem for Gulf Coast cities like Pensacola and New Orleans, where it was known as the "Strangers Disease" for its proclivity to attack unacclimated newcomers.

Over 100 years of medical research has shed light on yellow fever's secrets, but in 1878 uncertainty clouded most aspects of the disease. Yellow fever's horrific method of claiming victims was reason enough to cause panic, but the mysterious way it seemed to spread only added to the fear during epidemic years. By the 1870s, the medical community knew that the disease was transportable, but the exact method of transmission was unknown. Some doctors blamed miasmas in the air, others targeted poisonous "fomites" that they thought could latch onto freight and baggage, and many believed that filthy areas of cities bred the disease. Coastal quarantine efforts suggest that officials knew ships could import the disease, but beyond that yellow fever seemed to move with no discernible pattern. In 1853, the disease struck New Orleans, moving through the city in ways that seemed random to city officials. At every step, the disease confounded authorities and behaved in unexpected ways. The diversity of opinion on the method of transmission demonstrates that no one in 1878 really knew how yellow fever behaved.[7]

BY 1878, SOUTHERN RAILROADS had grown dramatically compared with the network that existed during the last major New Orleans outbreak in 1853. The much-touted "six lines of railroad" emanating from New Orleans, a key selling point for exposition boosters in 1884, were either complete or in their final planning stages, and northern capital in the form of the Chicago-based IC was in the process of rehabilitating the major rail corridor running north to Jackson, Mississippi, and beyond. Civil War destruction and Reconstruction-era stasis had given way to faster movement on these rail lines. So in the twenty-five years between the 1853 and 1878 epidemics, railroad development created a network in Mississippi for the disease to attack. Mississippi had only three railroad lines in 1853, but 1,127 miles of track crossed the state by 1880.[8]

In July 1878, New Orleans residents began falling ill with familiar symptoms, and officials soon realized yellow fever was back. The epidemic began like so many others beforehand, with a few scattered cases in New Orleans introduced by sea trade with infected ports in the Caribbean. Newspapers blamed tropical fruit dealers who "acted dishonestly" by concealing their travels before arrival in New Orleans.[9] Investigation would later reveal that the *Emily B. Souder*, a steamer from Havana, was indeed responsible for the disease's introduction.[10] From past experience, southern public health officials suspected that yellow fever could travel on boats, so it was no surprise that a patchwork of local quarantines popped up all across Mississippi and Louisiana when the New Orleans Board of Health announced the existence of yellow fever in the city. But these early quarantines were focused primarily on water routes of transportation.

As localities across the region mobilized to confront the threat of yellow fever, the press savagely ridiculed the areas that attempted to quarantine their railroads. As evidenced by these dismissive comments and complaints, plenty of people either did not take the threat seriously or doubted the possibility of yellow fever moving by rail. New Orleans merchants bitterly complained about quarantines that threatened to destroy their business, especially since many doubted the transmissibility of the disease. When Mobile declared a rail quarantine, shutting down the major rail route east of the city, the *Picayune* accused Mobile residents of having a "peculiar dread of cars, engines and mail bags." The editor found it ludicrous that Mobile apparently thought yellow fever was a "malady that attacks the rolling stock of railroads" and that as soon as a train reaches an infected town, "every car and locomotive engine instantly becomes diseased to such a degree that it scatters the infection all along the railway."[11] The *Atlanta Constitution* similarly mocked Mobile for seeing "Bronze John"—another colloquial nickname for the disease—lurking in every railroad car.[12] Another *Picayune* editorial in early August declared, "Small towns should keep away from railroads." According to the editorial, as a road passes through a state, small towns invariably pop up along the line, "issue a quarantine proclamation, and stop trains running if they choose."[13] Officials with the Illinois Central Railroad also saw little threat at this early stage of the epidemic. On July 31, an official noted that Mobile had quarantined against New Orleans, which cut a rival line's route, a fact that was actually boosting the IC passenger business. The official reported the "fever is of mild type and health officers believe it will not become epidemic only one death officially reported yesterday, 34 in all."[14] For merchants and railroads, quarantines were useless hindrances to trade, and it was illegal to arbitrarily halt commerce.

As further proof of doubt about yellow fever's mobility, many towns declined to issue quarantines. Some even took an entirely opposite approach. Holly Springs, a town in northern Mississippi along the New Orleans, St. Louis and Chicago Railroad (NOStL&C), invited refugees from infected towns to come and wait out the epidemic. The town had never experienced an epidemic before, and residents believed the area was impervious to infection. As a resident later explained, the people "were so confident that their location and the purity of their atmosphere rendered them safe, that they did not establish quarantine."[15] Towns mistakenly believed there was a "yellow fever zone" beyond which the disease would never spread.[16] They assumed that since an area did not have yellow fever in the past, it would be safe in 1878. For Holly Springs and other towns that welcomed refugees, the epidemic was an opportunity to prove their healthy climate and to profit from a stream of new visitors. Medical opinion supported this decision, as evidenced by a lengthy article from a Louisville doctor applauding Holly Springs for its decision to invite in refugees. Quarantine in areas as far north as Louisville, he contended, would be as rational as a yellow fever quarantine in the North Pole.[17] The surgeon general of the Marine Hospital Service even argued that land quarantines were useless, since only seafaring vessels could transmit the disease. He contended that freight could spread infection, but only after spending time in damp holds of ships.[18] The railroad was simply not widely acknowledged as a potential means of transport for yellow fever.

Despite repeated claims of health and safety in the Magnolia State, it became apparent that something was different about this epidemic in terms of both its virulence and its geographic spread. Instead of remaining in New Orleans, Yellow Jack began to rear its head in entirely new locations as residents fled. As a woman described the situation in New Orleans, "hundreds have flown from this city only to take the seed of the disease and spread it through the country."[19] Observers looking for a culprit first fixated on the region's original highway of commerce, the Mississippi River. Steamboats plying the river between New Orleans and Memphis had spread yellow fever in 1853, and when disease broke out in river towns like Vicksburg and Memphis, the steamboats again seemed to be likely vectors of transmission. One boat in particular, the *John Porter*, took much of the blame. An early history of the epidemic labeled the boat a "floating charnal-house, carrying death and destruction to nearly all who had anything to do with her."[20]

When poor Mrs. Fields's case was confirmed on July 26, Grenada became the disease's first inland foothold outside of New Orleans in 1878. Grenada may have served as the prime example of Yellow Jack's proclivity to ride the rails, but other Mississippi communities reached similar conclusions about the disease's transmissibility. Holly Springs, the town along the NOStL&C that invited refugees to come and wait out the epidemic, became another flash point of the epidemic when the first yellow fever case broke out there on August 18. Holly Springs was a short ride away from Grenada on the railroad, and yellow fever easily made the trip. Contrary to expectations that the disease would not flourish there, it struck with a vengeance, infecting 1,239 and killing 309 residents.[21] In the aftermath of the disaster at Holly Springs, it was safe to say the town would not invite refugees from future epidemics. A newspaper in Holly Springs came out in "favor of quarantining against all infected points, the whole coast of the United States, and even the rat-holes of Holly Springs" if yellow fever ever again threatened.[22]

Greenville, Mississippi, also became a site of tragedy, and residents were quick to blame the railroad for their woes. Greenville was located along the Mississippi River, in the Delta region. Spirits there were high when the town received its first railroad connection in May of 1878. The Greenville, Columbus and Birmingham Railroad, a narrow-gauge road in the northern part of the state, completed laying track to the town, and Greenville joined the railroad network. Commentators enthusiastically predicted the arrival of 20,000 bales of cotton on the new road in its first year of operation.[23] When the disease hit Greenville in early September, it struck with particular ferocity. Only thirty-three of the town's 1,350 residents escaped infection with yellow fever, and

387, including the mayor, died. At one point, only five white residents were free of infection. As a report afterward ruefully commented, "never did a town suffer so terribly."[24] Whether the railroad or river brought the disease is undetermined, but residents turned on the railroad as a culprit, blaming railroad employees working for the new road.[25] Instead of bringing the anticipated boom in commerce, new connections had virtually destroyed the community of Greenville.

By late August, newspapers and other observers could notice patterns in the way Yellow Jack traveled. Besides the Mississippi River vector, three clearly traceable paths spread the disease deep into the southern interior along railroads. The NOStL&C, which would soon become part of the IC, carved a northerly swath of destruction through the middle of the state, striking Holly Springs and Grenada, among other towns As towns along this line fell prey to the disease, corporate officials consistently underplayed the threat of the disease's spread. On August 16, a telegraph from J. C. Clarke, the vice president overseeing the company's southern operations, noted, "There is terrible panic among the people along our line, unnecessarily so."[26] The road's president, William Ackerman, tried his best to keep his road running, even as fever slowly crept north along his line. The arrival of yellow fever in Cairo, Illinois, led to at least four other Illinois towns quarantining against the southern part of the line, and Ackerman directed subordinates to remind these towns that it was illegal to block traffic on a road under contract to deliver U.S. government mail.[27]

As the epidemic continued, threats of vigilante action escalated against Ackerman's line, and he complained that the "fear of mob violence" was keeping the company from running trains in Mississippi. He noted that the Vicksburg & Meridian Railroad (V&M), the second main rail vector for the disease's transmission, ceased operation after "threats made to fire into the trains and wreck them."[28] Warnings of extralegal violence could not prevent the disease from spreading east from Vicksburg and the river to previously healthy towns in central Mississippi. Yellow Jack arrived in Vicksburg from the ill-fated steamship *John Porter*, and from Vicksburg the disease's march could be traced along the railroad line. When the disease hit the small railroad town of Lake, 239 of the town's 250 residents fell ill and sixty-four died.[29] Citizens at Meridian, another crucial railroad junction along the V&M, tried to stop the running of a medicine train to relieve Lake, but the superintendent of the road kept trains running anyway, and only the action of the state board of health got him to halt traffic.[30] These efforts to stop traffic were not enough to save Meridian, which developed an epidemic that infected 382 and killed eighty-two.[31] The first victim in Meridian was Lewis Carter, a black railroad employee charged with the task of bringing mail to trains from the post office.[32] In addition to infecting towns along the line, the disease took a heavy toll on the V&M itself. As the road's year-end report noted, "the prevailing disease of the past season did not fail to reap some of its harvest from the ranks of the Company's forces."[33]

Once the disease took root in Memphis, the Memphis and Charleston road emerged as a final rail vector. From Memphis the railroad spread yellow fever into small towns to the east in Tennessee. The situation became so dire along the road that the railroad company had to run special daily relief trains full of supplies. Correspondents traveling with these relief trains marveled at the devastation and noted the "fever is very prevalent along the line."[34] Another observer noted, "The cry of distress which we were forced to give utterance to six weeks ago, is now being echoed on every breeze that comes wafted to us from the small towns along the line of the Louisville, Memphis and Charleston, and Mississippi and Tennessee Railroads."[35]

The scene that unfolded over the next few months on Mississippi's railroads constituted a cruel inversion of how the railroad network normally operated. In Grenada, the same railroad that brought the disease largely abandoned the stricken town, as most trains neglected to stop in the town at all. Locomotives on the NOStL&C flew by Grenada on August 14, with their whistle blowing.[36] Trains manned by fearful crews treated the stricken town like a "veritable black hole," flying through the town at forty miles per hour with windows and doors sealed shut. When a train did arrive as a special request of a well-connected official who wanted to get his family to safety, a loitering crowd near the depot fled in a panic, vanishing within two minutes.[37] J. C. Clarke tried in vain to convince his employees to operate trains on the NOStL&C line. On August 28 he noted that many engineers were refusing to run trains through Grenada, and on September 5 told a subordinate at Water Valley that engineers had nothing to fear from the disease.[38] He directed the man to "tell them that no class of man are so apt to be free from taking it as engineer and trainmen" due to the continual change of air they experienced. If the men did their duties like "brave and honest men," they would survive.[39] In her autobiography, Ida B. Wells recalled a harrowing journey home to Holly Springs at the height of the outbreak. She knew the journey from an isolated farm to the stricken town was not safe, but she felt duty-bound to care for her sick family members. Passenger trains had stopped running, so she hitched a ride with a freight train. The caboose of the train was draped in black in memory of two different conductors who died of yellow fever. The conductor tried to dissuade her from her trip, but when she pointed out like him, she was simply doing her duty, he relented and let her ride.[40]

Yellow fever was clearly moving along rail lines, and reports from journeys along the rail corridors penetrating infected areas showed that southern attitudes toward their new connections were shifting as the epidemic progressed. On a journey from Winona to New Orleans along the NOStL&C, a correspondent noted the presence of heavily armed guards at every station. A farmer riding a wagon immediately turned his cart away as the train approached, and the train's arrival at a station crowded with blacks caused a stampede away from the tracks in all directions.[41] A doctor traveling through Grenada to the country to the north had a similar experience. As the train stopped to drop off nurses for Grenada, the nurses were told they had to jump from the train as fast as possible. The train could not stop any longer because of quarantine rules to the north. Apparently, other towns feared that even a short stay of a train in Grenada would poison the locomotive.[42] Another correspondent on a train traveling through the infected areas around Memphis poked fun at the fear of trains exhibited in the countryside, noting "an impression must be made that they used black vomit on trains as a common diet," and that area residents must have assumed that railroad men were purposefully breaking bottles of vomit in uninfected areas.[43] Jokes about rural fears of trains could be dismissed as the standard mocking of country rubes by city folk, but they also underscored a crucial fact, which is that these rural southerners clearly had begun to see the arrival of new trains as a serious threat.

Just as race structured mobility on southern railroads in more peaceful times, the same railroad network that allowed for the dissemination of pathogens and refugees hampered the movement of African Americans. Yellow fever was not colorblind, as it was historically less virulent among black populations. A doctor's assertion that "the negroes in this country are largely exempt from" the disease was to some extent a true observation.[44] Whether due to a genetic advantage from African blood or prior acclimation, yellow fever claimed a lower proportion of blacks than whites in every epidemic, though in 1878 it is clear many African Americans fell victim to the disease. Despite vivid demonstrations of the disease's devastating impact on blacks, in general, white southerners did not see blacks as vectors of transmission, due to their perceived immunity from the disease. In yellow fever's nightmare world, white southerners saw blacks as free from danger, and many used this assumption to fuel critiques of the black southerners who did try to flee.[45]

But while yellow fever may not have discriminated, the railroad network that let fearful southerners flee did. Impoverished blacks lacked the ability to pick up everything and leave when the epidemic struck, and the urban centers of many affected towns were almost entirely African American at the height of the epidemic. The situation in Memphis turned especially grim, as the depopulation of the city stranded black residents in an urban core lacking a functioning economy and reliable deliveries of food. For those lucky enough to avoid a deadly mosquito bite, starvation was a pressing danger. To solve this problem, authorities in Memphis removed 5,000 of the city's black residents to a refugee camp near a yellow fever hospital. A white man at the Memphis camp complained that the 5,000 African Americans at the camp "would not budge," and he claimed they were taking advantage of the situation to draw free rations. This man's horrific solution to this "problem" was to totally cut off railroad connections to this camp and simply let the refugees starve.[46] A manager with the Howard Association, which provided relief to affected communities, complained in a letter to Mississippi's governor that Grenada's "colored people" were "in subordination," and committing all sorts of "depredations," with the absence of white authorities. This must certainly be taken with a grain of salt, as these "depredations" may just have been efforts to secure food, but the letter speaks to the total breakdown of normal society in infected towns.[47] This pattern of white flight and black immobility was repeated all across infected areas. The railroad network facilitated the spread of the disease, but its denial of mobility to blacks ensured that poor blacks would most heavily feel the economic and social disruptions caused by the disease.

Railroads may have been responsible for spreading the epidemic, but to their credit, railroad companies did play a vital role in funneling aid to affected areas. News of the epidemic sparked a nationwide relief effort, a campaign that helped bring unity to North and South and heal some of the lingering wounds of Reconstruction.[48] As a report ruefully noted, "the railroad which had brought death now brought bread to feed the dying and coffins to bury the dead."[49] At the height of the epidemic in early September, J. C. Clarke tried to arrange meals for his employees at the largely abandoned stations along the line, arguing in a letter, "it's now more than ever before necessary to keep our road open for the benefit of the country through which we run our road." Railroads ended up serving as lifelines for devastated communities, delivering volunteer nurses, food supplies, and disinfectants.[50] After quarantines shut off normal traffic, the Mississippi and Tennessee Railroad ran solely to facilitate the work of the Howards and other charitable associations, and twenty-four employees died of the disease, most of whom fell at their posts.[51] These efforts notwithstanding, the lesson of the epidemic, that railroads could spread yellow fever, was plain to see.

Just as southerners became wary of the dangers of open commerce afforded by efficient railroad connections, they also improved the methods of tamping epidemics in the wake of these new developments. In a wave of postmortem reports on the tragic summer, investigators pinpointed the culprits with brutal clarity. The towns that did escape infection in Mississippi exhibited one of two characteristics. Some were isolated from both the river and major rail corridors. Despite the recent gains in railroad construction, Mississippi still contained many areas without railroads, and these towns found it easy to keep out infection. Yazoo City was inland from the river and lacked railroad service, and thus suffered only seventeen cases. Isolated from major avenues of commerce, yellow fever did not appear there until October 1.[52]

The other towns that escaped instituted rigid quarantines. For some small railroad towns in Mississippi, it was not hard to drop off the network altogether. In Macon, officials later noted they were "liable to contract the fever from travelers on railroad and by wagon roads, from tramps, from numerous refugees from the west, and from merchandise from infected districts." The town forbid stoppage of trains and shut its doors to all strange individuals, and was thus able to escape infection. Oxford was similarly exposed thanks to trains passing through on the NOStL&C, but strict quarantine kept yellow fever away. The most emphatic response to the state's questionnaire about quarantine practices came from Adams County, which hugged the Mississippi River and also contained a railroad. Officials in this county, which included the town of Natchez, concluded "vigilance, activity, fearlessness, and the double barreled shot-gun will give a community entire immunity from the yellow fever." The Mississippi Board of Health's official report summarized the results of its investigation, arguing that "the true cause of yellow fever is exotic and that it only exists in this state by importation, that it is transportable in vessels, railroad cars, clothing, goods, etc., and that efficient quarantine regulations are competent to exclude it from the State."[53] Dr. John Dromgoole, who chronicled the history of the epidemic, wrote, "This yellow-winged monster has taken a wide flight of desolation this year, but I fear it will be exceeded in after years." The reason, he continued, was "this year it has traveled by rail, and the fear is that rapid intercommunication hereafter may be a fruitful source of its reaching distant communities."[54]

The 1878 epidemic introduced the South to a recurring summertime railroad dystopia: the connectivity and the circulation of the improved railroad network proved a mortal threat to both lives and livelihood. The outbreak opened up the fault lines of a conflict that would rage every summer until the eradication of yellow fever in 1905. On one side stood merchants and railroad corporations worried about the deleterious effects of local quarantines, known as "shotgun" quarantines for the preferred method of enforcement. New Orleans merchants especially protested these local quarantines. If towns in the Mississippi Valley could shut down railroads at the slightest suspicion of yellow fever in the city, New Orleans would have no hope of trading goods in the summer.[55] On the other side of this debate were local communities wishing to assert their right to quarantine and control the movement of trains on their railroad lines. As a Memphis editorial argued, "Life is worth more than cities and commerce," and the Mississippi Valley must strictly quarantine against New Orleans every summer.[56] A paper in Jackson threatened that "the people would rise in their might and if necessary destroy every railroad and burn every steamboat coming with our limits" if yellow fever again appeared in the region.[57] With the health, and the very existence, of a community at stake, towns saw no problem with shutting down the network's movement via impromptu shotgun quarantines.

With the memory of the horrors of 1878 fresh in the minds of every railroad town, the shotgun quarantine would thus threaten to cut off traffic and choke off commerce every summer. How then would railroads and merchants sever the link between capitalism and disease? One strategy was to beef up state authority to manage epidemics. As a public health infrastructure emerged in southern states, commercial interests took the lead in these efforts. In New Orleans and other southern cities, businessmen were prominent in efforts to establish sanitary organizations and to create more standardized boards of health. Across the South, states established boards of health with the goal of providing for rational and orderly quarantines that would both keep the region healthy and allow for free commerce, in the event of an outbreak.[58] The federal government also responded to the epidemic with the creation of the National Board of Health. The epidemic directly inspired the legislation creating this board, and prevention of yellow fever was the focus of the overwhelming majority of its activities. The activities of this body also speak to the newfound fear that railroads were a vector for the disease's spread. In 1879 the board put out a series of rules and regulations for railroads that demonstrated they realized railroads could spread the disease, but they had no clue as to the exact method. As a general rule, railroad corporations were expected to keep roadbeds, tracks, and depots clean and "free from filth and impurities," an order that reflected the connection between unsanitary conditions and yellow fever. The board also suggested that railroad cars should be ventilated whenever possible, and upholstered seats, mattresses, pillows, curtains, and carpets in sleeping cars should be whipped or beaten periodically to keep out dust. The regulations stated that any car leaving a town with yellow fever infections had to be cleaned and fumigated with sulfur.[59]

The board's rules also attempted to provide orderly movement of trains in the case of epidemic, laying out specific regulations for travel between towns that were defined as "infected," which meant that they had any cases of fever, and towns that were labeled "dangerously infected," where cases were being transmitted within the locality. Any train leaving an infected city had to be inspected by a "competent medical man," who would provide the conductor with a certificate declaring that the train and its passengers were healthy. When a train ran through an infected or dangerously infected town, it would not be allowed to go slower than ten miles per hour. While sleeping cars or any upholstered cars were not allowed to leave "dangerously infected" locales, passenger cars could as long as they were fumigated. Passengers traveling on the network in infected areas had to carry certificates of health, which were distributed by a "competent medical man" who inspected passenger cars.[60]

The broader success of these measures can be seen in the fact that there was never another epidemic as devastating as 1878 had proved. Indeed, an outbreak in Memphis in 1879 fizzled out without spreading far outside the city limits, and the appearance of yellow fever in Pensacola, Florida, and Brownsville, Texas, in 1882 similarly did not lead to a wide-scale outbreak. It was unclear whether this is due to the board's work or just a case of good luck. Perhaps the outbreaks that followed the 1878 epidemic were simply less virulent, or the wide-ranging spread of the 1878 epidemic may have acclimated large portions of the South and decreased the number of potential targets for the disease.[61] The death toll may have dropped in subsequent outbreaks, but the virulence with which southerners contested the free movement of goods and people only increased. Public health institutions failed to keep pace with the rapid spread of railroads and the quickening pace of circulation on the network. The fear of yellow fever only intensified as railroads spread and further connected the region, as evidenced by an outbreak and a panic ten years after the summer of 1878.

YELLOW JACK'S NEXT MAJOR appearance, in 1888, demonstrated that quarantine problems were far from resolved and that the credibility gap between southerners' interests and the circulation dictated by the logic of capital only grew wider in the intervening years. When yellow fever showed up in Florida, a state whose geography was transformed dramatically by railroad construction in the 1880s, it threw questions about control of the rail network into stark relief. Richard McCormick, "a saloonkeeper and otherwise disreputable person," brought yellow fever to Jacksonville by riding a train from Tampa on July 28, 1888, touching off an epidemic that sent shock waves of fear throughout the South.[62] The disease found a fertile ground for expansion in Jacksonville, as both the city and the state had experienced dazzling amounts of growth in the previous decade. The rapid increase in population and economic activity might have been a boon for Jacksonville's pride. But for yellow fever, it meant more carriers to infect and more high-speed links with other communities. The 1888 version exploited a new network of connections, as the presence of new railroad lines and the memory of the 1878 epidemic transformed what in prior years would have likely been a localized nuisance into a public health crisis of the highest degree for the whole nation.

Yellow Jack had good reason to enjoy his sunny new surroundings. In 1888, Jacksonville was in the midst of a meteoric rise from a sleepy port to Florida's most significant metropolis and a quintessential example of a New South city forged by the railroad. Postwar Jacksonville continued to rely on the lumber trade until the railroad boom of the 1880s remade the city into the premier market hub for Florida. A historian of Jacksonville labeled 1879–81, the beginning of the railroad construction boom, an "epochal period in the history of Jacksonville," a period that led to Jacksonville's becoming the unofficial "gateway to Florida."[63] By 1885, a tourist guide enthusiastically proclaimed, "As all roads were once said to lead to Rome, so here, at least, all roads lead to Jacksonville."[64] Lady Duffus Hardy, a British traveler, lauded Jacksonville's railroads in 1883, describing an "immense amount of railway traffic, the iron roads running like the arms of an octopus in every direction" in which "trains are constantly passing to and fro."[65] Any tourist visiting Florida passed through the railway octopus centered at Jacksonville, either staying in one of its many hotels or continuing south to one of the hotels lining the St. Johns River.

The lines centering in Jacksonville tapped the entire Florida peninsula, which had seen rapid railroad development in the 1880s, thanks to an aggressive policy of state aid. Between 1880 and 1890, the state's railroad mileage shot up from 528.6 to 2,470.[66] The percentage increase in Florida railroad mileage from 1880 to 1890 was an incredible 367.4, while the national percentage increase was 86.2. The only areas to surpass Florida's spectacular railroad growth in this decade were wide-open western territories such as North Dakota and Washington.[67] More ominously, these railroads reached the southern half of the state, where yellow fever could linger year to year in subtropical climes. Yellow fever struck Tampa and Key West in 1887, two ports with close ties to yellow fever hot spots in Cuba, and the disease was never fully eradicated in the mild Florida winter.[68]

When yellow fever arrived on Florida's new railroads in 1888, it thus arrived in a state and a region that had seen a compressed period of dramatic change. Rapid railroad construction had outpaced the creation of government institutions needed to regulate commerce, as Florida lacked a state board of health. Instead, Florida passed a law allowing first cities, and later individual counties, to create boards of health.[69] The virulence of the 1888 yellow fever epidemic in Jacksonville was mild by historical standards. By the time November's frost killed the deadly pathogens, 427 people had died in Jacksonville. The disease did not actually spread far outside Jacksonville, either. Isolated cases appeared in Alabama and Mississippi, but the disease became epidemic only in Gainesville, Maclenny, and a few other small communities in North Florida.[70] But far more important than Yellow Jack's actual appearance in 1888, the mounting fear of yellow fever's spread held disastrous repercussions for the railroads recently connected to Jacksonville. Alarm over the epidemic traveled quickly over Florida's new railroad network and arguably did more damage than the actual spread of the disease. Actual cases of yellow fever were confined to a few areas, but the quarantine panic gripped the entire South, and fear again pulsed through the railroad network for a few months.

Mindful of the lessons from 1878, towns along rail lines emanating from Jacksonville quickly established shotgun quarantines to block traffic once the disease's presence was officially confirmed. A farmer in southern Florida remarked, "I fear that it will spread to the towns along the R. R.," as soon as he learned of yellow fever's arrival in Jacksonville.[71] Brief newspaper dispatches captured the wide geographical swath of the panic in Florida. The citizens of New Berlin, an unincorporated area outside Jacksonville, sent word that they "temporarily incorporated it a town, established a Board of Health and declared quarantine against Jacksonville."[72] Farmers with firearms greeted trains arriving in Hampton, and 250 men guarded the ancient city of Saint Augustine, an expensive but effective quarantine paid for with $20,000 from hotel and railroad developer Henry Flagler.[73] At the railroad junction of Palatka, 155 armed men turned back a grain shipment from Jacksonville.[74] In Gainesville, city authorities placed "a double cordon of guards around the city."[75] The guard in Gainesville made escaping the state even more difficult, since the town sat astride the only route north that did not pass through Jacksonville. Farther to the south in Ocala, citizens furiously interrogated each other as to their previous whereabouts, and the town council suggested not allowing any train to go slower than twenty miles per hour through Marion County.[76]

Florida's railroads were confronted with what amounted to an insurrection along their lines. Every line had to deal with shotgun quarantines, but the most intense conflict over quarantines happened just to the north of Jacksonville. As the disease became epidemic in the city, residents hoped to use railroads to flee to points to the north, where cities allegedly beyond the yellow fever zone offered asylum. However, shotgun quarantines in Waycross, Georgia, and Callahan, Florida, blocked the way. Caught between Jacksonville and the rest of the Georgia's railroad network, the junction town of Waycross had to account for all of Georgia's anxiety over yellow fever as well due to its rail connections to Savannah, Brunswick, Atlanta, and Macon. Atlanta may have welcomed refugees, but Savannah and Brunswick maintained strict quarantines against Florida passengers. When fever broke out in Jacksonville, shotgun-wielding citizens in Waycross took to the tracks to make sure no one left trains passing through the town. Under pressure from both the local citizenry and from other Georgia cities to the north, the Savannah, Florida & Western altered its schedule and stopped running all but one passenger train from Jacksonville to Waycross.[77] A newspaper correspondent called the situation on this one daily train "a pitiful sight." No one was allowed to leave the locked car at Waycross, and the crowded car was filled with hungry refugees crying out for food.[78] To further ensure that no yellow fever refugees made it to Waycross, the town council approved a resolution offering a $10 reward for anyone who arrested a yellow fever refugee in the town.[79]

A similar scene took shape farther down the Waycross Short Line, in the small town of Callahan, Florida. Hardly anyone lived in Callahan, yet it was a vitally important junction in northeast Florida, as passengers from the Florida Central needed to disembark there to catch the train north to Waycross and Georgia. On August 12, Callahan's leaders informed the Savannah, Florida & Western that neither northbound nor southbound trains would be allowed to stop at the town. According to their ultimatum, if any train stopped, the citizens would tear up the railroad track and cut off traffic for good. To show they meant business, citizens took to the tracks with guns to enforce the restriction, and Fernandina, a port city north of Jacksonville in the same county, sent a detachment of fifty militiamen to "keep a strict watch of the S, F & W trains." When members of an Atlanta baseball team tried to make a connection at Callahan to journey north, a train instead dropped them off a few miles from the town. They tried to walk to the railroad junction but were met by a "sheriff with two big pistols," who warned them against continuing their walk to the town. They wandered a few miles to another railroad track before a sympathetic conductor picked them up.[80]

The Savannah, Florida & Western found itself in an unenviable position, caught between shotgun-toting militias, the transportation needs of Jacksonville refugees, and the road's need to turn a profit. Before the yellow fever outbreak, the road's outlook for fall traffic was "never so good." The company was hopeful for a quick end to the epidemic so there would be no disruptions in shipping the lucrative orange crop out of Florida.[81] The quarantine also short-circuited the line's logistical operations when it locked up a large number of the company's much-needed boxcars in the town. In an interview with the *Savannah Morning News*, the corporate superintendent was reportedly "indignant" over the interference with the company's trains. He argued, "The company owns the right of way and proposes to use it," and planned to sell tickets to Callahan anyway, with the plan of letting passengers off outside of town if authorities interfered.[82] However, a few days later the paper reported that trains were still unable to stop in Callahan.[83]

Problems on the line worsened, as the number of new infections in Jacksonville began to rise and it became clear the epidemic was a major one. Not wanting to deal with yellow fever refugees anymore, and under pressure from Georgians and railroad town residents, the Savannah, Florida & Western eventually decided to close the Waycross Short Line to passenger traffic altogether on August 26, 1888. Railroad lines to the west of Jacksonville were similarly tied up by local quarantines, so the closing of the Waycross Short Line totally isolated the stricken city. Many citizens who had stayed in the city now wanted to leave, but quarantines kept them in Jacksonville. Angry editorials in Jacksonville's newspaper attacked the citizens of Waycross and the Savannah, Florida & Western Railroad, blaming both for hemming them in. Hot-headed citizens in Jacksonville even began to talk of using force to open traffic.[84] Jacksonville refugees in Atlanta lambasted the railroad company in a meeting, with one speaker claiming that they owned and ran the entire town of Waycross.[85] However, it was not just the railroad and railroad towns that kept Jacksonville isolated. John Hamilton, the surgeon-general of the Marine Hospital Service, sent a statement to newspapers and officials unequivocally denying Jacksonville's requests for more freedom of movement, invoking the memory of the past epidemic to make his argument. He wrote, "The dreadful ravages of yellow fever in the towns along the railroad lines leading out of

New Orleans in 1878 . . . is too fresh in the memory to risk its repetition along the Atlantic seaboard."[86]

To resolve these disputes, the surgeon general commissioned a special train to carry 291 Jacksonville refugees to the mountain community of Hendersonville, North Carolina, where high altitude was thought to protect against the spread of the disease. As evidence of the danger these passengers posed, John Guiteras, the official in charge of the trip, lamented that no keys had been furnished to lock the refugees in the cars. The train was delayed by a few accidents along the road, and the excursion began to run low on rations, but every time the train stopped in Georgia, communities refused to let the refugees leave the train, and opportunistic merchants only offered supplies at exorbitant prices. When this beleaguered caravan pulled into Atlanta, a reporter with the *Constitution* joined the excursion, later noting, "Never did I take a ghastlier ride" and that "it was apparent that Dr. Guiteras had lost control" of his wards.[87] After twenty-four hours the situation within the cars took a turn for the worse as symptoms of yellow fever began to appear among some of the travelers, leaving the passengers "truly panic stricken." "Stronger spirits" began to seize control of individual cars and make up their own quarantine rules. When one woman fell ill, the more radical of the passengers proposed simply kicking her off the train, until more humane minds prevailed, and the woman was simply moved to another car. *Leslie's Illustrated Newspaper* was able to capture this panicked scene in a drawing that shared Florida's railroad horror with the rest of the nation (figures 1 and 2). Individual cars desperately tried to quarantine against each other, and some frightened travelers simply jumped off the train and scattered into the countryside. At least four people went missing over the course of the trip, presumably fleeing to the presumed safety of other towns. Before the train reached the Carolina border, "every car was practically barricaded against every other car and there was quarantine all along the line."[88]

The dramatic situation within the train was nothing compared with the fear this excursion spread along the line. As the train moved north, the *Constitution* correspondent noted "a curious and ludicrous effect was produced" at every station the train passed. When the train first approached, a crowd would typically gather, but after learning it was "the yellow fever train, they fled like sheep." From the car windows, one could see "whole villages scudding around corners and taking for the woods as the dread train moved its slow and ghastly length along."[89] In Jesup, a resident complained, "it was understood" that the train would "come through with locked doors." But the train ended up lingering on the depot for fifteen minutes, and the man saw

FIGURE 1 "Scene on a Refugee Railway," *Frank Leslie's Illustrated Newspaper*, September 8, 1888. Passengers flee after a woman falls ill on one of the government-run trains leaving Jacksonville.

railroad employees board and leave the train, and even a few of the refugees briefly stepped out on the platform. "If there is any danger of any one contracting it by coming in contact with a train load of people," the man concluded, "we are in danger of having it here."[90] Even a week after the excursion, reports of escaped refugees continued to trickle in from all along the line, such as the story of five who hid in a cornfield somewhere north of Atlanta. The normally exciting moment of a train's arrival had turned into a terrible omen.[91]

The beleaguered caravan finally straggled into Hendersonville at 2 A.M. on September 13, two days after leaving Jacksonville. The *Constitution* compared the scenes at the journey's end, "when yellow faced, gaunt and nervous refugees were dumped" in Hendersonville to scenes of war, as families separated due to the trip's quarantine chaos rushed to tearful reunions. Guiteras feared that the hot, unsanitary cars would create a secondary center of infection, but residents of the town were lucky that their generosity was not repaid with a gift of yellow fever infection. Though the town's high elevation and inhospitable atmosphere for the *Aedes aegypti* mosquitoes forestalled any outbreak of disease, residents of Hendersonville also did not get what they expected out of their offer for refuge. One resident complained that while it was thought that the gesture would establish the city as a health resort and a vaca-

FIGURE 2
"The Yellow Fever Scourge in Florida," *Frank Leslie's Illustrated Newspaper*, September 8, 1888. Men with guns forcibly bar Jacksonville refugees from leaving the train. The image provides a clear depiction of the "shotgun quarantine" dreaded by railroad companies.

tion destination for wealthy Floridians, instead the town had become a "dumping place for whole train loads of temporary paupers averaging perhaps not a dollar ahead, one-third of them negroes."[92] Guiteras concluded removing refugees to high altitudes was a "desirable object," and if "the health department of the nation was endowed with the same liberality as the Army and Navy," they could set up "extensive permanent quarters in the mountainous regions, with a standing garrison of acclimated people, the fitting out of special trains exclusively under control of the Government." But as the train to Hendersonville demonstrated, at the present juncture "the experiment of excursions, insisted upon by the people of Jacksonville, is not a success."[93]

This vision of a permanent government-funded lifeline connecting mountains and fever districts never came to fruition, so in order to safely remove residents from Jacksonville, the surgeon general's office established two refugee camps outside the city, mirroring the solution to the devastation in Memphis in 1878. At Camps Perry and Mitchell, citizens could wait for ten days, then head north unmolested with a clean bill of health. Conditions at these camps were far from ideal at first. The tents were old and did not keep out rain, the heat was unbearable, and women and children were forced to eat at the same table with what the Board of Health described as "low Negroes" who made up half of the camp's residents. Federal funds made some improvements to the situation, ameliorating poor living conditions and establishing segregated living quarters for the black refugee population.[94] This solution mirrored the increasing segregation within southern rail cars. In Florida the legislature passed a bill segregating the state's railroads a year before this outbreak in 1887, and seven other southern states passed laws segregating railroads between 1888 and 1891.[95]

In another example of how the movement of southerners was structured by race, one only has to look at the situation in Jacksonville during the epidemic. Whites with money were able to secure passage on refugee trains and wait out the epidemic in areas to the North, but this option was not available for working-class blacks. A census taken in Jacksonville after most of the refugees had left in September found about 14,000 people in the city, and 9,800 of them were black. With the bulk of the city's business owners on the run, and with transportation links sundered, thousands were thrown out of work, left to fend for themselves in a city under siege. It was not just the suffering of yellow fever victims and threat of starvation that turned Jacksonville into a nightmare world. The normally sunny skies of the city were choked with smoke from fires set to ward off the disease, and the booming of cannons, brought in from Saint Augustine as another supposed remedy, constantly echoed at all hours. The city leaders created a Committee on Sanitation to provide jobs for the unemployed and to clean up dirty areas of the city. However, on November 18, the city abruptly announced that it was cutting the amount of jobs in half due to a money shortage. Only a massive mobilization under the auspices of the Knights of Labor convinced city officials to keep providing work for the working-class blacks stranded in the city.[96]

Moving potentially infected Jacksonville residents through the railroad network was hard enough, but in the rest of the state, merchants struggled to get goods through the chokepoints of quarantines. South of Palatka, Edwin Smith ran a country store not unlike the ones that proliferated across the South as railroads arrived. Smith attempted to order fertilizer from the Armour Company in Chicago, only to learn that they were not taking orders due to the closing of their Jacksonville warehouse.[97] He also tried Wilkinson and Co. Bone Fertilizers in New York, only to learn that they could not ship until quarantine was lifted from Fernandina.[98] The orange growers of his store's region had to farm without fertilizer in 1888, and many other Floridians went without essential products. Savannah wholesale traders, who supplied many Florida merchants, reported in August that country merchants were ordering cautiously due to the "unsettled condition."[99] However, Savannah eventually came to benefit from the epidemic, as South Florida merchants began ordering goods from there instead of Jacksonville. Instead of being transported on the Waycross Short Line, merchandise from Savannah traveled around Jacksonville, moving farther to the west before heading south into Florida via Gainesville.[100]

To solve the problem of unregulated quarantines and get commerce running again in Florida, Jacksonville officials organized a conference with health officials from ten counties and representatives from a number of Florida railroad companies on August 28. Jacksonville officials, unsurprisingly, opened the meeting with a complaint that the quarantine "had no precedent anywhere else in the history of yellow fever epidemics." When it "became impossible to send silver money by express to Tampa from Jacksonville, or iron pipe and machinery, to enable a saw-mill to continue operations, because of quarantine restrictions, it was time to inquire whether this quarantine is more rigid than the public safety demands." Lamenting the "scarcity of even the necessities of life" in South Florida, they sought a way to keep traffic open. The president of the Marion County Board of Health argued for the maintenance of quarantines. Under pressure from what he called "panic-stricken" residents of his county, he stated that he would not permit any goods from Jacksonville in his county. Angry over the unauthorized shipment of two cars of freight into his county from Jacksonville, he stated that "corporations had no soul," and that he "could not trust the railroad companies." He had no worry about shortages of provisions in his county, as he declared Marion County to be "the Egypt of Florida," with overflowing granaries that would be able to supply all of southern Florida.[101]

The difficulties of creating a fair quarantine policy that served both the interests of the people and the interests of the railroads was best illustrated by the presence of J. E. Ingraham, one of Henry Plant's top lieutenants in Florida, at the conference. At the Orange Park Conference he represented both the Osceola County Board of Health and the South Florida Railroad. As a railroad official, Ingraham was conscious of the need to make a profit for his employer. He declared that he "was keeping trains from running now at heavy cost to his company," and he argued that freight traffic needed to be opened before the maturation of the orange crop.[102] With men like Ingraham in charge of quarantine policy in some areas, one can see the basis for Marion County's mistrust of the proceedings. How could Floridians be certain that a railroad official would put the health of the public above the health of their corporation?

In the end, the representatives at the conference reached a tentative agreement over the movement of goods. Conference attendees adopted a resolution that said that "rice, grits, flour, sugar, coffee, bacon, lard, butter, potatoes, corn and oats in barrels; hardware and machinery, unpacked tobacco in any form, and cigars" could pass through their counties without quarantine. Merchants would now be able to order supplies from Jacksonville, and the problem of the local quarantine seemed to be solved. Jubilation over this settlement was short-lived, as most counties quickly sent word that they would still not accept freight from Jacksonville. Marion County "admits northing, and wants nothing except artificial stone and machinery, by special permit," and the Alachua County Board "will not consent to admit freights from infected points, whether fumigated or not." The only message confirming that a board of health would follow the agreement came from Osceola County, which promised to admit goods and wryly noted, "Our board is not composed of crawfish."[103]

The failure of this meeting demonstrated the danger of the vital commodities carried by Florida's railroads, and until December's frost allowed for the lifting of all yellow fever quarantines, it would be anyone's guess if goods shipped into or out of Florida would reach their destination. The frantic ravings of a letter sent to Edwin Smith by a northerner capture the fear of starvation caused by the quarantines. A mother sent the letter to her daughter who had recently immigrated to Florida. The mother had not heard from her daughter in a while, probably because of the disrupted mails. She had heard rumors that those in Florida were "suffering for food," and she wrote that it was the "hardest thing to bear" that her "own dear Mary should lack bread." A letter from Smith assuring her all was well assuaged the women's fears.[104] Despite widespread shortages, there were no reports of starvation from quarantines. Still, the lengths to which Floridians went to keep out "infected commodities" demonstrated how fear of yellow fever exacerbated an atmosphere of mistrust of railroad authorities.

This same potent blend of fever fright and antirailroad sentiment exploded across the South when isolated cases of yellow fever were found in Decatur, Alabama, and Jackson, Mississippi, in September 1888. These cases did not develop into a full-fledged epidemic, yet a few cases were all it took for a panic to start in areas that were hit hard in the 1878 outbreak. An official with the IC ruefully noted that from Jackson, residents fled "in such numbers as to create the wildest alarm in the towns in which they took refuge."[105] Quarantines entirely halted railroad traffic in the Mississippi Valley for about a week in September. As a Grenada paper argued, the town "cannot be too rigid with her quarantine. Our salvation depends on keeping 'Yellow Jack' out."[106] Mindful of the horror of 1878, some Mississippians even followed through on their threat to destroy railroads. A newspaper correspondent reported that the entire state was "one vast howling mob without any semblance of humanity" and noted the destruction of several bridges outside of Jackson.[107] All across the South, people looked back to 1878 fearfully. M. F. Surghnor, a woman in Monroe, Louisiana, recorded her fears in her diary as the disease threatened to move west from Jackson, a town through which "travelers are constantly coming to Monroe." As she recalled, the disease previously "came to all the Railroad Stations," and she feared for her family's safety in 1888.[108] At the height of the panic, the *Atlanta Constitution* wryly captured the magnitude of the scare, warning, "Northern tourists on southern roads who see squads of men armed with shotguns moving about in the bushes need not fear that another revolution is about to break out—it's nothing but a crowd of volunteer quarantiners hunting for bilious looking subjects."[109]

Mississippi had a more highly developed public health infrastructure than Florida, but the State Board of Health's edicts were largely irrelevant to people on the ground in Mississippi. After a case was found along the line of the Natchez, Jackson & Columbus Road, the board gave the railroad permission to continue running trains, but people in Natchez "rose up en masse and declared they would tear up the track if the running of trains could not be otherwise prevented." Faced with this threat to its property, the railroad was forced to halt traffic.[110] In Meridian, the local paper attacked the laxity of the city's quarantine, and accused officials of "knuckling to the railroads, to whom, of course, a strict quarantine is productive of much trouble and inconvenience."[111] A Grenada paper explicitly linked railroad activities to the Jackson outbreak, blaming some excavation work along railroad lines in Jackson for the handful of cases there.[112]

Just as in the 1878 epidemic, IC officials struggled to keep their employees at their posts. Three officers with the IC deserted their posts to bring their families to the north, which had a "demoralizing effect on the men, who naturally look to their officers for an example of wisdom and courage on such occasions."[113] An official with the railroad noted that during the 1888 scare the "few reliable ones were four or five of those who had been sent from north," while the old engineers "who had seen the epidemic of 1878" abandoned their posts.[114] Every time a paper or commentator would critique the quarantine effort, southern papers would invoke the memory of 1878. A Savannah paper responded to a New York City paper's attacks by arguing, "In 1878 for instance, the places along the Illinois Central Railroad which permitted no trains to stop within their limits, escaped the scourge, while those which permitted the trains to stop to put off the mails or to change engines became infected with it."[115] At least two men were even killed by the quarantine outbreak. After armed guards ordered a man to stay on a train in Durant, Kentucky, the man got off the train anyway and was shot to death.[116] Another man attempting to reach his daughters in quarantined Decatur was found "lying near the railroad track in a terribly mutilated condition," and authorities suspected he was either hit by a train or murdered and robbed.[117] At the high point of the panic in September, local quarantines held sway at over 150 points along the IC. In an interview, a manager of the road said he hoped "wiser council will prevail, and that system and method will take the place of the present practices."[118] But in September and October 1888, the "system and method" developed by public health agencies and railroad corporations had fallen to pieces. The increased rationalization and standardization of southern railroads only increased the potential for chaos when southerners feared infection.

The towns that set up shotgun quarantines had to balance the need to retain provisions with their desire for safety. Some towns were forced to relax quarantines as they ran low on supplies, but two towns along the IC, Winona and Durant, kept up the blockade, as "their supply of provisions seems to have been larger in proportion to population than other towns possessed."[119] Illinois Central officials quickly grew weary of accommodating every locality's quarantine regulation. After Yazoo City ran out of meat, town officials requested a special shipment of supplies, but E. T. Jeffrey argued against doing this, writing, "There is nothing that would bring these people to their senses quicker than a lack of food consequent upon their arbitrarily stopping the wheels of commerce."[120] After the scare, the IC even considered suing communities along the line where shotgun quarantine had prevailed. The road's president, Stuyvesant Fish, wrote to his general counsel in the South, "Now that the panic about the yellow fever is allayed and we have been robbed of, say, $120,000 of earnings," the company should gather testimony "on which to begin suits against the persons who unlawfully interfered with our business, doubtless the statutes of Mississippi, Tennessee and Kentucky prescribe severe penalties for interfering with the movement of trains."[121] In the end, the arguments of E. T. Jeffrey, who thought "it would be impolitic to do so," prevailed, but the thought that the company would resort to legal action speaks to the outrage they felt at the interference of traffic.[122]

When the 1888 epidemic finally subsided, finger pointing again erupted as authorities and railroad officials assessed the economic damage. Some southerners pointed blame at Florida's lack of regulation. In the years after the 1878 epidemic, all the other southern states organized boards of health to coordinate response to epidemics, and most were confident that another epidemic could be prevented. Florida, however, lacked a board of health, and many saw the state as a "weak link in an otherwise strong chain."[123] But the problems in 1888 were more than just a failure of state and federal health authorities. New public health agencies could not prevent 150 separate towns along the IC from setting up blockades, or widespread vigilante attacks on bridges and rail lines. The link between railroads and disease, seared into southerners' minds in the 1878 epidemic, overcame any efforts by officials to eliminate shotgun quarantines. Southerners fundamentally did not trust corporations to safely move goods and passengers in epidemic years. A quote from J. T. Harahan, vice president with the IC, in 1897, told all one needs to know about the trust Mississippians had for railroad corporations. Harahan had extensive experience with the L&N Railroad in the previous epidemics, and he wrote to the IC president that there would not be shotgun quarantines if "the people had confidence in the management and felt that it would do whatever was necessary to protect them as well as to prevent the disease from spreading."[124] In an interview, an old Mississippi doctor, who even lived through an 1825 epidemic in Natchez, remarked on the surprising amount of havoc a "rather moderate epidemic" caused, telling a reporter that "the alarm, public excitement, furor and national disturbance exceeds anything witnessed before by ten or forty fold." The reason for this was clear: the "rapid and multifarious railroad transit" which dwarfed the "slow, once-a-week steamboat travel" of past years.[125]

E. P. SKENE, LONGTIME TELEGRAPH operator with the IC, stood at his post in Jackson in disbelief in September 1897. Yellow fever had again appeared in the Magnolia State, this time in the small town of Edwards on the old V&M line. Quarantine actions erupted across the state, and Skene was receiving telegram reports of the chaos engulfing his line. On September 16, several quarantine officers shot into a cab of an IC train at Durant to try to stop the train. And two days later, unknown residents of Jackson tore up part of the Alabama and Vicksburg Railroad's track and burned a bridge two miles outside of town.[126] The *Jackson Daily Bulletin* condemned this act, yet agreed with the sentiment behind the destruction, accusing the road of "persistent and defiant disregard of quarantine regulations."[127] A. J. Greif, Skene's contact in Jackson, noted that a mass meeting was being held "under the leadership of some very radical men" and there was "no telling what measures they may adopt."[128] In Washington County, the head of the Yazoo and Mississippi Valley branch of the line expressed fear that "the people of Washington County will dynamite our trestles." Skene and other officials hoped to move a shipment of grain from Memphis but declined, as they would "have serious trouble on the main line of the IC road" if residents found out about the movement of goods from a city where yellow fever was suspected.[129]

By 1897, nineteen years after the 1878 outbreak, public health officials still had not solved the riddle of yellow fever's travel by rail. Authorities and railroad officials agreed that the only answer was for the federal government to get involved. IC general counsel James Fentress argued forcefully for a federal quarantine act in a letter to the president of the road, noting, "It is very difficult to show any difference between a foreign enemy sending troops upon our shores and destroying our people and a foreign disease imported from foreign shores, that kills more than are killed in battles."[130] Legislative action after the 1897 epidemic centered on a bill that would have strengthened the powers of the Marine Hospital Service, but just as this bill was being debated, the U.S.S. *Maine* exploded in Havana Harbor, leading the United States into war with Spain, and ending the push for more federal involvement in quarantine matters.[131] When the United States took control of Cuba from Spain, officials used the control and suppression of the yellow fever threat as a motivating factor in the occupation of Cuba. As the argument went, occupation would allow the United States to clean up the "dirty" sections of Cuba, stop the constant importation of yellow fever germs, and salvage the South's economy.[132] Ending the yellow fever problem became a question of foreign affairs, and not control of circulation or regulation of railroads.

This occupation of Cuba would finally solve the problem of the shotgun quarantine, though not in the exact way advocates had intended. Cleaning up the streets and sewers of Havana was not as important as Walter Reed's experiments with soldiers stationed in Cuba. Reed definitively discovered the mosquito vector responsible for transmission, and demonstrated that mosquito control efforts, and not shotgun quarantines, were the most effective way to manage epidemics. The South's last epidemic, in New Orleans in 1905, was managed by a concerted campaign to halt mosquito breeding. Crews patrolled urban centers, dumped out stagnant water, and cleaned open sewers, destroying potential breeding grounds for the *Aedes aegypti*.[133] This campaign was a success, but on southern rail lines, the situation in 1905 was still unsettled. Health officials continued to place inspectors on railroads and recommend ventilation, and even with growing evidence to support the mosquito theory of transmission, doubts lingered. In August, Mississippi turned again to a time-honored tactic and quarantined against the entire state of Louisiana. Defending this decision in a letter to his Alabama counterpart, Dr. W. H. Saunders, a Mississippi health official, argued that the reckless actions of the Gulf and Ship Island Railway had "Mississippianized our Gulf Coast to such an extent that never again will it willingly throw itself in with New Orleans or any other fever infected port." Years of shotgun quarantines had so impacted the state that the man was able to use Mississippi as an adjective to justify his recent actions.[134]

The links between railroads, capitalism, and disease, and the clear tensions between southerners and the interests of railroad corporations in epidemic years, clear to observers from 1878 to 1905, have since been obscured. The responsibility for this disremembering lies with both nineteenth-century and more modern chroniclers. In the competitive economic climate of the New South, towns and cities were loath to admit the existence of outbreaks. For example, ephemera associated with the New Orleans Exposition, an event that took place only a few years after the 1878 epidemic, either ignored the tragic history of the city or took pains to comment on how healthy New Orleans was. One guidebook noted the city was "erroneously supposed to be the most unhealthy city of the United States," due to an "immense floating population that often imports with it new diseases," but despite this, yellow fever was "stamped out" and the average general health was excellent. Railroads seeking immigration and economic growth along their lines took a similar approach. The IC released an 1889 guide to its southern rail territory that incredulously noted that compared to other towns, Holly Springs had a "lower rate of mortality than any other in the world."[135] The boosters who wrote the story of the alleged New South economic miracle were also quick to omit accounts of fever from their tales of regional progress. A reputation as a fever hole could doom a city, and the persistence of yellow fever could undermine the entire New South project. Historians, too, have helped divorce the history of disease from the capitalist system that often helps spread these outbreaks. Yellow fever has certainly attracted scholarly attention, but tales of epidemics often get stuck in medical history and isolated from the broader narrative of southern history or of the history of capitalism.[136]

Whether the threat was Black Death in the fourteenth century or Ebola in the twenty-first, epidemics were historical moments that revealed connections and the often-arcane workings of market forces with brutal clarity.[137] A Grenada resident may have pondered the origins of newly available commodities like fresh Gulf oysters or stylish big-city fashions, but not with the same urgency that resident would have when yellow fever appeared on southern railroads. The mundane movements of a Tampa barkeep to Jacksonville by rail also would have been lost to history, were it not for the deadly pathogens he carried. And the ability of a black family to pack up and leave their home for an unknown safer destination would not be considered in normal times. Every time yellow fever appeared, it flipped the railroad dream to a nightmare and inverted the meaning of the South's railroads. When Yellow Jack was riding the rails, a railroad map became a guide to which lines to quarantine, and a timetable became a schedule for when to hide from an arriving train full of potentially dangerous victims.

The response to these epidemics constituted an upside-down version of the New South creed, as residents of endangered areas fled the sweltering South, sought to halt commerce, severed connections, critiqued corporate greed, invited federal regulation, and turned their back on the railroad's circulation of goods and people. Under the fever regime of disconnection and halted movement, towns that had hitched their future to the railroad learned just how crucial the railroad had become. Within the South's urban cores, capitalism similarly broke down, stranding mostly African American and working-class populations without income or sustenance. In these outbreaks, the white South's attempts to reinforce the barricades of white supremacy echoed and fed into similar attempts to manage and segregate rail travel. Authorities in desolate city centers in Memphis and Jacksonville argued that the African Americans left behind from the exodus deserved their grim fates, as these stranded men and women seemed to bolster white claims that blacks were lazy and stagnant. And in a time when segregation advanced within rail cars, it was no surprise that refugee camps and evacuation trains also became battlegrounds in this struggle. Though yellow fever may have been the most grisly nightmare of the railroad, it was not the only example of how the adoration of the railroad could instantly turn to horror. If yellow fever constituted a yearly threat, a problem to monitor as the weather turned warm, the train wreck—the quintessential disaster of the railroad—was a more ever-present menace.

CHAPTER FIVE

Damnable Conspiracies

From whence came this, inhuman wretch,
Deserving of man's blighting scorn?
By natural means, no womb could fetch,
Into the world, such creature born!
—"The Train Wrecker," a poem in the *Birmingham State-Herald*,
December 30, 1896

In the middle of a hot August night in 1891, Train No. 9 on the Western North Carolina Railroad steamed west through the Carolina Piedmont. Soon the train would begin its ascent up the mountains, a twisting route on the Old Fort Loops that formed the only way through the Black Mountains to Asheville. But before it could make this climb, disaster struck on Bostian Bridge, an imposing stone edifice just west of Statesville. As it crossed this structure, something went wrong, and the train flew off the bridge and crashed into the water below (figure 3). Statesville citizens rushed to the area of the disaster to assist the wounded, but morning's light revealed a ghastly scene, "a charnal-house in Third Creek on its banks." Early arrivals to the site of the wreck witnessed "a harrowing spectacle and harrowing sounds," and saw the engine turned on its side just to the west of the stream. In the water, the first-class car was piled on top of the combination second-class and baggage car. Twenty-two passengers had died, making the wreck the deadliest in the history of the state and the worst disaster in a year plagued with railroad disasters.[1] Five years later, on a December night in 1896, the entire length of a passenger train on the Birmingham Mineral Railroad mysteriously plunged off a bridge over the Cahaba River near Blocton, Alabama, falling 110 feet to the shallow river below (figure 4). While a few passengers were killed on impact, most of the twenty-two killed victims were roasted alive in the cars, which caught fire from the train's overturned heating stove.[2]

These two New South calamities are reminders that the train wreck was the ultimate bogeyman of the railroad. As soon as railroads began to propel people through space at previously unimaginable speeds, a fear lurked in the back of the minds of every traveler: what would happen if this train were to crash? In 1829, a British politician observed an early train ride and argued it "was impossible to divest yourself of the notion of instant death to all upon

FIGURE 3 An engine and passenger cars lie beneath Bostian Bridge outside Statesville, North Carolina, after an 1891 wreck. Courtesy of the State Archives of North Carolina, N.88.9.12.

the least accident happening." Even after decades of improvements in speed, systemization, and safety equipment, the train wreck remained terrifying, and in some ways wrecks became even more terrifying, in this latter stage of railroading. Rather than the nagging anxiety that accompanied the raggedy and bumpy railroad journeys on early railroads, a wreck on a well-established railroad was a thunderbolt out of the blue, a moment that instantly shattered the reverie of a train ride and turned railroad magic to railroad horror.[3] The piles of wreckage in Third Creek and the Cahaba River, and the many other wrecks on the South's distinctively dangerous railroads, were more than just personal tragedies for the victims and their kin. These sites undercut the message of the New South railroad revival.

A train wreck thus always held significance and meaning far beyond the actual wreck scene itself. Who caused these disasters, and who was to blame? In these two wrecks in North Carolina and Alabama, the press reached a horrible conclusion: these disasters were caused by malicious intent. Specifically, the press blamed train wreckers, gangs of criminals who deliberately derailed

FIGURE 4 The aftermath of a train wreck in the Cahaba River in 1896, near Blocton, Alabama. Courtesy of Louisville & Nashville Railroad Collection, Archives and Special Collections, University of Louisville, Cahaba1-L&N.

trails to plunder and rob the wreckage, and the press heaped scorn on these culprits. After the Bostian Bridge wreck, the *Morganton Herald* expressed shocked that "we have here among us fiends with hearts so black and minds so devilish and impulses so hellish that they would plan and consummate such a wholesale murder of innocent people."[4] The *Birmingham News* declared "A Death Trap Had Been Set by the Removal of a Rail," and it proclaimed the Cahaba wreck a "startling story of robbery and pillage."[5] This menace had a life that went far beyond these two disasters. Indeed, train wreckers seemed to be at work on southern rail lines in the 1890s, and throughout the 1880s and '90s, the southern press reported over 300 instances of train wrecking. In 1896, the humor columnist with the *Atlanta Constitution* even joked that "if the train wreckers don't let up, the passengers will have to walk and escort the trains from place to place."[6]

At first blush, train wrecking would seem to be a petty act of criminal desperation, an act of politically motivated terrorism, or a statement of resistance against advancing railroad corporations. The rapid advance of capitalist social and economic relations typically invited resistance and contestation, so could we see train wrecking in this frame? The farmer throwing a log on the track of a train to exact revenge for the grisly death of a beloved cow, or the striking brakeman's sabotage of a switch, would then be analogous to the English weaver smashing the loom that would soon take his job or the coal miner tossing a stick of dynamite in the tent of a particularly overbearing boss.[7] But investigating the inner workings of these wreck scenes reveals a more interesting conclusion. In both of these wrecks in North Carolina and Alabama, and in countless others in the South, the train wrecker never existed. Just as "Yellow Jack" seemed to lurk in every passing train, white southerners feared the imaginary black train wrecker, a mythical figure deployed by corporations to deflect public outrage.

SADLY SCENES LIKE THAT outside Statesville or at Cahaba Bridge became all too common in the 1890s. Train wrecks were by no means a new threat in the 1890s, but the decade formed a critical turning point in the history of railroad disasters. Train wrecks surged nationwide in the 1880s and '90s, peaking between 1890 and 1893. Some of this can be attributed to the spectacular growth in American rail mileage and the increase in efficiency demands that drove up the average weight of trains and placed an additional burden on tracks. But it is clear that some of this growth was due to the proliferation of cheaply constructed new railroads in the South and the West.[8] The distinctive flimsiness of the southern rail network was a direct result of the larger structural factors that consistently hampered southern industrialization: lack of capital, dearth of technical experts, and low levels of regulation.[9] Southern roads had less money on hand to begin with, leading to cheaper construction materials and dangerous shortcuts. A road that lacked capital would likely struggle to pay the yearly interest on its initial bonds, let alone keep up the expensive work of maintaining its tracks and rolling stock. Bridges in particular required constant upkeep and maintenance to ensure their safety.[10] The depression of the 1890s, when over thirty-three different southern lines fell into receivership, had an especially crippling effect on financial health and stability of southern rail lines.[11] A safety inspector with the Southern Railway, a company that took on the unenviable task of rehabilitating many of these bankrupt lines after its birth in 1894, reported that the company's first year was one of "necessary heavy work," since "the bridges and trestles were in worse condition than was realized by anybody until we began to get at them."[12]

With conditions like these, it was no surprise that southern railroads were the most dangerous in the nation for both passengers and employees. The

Interstate Commerce Commission, created in 1887, began to tabulate passenger fatalities and injuries in 1890. The commission sorted the data by region and in 1891 concluded that travel in states south of the Ohio River and east of the Mississippi was more dangerous than any other area of the country.[13] In 1893 the ICC further broke down this data, dividing the nation into ten groups. Over the course of the 1890s, Group IV, which included South Carolina, North Carolina, Virginia, and West Virginia, and Group V, which included Florida, Georgia, Alabama, Tennessee, Kentucky, and Mississippi, were consistently the most dangerous in the nation for passengers. Between 1892 and 1900, a traveler on a Deep South railroad was 2.48 times more likely to be killed and 2.76 times more likely to be wounded than a traveler in the nation at large. And a passenger on one of the Upper South's railroads was 1.84 times more likely to die and 2.3 times more likely to be injured.[14]

This heightened frequency gave southerners an intimacy with railroad disasters that other sections of the country lacked. Towns along southern rail lines became familiar with a tragic routine as wrecks piled up on the region's lines. First came the shock of the disaster, reverberating through town, region, and nation, as telegraph wires buzzed with the grim news. All across North Carolina, papers reported that the public clamored for any updates on the Bostian Bridge wreck. Charlotte's telegraph office was packed with residents until authorities sent final confirmation that no Charlotte residents were involved.[15] In Raleigh, telegraph lines became so clogged that correspondents stationed there had difficulty doing their jobs, and as far away as Wilmington, crowds thronged telegraph offices for news of the wreck and the affected passengers.[16] A more well-developed network of telegraph lines and newspapers meant that news of the wreck carried farther than would news of a wreck in earlier years, and a more connected railroad network meant that the wreck's victims were drawn from a wider range. So the rapid development of the South's infrastructure did more than just lead to more wrecks; it also amplified the impact of these disasters.[17]

Technological advancements designed to further integrate southern railroading also could be a cause of a wreck itself. In the fully integrated rail network of the 1880s and '90s, it only took one mistake to lead to a systemic failure. Though a fictional account, an "old contributor's" story in the Atlanta journal *The Sunny South* in 1892 betrayed such anxieties about the reliability of the railroading infrastructure. In a small station "situated on one of our southern roads," a brand new dispatcher, Nellie West, settled in for her first day of work. In a flurry of activity, Nellie hurriedly sent messages to trains traversing the network until she received a confusing telegram from the railroad's dispatcher. The order was to clear a train to travel to Oakville, but she wondered if the dispatcher meant Oakvale instead. She relayed the message as given to her, telling the conductor to continue on to Oakville. As he neared the next station, he turned pale, spotting another approaching headlight on the same track. It was too late to save the trains, and "two engines clash together like living demons, and in a moment two hundred souls have gone out into eternity." Nellie was innocent, having only relayed someone else's incorrect order, but the other dispatcher pinned the blame on the newly employed woman. Nellie was arrested, and the case went to trial. All hope seemed to be lost for Nellie, until at the last minute another railroad official burst into the courtroom with evidence of the cover-up. The lessons of this story were clear to readers: all it took was one miscommunication for the railroad network to send 200 innocent passengers to their graves.[18] An editorial after the Statesville wreck spoke to a similar fear. Noting that "a horrible wreck" is recorded in a paper nearly every week, the editorialist commented, "In this great system many lives are hung upon the many liabilities of a great army of employees." The rationalization and construction of a southern railway system had exposed millions of travelers to new dangers and "human life is still very cheap."[19]

Tracing a victim's contacts gives another window into the speed at which news of train wrecks spread. Bennehan Cameron, a young man on his way to a career among North Carolina's business and political elite, survived the Bostian Bridge wreck and received reams of correspondence from business contacts, friends, and family as he recovered. Beyond expressing relief at his survival, the letters attempt to grapple with the shock of the event. Many saw his survival as proof of his piety and "noble acts."[20] The emotional ripples of one man's injury spread to Baltimore, where his fiancée was horrified to find his name on a list in a newspaper. Dread stalked her until she got a telegram stating he would make it, and she declared it "was nothing short of a miracle" that Cameron survived.[21] But along with telegraph connections, Cameron's correspondents claimed to have experienced telepathic warnings of danger. P. D. Cameron wrote that he "had a most distinct mental impression that you were on the train, a premonition and usually considered to be something bad. In my case they were happily translated into something exceptionally fortunate."[22] A business contact who owned a cotton mill wrote, "Just why I cannot say, but I felt almost certain you were on this ill-fated train, and so told my friends here."[23]

Faced with an unexpected horror, people often turned to the supernatural to explain a wreck. After the wreck at Cahaba Creek, a conductor who claimed he did not believe in visions told a reporter that the last time he crossed this bridge, he saw a red light "flashing like a meteor" and stopped the train on the bridge, jarring his passengers. The man claimed he did not believe in visions, yet he was grateful for this warning, which ended up saving him.[24] The history of southern railroading is littered with folk tales like the Maco Lights, red lights visible in eastern North Carolina, where a spectral signalman allegedly continues to hold his watch. And to this day, ghost hunters and other aficionados of the supernatural swear that the Bostian Bridge site remains haunted.[25] Wreck scenes became enchanted sites that held power long after the calamitous crash of a train.

Bennehan Cameron was lucky enough to survive his train wreck, but the relatives of unfortunate victims struggled to make sense of the instantaneous loss of their family members. The father of a woman killed in the Statesville wreck, S. P. Read, wrote to a surviving passenger, and he tried to find comfort in a religious interpretation of the calamity. He wrote "that the creator determines all results and then results can only be for the best," but as he sadly related, "If my heart could grasp these truths as does my intellect oh how happy I could be." He struggled to reconcile the random destruction of a train wreck with God's plan for him and his family.[26] The trauma of train wrecks was amplified by the manner in which they destroyed Victorian notions of a "Good Death." Nineteenth-century Americans were supposed to peacefully die in a planned affair at home in bed, while surrounded by praying friends and family.[27] But victims of train wrecks died sudden, violent deaths, far from home, and family members yearned to know the exact details of their loved ones' demise. Ophelia Moore's mother wrote a letter to Statesville's Dr. Hill, inquiring how exactly her daughter had died. A man had told her they heard Ophelia's shrieks, and others told her that Ophelia had been calling for her before her death. Another doctor told her that Ophelia probably had not suffered, and she concluded, "God was merciful to take her before many hours of suffering."[28]

Surviving a wreck took more than faith and good deeds. For all of Cameron's piety and luck, a letter from another friend pointed to the real reason he survived the wreck. A friend attributed Cameron's survival to the fact that he "preferred using a Presidential Car to riding with ordinary people." For this man, "paying up fare" and always traveling in the most expensive accommodations were the most useful lesson from the wreck.[29] Early rail travelers, especially those from Europe, marveled at the lack of class distinctions within American railroads. As one antebellum British visitor wrote, "On the railroad there is but one class and one price." Rail boosters also claimed that rail travel was a democratizing force, by arguing that railroads brought together people from all walks of life.[30] Every wreck scene had its own grim calculus as to which car would suffer the most, but in general, train wrecks destroyed this notion by demonstrating how poorly constructed and crowded second-class cars often bore the brunt of derailments. Indeed, the arguments of Cameron's friend were correct, as most of the victims from the Statesville wreck were drawn from the second-class car. The first-class car ended up falling on top of the second-class car, crushing those inside and making it much easier for the more wealthy passengers to escape the wreckage. In the South, second-class cars were the Jim Crow cars, a fact that added another element of danger to the already fraught experience of travel for African Americans.[31]

After the shock of the accident and the immediate rescue operations came the spectacle, as gawkers converged on the scene of wrecks. Few events could bring out a crowd like a train wreck, as wrecks like that at Statesville fed the public's lust for two repressed desires: death and technological failure. When a huckster staged a deliberate train wreck in Texas—the "Crash at Crush"—in 1896, thousands turned up for a chance to witness a real live train wreck. Two forty-ton engines dressed in "holiday attire" hurtled toward each other at forty-two miles per hour, and collided spectacularly in front of 60,000 cheering spectators. The frenzied crowd roared at the moment of the wreck and then surged toward the carnage. As onlookers crawled through the wreckage in search of relics and souvenirs, the boiler exploded, filling the air with flying shrapnel. A shard of metal decapitated a woman, a flying bolt fatally impaled a photographer, and two others were fatally injured in the explosion. Despite the grisly end to the affair, a reporter judged the event "one of the greatest picnics and all round pleasure making days ever known in the history of Texas."[32]

The Statesville crowd never reached this level of excitement, but the cleanup of the site still became a tourist attraction. Three days after the wreck, crowds of citizens, tourists, and "country people" braved a cold driving rain, and gathered at the scene at an early hour. The *Atlanta Constitution* noted they "jostled each other, anxious to see every little detail of removing the debris." The excitement was so intense that business in Statesville was totally suspended for days after the wreck.[33] Visitors also clamored for souvenirs to commemorate their visit. Mr. John E. Cochrane of Statesville had the bright idea to make walking canes out of the wreckage. He presented one to a reporter, who noted it was "of cherry, of handsome finish and was most likely part of a sleeper car."[34] These scenes of hysterical southerners clamoring for a view of a horrific site and yearning for some kind of keepsake all speak to the emotional trauma a wreck inflicted on a town. And they bear an uncanny resemblance to another display of community violence in the New South, the spectacle lynching. In lynchings, the ritualized gathering eased anxieties caused by an alleged crime or transgression of the racial order, and in the spectacle of the train wreck, community solidarity helped absolve the failure of the railroad network.[35] Train wrecks occurred wherever train tracks went, but given the high per capita rate of wrecks in the New South era, this was a time and place peculiarly familiar with these grim rituals of shock, rescue, cleanup, commemoration, and mourning.

AS SOON AS THE RESCUES were complete, authorities' most pressing concern at a wreck site was typically the investigation into the cause. Affixing ultimate responsibility for these wrecks riveted the attention of locals and could tear towns apart. These were more than just local affairs. The results of these investigations mattered for railroad companies working to solidify their standing in the region at large. The aftermath of a train wreck constituted a dangerous time for railroad companies. First of all, their employees could be in immediate peril. When an inattentive engineer's error led to a collision on the Richmond and Atlanta Air Line near Greenville, South Carolina, in 1887, the engineer ran into the woods to flee retribution from locals.[36] More ominously for railroads, anger could easily spiral upward to those higher on the corporate ladder. In 1891, a New Orleans editorialist noted that the South's increase in wrecks could hardly be blamed on lowly engineers and brakemen. As "railroad accidents are often the result of inferior and insufficient material and methods used in the construction of the roadway," authorities should hold the upper management of roads responsible for wrecks.[37] After the wreck at Statesville, the *Concord Weekly Standard* invoked the wreck to attack railroad authorities. As the editorialist wrote, "When you thrust power upon some people they become tyrants, bigots, and, in plain English, fools." The paper predicted that the "boiling and sizzling" of public anger now was "only a forerunner of what is coming."[38]

The uptick in train wrecks in the 1890s came at the same time that northern-backed corporations like the Southern Railway were consolidating control of southern rail lines and trying to win favor in towns they served, a fact that made this potential "boiling and sizzling" a critical danger. When a Southern Railway train derailed at Stone Creek trestle outside Macon, Georgia, in March 1896, investigations into the cause of the wreck became entangled with local opposition to corporate consolidation. The South's purchase of local rail lines was a sore point for communities like Macon, which had been previously served by independent lines. In the end, this wreck, which killed three, was one of the few that we probably can pin on train wreckers. Warren Criswell and Tom Shaw, two down-on-their-luck white men, plotted the wreck to kill their wives and collect the insurance money. After a lengthy investigation and trial, Criswell and Shaw were sentenced to jail for life in November 1897.[39]

But as this investigation and trial dragged on, Macon residents' opinion on the cause of the wreck coalesced around the two sides of the railroad consolidation debate. Citizens held a mass meeting in direct response to the wreck, where half the crowd pushed for a resolution denouncing the as-yet-unknown wreckers and the other half held the views of a Mr. Small, who rose to his feet and argued that such a resolution would advertise to the world that Macon was host to such criminals. He blamed a rotten trestle for the wreck and warned there were "other trestles between Macon and Brunswick that the point of a walking stick could be driven into."[40] Railroad lawyer N. E. Harris arrived and took pictures of the site "because of the strong feeling here in the city and of the continual suggestions being dropped every where that the trestle was rotten."[41] The subsequent trial of the two suspects was also infused with antirailroad politics. The judge dismissed a juror after someone overheard him say he would acquit the wreckers just because "he was opposed to railroad corporations and believed in fighting them in every way possible." And Shaw's defense lawyer framed his client's battle in broad terms, arguing, "This man is alone, standing here before you oppressed by this great corporation, extending from Virginia through Georgia."[42] Foes of the Southern Railway blamed a rotten trestle and a corporate conspiracy to frame Shaw and Criswell, and defenders of the corporation blamed train wreckers, so in effect, the entire aftermath of the wreck became a referendum on the Southern Railway's presence in Macon.

Hundreds of communities were torn by similar questions, as train wrecks opened up debates on regulation of corporations and the benefits of consolidation and rapid railroad development that the New South leaders and their corporate allies hoped to avoid. Every train that tumbled off a bridge or that slammed into the back of another engine shattered the phantasmagoria of the railroad. If trains were a symbol of revival, the train wreck could easily undo this claim and expose the dark side of capitalism. In an ominous sign for the boosters, editorial writers at the region's most prominent papers were beginning to pay attention to the carnage on the rails as the wrecks piled up in the 1880s and '90s. A few months before the Statesville wreck, the *New Orleans Daily Picayune*, one of the South's largest papers, noted that railway accidents were "becoming alarmingly common," and it blamed this on the fact that "many railway companies are bankrupt," which meant "their bridges are out of repair, their trackways are decayed and unsteady," and their "general business is run upon a scale of economy that is constantly dangerous."[43]

Questioning the benefits of new railroad construction opened the door for critiques from groups like the Farmers' Alliance, Knights of Labor, and the Populist Party, who challenged and offered alternatives to the New South status quo. Train wrecks could lead to calls for more regulation and sharpen the mission of state railroad commissions, or these disasters could bolster the electoral success of antirailroad candidates. There was a precedent for increasing regulation and government intervention after train wrecks, especially in the North. An 1871 wreck in Massachusetts threw the issue of railroad safety into the public spotlight, and inspired efforts to improve regulation and adopt safer technology. Charles Adams produced comprehensive post-wreck reports that suggested the use of technological improvements to increase safety.[44] Similarly, an 1882 collision at Spuyten Duyvil, New York, killed eight passengers and led to a legislative investigation and a total reorganization of the state's railroad commission.[45] Southern states were in the process of establishing railroad commissions in the 1880s and '90s, but these bodies were often uncertain in their powers and duties. For example, the newly created North Carolina Railroad Commission got involved with the Statesville wreck, making the aftermath of the wreck crucial in determining the direction this commission would take.[46] Simply put, train wrecks captured the attention of a community like few other events, and the closely followed investigations into wrecks held serious implications for both companies and governments.

It was in these moments of tension and ambiguity that the figure of the train wrecker, and the notion that train wrecks were caused not by busted-up tracks, rotten trestles, or negligent employees but by malicious villains began to appear. The idea that someone would deliberately derail a train was not a total fabrication, as it was based on a kernel of truth. As more and more southerners encountered railroads for the first time in the 1880s and '90s, plenty had reason to oppose the arrival of the railroad.[47] New railroads were a source of joy and a reason for celebration for boosters and town elites, but there were many reasons why a line could be targeted for an attack. Railroads blasted noise and smoke through previously tranquil landscapes, bisected properties, annihilated wandering livestock, endangered civilians, and dispossessed farmers of their land. A railroad often was the most tangible manifestation of the New South ruling order, so striking a blow at a rail line could potentially be a strategy for labor unions and antirailroad political groups like the Farmers' Alliances.[48] For many southerners, attacking railroad property was the only way to strike back against the larger and often impersonal forces that shaped their lives.[49]

Some wrecking attempts were directly linked to overtly political grievances. A reporter with the *Railway Gazette* attributed a spate of attacks on Mississippi trains in 1884 to the defeat of a recent antirailroad law in the state's courts.[50] Similarly, in 1893 a *Picayune* journalist attributed the removal of a rail near Beauregard, Mississippi, to town citizens angry about the Illinois Central's recent decision to remove the town's depot.[51] Labor struggles could also lead to attempts at train wrecking, as in the case of the three African Americans arrested near Vicksburg in 1890 for allegedly removing a rail. The men had been employed in a laboring force on the line and were recently discharged from their positions.[52] In a similar example, an engineer in Alabama wrote a letter to his family after two disastrous wrecks in 1894 on his road. Two trains met in a head-on collision, and his train fell off a burnt trestle. If it had been dark out, he surely would have been killed in the latter of these two wrecks. As he related, "We are having a big coal strike here and some think that the tressle [*sic*] road was set on fire by striking miners, but no one knows."[53]

Criminals also targeted trains for economic reasons. Tom Shaw and Warren Criswell's attempt to kill their wives for insurance money outside Macon surely ranks as the most far-fetched of these schemes, but a far more common way to make money off train wrecking was to rob the ruined train, and it was no coincidence that southerners began to fear conspiracies of robbery in the 1890s. After Reconstruction, the South had been almost untouched by a string of train robberies, perpetrated mainly by Jesse James and his gang. James had his roots in vicious Confederate guerilla organizations, but he mainly terrorized Midwestern states like Missouri and Iowa. By 1890, train robbers like Rube Burrow, Eugene Bunch, and Railroad Bill were more active in the South, and the techniques used to rob trains ensured that robbery would be linked with wrecking. A common method, pioneered by Jesse James and his gang, was to place some sort of obstruction on the track. Either a robber would wait by the obstruction to flag down the train, or the engineer would simply see the danger and stop the train. Skilled robbers typically avoided wrecking trains and causing casualties, simply because they did not have to.[54] But unskilled copycats could easily replicate these tactics for their own crimes, a fact that concerned detective William Pinkerton, who blamed the proliferation of sensational dime novels for an uptick in robberies in the 1890s.[55] These novels, periodicals, and newspapers amplified the cultural impact of a small group of train robbers, so by the middle of the 1890s, many began to suspect robbery was the motive for wrecking attempts.

The train wrecker was based on a horrifying but rare reality, but by the 1880s the train wreckers menacing rail lines were not always real. In fact, they were just as often imaginary diversions created by railroad companies. Examining the incentives of railroad employees explains why corporations were keen to use this scapegoat. On a most basic level, the financial motivations of railroad legal departments led many to blame wreckers. By the 1890s, railroad corporations were growing greatly in size, and legal departments became increasing organized and powerful. Even though the management of these large systems may have been in far-off cities, corporations retained respected lawyers in local communities. The influence these railroad lawyers wielded was substantial. Not only were these men already drawn from their town's elite, they also were backed by the financial resources of a large system. In the post-wreck environment, these lawyers quickly tried to establish control of the accident scene and manage investigations at an early stage, with two main goals in mind: to deflect blame and public anger away from their employers, and to minimize the payout of damage claims.[56]

Lawsuits from victims and their families began to pile up after wrecks, so to beat these potentially expensive cases, railroad lawyers often tried to prove that wrecks were not due to negligence on the railroad's part. The company would not have to pay damage claims if the company was not found negligent. The most convenient way to do this would be to pin the blame on an outside party like a train wrecker. For corporations, whose very existence hung in the balance in a tight economic climate, damage claims could be devastating. An editorial in the *Charlotte Chronicle* named Jay Gould as a potential beneficiary of the Bostian Bridge wreck. The paper conjectured that Gould wanted to "wrap his octopus limbs about the R&D system" and his attempts to consolidate the system would be aided if the R&D was forced to pay out large sums in damage claims.[57] In the trial of Tom Shaw, the defense attorney claimed that the railroad "had dragged the whole country with a fish net for the purpose of fixing the responsibility for the wreck on some party or parties" to absolve the railroad of guilt.[58] Even though Shaw lost this trial, the incentives of the railroad were to pin the Stone Creek wreck on him to avoid paying damage claims.

A similar strategy on the part of a railroad legal department could be seen when a Southern Railway passenger car crashed through an open switch in Scotland, Georgia, in March 1895. The presence of Roland Reed, a well-known actor, added to the public intrigue in this wreck. Not only did the wreck injure members of Reed's troupe, but the accident also delayed his company's travel, forcing them to miss a number of performances in Florida. Reed and others on the train claimed the train was going sixty miles per hour, way too fast for the section of track. A coroner's jury agreed, blaming the railroad for negligence and carelessness both due to the speed of the train and for leaving the switch open. The monetary losses from the canceled tour, and Reed's fame, meant that the ensuing lawsuits could exact a heavy toll from the Southern Railway. About two weeks after the wreck, railroad detectives arrested Charles Nelson, an African American laborer who lived near the train tracks, after circumstantial evidence linked him to the wreck. As a reporter noted, the railroad "would be relieved of all responsibility if the alleged wrecker is finally convicted in higher court."[59] The evidence supporting the arrest was undoubtedly flimsy, as Nelson was never convicted. When the case finally went to trial in 1897, the railroad trotted out "a little army of witnesses," all trying to prove that Nelson caused the wreck.[60] Reed won the case, but the railroad's version of the story, the version backed by the power of the large Southern Railway corporation, blamed wreckers—specifically an already marginalized working-class African American—for the derailment of its train.

THE INVESTIGATIONS INTO TWO of the New South's most calamitous wrecks, at Bostian Bridge and the Cahaba River, further demonstrated the power of the imaginary train wrecker narrative.[61] As cleanup crews carted away the wreckage under Bostian Bridge, the Iredell County coroner's jury convened and interviewed over forty witnesses from the community. The testimony, printed in full in the *Statesville Landmark*, spoke to the difficulty in making sense of such a chaotic scene, but two clear versions of the wreck emerged. One clear theme was the presence of rotten ties and timbers on the bridge. "You could kick them to pieces," argued Col. S. A. Sharpe, and "occasionally you could find a sound one but not many." W. A. Eliason agreed, and concluded his testimony with the caveat, "I have no feelings of animosity against the railroad except in regard to the accident." R. B. Linster noted that as soon as the convicts employed by the railroad to clear the scene arrived, he "noticed that they were throwing broken crossties off the bridge into the creek." Five other witnesses besides Linster repeated this story about convicts destroying evidence.[62]

The R&D presented its own version of the wreck, aided by a cadre of lawyers the company had sent to Statesville. The Iredell County coroner's jury testimony clearly identified the witnesses introduced by the railroad, which made the version of the accident that the railroad attorneys sought to push quite obvious. D. L. Hutter claimed to see spikes on the track, W. G. Wright saw some spikes and "evidence of wrecking," T. J. Allison found a warped rail that he thought the engine passed over, and Bennehan Cameron saw a detached rail. L. Kale, the road's section master, said he had done no work on the road for a month, but thought it was sound. He said his tools were in his house, but the door was unlocked and someone could have gone in and taken them. In addition to pointing out the physical evidence of a maliciously caused wreck, railroad witnesses also suggested potential culprits. Two witnesses spoke of a mysterious white man in a black suit and a black slouch hat seen around Statesville before the wreck.[63]

Other railroad witnesses pushed the idea that the train had been wrecked for the purpose of robbery. Mrs. Moore testified that when she got out of the ruined train, a diamond pin that she had been wearing earlier was gone, as was a check for $200 and a note for $2,000. Miss Luellen Pool said that as she lay in the cars, a man with a hat pulled over his face "came creeping along the top of the car and put his hand in the window as if feeling for something." After another passenger asked him what he wanted, the man "left creeping away." In the same car as Miss Pool's, Colonel Sanderlin awoke to find a black man around the age of twenty or twenty-two staring at him through the window making "suspicious movements." After the man would not respond to Sanderlin's queries, it "instantly dawned on me that he came there to rob us." Henry Demming spoke of "two colored men" who came toward the wreck from Statesville and a man with "African blood" moving very deliberately around the scene of the wreck. He was "the coolest man I ever saw," and he "asked no questions and seemed to be helping no one."[64] S. P. Read, a man in Memphis whose daughter died in the Statesville wreck, later wrote Bennehan Cameron asking for details about his daughter's death, "down to the minutest details." From what the man had heard, his daughter had survived the initial wreck, and Cameron had removed her from the car, but after Cameron returned to the scene of the wreck the woman was dead. He suggested in his letter that "during your chance when you left to ring the alarm at Statesville, some villain may have murdered her to take from her person the insignificant valuables she possibly had."[65]

Suggestions of a planned robbery fixated on the presence of mysterious African American men who descended on the scene after the wreck, but the four black men who testified before the coroner's jury, Henry Nesbit, Henry Hart, Joe Chambers and Jesse Freeze, offered a much different take on the matter. Clearly identified as black, as the Jim Crow court system dictated that their testimony required an extra signature, these men presented a version of the wreck's aftermath that cast serious doubt on the robbery rumors. Henry Nesbit hurried to the bridge after hearing a crash and saw "some big fat man," who was "calling for his gold specks, gold cane and hat." Nesbit got an axe and used it to cut a man free. He saw no one robbing the cars, and saw no mysterious strangers. Henry Hart said he met Nesbit on the way to the wreck before joining him at the scene to help get the wounded and killed passengers out of the train. Jesse Freeze saw several men entering the ruined cars, but instead of robbing passengers, they were merely trying to get victims out of the cars, which were rapidly filling with water from the creek. Joe Chambers also saw "some old fat man" sitting on a young lady. When rescuers finally removed him from the car, the man told Chambers to "stop until I get my umbrella, walking stick and spectacles."[66]

The fat man turned out to be none other than Colonel George Sanderlin, who was so insulted by this testimony he sent a letter to the *State Chronicle*, which was reprinted by papers across the state. He denied sitting on a lady, instead claiming he was resting on a mattress after Bennehan Cameron, and not one of the black men, pulled him out of the wreck, and he argued that the testimony about his concern for his personal effects was exaggerated. He only wanted to get the cane since it was valuable, and he suggested the black men wanted him to leave it behind so they could steal it. Sanderlin wrote he asked for his pants because he was cold, and he needed his glasses since he was nearly blind without them. As he concluded his letter, he "received many painful wounds and bruises in the wreck, but not one has hurt me so much as the picture drawn of my inhumanity and of my great concern over small things."[67] In light of this testimony from both sides, it is more than likely that the alleged robber seen by Sanderlin and Miss Pool was simply one of the four black men working to free trapped passengers.

In grappling with these two competing narratives, the report issued by the Iredell County coroner's jury was noncommittal as to the cause of the wreck, blaming both "some person or persons unknown" for removing a rail, and the railroad company for leaving tools in an accessible shed, for failing to maintain crossties on the bridge, and for running the train too fast over the bridge. Even the jury itself was not confident in its verdict. A paper later reported that J. S. Ramsey of the jury signed the report but did not believe that any rail was removed or misplaced before the wreck.[68]

The diary of David Schenck, the Richmond & Danville's head lawyer on the case, also suggests that the wrecker story was a fabrication. When the R&D system was reorganized as the Southern Railway in 1894, Schenck was forced out of his position. In a bitter diary entry, Schenck attributed his dismissal to his reluctance to carry out his duties after the Bostian Bridge wreck. As lawsuits for damage claims wound their way through North Carolina's courts, the company tried another common strategy to contest the claims. It attempted to get the cases removed from local courts in Iredell County to Circuit Court in Charlotte, where the railroad would not have to deal with a jury from the community traumatized by the wreck. Schenck recalled that he would not swear to the petitions for the removal of the cases "because they contained falsehoods." Unfortunately Schenck's diary does not elaborate the character or source of these fabrications, but the entry shows that even an experienced railroad lawyer harbored doubts about the company's tactics.[69] In the end, we will probably never know what actually caused the wreck outside Statesville. But it is clear that lawyers with the R&D did all they could to blame the wreck on wreckers who were never found. About a year after the wreck, the *Landmark*'s editor wrote, "The contention of the *Landmark* has been that the train was not wrecked, and we are satisfied, in view of the railroad company's ridiculous failure to make it appear that it was, that the public believes by this time that the *Landmark* was right." And in 1966, on the seventy-fifth anniversary of the wreck, Statesville's newspaper still noted the cause of the wreck was "controversial."[70]

Though the *Statesville Landmark* continued to contend that the R&D was lying about train wreckers, the editorial tone of other southern newspapers clearly shifted once the coroner's jury concluded that wreckers were behind the derailment. Immediate response to the Statesville wreck had focused on the broader systemic flaws behind the wreck. However, a number of papers clearly changed positions in light of the intimation that wreckers caused the accident. In the first issue published after the wreck, Leonidas Polk's *Progressive Farmer*, a Populist publication typically hostile toward rail corporations like the R&D, noted that whatever the cause, "it does not do away with the idea that every high bridge ought to be inspected before crossed by a train, and that trains ought to be run over bridges at a very slow rate of speed." The practice of fast trains to try to make up time by running fast should be "stopped at once." But after the coroner's jury report, the paper switched tack and defended the railroad, arguing that "it is absurd to say that they carelessly allow anything to occur that entails such a great loss." The paper suggested the "well-dressed stranger" was the culprit, positing the theory that he may be a "Jack the Ripper kind of fellow who thinks his mission here is to wreck trains." A mere day after an editorial suggesting safety improvements, the *Richmond Dispatch* noted that train wrecking had become too common, a "menace to all who ride upon railroads," and that to "flay them alive would be all incommensurate with the condemnation due their dastardly deed."[71] The rhetorical fire of editorial pages, once trained squarely at the R&D or at the broader railroad system, was clearly redirected toward the unidentified wreckers.

FROM HIGH ON DOWN, corporate officials used train wreckers as a scapegoat, as the aftermath of the 1896 Cahaba Bridge wreck demonstrates. The response to the wreck was complicated by the fact that two separate corporations potentially could have been held liable for the smoldering pile of wreckage in Cahaba Creek. Because of a lease agreement, the Southern Railway owned the track, but the L&N owned the ill-fated train. Immediately, Southern Railway officials scrambled to avoid responsibility after the wreck. The road's president, Samuel Spencer, wrote to his vice president W. W. Finley, directing him to "take no steps that will commit us in any way to responsibility for the accident until all facts as to cause are known."[72] Spencer also told a subordinate "arrangements should be made to prevent the papers from using the Southern Railway company's name in headlines in connection with the accident." The name of the more obscure Birmingham Mineral Railroad instead appeared in much of the subsequent press coverage.[73] The L&N wanted to cooperatively issue a reward with the Southern, but Finley questioned the wisdom of this move, arguing that "it might induce suits against the companies jointly thus calling us to defend suits which might not otherwise be filed against us."[74]

In this case, records from the L&N, the line that owned the track, confirmed definitively that a faulty bridge, and not malicious parties, caused the accident. R. Montfort, chief engineer with the L&N Railroad, arrived on the scene on January 11, 1897, to make a detailed inspection. He found serious and debilitating flaws in the bridge's design and concluded there was nothing that "justifies or supports the theory that the accident was the cause of wreckers," and he attributed the popularity of this theory to hysteria over a rail removed from a nearby trestle two weeks ago.[75] Montfort's observations were confirmed by the fact that press coverage similarly conflated these two distinct incidents. A *Birmingham News* report on the Cahaba wreck noted that three rough-looking men were seen at the scene of both wrecks, and at another train robbery in Fayette County, and it posited that this gang of three was responsible for all of these crimes against trains.[76] As Montfort continued his investigation, he found that the original design of the bridge "was not in accordance with L&N specifications." An L&N official supervising the project never actually approved the design, yet it was built anyway.[77] A week later

Montfort found the smoking gun in his investigation when he uncovered a critical error in the original blueprints for the structure, an error "that reduced the strength of the bridge by over fifty per cent." This mistake was so egregious he worried that the publication of this "inexcusable blunder" would "amount to utter ruination for the reputation of the bridge building department of the Carnegie Steel Co."[78]

Instead of releasing this information, Montfort looked for ways to conceal the fatal miscalculation and found witnesses who would lend more credence to the wrecker story. His plans settled on an engineer with the East Tennessee Virginia, & Georgia system named Mr. Lum. Lum also visited the wreck, and though he also acknowledged that the bridge design was defective, he suspected that wreckers still might have played a role. Montfort suggested that Lum was "just the man we were looking for," and hoped the company could have him testify that the accident could have been caused by train wreckers.[79] Montfort wrote an official with the bridge company that the L&N "would be very glad indeed if he could convince everyone that the accident was due to wreckers," and the company president responded that he would help in any of these efforts. So instead of pressing a claim against the bridge company, the L&N's chief attorney advised covering up Montfort's damning evidence and working with the Carnegie Steel Company in an attempt to prove that the bridge was safe. Montfort and another man who noticed flaws in the bridge design were not going to be part of the railroad's legal strategy, as their opinions were "such to preclude our calling on them as witnesses."[80] Investigators from the Southern Railway, which owned the train that wrecked, also doubted the wrecker theory, but pushed it anyway. An investigator with the Southern noted, "We were very careful not to say anything, or question anything, to deprecate that theory, which seemed to be a popular one."[81] After a man with the Southern wrote that evidence from the site "disposes of the wrecker theory," Vice President W. W. Finley warned the investigator not to share this information, noting, "It is extremely important that there shall be no controversy upon that question at the present time."[82]

So in the case of the Cahaba Bridge wreck, it is clear that both the Southern and the L&N conspired to blame a wreck on wreckers.[83] Ultimately, the L&N attorneys settled sixteen of the Cahaba bridge cases in November 1897, though not before a lawyer delivered a harangue that the L&N did not think the road was liable, and that they were only settling the cases since they "preferred to live in all amity with the citizens of the country through which the road runs."[84] The legal battle may have been ultimately lost, but on the pages of southern newspapers, the strategy was a success. A banner headline in the

Birmingham News screamed, "A Death Trap Had Been Set by the Removal of a Rail," and it proclaimed the wreck a "startling story of robbery and pillage."[85] "Train Wreckers Take Twenty-Eight Lives" announced the large headline on the front page of the *Constitution*. The paper blamed the wreck on nameless people who "took refuge in steep crags of their mountain homes" and noted that Birmingham's citizens were ready to burn at the stake any train wreckers they caught.[86] Editorial response focused not on the lapses in safety and inattention to engineering detail that led to the wreck, but on the dastardly deeds of the wreckers. In a clear analogue to the false rumors of robbery in the Statesville wreck, one paper proclaimed, "After the crash robbers rushed the scene and plundered the dead and dying. There seems little doubt that these robbers removed the rail which was missing from the bridge."[87] The *Birmingham State-Herald* declared, "No quarter to train wreckers should be the shibboleth of every honest citizen," the *Wilmington Messenger* noted the whole incident "reads like it might be a page from the devil's own diary," and the *Milledgeville Union Recorder* marveled at the $10,000 reward offered by the railroads and argued that "hanging would be too easy a punishment for the train wreckers and robbers."[88]

Underneath these headlines, there were, of course, some doubts. A letter to the *Birmingham State Herald* from a Blocton resident disputed the railroad company's account. Everyone is so fixated on the one report of men pilfering cars, he argued, that they overlooked the fact that the train was going forty miles per hour, way over the fifteen miles per hour that the railroad had reported.[89] Other local residents similarly contested the robbery story, saying the alleged robbers were merely locals trying to assist victims.[90] But these dissenting voices ended up buried deep inside newspapers, obscured by a fantastical but horrific tale backed by the power of the South's largest corporations.

RAILROAD COMPANIES TOLD a clear story about the cause of wrecks, but the broader impact of this narrative can be seen in its dissemination in the southern press. Given a few real-life examples of train wrecking, and helped by the encouragement of railroad corporations, newspapers gladly played up the sensational nature of train wrecking. Many papers in this period had direct financial backing from railroad companies, as the close links between Henry Grady and the L&N demonstrated. As wrecks surged in the region, train wreckers began to appear more frequently on the pages of the southern press in the 1890s. The pages of Grady's *Atlanta Constitution*, the region's foremost newspaper and standard-bearer for the New South movement, reported

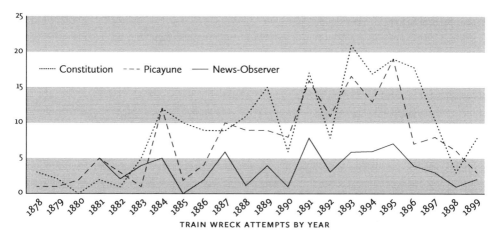

GRAPH 1 Train wreck attempts by year. This graph shows the dramatic rise in train-wrecking attempts as reported on the pages of the *New Orleans Picayune, Atlanta Constitution,* and *Raleigh News-Observer.* Created by author with the assistance of the University of North Carolina Press.

212 instances of train-wrecking attempts in the states of the former Confederacy between 1878 and 1900, of which ninety succeeded in actually derailing or damaging the train[91] (graph 1). While train wrecking was almost entirely absent from the newspaper in the 1870s and early 1880s, instances of attempted wrecks jumped in 1884 and eventually peaked in 1891 and 1896. Similar trends are apparent in the *New Orleans Picayune,* which contained 167 instances of attempted train wrecking between 1878 and 1900. Like in the *Constitution,* train-wrecking articles clearly jumped in 1884, and in the years between 1891 and 1895 before declining toward the end of the decade.[92] The *Raleigh News-Observer,* a smaller paper more focused on local news in North Carolina, also showed an increase in wrecking attempts in the 1890s, though the peaks and valleys are less dramatic due to the smaller sample size.[93]

This mass of reports is significant both for how it captures press interest in the topic and in how it charts the widespread fear of wrecking. It is clear that the attention of the press was fixated on this threat, and that a certain subset of the southern population, namely, the white, middle, and upper-class "New South"–oriented business class, was reading more about attempts to wreck trains. As a brief editorial in the *Constitution* argued, "a purely accidental railroad wreck does not have one-fifth the effect on the traveling public that a report of a malicious train wreck has."[94] Beyond demonstrating public interest in the phenomenon, these articles also revealed common trends in the suspected method used to wreck trains. The most common and least technically sophisticated way to wreck a train was by placing some sort of obstruction on the track. The *Picayune* reported seventy-three attempted wrecks caused by an obstruction, while the *Constitution* reported ninety-six between 1878 and 1900. Crossties, a common item found near train tracks, were a favorite choice, but wreckers could use a wide variety of obstructions to wreck trains. Rocks, logs, trees, dead or living animals, other cars, and more could be placed on tracks. The second most common way wrecks were attempted was by tampering with a switch. All it took was a switch in the wrong position to send the locomotive in the wrong direction, either off the track or into another track with an obstruction. When it came to misplaced switches, the *Picayune* reported thirty-six, while the *Constitution* mentioned thirty-nine. A final method of destruction was to tamper with a rail in some manner. Removing a rail at a particularly perilous point like a bridge could cause a derailment, as could driving spikes into a rail. The most devious of these attempts would happen on bridges or trestles, but newspapers reported on tampered rails in a wide variety of situations. In this category, the *Constitution* listed thirty-three, while the *Picayune* showed thirty-one from 1878 to 1900.

Though news articles seemed definitive in their declarations of wrecking, in all three of these methods, there was a great deal of uncertainty associated with the investigation of the crime. Crossties and other track obstructions could just as easily be dropped by another train, or left by careless workers, and switches could be accidently misplaced by employees or simply break on their own. In addition, the investigation of derailments was extremely complicated. When a train derailed, it would typically strip the rails off the track, making it exceedingly difficult to pinpoint how exactly the train derailed. In short, each of these methods of wrecking could just as easily be accidents or startling coincidences. Yet the first instinct of the press was to present these small pieces of evidence as proof of malicious intent.

An attempted train wreck near Birmingham in 1896 demonstrated the extent to which journalists weaved wrecking attempts into vast conspiracies. The plot to plunder the train was unsuccessful, as the wreck never actually occurred, but investigators soon made a few arrests and extracted confessions from an alleged gang of African Americans. The *State-Herald* printed this sensational story on the first two pages of the Sunday paper. The article detailed the confessions of the group of men who had confessed to the attempt to wreck a train at McComb's Trestle, an attempt that would have constituted "the most diabolical crime in the history of the South." According to the confession, the men planned to wreck a Southern Railway train with over 200 passengers so they could rob the cars and get some Christmas money. The gang lacked guns, but figured it would be easy enough to plunder the ruins of the train once it tumbled off the trestle.[95] The degree to which this motley crew represented an actual threat is debatable, as is the validity of the confessions extracted by the Birmingham police force, but the *State-Herald's* extensive coverage speaks to how the press played up the threat of train wrecking. Advertisements printed all week long hyped up this story, presented by the paper as "A Damnable Conspiracy," and the paper promised "every minute detail given of a plan which exceeds in Deviltry Anything Ever Conceived by Mortal Man." The story of a gang of African American laborers so heartless they would derail a crowded passenger train just to get some spending cash confirmed white thoughts about African Americans and train wrecking, and it surely got a few more Birmingham residents to pick up a Sunday paper.[96]

As further proof of the public interest in train wrecking, fictional train wreckers also began to appear in the southern press. In a fictional narrative, "The Hut by the Wateree" (1885), an author told the tale of a journey gone bad in South Carolina's swamps. As a train made its way through the foggy swamp in the middle of the night, the engineer saw a woman in the track, and he halted the train. Though the narrator at first suspected this woman of ill intent, he later found that her actions had spared the train from a calamitous plunge off a damaged trestle up ahead, a trap laid by a criminal hoping to kill a man on the train. In melodramatic fashion, the story related the twisted love triangle involving the woman that led to this scenario, but perhaps the more pressing lesson from this saga is the danger that lurked in distinctively southern landscapes like the South Carolina swamps.[97] An 1893 story in the *New Orleans Picayune* entitled "A Deadly Dilemma" presented train wrecking as a dire moral quandary. Down by some train tracks, a man had a quarrel with his lover "Nettie" that ended badly, and they parted ways. The man watched the woman leave, and to his horror, she tripped and fell onto the train tracks. As she lay unconscious on the track, the man heard the sound of an approaching train, and he was presented with a "deadly dilemma," to either wreck the train or watch Nettie be crushed. Rushing to save Nettie, he threw a telegraph pole onto the track. But he was soon confronted with the gravity of what he had done. This act was nothing short of murder, as "there were people on that train—innocent human beings, men and women like himself who would next minute be wrecked and mangled corpses, or writhing forms, on the track before him." He removed his obstruction in the nick of time, managing to stop the train and save his lover without serious damage. The newspapers the next day were "equally divided between denunciation of the miscreant who placed the obstruction in the way of the train, and admiration for the heroic and unrecognizable stranger" who had prevented a calamity. However, only Nettie knew the truth, that her lover had risked his life to save hers.[98]

Even young boys got into the business of hunting wreckers, as related by an 1896 story in the *Atlanta Constitution*. On the eve of the fourth of July, two boys, Larry and Howard, set out to fish, traveling along a railroad line to reach their desired spot. On the way they encountered a nervous-looking man, who made awkward conversation with them before he accidentally dropped a piece of paper that betrayed his plans to wreck and rob a train. They quickly gave the message to a railroad official, who invited them to join the hunt for the wreckers the next day. Larry hid under a blanket in the cab, with instructions to blow a whistle as the robbers entered. Per the discovered plan, robbers stopped the train and entered the car, but after Larry blew the signal, detectives swarmed the cab and arrested the wreckers. The robbery was foiled, but once again a southern railroad had been targeted by a "gang of wreckers."[99] These fictional wrecking attempts were sanitized versions of the stories that flooded southern newspapers at the time. No one ever died in these stories, and the plots were all resolved with an affirmation of love or a reward for adolescent curiosity. Yet the very appearance of these stories, as well as the implied threat of a cataclysmic wreck, speaks to the widespread nature of the train wrecker narrative. As innocent men, women, and children traversed the southern railroad network, all it took was one act to send them to horrible deaths.

In perhaps the ultimate irony, advertisers exploited the public's fascination with train wrecking. A shoe company in Columbus, Georgia, in 1893 compared the proliferation of train robberies and wrecking attempts with the "horrible wrecking" its stock had recently received from voracious customers. Along with this text, the company included a shocking depiction of gigantic robbers literally holding up and shooting trains, while passengers tumbled to the ground below[100] (figure 6). A medicine salesman in North Carolina used a drawing of a train crashing off a bridge to link the danger of train wrecking to indigestion, a problem that threatened not only travelers but those at home as well (figure 5). Like train wreckers, indigestion "undermines the supports that hold up the bridge of life and yearly precipitates thousands into the dread valley of consumption."[101] A year later, the same company ran an ad with a picture of a smashed-up train, reminding the reader that consumption "does kill tens of thousands for every one that is killed by accident."[102]

Travelers shudder with horror at the thought of the train-wrecker who stealthily undermines the supports of a railway bridge and precipitates a passenger train with its load of precious human freight to a horrible death by fire and water. There is a deadlier enemy than the train-wrecker that menaces not only travelers but stay-at-homes. Its name is indigestion. It slowly undermines the supports that hold up the bridge of life and yearly precipitates untold thousands into the dread valley of consumption. If people will only take the right precaution they can avoid this calamity and even remedy it after it has occurred if they will act in time.

All cases of indigestion and every disease that has its inception in indigestion or faulty nutrition are cured by Dr. Pierce's Golden Medical Discovery. It cures 98 per cent. of all cases of consumption. It cures wasting diseases. It is an unfailing remedy for nervous prostration. It is the great blood-maker, flesh-builder, and nerve tonic. Thousands have testified to its merits. There is nothing else "just as good." Druggists sell it.

FIGURE 5 An advertisement referenced the increasing dangers on southern railroads and compared train wrecking to stomach ailments. *Raleigh News-Observer*, July 8, 1897.

ONE COULD ENCOUNTER train wrecking in any geographical context, but on the exceptionally dangerous railroads of the South, train wrecking merged with white assumptions about the inherent criminality of African Americans and with new, railroad-fueled fears of black anonymous travelers. The spike in train wrecking neatly tracked a spike in lynchings, extralegal killings of blacks fueled by fears of miscegenation and the mythical black rapist. The truth was not always what it seemed in lynching cases, and the vast majority of these "crimes" were imagined, exaggerated, or minor transgressions of strict racial codes. The same newspapers that whipped up fantastical crimes

FIGURE 6 Another advertisement used shocking imagery of a literal "hold-up" to sell shoes. *Atlanta Constitution,* October 29, 1893.

committed by lynched African Americans reported on train-wrecking conspiracies. Quantitative data from the newspaper accounts of train-wrecking attempts demonstrates how the train wrecker was very often black. Not all the wrecking attempts in the *Constitution* and *Picayune* named a culprit, but in the cases where a suspect was either captured or named, forty-nine out of the seventy-six train wreckers (64 percent) in the *Picayune* were black, as were forty-nine out of the eighty-four (58 percent) in the *Constitution.* The *News-Observer* reported an even higher percentage, with eighteen out of twenty-two (82 percent) wrecking suspects labeled as black.[103] These newspapers were, of course, published by white elites, but they give a window into how white southerners came to see the train wrecker as a black figure. Just as survivors of the Statesville wreck labeled their black rescuers as robbers, the region-wide tendency was to put a black face on the heinous crime of train wrecking.

On a most basic level, this racialization of the train wrecker was influenced by the fact that African Americans were typically present in large numbers along southern rail corridors. Industries that flourished along new rail lines, such as logging, sawmilling, and turpentine production, all made heavy use of transient African American labor. A detective involved in the hunt for some suspected train wreckers in Alabama in 1897 attested to the difficulty in investigating wrecking attempts along isolated rail lines. Sent to the sparsely settled area around Wilcox, which was almost entirely settled by blacks, he found it almost impossible to get any evidence of a tangible nature. For obvious reasons, local blacks refused to give any information to the white outsider associated with the railroad company. He arrested a few black men on suspicion, only to later find they were innocent. The day before the wreck was payday, which meant "the negroes from the different gangs were leaving, and moving up and down the road," which made it "difficult for us to run a line on the guilty ones."[104]

A rail corridor held a clear meaning to railroad corporations: it was for the travel of trains. But for others less involved with the railroad network, the tracks snaking through the southern countryside could serve any number of purposes unrelated to the transport of goods. Rail lines invariably ended up in towns, so they could be a convenient path home for a traveler. Accident record books are littered with examples of southerners who paid the ultimate price for their unfortunate decisions near a track. In 1881, an engine struck Robert Battle, a seven-year-old black boy, and threw him some distance. As the report from the St. Louis, Nashville & Chattanooga read, "the boy was gathering up old fish plates and spikes and was one of a party of three or four boys all of whom had sacks in which they were putting the iron. He started to run across the track and [the] engine struck him."[105] And in a one-month period, the same railroad reported two examples of passed-out drunk men getting hit by trains.[106] For many southerners, intoxicated or otherwise, rail lines were clear markers of one's geographic position, which made them convenient walking paths to find a way back into town. But many had trouble perceiving the speed of trains. Robert Harrison, an "old colored man" from Summerville, South Carolina, was hit by a train in 1894, and a report from the road noted "he was walking on side of track and heard train coming and moved to one side, as he thought far enough, but was struck on shoulder by end of bumper on pilot of engine."[107]

Beyond blacks' presence near rail lines as laborers and pedestrian travelers, the very nature of the railroad network and the economy it created produced a class of constant outsiders and "strange negroes" easily targeted for crimes. Combined with white assumptions about inherent criminality of blacks, this created a combustible situation along southern rail corridors. Lynchings and other forms of extralegal violence against blacks surged in the 1890s, and while the entire South was wracked with racial violence in these years, the highest lynching rates were in rapidly industrializing areas along new railroad lines.[108] The dynamics that led southerners to fear strange black rapists similarly led them to link unfamiliar blacks with train wrecking and to assume, as in the Statesville wreck, that altruistic black rescuers were robbers. Just as unrecognized faces could pose a threat to the virtue of white women, the countless anonymous black laborers around rail lines could just as easily be diabolical wreckers. A stranger was more likely to be targeted for lynching, and when a train mysteriously derailed, a stranger would be an obvious target.

These assumptions often played out when a train would wreck near African American areas of settlement. When a passenger train on the IC line wrecked near Ponchatoula, Louisiana, authorities arrested at least five different blacks on suspicion of tampering with the switch that caused the derailment. As with most cases, the evidence was merely circumstantial. The conductor had seen the black men loitering around the track, and "did not like the appearance of two of the men."[109] After a wreck near Opelika, Alabama, on the Central of Georgia, authorities used bloodhounds that led them to a "negro cabin," where they arrested what they called a "worthless, idle negro preacher" and a "strange negro."[110] In the post-Reconstruction South, whites linked African Americans with all types of criminal behavior, and train wrecking was no exception. If the "bad nigger" or "black rapist" became an archetype in the mind of the white South in the late nineteenth century, the dastardly black train wrecker similarly became a stock character that gripped white fears.[111]

In fact, lynching and train wrecking directly merged in more than a few instances. In December 1884, a passenger train on the recently completed New Orleans and Northeastern Railroad flew off a curve, killing the engineer and the fireman. After noticing that a switch had been deliberately misplaced, detectives immediately went to a nearby settlement and arrested Tom Parker, an old black man. Forty heavily armed men, enraged over the death of the train's engineer, rode a special train to Poplarville, sprung Parker from the jail with a railroad iron, and tortured him with hot coals from the train until he confessed. In plain view of passing trains, he was tied to a post with a note attached to his breast declaring, "This should be a caution to all other train wreckers." Once these preparations were completed, the lynch party emptied hundreds of bullets into this displayed corpse. The violence of the Poplarville lynching and Parker's confession made headlines across the South. Instead of questions about the wisdom of applying lynch law, the press largely applauded this punishment. The *New Orleans Picayune* concluded that the intervention of "Judge Lynch" was entirely appropriate in this case, arguing the "atrocity of the crime of train wrecking" and the difficulty of procuring proof justified such measures.[112]

But as with most wrecking attempts, the truth was much murkier than what the lynch mob had presumed. The "confession" that made headlines had been extracted only after torture with hot irons, and the only real piece of evidence was a claim from someone who overheard Parker threatening to "ditch the damn train," after the railroad company refused to compensate him $2.25 for a pig hit by a passing locomotive. Other witnesses provided an alibi for Parker, noting he was at home in the hours before the wreck, and arguing that he only went to the track after the wreck to flag down and warn any other approaching trains. His only real crime seemed to be the fact that he was an African American with a "bad reputation" who lived in a swampy area near the railroad tracks. Whatever the guilt of Parker, the railroad company—still a new presence in the community—certainly benefited from this reaction.[113] The wrecker story, whether true or not, caused the community to rally around the railroad, instead of against it. The grisly display of the mutilated body on the train tracks clearly assigned guilt for the wreck on Parker, and not on the corporation.

A similar incident occurred in 1888, when a deputy near Greenville, Mississippi, found seven crossties on the track of the Yazoo & Mississippi Valley Railroad. Suspecting a plot to wreck the train, he set off to try to find whoever was responsible. Seeing a black man walking on the track with crossties, he drew his gun and arrested the man. Meanwhile, the oncoming train had stopped short of the obstructions, and angry passengers quickly came upon the scene of the arrest. The passengers held an impromptu vote, and opted in favor of hanging the suspect. If not for the efforts of the train's conductor, who interceded and got the passengers to turn the suspect over to authorities, the man surely would have been lynched on the spot.[114] Once again, the guilt of the suspect is unclear but the case shows the willingness of southerners to apply lynch law to African Americans suspected of train wrecking, and the lengths to which whites would go in order to protect their trains from real and imagined threats. As troops began to head to Florida's Key West for deployment in the Spanish-American War, a doctor wrote a letter to Georgia's governor, warning of a plot by the Spanish to wreck trains full of soldiers.

However, the Spaniards themselves would not be the train wreckers. "It has been ascertained," he wrote, "that they intend to employ Negroes to work in front." By 1898, a plot like this may not have seemed so far-fetched to white southerners used to a drumbeat of stories linking African Americans to train wrecking.[115]

The fear of train wrecking helped feed into the spike of lynchings in the 1890s, and there were also directly traceable legal consequences. At least in Alabama, the aftermath of the peak of wrecks in the 1890s led to introduction of more legislation to protect rail lines. In February 1899, the first full meeting of the legislature since the Cahaba wreck, Alabama's legislature passed a whole series of laws to crack down on illicit activity on the state's railroads. These criminalized tampering with the operations of a train and messing with signals, and banned anyone from "beating their way on railroad trains in this state," or firing weapons on trains.[116] So in the aftermath of the Cahaba train wreck, which was blamed on wreckers based on deliberately concealed evidence, Alabama's legislature moved decisively to protect railroad corporations and militarize railroad corridors.

EVERY TIME A train wreck occurred—and this happened with depressing regularity in the 1880s and '90s—these scenes offered a glimpse behind the veil of the railroad phantasmagoria. Wrecks revealed the shoddy details of how southern railroads were built and maintained, and the results were not pretty for railroad companies. Smoldering piles of wreckage and mangled bodies stacked in makeshift morgues provided tangible evidence of the failures of capitalism and the New South project.[117] The train wrecker, a largely fabricated phantom that preyed on white assumptions about black criminality, served as a convenient red herring that harnessed the power of the state on the side of the corporations and distracted from the systemic failure that a train wreck represented. Believers of the train wrecker narratives saw these catastrophes not as systemic breakdowns or corporate errors but as confirmations of black depravity. The black train wrecker was a demon that seemed to come from outside of capitalism, a villain so hopelessly oppressed or divorced from the system that he resorted to train wrecking. The link between assumptions of African American criminality and train wrecking, and the South's high rate of train wrecks meant the train wrecker was in some regard a uniquely southern menace.[118]

But while the use of the train wrecker helped to sustain the railroad's glory and the rule of New South Bourbon Democrats, it is important to note that this was an incomplete victory. Passengers surely did not feel any safer with the notion that wreckers stalked their travels. Would their next train ride be their last? And were wreckers lurking around the corner of the bend? As the *Durham Globe* remarked in the aftermath of the Bostian Bridge wreck, "Now that the railroad has been exonerated, let another wreck take place."[119] And when some southerners actually did take the lessons of Jesse James to heart and successfully rob trains, the results would similarly shock the public.

EVEN LONG AFTER the smoke cleared from the wreckage, the train wrecks from the golden age of southern railroading, these disasters of New South capitalism, lived on through song. Tunes like "Wreck of the Old 97," "Engine 143," and "Wreck of the Virginian" commemorated tragedies on the rail, and ensured that the memory of these wrecks endured beyond the date of disaster. The train wreck ballad is not unique to the South, but two factors ensured that the majority of the songs have a southern setting. One factor is that the exceptional danger of southern railroading produced plenty of subjects for aspiring balladeers. The other factor is that the mountain hollers, sharecropping settlements, and mill towns of the South held a reputation for authenticity that lured song collectors and record labels searching for a "country" sound.[120] On the surface, the purpose of the train wreck ballad is to tell a story and report the news. The songs report basic details like the date, location, and mission of an ill-fated train, before going into the gory details of the wreck. The tradition of the ballad, a centuries-old mode of expression brought by Scotch-Irish settlers to the mountain South, was thus upgraded for a new technology and new form of calamity. So while newspapers and telegraphs quickly disseminated the initial news of a wreck, the ballads more slowly cemented these stories, and the dark link between southern railroads and death, in the national consciousness.

The ballads did more than just report news, as they also spoke to deeper anxieties about the rapid modernization of the South, such as the enduring tension between speed and safety. Boosters and railroad companies celebrated speed as proof of the southern revival, but reckless rates of speed were at the root of many of the ballads. "Wreck of the Old 97" tells the tale of the Southern Railway's Train No. 97, which carried mail from Washington to Atlanta and New Orleans. Old 97 was the fastest in the South until it flew off a trestle in Danville, Virginia, in 1903. Coming into Danville, the train was an hour behind time, and the engineer, unfamiliar with the nuances of the route, reportedly pushed the train to speeds of up to eighty miles per hour as it approached the perilous curve. A failed quest to make up lost time is also at the heart of the ballad of Casey Jones, who was killed when his mail train smashed into a freight train on the track at Vaughn, Mississippi. As the song relates, Casey Jones yelled, "We'll be on time or we're leaving the rails" as he sped his engine up south of Memphis. Similarly, Ben Dewberry "looked at his watch and shook his head," ruing that "we may make Atlanta but we'll all be dead" before his train flew into a ditch. And the ballad "Engine 143" describes George Alley's Fast Flying Virginian train as the "swiftest on the line," running "just twenty minutes behind." His mother even warned him before the wreck to be careful, "for many a man has lost his life in trying to make lost time."[121]

Railroads and capitalism compelled obedience to the clock. One cannot make a train without knowing the time, and the arrival of trains at regularly scheduled intervals brought the notion of "railroad time" to small towns that had been more attuned to nature's time. The spread of time consciousness and time discipline neatly matched the advance of capitalist values throughout the world.[122] As these ballads show, wrecks were moments that flipped the meaning of railroad speed, this all-important marker of time. So instead of a boast about No. 97's impressive speeds, the Southern Railway tried to downplay the route's speed records, and the company claimed the train was only going thirty to thirty-five miles per hour.[123] Post-wreck editorials often echoed this critique. After the wreck at Bostian Bridge, an author warned, "We must either restrain our ambition to get over the globe in such a hurli-burly, or increase the safety of the process."[124]

While this systemic critique lurked in the background of train wreck ballads, the songs' more enduring function was to make heroes out of the engineers, who as the songs go, all stayed with the engine until the very end to save passengers. As Casey Jones's train neared its collision, the fireman leapt out of the engine, but Casey stayed at the helm to apply the brake and slow the train as much as possible. The collision still happened, and Jones was killed in the eventual collision, but the speed had slowed enough so passengers were unharmed. Even though Steve Brady of the Old 97 was in reality thrown from his cab in the wreck, in the ballad, he was found dead with his "hand on the throttle, scalded to death by the steam." Engine 143's George Alley reckoned with his maker as he expired, saying he was "nearer, my God, to Thee." Even though the actual history of their disasters may have slightly deviated from the songs, these men have since become legendary figures for their heroism.[125]

The ballads' valorization of the individual at first seems to exist in an uneasy tension with this systemic critique of speed. What message do listeners take from these songs? But like the train wrecker panic, the ballads' focus on stories of individual heroism deflected blame from larger structural issues

with the operation of southern railroads—such as unsafe operating proce-
dures, rushed timetables, poorly maintained track, and foolhardy and reckless engineers—by reducing the wrecks to personal dramas about white
southern men trying and failing to make up lost time. The fates of these ruined trains and the doomed men who ran them can thus be seen as both a
warning and a metaphor for how southern railroading typically lagged behind
the national story.

CHAPTER SIX

Ubiquitous, Promiscuous, Frequent, and Numerous

It is as easy to hold up and go through a train as it is to rob a hen's nest.
—Rube Burrow

Chester Hughes crouched in his train car and clutched his Winchester rifle tightly in nervous anticipation. It was December 16, 1888, a dismal night in central Mississippi, and Hughes was traveling with his recently widowed sister from New Orleans to Memphis on the main line of the IC. His tight grip on his gun was due to the three men who climbed aboard the train and disrupted his peaceful journey north. While the train's engineer, Al Law, first assumed the men were tramps and thought nothing of their presence, his disinterest turned to terror after they burst into his cab and shoved their pistols in his face. In the middle of a dense swamp, Law stopped the train, and horrified passengers contemplated their fates. Ladies began praying, and many men cowered in fear behind their seats. Law screamed out to passengers for help in defending the train, and Hughes saw his chance to shine. He could become a hero, stop a robbery, save a train full of travelers, and see his name emblazoned on the front page of all the next day's papers. Hughes sprung from his seat, ran outside the train, and readied his gun to fire, but his moment of glory was brutally ended when a hail of bullets from the robbers cut him down. As he bled out on the ground, other passengers rushed to comfort him with whiskey, but his vision soon began to fade. One of his last sights may have been of a bearded, grizzled, white man, clutching bags of money, a man none other than Rube Burrow, a known tormentor of southern rail lines.[1] Hughes died an innocent victim of the first train robbery in the entire state of Mississippi, and the now-notorious Rube Burrow vanished into the night with $4,000.[2]

Seven years later, a reporter from Montgomery took the morning train south to Brewton, Alabama, to investigate some curious developments. As his train pulled into Brewton on a swelteringly hot August day in 1895, the sights he witnessed shocked him. The first sign that something was amiss were the armed guards posted along the L&N line into town. When the reporter left the train, he encountered a veritable army of over 200 men with

Winchester rifles patrolling the area around the depot. Armed citizens, local sheriffs, railroad men, and detectives all combined to form this motley and restless crew. Were he perceptive, he may have even noticed the presence of William Pinkerton, perhaps the country's most famous detective. At the town center, he encountered an eerie calm as the local businesses were almost all shuttered. One barber complained he had not shaved a man in a week. As the reporter would later write in his dispatch, the scene suggested a "frontier town on the verge of an expected attack by Indians."[3] Another reporter would recall that "every tom, dick and harry with a gun" had turned up to Brewton.[4] The same two words were on the lips of every man in this ragtag militia, the name of the threat that had so paralyzed the community, "Railroad Bill"—an African American train robber who, if the words of locals were to be believed, had acquired magical powers. He was impervious to bullets, some said, while others claimed he could shape shift into different animals.

These two men, the unfortunate Chester Hughes and the *Montgomery Advertiser* reporter, had stumbled into encounters with two of the most legendary train robbers in southern history, Rube Burrow and Railroad Bill. Rube Burrow was a grizzled white man from Lamar County, Alabama, who stunned southern railroad officials when he robbed a train on the St. Louis, Arkansas and Texas Railway near Genoa, Arkansas, in 1887. This robbery was the first to occur in the territory of the Southern Express in seventeen years.[5] After this attack, he gained more notoriety in Alabama after he and his gang engaged in a shootout on the streets of Montgomery that led to the arrest of a compatriot and the killing of a compositor for the *Montgomery Advertiser*. In between periods spent in hiding, he robbed an IC train at Duck Hill, Mississippi, in December 1888; a Mobile & Ohio train near Buckatunna, Mississippi, in September 1889; and an L&N train at Flomaton, Alabama, in September 1890. These robberies were punctuated with various manhunts that erupted in areas where he was rumored to be.[6]

For two years, Railroad Bill cut a similarly lawless path across a corner of southeast Alabama and northwest Florida. His robberies began in 1894, targeting trains on the Mobile & Montgomery division of the L&N. Railroad Bill burst onto the pages of southern newspapers in April 1895, after gunning down J. H. Stewart, an L&N section master engaged in hunting Bill. Three months later, Bill killed the sheriff of Brewton, touching off a massive manhunt that lasted throughout the summer of 1895. After a number of close calls, Railroad Bill went into hiding until December, when he emerged to rob another train. In March of 1896, his career ended when he was unceremoniously ambushed and shot down in a general store in Atmore, Alabama.[7]

It is easy to see why train robbers like these men captured the imaginations of Americans. In the abstract sense, train robbers embodied a challenge to the forces that increasingly came to dominate American life toward the end of the nineteenth century. Robbers struck against faceless corporations like banks and railroads, and to Americans at the mercy of distant financial instruments and economic forces far beyond their control, cheering a robber's exploits could be a way to fight back. Both the contemporaries of robbers and later generations of historians often have slipped bandits and train robbers into this convenient Robin Hood frame, and they have viewed the crimes of these robbers as a way to strike against the rich and enrich their communities.[8] But the panicked reaction to Burrow and Railroad Bill suggests another way to read their lives. What if instead of foes of the railroad network, they were creations of it and human embodiments of the powers of capitalism sweeping over the region? As accounts of their actions veered wildly into the supernatural, the railroad phantasmagoria took on an entirely new and terrifying form. These two robbers, one white and one black and operating in a similar area and time frame, also provide an intriguing test case for how southerners reacted to new forms of criminality abetted by the forces of the railroad. Though both exploited the railroad network for their crimes, the reactions of law enforcement, communities, and vigilantes contrasted markedly.

BOTH MEN HAD SIMILAR origins as products of the mobility of labor touched off by southern railroad development in the 1880s. Despite the portrayal in the press of Rube Burrow as a country bumpkin, he did not simply crawl out of the Alabama foothills and start robbing trains. He moved west to Texas in 1874, where he helped build railroads like the St. Louis and San Francisco Railroad, and he worked on the Mexican Central Railroad before settling down to a more pastoral life on a farm. His experience with the railroad industry must have sparked an interest in using railroads for more nefarious ends, and after failing as a farmer in Texas, he turned to train robbery as a profession.[9]

The details of Railroad Bill's life, at least before he began robbing trains in 1894, were much murkier than Rube Burrow's. His early career was the subject of much debate, but most reporters on his trail concluded that he had come out of a turpentine camp. Folklorist Carl Carmer began his Railroad Bill legend with an apocryphal tale of how "Morris Slater, turpentine nigger out of the pine woods of Escambia County, went to town one day with a rifle under his arm." A policeman stopped him and tried to get him to hand over the gun. Slater refused, and shot the policeman when the policeman made a move toward him. To escape, Bill hopped on a freight train that was leaving the station. Bill's pre-escape occupation in turpentine camps placed him in an industry that was closely tied to railroad growth. Based in the Carolinas before the Civil War, the industry moved into new areas as new railroad lines plunged into the vast piney woods of Georgia, Florida, and Alabama. All along newly constructed railroads, turpentine camps sprung up and black workers—men like Slater—flooded into the rail corridors, either as free laborers or under some sort of coercive labor arrangement.[10] Other origin stories link him to a traveling circus, where Bill mastered an array of tricks and ruses and gained a flair for showmanship that would aid his robberies. His alleged name Morris Slater does show up in the census, so if one believes this to be his real name, he was born in 1850 as a slave in North Carolina, and by 1885 he was working on the Northern Railroad and living in Suwannee, Florida.[11]

In a sense, the nickname given to the outlaw was more significant than any real history of his life. A collector of folk ballads claimed that Morris Slater earned the nickname "Railroad Time" for his fast work habits, and at some point, "Railroad Time" became "Railroad Bill."[12] To work at railroad time was to match the acceleration of the pace of both work and life that railroads introduced, so no matter who gave this name to the outlaw, it was a direct acknowledgment of his birth in the new railroad economy. Another postmortem account of Railroad Bill's history, given by a deputy sheriff, claimed Bill had a slightly different origin, linking him directly to a railroad job. A detective with the L&N claimed the outlaw's real name was Bill Jerome, who had worked on the L&N as a brakeman. According to this account, he first fell into trouble when the road charged him with stealing and selling their brasses, and he then became jealous of his wife and beat her. He was arrested, but escaped and slipped away on a train, after which he took the name Morris Slater and began robbing trains.[13] Whether he worked for a railroad, traveling circus, or turpentine camp, it was clear that both the mobility and the quickened tempo of the railroad network defined his pre-outlaw career.

Whatever their exact origins, these two robbers emerged at a critical juncture in the growth of the southern railroad network, and they took advantage of these new developments in transportation. The spread of the railroad to new areas—the incorporation of new space into the network—meant that trains laden with valuables now traversed isolated areas ideal for robberies. The sites of Burrow's thefts were typically in heavily wooded areas, far from the reach of authorities. Burrow's robbery at Flomaton, Alabama, was in an ideal spot, an isolated bridge over the Escambia River surrounded by dense woods on both sides, which shut out the moonlight.[14] On September 25,

1889, Rube Burrow and two accomplices robbed a train on the Mobile & Ohio line near Buckatunna, Mississippi. The robbers forced the engineer to stop on a bridge, so passengers could not interfere, and then they forced the express messenger to open his safe. Fearing such a crime, the road had recently armed its employees with Winchester rifles, but the only detective on this train was asleep during the crime.[15] At Duck Hill, Burrow robbed the IC line at an open low marsh, and then ran into a nearby swamp to hide.[16] Distinctively southern geographic features such as swamps, dense piney woods, and the rugged foothills in Lamar County aided his exploits by providing convenient hiding spots.

Railroad Bill traveled less than Burrow, focusing his robberies in the isolated southeast corner of Alabama, a swampy, heavily forested region between Mobile, Brewton, and Pensacola. In the decade before Railroad Bill's robberies, the area in which he operated had been swiftly and dramatically transformed by changes in the railroad network. Like large portions of the South, the railroad was late in coming to the Florida panhandle and southeastern Alabama, not arriving in force until the 1880s. At the dawn of this decade, the Mobile & Montgomery line connected the port of Mobile with Alabama's interior, but the other major city in the region, Pensacola, was still more oriented toward water trade with other Gulf ports. Florida's Reconstruction government made efforts to connect Pensacola with Jacksonville and the rest of the state, but these efforts bore little fruit. The panhandle's isolation was so severe that area legislators had even floated the idea of seceding from the rest of Florida to join Alabama, which offered more generous aid for railroad construction during Reconstruction.[17]

It would take the efforts of one of the South's largest rail conglomerates, the L&N, to improve transportation links in the area. Dubbed "Newcomb's Octopus" by both admirers and detractors, the road steadily moved south from its original territory in Kentucky after the war, acquiring important lines through Alabama. In an atmosphere of intense competition for new territory, the L&N set its sights on the greater panhandle region, with its ample untapped lumber supply. To first gain a foothold in the area, the L&N purchased the Mobile & Montgomery road in 1880, and it completed an unfinished line that connected Pensacola with Selma. The Mobile & Montgomery had fallen into financial duress in 1872 and was in an extremely dilapidated condition when it was purchased by the L&N, and ownership by a large corporation dramatically improved operations on the line. To further conquer the area, the L&N bought the Pensacola & Atlantic, a line finished in 1883 that stretched east from Pensacola, in 1885 at foreclosure. As this road moved into this new terrain, tales of the fantastical followed its march. A construction worker on this line recalled an interview with a local who thought trains had life and who asked if the train would be able to get into the door of his house.[18] The timing may have been late, but for better or worse, the area was fully connected to the national rail network by the end of the decade.

Railroad Bill terrorized white citizens in burgeoning L&N railroad towns like Atmore, Brewton, Flomaton, and Pensacola, whose economic hopes and dreams were inextricably linked to this new railroad development. Atmore, Alabama, for example, was named after C. P. Atmore, a general pass agent with the L&N, who had purchased the land and laid out the plots for the new town along the L&N route linking Pensacola and Brewton. Brewton's main newspaper even dubbed itself the *Standard Gauge*, in a celebration of the road's decision to change its gauge from the southern 5-foot gauge to the northern or "standard" 4-foot 8½-inch gauge in 1886. In an effort to lure investment and new settlement, the *Standard Gauge* consistently touted improved rail facilities that meant trains could reach up to fifty miles per hour, and C. P. Atmore himself wrote that trains on the line were "equipped with all modern appliances, and a through service to all cities of the North at a speed not attained by many roads as passenger schedule."[19] The areas between these towns, the deep, dark swamps and forests recently reached by the L&N, were convenient hiding spots, and Railroad Bill made use of the wild and unsettled nature of the country in which he operated. Anyone with intimate knowledge of the swamps could hide from railroad employees fearful to venture far from the tracks. Even the terrain seemed to hold supernatural qualities. A railroad official complained that the area between Pensacola and Mobile was like Africa, full of thirty-foot alligators and gigantic mosquitoes. Bill had plenty of friends in the swamps; as the detective argued, "The darkies will protect him if the bears won't."[20]

Though railroad corporations provided the tracks, cars, and locomotives attacked by Alabama's train robbers, large national corporations like the Southern Express provided the capital. Express companies first arose in the 1850s as a way for wholesalers to quickly send commodities over multiple rail lines. A shipper could contract with an express company to send an item, and the company would ensure that the shipment arrived as fast as possible by sending it in specially marked cars. Much of the success of the express companies derived from the way in which they smoothed over difficulties that often arose from the multiplicity of independent southern rail companies. As the name implies, the Southern Express was an explicitly "southern" express company. The company was born during the Civil War, when the Adams

Express Company split in half to serve the respective combatants. After the war, the company remained in place, and even though its president lived in New York, it attempted to keep the "southern" brand. As a report on the business in 1881 related, the "stockholders are southern men and it looks to the South exclusively for its support."[21]

Acting essentially as the nervous system for the disparate southern railroads and a channel to direct shipments of money and goods, the Southern Express grew in the 1880s and '90s, as the southern railroad network expanded to incorporate new areas. The end of Reconstruction and the depression of the 1870s led to a revived national economy and renewed economic development in the South, which meant more capital and cash coursing through the veins of the railroad network. This also created more targets for robbers like Burrow. Newspaper accounts invariably printed the tally of each of Burrow's crimes, marveling at his hauls. In the Texarkana robbery, Burrow took about $10,000 worth of Louisiana Lottery money from the express car of the St. Louis, Arkansas and Texas train, and he got $3,000 from the express messenger at Duck Hill.[22] At Buckatunna, Burrow made off with $2,700 that belonged to the Mobile and Ohio Railroad Company, though his gang had to leave behind $7,000 in silver government money bound for Florida.[23] In Burrow's last robbery, a rushed affair in Flomaton, Alabama, his lack of preparation was apparent. Instead of robbing the No. 2 limited express train, which was carrying $17,000 worth of lottery tickets on its way to the Louisiana Lottery Commission, he robbed Train No. 6, which had a much less lucrative haul. The best target for robbers were through trains, which stopped less frequently and carried commodities and money at higher rates of speed.[24]

Railroad Bill dealt more in goods than large sums of money, as he exploited the commodities traversing the area on L&N freight trains. In one of his typical robberies, he surreptitiously boarded an L&N freight train and pointed a Winchester rifle at a brakeman who spotted him. Telling the brakeman not to tell the conductor, Bill grabbed a box of clothing worth $200 and threw it off the train.[25] A week after this robbery, an L&N official reported that upwards of $1,000 of stolen merchandise was scattered throughout the countryside, and the railroad sent detectives to find both the goods and the robber.[26] After a robbery, Bill often distributed his ill-gotten gains along the line, so either he or his compatriots could gather them up later. Folklorist Carl Carmer claimed that after one robbery of a freight train, "canned food was cheap along the L&N for a while." For local blacks, Railroad Bill seemed to serve as a Robin Hood–type figure, redistributing commodities that otherwise would have passed them by. Though his usual customers were blacks, who Carmer claims were forced to buy from him, even white men bought his goods, since he "was underselling the lumber company stores."[27]

One of the most touted new features of the improved southern rail network was the regular and punctual arrival of trains. The ability to post and hew to a consistent daily schedule was an ultimate goal of any railroad corporation, but the same schedules that made travel convenient for passengers and freight shipments reliable for merchants also made robberies easier to plan. Rube Burrow's robberies were carefully researched, taking advantage of times when trains entered isolated areas, like the swamp near Duck Hill, or a bridge over a river near Flomaton. Word that Burrow was operating in an area caused railroads to alter their normally scheduled shipments. After an engineer reported a suspected Burrow sighting near Decatur, the L&N sent its pay train carrying thousands of dollars up the track earlier than scheduled, with a guard of a dozen armed men, to ensure its safe arrival.[28] An official with the express company claimed Burrow's light haul of $250 in the Flomaton robbery was due to the fact that the company had simply stopped sending "any considerable amount of money or valuable on any of the night trains in Rube's territory."[29] A large part of Bill's success came from the way in which he was able to master the regularly scheduled and rapid movements of trains through the area's rail lines. He even had favorite trains that he targeted on a consistent basis. A detective hunting him told a reporter how Bill frequently robbed the No. 74 train on Saturday nights, boarding the train in an area where it moved slowly up a high grade.[30] Trains that arrived at certain places at regularly set times were easier to board and rob than trains that came erratically.

RUBE BURROW AND RAILROAD BILL'S robberies began as problems limited to the rail corporations they attacked, but as the robberies piled up, their activities sparked fearful discussions in the press that touched on broader unease surrounding railroad development. Rube Burrow's southern robberies began at a time of heightened anxiety about the security of property and lives on southern railroads. In November 1888, the *Picayune* noted a "revival of train robbery," and expressed shock at the news that someone had tampered with shipments of money sent to New Orleans from Washington. This robber was not the "lone highwayman," but a "quiet, silent, ingenious person."[31] In 1889, authorities captured a group snatching trunks off of the New Orleans and Northeastern Road. Using false keys, the culprits stole jewelry and other valuable from passengers' trunks and deposited the haul in a New Orleans boarding house run by a woman "who did not enjoy a very savory reputation." Upwards of fifteen people were implicated in these robberies.[32] So

Rube Burrow's spectacular overt attacks on the area's railroads coincided with more covert, and more common, forms of rail theft.

The novelty of Burrow's crimes was also not lost on southern observers. He targeted corporations and states that had never seen such activity. Burrow's 1887 robbery in Arkansas was the first in the territory of the Southern Express in seventeen years, and his crimes in Mississippi, Alabama, and Florida marked the first outbreak of train robbery in these states. The obvious reference point for a southern train robber, Jesse James, was most active in the west, and his pro-Confederate sympathies hardly made him a bogeyman for southern elites.[33] Rube Burrow's crimes were especially frightening to southerners due to the way in which they put passengers of railroads in Burrow's territory directly in harm's way. Commenting on train robberies in general, the *Railroad Gazette* noted "passengers are profoundly interested in these affairs . . . the terrorizing is, for many passengers, worse than the loss of watches and purses."[34] The Duck Hill robbery, in which Chester Hughes was shot and killed, proved particularly frightening for travelers. During the robbery, the train's passengers were reportedly "panic stricken, and sat shrinking and quaking in and under their seats, hiding their valuables in the most available places."[35] Observers also recognized the extent to which Burrow used the latest railroad technology for nefarious ends. The *Memphis Appeal* wondered, "Why is it that in these days of perfect railroad systems the officers and passengers of a train can be so taken by surprise as to be rendered entirely defenseless and at the mercy of even a single man?" The paper blamed the Westinghouse air brake, which saved labor, thereby reducing the size of train crews, leaving engines defenseless in the face of criminals like Rube Burrow.[36] Creating a cohesive railroad system allowed for faster transit, and improved service, but it also created space for the actions of a robber like Burrow.

For railroad corporations, the danger of Rube Burrow's robberies went beyond the stolen money, as the apparent ease with which Burrow robbed his prey caused some editorialists to train their ire on the railroad companies themselves. The most famous quote attributed to Burrow, a man who did not leave much of a verbal record, was that it was "as easy to hold up a train as it is to rob up a hen's nest."[37] The *Constitution* cracked that criminals who were thinking of burglarizing a house should instead rob trains, as the "safest robbery in the world is for one resolute man, with a couple of pistols, to capture a passenger train and go through it."[38] As the *Constitution* argued, "train robbing is a crime that causes every citizen to feel a sense of personal danger. When he trusts his person or his property to the care of a railway company he feels that it is his right to be guaranteed a reasonable amount of safety."[39] The

Picayune contended that one of his robberies was "a repetition of an event that has become too common to excite astonishment." The paper blamed railroad companies for being unprepared and accused railroad employees of cowardly responses to incursions. The "profession will continue to thrive just so long as it is free from danger and fairly profitable," so the only remedy was the shotgun.[40] These outbursts from the press could not only harm railroads in the court of public opinion, they also threatened to directly harm the companies' bottom lines. If southern railroads became too lawless, would passengers continue to ride, and would corporations trust them with their freight?

As Burrow's tally of hauls grew, a wide array of actors joined the hunt for Rube Burrow. The Southern Express was his most dogged pursuer, but Alabama's governor got involved as well. On two different occasions, he deployed troops to areas where Burrow was alleged to be. Once he sent the Birmingham Rifles to Blount County, and on another occasion he deployed a unit to Lamar County.[41] Alabama's governor even received unsolicited letters from detectives hoping to join the hunt. George Bartholomew, from Hannibal, Missouri, wrote the governor in 1889, "having heard of the futile attempts to arrest Rube Burrow." As long as his expenses were paid, he pledged to capture Rube Burrow in four months if Burrow was in the country, and within six months if Burrow had left. He closed his letter by writing, "Don't think this the ravings of a crank, or an aspirant to become a detective," and to prove this point the man even enclosed three letters of recommendation from Pinkerton detectives.[42]

Just as Rube Burrow spoke to broader anxieties about the security of southern railroading, Railroad Bill's arrival on the scene coincided with an uptick in worry about the impact of mobile labor, or the "tramp problem." In the aftermath of the Panic of 1893, out-of-work men descended on Florida, drawn by its warm climate and more accessible rail connections, and local papers took notice. In February 1894, a story claimed that Pensacola was infested with "Negro tramps," claiming they were responsible for three robberies in the past four days.[43] In November a self-described "jolly mill man" reported that the tramps were so "numerous and warlike" near Escambia that he had to take bodyguards with him when he traveled.[44] A month later a letter to the editor complained how tramps invaded homes without even knocking and harassed local women, including an eighty-year-old woman who fainted while confronted by a six-foot-tall man and a mother who had been forced to feed and clothe over a dozen tramps in the last day. If the police were unable to solve the problem, the man said the mayor could call on the citizens and "he will find himself at the head of an army of good men, many of whom are old soldiers."[45]

When Railroad Bill gained notoriety, he put a distinct black face and a catchy nickname on these broader anxieties, and when he began killing his pursuers, his activities seemed to threaten entire communities. Railroad Bill's crimes along the railroad corridor, using the advantages of the new railroad network to his advantage, occurred on a low level for a while, and he started out as mainly a nuisance for L&N employees, but he became a regional bogeyman after a botched capture attempt in early 1895. After an L&N freight conductor found Bill lying asleep at a tank by the rail line, the conductor gathered some other railroad men to help apprehend him. As the impromptu posse approached, Bill woke up, attacked the men with revolvers, and forced them to retreat and regroup. A second train showed up, but Railroad Bill captured this train and imprisoned the crew. Some white men formed yet another posse and pursued Bill to Bay Minette, and Bill shot one of these men, James Stewart, through the heart.[46]

After this incident, the sheriff of Brewton swore he would capture Railroad Bill. As an apocryphal version of this story goes, when Bill heard this, he allegedly wrote a taunting letter to the sheriff that said "I love you and do not want to kill you so do not come after me."[47] But the sheriff did go after Bill, using a black informant to get close to Bill's hideout. As the mayor's party approached the spot on July 4, 1895, Bill ambushed them, mortally wounding the sheriff and casting a pall on the town's Independence Day celebrations. Brewton's local paper, the *Standard Gauge*, claimed that the informant had set up the whole attack and betrayed the mayor.[48] Some did not believe Railroad Bill was responsible; at least one Escambia County resident floated the theory that Bill was nothing more than a scapegoat for the murder. They argued that Bill had never before been seen in this area, and the real culprits were Sheriff E. S. McMillan's political enemies.[49] Newspapers debunked this theory a week later, but the fact that this story was out there speaks to the ambiguity surrounding the search for Railroad Bill.[50] Whatever the cause of the Independence Day incident, the impact was immediate. After word spread of the killing of the sheriff, hundreds of armed men descended on the area to take part of a massive manhunt of the type never seen before in the area. The train robberies were a nuisance, but the murder of the sheriff threatened the entire community. Brewton became an armed camp, but the same railroad network that inspired Railroad Bill's crimes, and that gave the outlaw his name, would also aid in his escape from the law.

AS RAILROAD OFFICIALS, local authorities, amateur gumshoes, and bounty hunters doggedly tracked Rube Burrow and Railroad Bill, both men used the attributes of the railroad network to elude capture. While on the run, Rube Burrow took advantage of the network's ability to produce anonymity. With so many trains constantly carrying passengers throughout the South, it was quite easy for him to become lost in a sea of similarly scruffy white men. As Rube Burrow traversed various points in the southern railway network and as his legend grew, he seemed to be everywhere at once. In November 1889, a passenger agent of the Kansas City, Memphis & Birmingham Railroad saw a "rough looking fellow," with "blood in his eye," who looked like he "was capable of doing anything." Another man with the passenger agent swore this mysterious stranger was indeed Rube Burrow, and the agent rushed to a *Birmingham News* reporter to report his findings. By this point, alleged Rube Burrow sightings had become so common that the paper noted, "Like every other man you meet nowaday's, Bowden 'has just seen Burrows and is dead sure it was him.'"[51] The very next day, the same paper reported Rube Burrow sightings in Irondale and near Sand Mountain, two towns on opposite sides of Birmingham. At both locales, someone saw a suspicious group of heavily armed white men, and they assumed one must have been Rube Burrow and his gang.[52] A Blount County newspaper pointed out recent reports of his presence in Etowah, Cleburne, and Jefferson Counties and noted, "There must be several Rube Burrows operating in this state from what the newspapers say." The paper concluded he "was a sort of ubiquitous fellow" and noted that "should these rumors continue much longer people will conclude that Burrows is a myth."[53] Even a mere rumor about the presence of Rube Burrow could shock an area. After Rube was said to be in the county, residents of Fayette County, Alabama, became terrified and "hourly expectant of more mischief at his hands." A rumor spread that a man had smuggled in six Winchester rifles in order to help Burrow "make war" on the pay train of the Georgia Pacific or the Kansas City railroad.[54]

Rube Burrow became so well known that most people simply assumed he was responsible for all robberies in the South. Before the investigation of the Flomaton robbery was complete, the *Advertiser* noted the public's opinion on the matter, writing "it was the work of Rube Burrows said nine men in ten and the tenth man was forced to admit that it looks like the handiwork of the Lamar county outlaw and desperado."[55] A Birmingham paper poked fun at this tendency to blame Rube Burrow for all the crimes committed in the South, jokingly announcing, "Rube Did It" at the top of a headline about a train robbery in far-off Indian Territory.[56] As further evidence of the confusion surrounding his crimes, Rube Burrow was often conflated with Eugene Bunch, or "Captain Bunch," another train robber who operated in a similar territory.

Bunch was a Louisiana schoolteacher-turned-brigand who gained notoriety for robbing a train sixty miles north of New Orleans on the New Orleans and Northeastern road in 1888. His exploits were mostly confined to an isolated corner of southern Mississippi, meaning his crimes never reached as wide of an audience as Burrow's.[57] In one humorous incident, Bunch robbed a New Orleans express train of securities, but lacked the expertise to know their value, so he sent a letter to the New Orleans Board of Trade inquiring about the worth of his ill-gotten gains.[58]

Burrow also used the South's new connections to keep abreast of the actions of his pursuers. Even while on the run in the isolated Florida panhandle in 1889, Burrow was able to use newspapers to track the movements of his pursuers. The *Atlanta Constitution* crowed that Burrow "knew a good paper when he saw one" after a special detective with the L&N noted that a number of yellowed clippings from the *Constitution* were found on Burrow at the time of his capture. The detective learned from people he stayed with that Burrow would insist on having a subscription to the paper wherever he went, so he could track both the news of his own exploits and the efforts of detectives on his trail. He asked for the paper at every house he stayed at, noting it was the "best paper in the South."[59] This discovery highlighted the importance of modern connections to Burrow's success, as even the swamps of the Florida panhandle could receive timely copies of an Atlanta newspaper. But more significantly, the episode also revealed the symbiotic relationship between Burrow and the southern press, which was all too eager to publicize and sensationalize his robberies to sell papers. Rube Burrow also took advantage of the new consumer goods offered by the railroad. While holed up in hiding in Lamar County, he ordered a disguise of false whiskers and a wig from a Chicago mail-order house, but after the postmaster got suspicious and refused to deliver the package, Burrow shot him through the heart and killed him.[60]

Perhaps the best assessment of Rube Burrow's ability to exploit new railroad connections and his links to the spirit of capitalism sweeping the region came from Rufus Sanders, a Sunday columnist with the *Montgomery Advertiser*. In a post-mortem summary of Burrow's life, Sanders described how Burrow "flitted about from the hills of his native Alabama to the murky swamps of Mississippi, from the bald prairies of Texas to the everglades of Florida." Sanders lamented that Burrow was "here yesterday, and there to-day and somewhere else tomorrow," and he concluded that Burrow was "at once ubiquitous, promiscuous, frequent and numerous." Rube Burrow was just one man, and even at the peak of his crimes, his gang never had more than a few other members. But his rapid movement through the railroad network, the widespread news reports about his actions, and the ease at which one could blend in while traveling made him omnipresent to observers.[61]

While Sanders clearly saw Burrow's elusiveness as a product of the railroad network, he also argued that there was more to the cultural reaction to the bandit. He described Burrow as a distorted manifestation of the mood of progress sweeping the South, as an intensely ambitious man with no higher goal than to win what Sanders called "the mad race for the almighty dollar." Burrow, the columnist explained, had "a bad case of money on the brain," and instead of making money the usual way, he opted for the quickest route to wealth and was "warped beyond reproach by his lust for money."[62] The last train robber to become a southern media sensation, Jesse James, attracted much more sympathy due to his political stances, namely, his written broadsides against Reconstruction and northern aggression, and his targeting of symbols of northern capital like banks and railroads. James may have been celebrated as a defender of traditional values, fighting back on the South's behalf, but Burrow was something different: a violent and repulsive expression of the New South quest for profit.

Just as Rube Burrow's skill at manipulating rail connections induced a sense of ubiquity, Railroad Bill's mastery of the rhythms of the movements of trains along the L&N line aided his attempts to elude his pursuers, who had become increasingly numerous after he shot Brewton's sheriff. Whenever Railroad Bill seemed to be surrounded, he hopped on a passing train to ride to a safer area. Because of his past experience in the railroad industry, Bill was able to board any train as long as it was going below its normal speed. He also allegedly rubbed turpentine on his shoes to throw off the bloodhounds on his tail.[63] Authorities eventually realized that the only way to catch a criminal like Railroad Bill was to stop the circulation of the railroad network. As authorities closed in on Bill near Castleberry, L&N officials ordered their train to continue through the town without stopping to keep Bill from making an escape by rail.[64] A few days later, the superintendent of the L&N ordered all trains to "run at a rapid rate and not stop between Evergreen and Brewton," the reason being that "it was believed that Railroad was intending to catch a train for the neighborhood of Bay Minette or Bluff Springs."[65]

For the men who joined in the hunt, the attempt to find Railroad Bill was marked by confusion, bewilderment, and fear. In the eyes of some whites, Railroad Bill's activities were a threat to anyone traveling on the area's rail lines. Atmore's *Pine Belt News* noted that while "he shows up today in one place, tomorrow his whereabouts are shrouded in mystery." It was now dangerous to travel in the area, as anyone could mistakenly stumble upon Bill, who would "shoot them on sight."[66] In an interview with a reporter, a man who went to Brewton for the manhunt noted that everyone came to town "loaded down with Winchesters and revolvers and scared of their own shadow." He admitted that he personally did not want an encounter with Railroad Bill and would much prefer to find the outlaw then pass him off to the sheriff or another officer.[67] Indeed, Railroad Bill was so frightening to the white public, and his pursuers, because he seemed to be everywhere. At the height of the panic, Railroad Bills were found all across the South. A reporter tagging along on a manhunt captured the ubiquity of Railroad Bill by noting he saw about "414" Railroad Bills lurking in the Alabama swamps. "How is this?" asked the *Montgomery Advertiser* on a day in which four different reports placed Bill in Houston, Mississippi, Birmingham, and southern Alabama.[68]

Due to his skill at manipulating railroad connections and his success at avoiding the numerous posses on his trail, southerners began to attribute supernatural powers to Bill. A folklorist noted that blacks in the area remembered him as a "conjure man" who could change himself into any kind of animal he wanted to. While being pursued by a posse, he changed into a sheep, and then watched the policemen pass. On another occasion, he turned into a dog, and joined the pack of bloodhounds pursuing him. The bloodhounds lost the scent and the search ended in failure. Another time he turned into a fox to elude a white man hunting him.[69] A detective with the L&N later recalled that many thought that an ordinary leaden bullet could not kill him. Only a "solid silver missile" could slay Railroad Bill.[70] Newspaper accounts from the manhunt reinforced the link between Railroad Bill and supernatural powers for a wider audience. A reporter on his trail noted that both blacks and "white people who should know better" thought Bill had superhuman powers. One woman swore she saw him transform into a large white cow. A livestock dealer described as one of the most popular men in Brewton had not believed these stories, and he told a reporter "the negroes had been telling so many of those marvelous tales about Railroad's changing his form at will that it was getting monotonous." But while around a railroad depot at night, he noticed a dog lurking around the station and the telegraph lines. It looked like the dog was scouting the area, and a detective with the man was certain the dog was Railroad Bill looking for information. Having witnessed Railroad Bill's magic with his own eyes, he no longer doubted the "marvelous tales."[71]

In the manhunts for these two robbers, authorities, journalists, travelers, and those following these exploits in the press encountered the bewilderment that the railroad network could produce. The rapid circulation of the network threatened to bring robbers from capitalism's forgotten hinterlands to the area and made it entirely too easy for them to slip away. And these men's faces began to appear in the crowds of anonymous travelers that inevitably swarmed crowded urban depots. New connections seemed to bring these men to the doorstep, collapsing the once-significant distances between various points in the South. To master the rhythms of the network, as Railroad Bill did, was to become a magical illusion. The railroad magic that boosters claimed was reviving the region economically became something darker in the hands of skilled train robbers. Their use of faster rail connections made them seem ubiquitous, and only the language of the fantastical could explain the skill with which they evaded pursuers. Mass media fed into the panic, spreading stories about these men to readers around the region and nation. In a systemic sense, this was an outbreak of criminality that undermined the New South message of railroad progress and in Railroad Bill's case directly challenged white supremacy.

THE SEARCH FOR THESE train robbers, which in both cases dragged on and frustrated authorities, eventually implicated broader portions of their community. While both Burrow and Bill could draw on the railroad network in similar ways, their different races led to widely divergent reactions. With so many potential Rube Burrows running around the South, railroad officials consistently assumed a broader conspiracy was behind the robberies. After the robbery at Duck Hill, Mississippi, an official with the Illinois Central claimed that he could place his hands on "every man connected with the outrage." He pinned responsibility for the robbery on a gang living near Duck Hill that was known to residents and neighbors. Whenever this gang visited a town, the official argued, "an organization is effected to prevent surprise and arrest by prowling detectives," and he rued that the complicity of the local populace would mean there would be no arrests for this robbery. Duck Hill's citizens were outraged, and held a meeting to denounce both the statement and its author, and to declare that they were doing all they could to capture the robbers. In the end they forced both the IC and the *Memphis Appeal*, the paper that first printed the claim, to apologize.[72] The IC also linked Rube Burrow to an attempted train wrecking on the main line. Less than three weeks after the Duck Hill robbery, someone misplaced a switch at Brookhaven, over 150 miles South of Duck Hill on the IC mail line, and an official with the road suggested, "Perhaps it is done by someone to distract attention from the train of the Duck Hill train robbers."[73] To officials of the IC, it seemed that a wide array of interests along their line in Mississippi were conspiring to rob their trains.

Authorities and railroad officials also targeted Lamar County, the county where Rube Burrow had grown up, and where many family members remained. For Lamar County authorities, the implication that Rube Burrow used their county to hide was a slander of the highest order, one that threatened the community's safety. At the height of the hunt for Burrow, the County Probate officer penned a desperate letter to Alabama's governor. Burrow was hiding in Lamar County, but the Pinkertons and various detectives were having no luck in apprehending him. The probate officer argued the "citizens cannot be censured for their seeming lack of trying to apprehend him for he regards human life as little as anyone who ever lived." It was impossible to find him, as "Burrow can stay here with less danger to himself than any place in the world. He has relatives and friends here more than any other place and he is familiar with each hilltop." Rube Burrow's presence also threatened the economic future of the community, as "life and property here are not considered secure and if this man is not gotten out of this county" then many respectable men would flee. The officer lamented that "a blight has settled itself upon us that may take the lives of some of our best citizens to wash away," and he begged Alabama's governor to "bear everything within the power of yourself as governor of the state to help us rid ourselves and the state of such a character." In closing his plea, the officer contended that Burrow's "crimes, daring and powers of resistance have not been greatly magnified in the newspapers and our situation here is almost intolerable."[74]

Indeed, the stakes were high for Lamar County, as the area desperately sought new investment for railroad development. On the pages of the local paper, the *Vernon Courier*, denunciations of Burrow's actions mingled with pleas to turn "the eyes of the railroads to Lamar County."[75] Unless Burrow's "blight" on the community was not lifted, the attention of outside railroad corporations, so crucial to the county's future, could elude the area. In a microcosm of the threat robbers posed to the New South dream, Burrow could doom local economic goals. Lamar County elites made quick disavowals of his actions, and in August 1889, citizens held a meeting in Vernon and adopted a lengthy resolution, alluding to people in the county who had been receiving "firearms and disguises" for the Burrow gang, and declared "various threats have been made against our citizens by those who are supposed to be harboring, aiding and abetting" the gang. The citizens denounced the outlaws in their midst, and warned that further outlawry would be punished. Referring to attempts to lynch a captured friend of Rube Burrow, the resolution hoped that only "lawful methods" would be made to secure peace.[76] So while some in the county, especially Burrow's family, may have helped him hide, the robber lacked the broad base of support enjoyed by men like Jesse James, who drew on sympathetic ex-Confederates and friendly newspaper editors.

The confusion about Rube Burrow's whereabouts and identity also endangered other white men with similarly grizzled appearances. At the height of the manhunt in November 1889, the local paper in Blount County, Alabama noted, "The county has been fearfully excited over the advent of two men heavily armed, who were passing through the country, and were supposed to be the notorious desperado Rube Burrow and one of his pals."[77] In response to this alleged sighting, the sheriff of the county telegraphed the governor to ask for troops, and the governor immediately sent twenty-five soldiers with dogs.[78] They engaged the alleged Rube Burrow gang in a shootout, but in the end, the men turned out to just be two local moonshiners on the run after a fight with a U.S. deputy marshal.[79]

While this was certainly a dangerous situation for the moonshiners, Rube Burrow's whiteness prevented a more generalized outbreak of violence against men who looked like him. The notion that Rube Burrow drew support from local communities threatened economic development and drew condemnation and harsh words, but when officials suspected that Railroad Bill drew support from local African Americans, the reactions from the white South were much more fearful and violent. As Lamar County elites reminded authorities, this was an issue of a small group of lower-class whites, and not the community at large. But for the black population of southeast Alabama, it would not be as easy to separate from Railroad Bill. So it is clear that while the race of the robbers themselves was not a huge factor in explaining their success in robbing trains, it did lead to different outcomes for the population that was alleged by authorities to have helped shelter them. The confusing ubiquity of Railroad Bill that was amusing to newspaper reporters and frightening for ordinary travelers became a nightmare for African American populations along southern railroad corridors.

Frustration with the hunt for Railroad Bill quickly turned into rage against the entire population of African Americans in the area. The *New Orleans Picayune* complained about how Bill received aid from local blacks, and it suggested Bill was coercing aid from local blacks with violence. It argued these people were "between the devil and the deep blue sea," stuck between the demands of Railroad Bill, who was "more than liable to perforate their anatomies with sundry pellets of lead," and the white hunting parties who were sure to "inflict summary punishment" on anyone found to be helping the outlaw. The author's solution was to totally clear out the black population of the area, as he asked, "Would it not be better for those negroes to leave that section of the country?"[80] Another railroad official told a correspondent that African Americans in Baldwin County were harboring and protecting Bill. He argued "they are afraid of him and seem to look upon him as something inhuman, they believe his life is bewitched, and this superstition serves the purpose of defeating our plans for capturing him." Railroad Bill's magic thus became justification to suggest what amounted to a racial pogrom in the region.[81]

As the Railroad Bill panic reached its height in the aftermath of his killing of the mayor of Brewton, black men on railroads in the area encountered violence, force, and disconnection from the rail network. Legal and extralegal groups of white men in southern Alabama began to stop and arrest every African American rail traveler in the area. Other blacks were rounded up and kept in a guardhouse to keep them from slipping information to Bill.[82] One African American woman in Mobile received a letter from her husband in Pensacola informing her that he would not be able to visit her unless he walked. Traveling by rail was too risky a proposition for this man, as he noted that two suspected Railroad Bills had already been killed along the railroad between the two towns.[83] Another African American named Bill Thomas, a turpentine worker who allegedly shot a sheriff, was killed in a shootout in Chipley, Georgia. Some officials suspected Thomas and Railroad Bill were the same person, so the L&N dug up his body and shipped it to Montgomery for further inspection.[84] Authorities in Jacksonville, Florida, also thought they caught Railroad Bill, so they sent officials in Brewton a telegraph informing them of his capture. After a comparison of pictures, they realized they had a man named D. McCoy, who had ended up in jail after threatening another man with a revolver.[85] Officials in Evergreen, Alabama, caught a suspected Railroad Bill, and the man was held in jail for a few days, but authorities released him after L&N officials confirmed the man was not the outlaw. Once free, the man with an unfortunate resemblance to Railroad Bill had no choice but to flee the area, heading to Atlanta "as fast as his 'nether limbs could take him."[86]

Even southern blacks were confused about the true identity of Railroad Bill. At the height of the panic an "old Negro" named Bill Vaughn, who made his living selling gumbo ingredients, hosted a guest in his Pensacola home. But after his visitor began to act suspiciously, Vaughn attempted to capture him for the reward money, and he shot the suspected Railroad Bill full of buckshot. After the confrontation, Bill Vaughn ended up in prison and the suspected train robber ended up in a hospital in critical condition. Vaughn claimed he was certain that he had caught Railroad Bill, but a detective on the case viewed the wounded man and said it was not the infamous train robber. The manhunt did not end after this incident, so in all likelihood another innocent man had been caught up in the violent search.[87] In its summation of the outlaw's life, the *Advertiser* wrote that "the number of Negroes who were killed under the impression that they were Slater will never be known," but it noted that "several were shot in Florida, Georgia, Mississippi and even out in Texas."[88] An advertisement in the *Pensacola Daily News* cracked that "Railroad Bill has bobbed up serenely in so many different localities that he now ranks with Marti, the Cuban patriot, so far as diversified death goes."[89] Whatever the ultimate death toll, it is clear that the summer of 1895 was an especially horrific time for black residents of the South.

Railroad Bill, the man, was nothing more than a minor nuisance for the L&N, and a threat to law enforcement in small towns such as Brewton and Atmore, but on the pages of the media, Railroad Bill became a menace to the entire region. In the eyes of the white South, he came to embody the ways in which railroads and capitalism could empower black men, who in turn could uplift and enrich entire communities with ill-gotten gains. This was not the lost, wandering, disconnected black figure that appeared in so many white travel narratives. Railroad Bill had fully harnessed the railroad's powers. Such a threat could not be simply be legislated or written out of the story; it had to be confronted with violence against the robber and the entire African American community. Rube Burrow may not have defied the race line, yet his robberies still embodied a challenge from an area of disconnection and stagnation. Hailing from a county desperate for railroad links, Burrow became a stand-in for lower-class whites—the moonshiners, mountaineers, country bumpkins, and more, who were severed from the railroad world. Burrow was a creation of New South railroad, but for southern elites, there was no place for men like Burrow in their visions of progress.

IN THE END, these two men could only run for so long, and both met bloody ends. Rube Burrow tried to escape from a jail in Linden, Alabama, only to be gunned down in the street. After a lengthy manhunt, Railroad Bill's death was surprisingly mundane. On March 11, 1896, he walked into the Tidmore & Ward general store in Atmore, and Mr. Tidmore, the store's owner, set a trap for Bill. As the outlaw strolled into the store to buy supplies, a posse of white men shot him dead. Even with the readily viewable evidence of the physical bodies, some wondered if Rube Burrow and Railroad Bill were actually dead. A story in the *Pensacola News* told an anecdote from a man who met a strange traveler who claimed that the body claimed by Burrow's family was a fake.

After the stranger failed to deny that he himself was Rube, the man suspected that the mysterious stranger was none other than the outlaw himself.[90] A letter from the *Standard Gauge*'s correspondent in Canoe wondered "who all the mischief and mean acts will be laid to," now that Railroad Bill had been laid to rest. For this writer, Railroad Bill was a bogeyman and an easy scapegoat for a wide variety of criminal activity in the area.[91] Others even doubted whether Railroad Bill existed at all. A man from Evergreen claimed that Railroad Bill was entirely fabricated. He described an amateur detective named Hendrix from Texas, who was part of the posse of detectives chasing Bill, and who had brought a black man with him to Alabama. Hendrix allegedly had the black man sneak around and scare locals by dramatically informing them that he was Railroad Bill. If this story was to be believed, the manhunt was nothing more than a plot by Hendrix to keep up excitement and draw a paycheck from the L&N.[92] As late as the 1920s, some still believed Railroad Bill was alive. After his travels through the state, folklorist Carl Carmer wrote that there were "people in the little shacks far back in the woods who do not believe that Railroad Bill is dead."[93]

Even the deaths of these two men failed to quell the panic around their lives, and like most legendary figures, fable and fact blended and spun these stories in new directions years after the fatal shootings. Yet, the affected towns, and the region at large, tried to move on as best they could. The various challenges these men embodied—to the New South order, to the idea of the railroad as a symbol of progress, and to racial hierarchies—needed to be suppressed. So how, then, were these anxieties normalized?

Rube Burrow's white skin color may have softened some of the outrage over his crimes in the press, and there was not the same level of extralegal violence in his pursuit, but he still demonstrated that men marginalized by the New South economy could still strike back against the system and cause sensational crimes. William Pinkerton, the man in charge of the detective agency that had doggedly pursued Burrow across the South, worried that others would follow in his example, and he blamed the proliferation of robberies in the 1890s on "the reading of yellow-covered novels," noting that "country lads get their minds inflamed with this class of literature." He noted that "the majority of these robbers are recruited from among the grown boys or young men of small country towns."[94] Rube Burrow's crimes underscored the notion that southern rail travel had become increasingly dangerous and violent, which could undercut booster claims of a New South safe for northern capital and tarnish the reputation of the entire South. In a December 1890 editorial, the *New Orleans Daily Picayune* complained, "There has been a tendency of late to credit the South with a monopoly of train robbers and wreckers."[95] Rube Burrow's robberies surprised southerners unaccustomed to robbery in this section of the country. Even though Flomaton was just north of the Florida border, a Jacksonville paper declared it was startling that such a crime was committed "within the borders of law-abiding Florida," as "one associates train robbery with the wild and woolly West."[96] For white elites, it was essential to sever these misdeeds from the railroad network that abetted them.

For Rube Burrow, the process of mythmaking was in full swing by the middle of his career, and the New South press resorted to two frames to marginalize Burrow and downplay the significance of his crimes. One common response among those searching for Burrow was to see his crimes as symptomatic of the sentiments of uncivilized rural country folks. Railroad publications explicitly linked the crime of train robbery with notions of "civilization." When it came to train robberies, the *Railroad Gazette* suggested the only "rational remedy is to civilize our country."[97] In another editorial, the *Gazette* lamented "there is no civilized nation on the face of the earth in which such train robberies can happen."[98] Thus, chroniclers of Burrow's life made much of his origins in the allegedly backward and uncivilized Lamar County. G. W. Agee, the Southern Express official in charge of the manhunt, noted that the part of Alabama had "excellent citizenship," but had "not until the last decade possessed of the advantages of development which more fortunate sections have long enjoyed." Burrow was reared "amid the environments of ignorance and superstition," son of a "rugged pioneer," and the official claimed that "it is from such strong and rugged natures, uneducated and untrained in the school of right and honesty, that comes the material of which train robbers are made."[99] From the perspective of the railroad network, there was some truth to Agee's contention that Burrow's corner of Alabama lacked development. But Burrow's past working for railroads, his travels out west, and Lamar County residents' vigorous denunciation of his activities demonstrated that he was as much a creature of the railroad network as he was a country bumpkin.

Focusing on Burrow's uncivilized origins was one tactic to downplay his actions, but another was to paint him as a redistributionist Robin Hood figure. One of the most prolific chroniclers of Rube Burrow's career was E. W. Barrett, an enterprising correspondent with the *Atlanta Constitution*, a publication that more than any other epitomized the values of the New South. Seeing an opportunity to hitch his journalism career to the train robber's rising star, Barrett traveled to northern Alabama in fall 1889 at the height of public interest in the robber, to get the story behind the legend and hopefully secure an interview. He never actually got the interview, and instead he fabricated an encounter with Burrow, in an attempt to "scoop" the *Constitution*'s rival newspaper in Birmingham. After the fake interview was printed, a special train rushed thousands of copies of the *Constitution* to Birmingham.[100]

Despite the falsehoods, Barrett's full-page feature article "Red Rube" offered a revealing window into the meanings journalists placed on Burrow's crimes. The name of the article itself points to Barrett's interpretation of the outlaw as an expression of an anticapitalist challenge to rail corporations. The reporter exaggerated the physical characteristics of Burrow, labeling him a "splendid specimen of manhood," who had "never been beaten in a foot race or thrown in a wrestling match." Furthermore, Burrow had "seldom fired at a man at a range of five hundred yards or less, without the bullet going true to the mark." Barrett then recapped Rube's robberies and crimes, as well as the failed efforts to capture him, and he reprinted excerpts from his interview with family friends of the Burrows. The fake interview, appearing two days later in the *Constitution*, continued the construction of the "Red" Rube Burrow. When Barrett pressed Burrow to explain why he robbed trains, Burrow said, "My folks ain't goin' to live in want while trains run and tote money." Burrow also denied robbing country stores, claiming he "never robbed a poor man," and he never "robbed a little storekeeper or farmer." The article concluded with a warning that "it will not be long before Rube Burrow will be heard from again in a reckless and daring train robbery."[101]

This portrayal of Rube Burrow as enriching impoverished Alabamans with his ill-gotten gains hardly squares with other evidence. In fact, when captured, he was filthy and destitute, on the run and hounded by express companies, railroad detectives, and policemen.[102] He lacked a broad base of support, as residents in Burrow's home of Lamar County were quick to disassociate themselves from his actions as his career became notorious. In August 1889, they even went so far as to adopt a resolution, attacking people in the county who had been receiving "firearms and disguises" for the Burrow gang, and denouncing the outlaws in their midst, and warned that further outlawry would be punished.[103] A folklorist has debunked an apocryphal tale told about Burrow in which he gave a destitute widow money to pay rent. The story lacked any documentation, and it closely mirrored a key element of the Jesse James legend, leading this scholar to believe that Alabamans may have confused the two stories.[104]

As further evidence of the power of the Jesse James story, observers sought to inscribe the same sort of neo-Confederate, anticapitalist motivation behind Burrow's robberies. The *Abbeville Times* bragged that "he was the only man that has ever been known to down the railroads and express companies, while those monopolies are allowed to go daily robbing the people." A family acquaintance from Lamar County later claimed Rube Burrow robbed trains to avenge the Southern defeat in the Civil War. As a youth, Burrow had been exposed to tales of Yankee atrocities, and he robbed railroads since he associated them with Northern influence.[105] In his fake interview with Burrow, E. W. Barrett claimed Burrow was "led astray" by Jesse James.[106] And a newspaper in Florence claimed that the Burrow boys grew up in the county, and served in the local Confederate regiments. However, it would have been impossible for Rube and his brother, who were both born around 1860, to serve in the Confederate army.[107] Jesse James drew strength and sympathy from the notion that his robberies were revenge for Reconstruction-era northern abuses, but there is hardly any evidence that Burrow was fighting the same sectional battles.[108] One man even wanted to use Rube Burrow to teach Christian values of forgiveness. A self-anointed "prophet and exile," John McClure Tate, wrote Alabama's governor and asked for "a general perpetual, everlasting and eternal amnesty proclamation" for Rube Burrow, as long as the outlaw would "return, confess, repent and in the future lead a more honest, peaceable, law abiding and god fearing avocation." This would set an example for others to follow and end the bloody and expensive chase.[109]

Rube Burrow's whiteness clearly invited sympathy from the New South press, which inflated his deeds and presented them in a more favorable light. The same white southern editors who celebrated Jesse James's robberies as resistance to northern dominance and the policies of Reconstruction tried to slip Burrow into a similar frame. The imaginary versions of Rube Burrow, neither the "Red" Rube Burrow, totally fabricated by E. W. Barrett in an effort to sell papers, or the ex-Confederate robbing trains to exact vengeance from the Yankees, were more compelling than the real Rube Burrow. In the decade after Burrow's death, other dime novels followed in this trend of romanticizing Burrow with an assortment of colorful stories like "Rube Burrow, the Outlaw," or "Rube Burrow of Sunny Alabama: The True Story of the Prince of Train Robbers." Another account explicitly linked Burrow to Jesse James, "Jesse James, Rube Burrows & Co.: A Thrilling Story of Missouri."[110] The novels transmuted the very real threat that Burrow posed to travelers' lives or investors' capital into a familiar narrative of resistance. With little evidence to support these fables, an expression of capitalism's dark powers became a way to express grievances about railroad corporations. Linking Burrow to heroes like Robin Hood or Jesse James downplayed the novelty and violence of

Burrow's crimes, and turned a menace to travelers' lives into a more familiar outlaw figure that could be celebrated by white southerners.

The meaning of Railroad Bill was similarly up for debate in the aftermath of his grisly death, but the outlaw's race ensured that his memory would be filtered through multiple lenses. The white press emphasized Bill's race to cast him as a villain perfectly suited for a decade that witnessed the consolidation of Jim Crow racial hierarchies. For white Alabamans, his life confirmed the notion that African Americans were criminal and black mobility was dangerous. He seemed to confirm arguments that blacks were destined for criminality in a post-Emancipation world, and he flipped on its head the idea of Odum's Black Ulysses, the black man disconnected and alienated from the forces of capitalism. African Americans in the area of his actions clearly followed his story, and for them, Bill's defiance of white authorities made him a heroic figure and placed him in the pantheon of legends like John Henry. Just as John Henry embodied a bottom-up narrative of resistance and racial pride, black Alabamans could cheer Railroad Bill's various escapes and celebrate his resistance against the white power structure.[111]

But along with casting Railroad Bill as evidence of black criminality, white Alabamans expunged the anxieties of his criminal activities by commodifying all aspects of his life. Just as Rube Burrow was transformed into a media commodity, a stock character aping elements of Jesse James's mythic life, white Alabamans reduced Railroad Bill to a salable item immediately after his violent death. This process started with a vigorous contest between his various captors over the reward money. The self-proclaimed "hobo correspondent" for a Texas newspaper even claimed he deserved part of the reward, due to his article that described a meeting with the outlaw on a train between Mobile and Pensacola three weeks before the killing. In the end, J. L. McGowan got half the promised money, as well as a lifetime free pass on the L&N.[112] In the same issue of the *Pine Belt News* that announced Bill's death, the Chicago Photo Company, based in Brewton, ran an ad offering "photos of the desperado as he appeared after death for FIFTY CENTS." To make potential consumers feel even better about their purchase of a Railroad Bill memento, the ad noted that a percent of the proceeds of the sale would go to the family of the slain sheriff of Brewton.[113]

These blatant attempts to claim Railroad Bill's life as a commodity did not occur without resistance from local blacks, as from the beginning it was clear that Railroad Bill meant something entirely different to local African Americans. Railroad Bill's body itself was a contested item, as both races sought to gain possession of his remains. Immediately after the shooting, authorities moved quickly to prevent blacks from taking the body. Sheriff James McMillan telegraphed L&N superintendent McKinney with an urgent request. He asked, "Can you possible [*sic*] get me to Atmore with switch engine? Am afraid negroes will take body away from McGowan."[114] The *Mobile News* reported the "entire country around Perdido was at once aroused, and bold threats were made by the immense mob of Negroes gathered there that they would take the body." After McMillan's urgent telegraph, the L&N sent a special train from Flomaton to Brewton to pick up the body. The train flew down the track so fast that "it is possible that never before in the history of the M. and M. road has any switch or any other engine gone over the road with such terrible speed." White authorities spirited the body away from the scene before any violence, but African Americans in the area continued to show interest in the remains of the robber.[115]

With Railroad Bill's corpse securely in the hands of the white authorities and the men who killed him, his body became a trophy and a means of profit. The man who killed Railroad Bill, J. L. McGowan, brought the body to Montgomery, where L&N officials viewed the corpse and confirmed that it was indeed Railroad Bill. When a crowd of curious watchers gathered at the depot upon the body's arrival, the enterprising sheriff decided to charge admission to view the body. Visitors could even pose for a picture next to the bullet-riddled corpse, and images of the slain bandit spread far and wide.[116] After spending a few days in Montgomery, where the public could view the corpse for twenty-five cents a look, city authorities intervened to shut down the macabre display, and they forced McGowan to move to a new town. He then tried public exhibitions in Pensacola and Mobile, with the same result, and he ended up taking the body to Birmingham for embalming, where he set up yet another exhibition of the body.[117] By March 13, the body had arrived in Pensacola, where an "immense crowd of people, principally colored," had gathered at the depot to await its arrival. A force of policemen was on hand to preserve "good order" and escort the body to an undertaker, who opened the casket and found the body in an "excellent state of preservation." The next day the body was taken to Palmetto Beach, where the public could view it. Interest in this attraction was so intense that the railroads even ran extra trains to the beach starting at 10:30 A.M. and leaving every hour, to accommodate the crowds.[118] A detective with the L&N later estimated that about 3,000 people gathered at one of these displays, including those who "came from all directions in ox carts, on mule-back, walked, and in every other way they could come through the pine woods" to see Railroad Bill.[119]

McGowan's efforts to profit off of Bill's death were so blatant that editors began to criticize the unabashed commodification of Railroad Bill's body. The *Montgomery Advertiser*, hardly a friend to Railroad Bill, was aghast at the exhibition of the body. The paper opined "it can be said to the credit of the community that comparatively few people paid an admission price of 25 cents" to view the "gruesome and sieve-like corpse." The exhibitors justified the showing by claiming it would serve as a warning to other robbers, but the *Advertiser* argued this class already viewed Bill as a hero and the exhibition of the body was thus nothing more than "a money-making scheme" that deserved condemnation. The paper hoped the whole matter would end with the burial of the body, "for after all he was a human being."[120] Others attacked McMillan's widow for profiting from the wreck. After the *Mobile Daily Register* ran a story that mentioned that the widow of the sheriff whom Bill killed in 1895 had been collecting money from the exhibitions, the widow wrote a letter to a few Alabama newspapers denying that she had profited from the exhibitions.[121] Bill would not be laid to rest until the end of March, when he was buried in St. John's Cemetery in Pensacola. A local undertaker and two black gravediggers carried out the task, but first they made sure to take the dead man's bloodstained rifle and pistol from the casket.[122]

White southerners recast Rube Burrow's story into one more comforting and familiar, and they used ritualized displays to fully expunge the horror of Railroad Bill's crimes. The ceremonial method of displaying Bill's corpse and commemorating his death closely mirrored the aftermath of lynchings. After lynchings, whites rushed to commemorate the occasion by disseminating souvenirs and postcards. Turning the event into a spectacle with highly ritualized actions, large crowds, and these commemorative impulses alleviated the collective anxieties caused by the alleged crimes and reified white supremacy in the affected community.[123] The macabre carnival atmosphere of Railroad Bill's death performed a similar function for white railroad travelers in Alabama. In fact, his drawn-out funeral rituals directly inverted the horrors of his criminal actions. In life, Railroad Bill used the speed and reliability of the area's railroads to his advantage, but in death, rapid rail transportation spirited his corpse away from blacks and aided the carnival-like display of the man's body that reassured fearful whites that the outlaw was truly dead and gone. As he passed into the railroad network as a dead body and a commodity, Railroad Bill went from an extraordinary figure to something more mundane and ordinary in the New South—a black body, up for sale, dismembered, and on display for white consumption and viewing.

IN 1898, AN EXASPERATED Atlanta judge looked down his bench at a black girl nicknamed "Baby," who was brought before the court for disturbing the peace. She had been annoying another black woman by singing a song repetitively in front of her house. Asked to explain her actions, Baby professed innocence and in her words claimed, "All I ever did wus to sing a song called 'Railroad Bill' in front of her house, and dat song is nice enough fur de opery house."[124] The ultimate fate of Baby and her singing career is unknown, but it is clear that less than two years after Railroad Bill's violent demise and his corpse's grisly tour of the rail depots of southeast Alabama, his actions had already been translated into song. When Carl Carmer, a northern professor visiting Alabama, toured the state in the 1920s, he found Railroad Bill songs all throughout the state. Carmer wrote in his typically dramatic fashion, "Black boys were tuning their banjos" and preparing to sing songs about Bill's deeds as soon as he died.[125] The same railroad network that created Railroad Bill's career immortalized him in song as his legend spread, cementing his status as a folk hero and twisting his story in new ways. In work camps in the piney woods, in far-off rail depots, and among transient laborers, Railroad Bill's story quickly spread through the South via song.[126] The story of Railroad Bill clearly did not end when his decomposing body was put in the ground.

Carmer attempted to get to the root of the true story behind the song, but other white folklorists, such as Howard Odum, have more obsessively charted the song and its many variations. Odum wrote that Bill was "the Negro's hero of the track" and argued that "one must take all the versions of the song in order to appreciate fully the ideal of such a character." Indeed, the format of the song lent the story of Railroad Bill to open interpretation. Once the song started up, singers would make up verses that both said something extraordinary about Bill and that rhymed with the previous verse. Odum identified four different variants of songs about Railroad Bill.[127] Norm Cohen, a chronicler of railroad folk songs, fit the various Railroad Bill songs under the broad rubric of "blues ballads," narrative folk songs with loose organization that differ from the "temporally correct sequence" of more structured broadside ballads.[128] So as the Bill songs spread and took on new verses, the man took on a whole other life, and his legend grew to encompass a wide range of activities.

In one version Odum collected, Railroad Bill "never worked and he never will," stole from a farmer, attempted to kill the singer, and stole from his wife.

None of these activities were associated with the actual Railroad Bill; indeed they could have described virtually any man who was up to no good. In another song, "Right On, Desperado Bill," the singer laments his missing woman, begs for more money to buy beer, expresses reckless attitudes toward gambling, and celebrates how Bill "shot all buttons off a high sheriff's coat." Odum wryly noted that "other still less elegant verses must be omitted," but it is clear that in this version, Bill's misdeeds are celebrated and folded into a wide range of rebellious behavior that any down-on-his-luck black man could relate to.[129] A second song found by Odum, entitled "It's That Bad Railroad Bill," retained more historical accuracy in that it detailed the actual manhunt for Bill. Each of the ten verses of this song listed a different train looking for Bill. In the process the singer just misses Bill by a minute, sees Bill "marchin' to an' fro," gets shot at with a "forty-fo," and gathers ten men to "run po' Railroad Bill in." A similar version, entitled "It's Lookin' for Railroad Bill," even more explicitly referenced his crimes. One verse reports that "Ole McMillan had a special train / When he got there wus a shower of rain," while another says "Railroad Bill was the worst ole coon / Killed McMillan by de light o' de moon." After each couplet, which gives exaggerated versions of various other bad things done by Railroad Bill, the singer sang, "lookin' fer Railroad Bill." And a final version performs a similar task as the stories linking Burrow to Jesse James. The singer has Bill go west, where he meets Jesse James and finds he is no match for the Missouri desperado.[130]

The Railroad Bill folk songs have given the robber a life well beyond his few years of train robbing. Their persistence among African Americans speaks to his importance as a folk hero who took on the emerging Jim Crow system. He became an archetypical "bad man" who flouted conventions, escaped the law, and generally did whatever he pleased, and it was easy to see how this would appeal to black southerners. But in a sense, the songs further whitewash the real story of Railroad Bill. All of these songs were stripped of the most threatening elements of the violent events of the summer of 1895. While the actual hunt for Railroad Bill was a moment of confusion, terror, and random violence, the folk songs sanitized the story, folding it into other narratives of black "bad men." Gone are the fears of tramping and anxieties about mobile labor, the calls to defend the honor of white women, the nervousness about strange men lurking around rail corridors, the frightening supernatural qualities of his escape, and the outburst of extralegal violence directed toward random African American travelers.

In the Rube Burrow and Railroad Bill stories, two different agents were responsible for myth making: the New South press and traditions of African

American folk song. But the conclusion is the same. The legendary versions of Rube Burrow and Railroad Bill both depict them as resisting capitalism and fighting modernity by robbing trains, or in Railroad Bill's case, by fighting back against the emerging Jim Crow segregation regime. Portrayals of these men as Alabama versions of Robin Hood, one for the rural white population and one for blacks, paints them as redistributive foes of the market or as "social bandits" fighting for an oppressed peasant class.[131] As railroad corporations increasingly became the target of political attacks in both Alabama and the nation at large, first by the Populists, and then by Progressive-era regulators, it was easy to frame their actions as opposition or resistance to railroad.[132]

But these depictions miss the point and sever their crimes from the enchantment produced by capitalism and the railroad. As men driven by a lust for accumulating wealth and profit, aided by the rapid expansion and systemization of railroads, and fueled by sensationalist media, they were capitalism distilled to its purest and most violent form. Railroad Bill and Rube Burrow transmuted the magic of the railroad into criminality with terrifying results for southerners. The sense of bewilderment, confusion, and panic seen in accounts of their hunts revealed the railroad's circulation and connection run amok. And in their plunder of wealth and commodities, the two robbers proved a particularly avaricious version of booster efforts to lure investment, exploit natural resources, and sell the South. In this, they were able to transcend the southern racial divide in some way.

While both white and black men could twist the railroad to their own devices, the white South's position in authority meant that the hunt and aftermath of the black Railroad Bill's career would be marked with more violence and a concerted effort to display his corpse and prove his passing. Railroad Bill was, in white eyes, a common black man animated and transmuted into something terrible and fearsome by the forces of the railroad. And the violence directed against his community spoke to how this terror was applied to black men and black women across the region. Black mobility, as we have seen, was denied by ideological and legal efforts, and in the grisly denouement to the Railroad Bill saga. In the end, the same railroads Railroad Bill preyed upon transported his rotting corpse from station to station for display, taming his magic and replacing the chaos of his crimes with the usual well-ordered movement of the railroad. These robbers struck fear into the South from the ground up, but the final monster of the New South railroad would come from the highest of corporate perches: the desk of J. P. Morgan himself.

CHAPTER SEVEN

Fighting the Octopus

The Southern Railway is one of the greatest corporations in the country, and it's by long odds, the mightiest corporate monopoly the South has ever known.
—John Temple Graves, writing to the *People Party's Paper*, 1896

On June 5, 1897, Georgia residents and railroad men across the South woke up to quite a surprise. W. B. Sparks of Macon and a number of his allies had presented a petition to put the Southern Railway, the largest railroad system in the South, into the hands of a court-appointed receiver due to its violation of the state constitution's antimonopoly clause.[1] Momentum for this attack had been building for months in Macon, where the pages of the *Macon News* were full of attacks on the Southern since the road's purchase of the local GS&F. On April 27, 1897, the paper published a manifesto declaring that Macon had been "bottled up." Macon's residents, Sparks argued, "will probably awake to a knowledge of their true condition after the chains have been permanently fastened about them." Because of the company's recent acquisitions, nearly all the railroad lines into and out of Macon were now under Southern Railway control. Without competing freight rates, there was no way for Macon to become the commercial center of the state, and the town's merchants would be doomed to forever play second fiddle to other Georgia cities.[2] In another journalistic broadside, the paper rued that Macon's citizens had spent more on railroad building than "any two cities in Georgia," with the goal of making the city a railroad center, but "professional wreckers and monopolists" had foiled the city's plans. Eleven railroads centered on the city, but only one was independent.[3]

The stakes of this antimonopoly petition were high. The *Macon Telegraph* argued, "If the Southern, which is now in the full tide of its development as one of the greatest of American trunk lines," would be broken up, "its service would be seriously crippled and untold loss would be inflicted upon the owners of its shares and its securities."[4] Defenders of the road turned to a message of regional salvation and linked the corporation's success with the South at large. An attorney in Macon argued that a receivership for the Southern would "strike a blow from which the South would not recover in twenty five years."[5] The Southern, as its backers argued, was of utmost importance to the development of the region, and its consolidation efforts seemed like the best solution to the South's overcrowded railroad landscape and the puzzle of mass financial insolvency of southern railroad companies.

The success of capitalism as an economic system has always been predicated on the constant churn of creative destruction and corporate consolidation. Old firms and business go under and are replaced with more innovation or more efficient successors. Companies that fail or die can find another life when larger, more successful competitors purchase them. For many firms, bigger is better, as the all-consuming logic of the market pushes companies to consolidate for efficiency gains.[6] The Southern Railway formed the clearest example of how this trend toward corporate consolidation accelerated in the South after the Panic of 1893. By 1900, five major companies, the Southern Railway, Atlantic Coast Line, Seaboard Air Line, IC, and L&N, controlled roughly 60 percent of southern rail mileage.[7] These were the largest corporations the region had ever seen, and they were backed mostly by northern or foreign capital. With the rise of these companies, large systems, oriented toward interstate trade, finally supplanted the locally oriented or state-owned roads that before had dominated southern transportation.[8] The rise of the southern rail conglomerates was the natural result of capitalism's Darwinian process of consolidation and the logical conclusion to the excesses of the 1880s railroad boom.

But the public hostility toward the Southern demonstrated that this was a highly contested victory. Indeed, by 1898, the road's officials were so perplexed about the hatred for the company in its early years that they sent out a series of letters to subordinates asking why this was so. As one respondent noted, "the public at large . . . at first was very distrustful of the management of the Southern (largely on sectional grounds)" and "there was also a certain amount of jealousy created by the size and success of the Southern."[9] Another drummer argued that nearly every merchant he met "had some unkind thing to say about the road."[10] Complaints like these turned to legislative and political action in both Georgia and North Carolina, two states critical to the shape of the Southern's main line. At the same time the Sparks petition electrified the Georgia press, North Carolinians from all three major political parties raged against the company's ninety-nine-year lease of the state-owned North Carolina Railroad.

In response to the rise of companies like the Southern, a new monster—the "octopus"—came to the New South. While the Southern cloaked itself in a familiar message of regional rebirth, its detractors framed their arguments in the language of monstrosities and dark conspiracies, painting the Southern and its fellow railroad conglomerates as grasping behemoths and all-consuming octopi that would strangle the region, devastate localities, and deliver southern railroads to a Wall Street cabal. The wonder of the railroad's corporate machinations bred a new horror that in turn fed a Populist insurgency that threatened to tear the white South's unity asunder. The question at hand in these conflicts was not just regulation, which Progressives would continue to fight for, but the very shape, size, and purpose of the railroad company itself. Should the South be host to railroad monopolies? The newfound presence of these corporate behemoths marked an inflection point in the regional economy. Would the New South order of northern-backed large corporations win out over sectionalist critiques, local pushback, and the antimonopolist arguments of the Populists? As we will see in Georgia and North Carolina, two states critical to the Southern's main line, the ultimate defeat of this antimonopoly critique had dire implications for the Populist insurgency and its political challenge to the New South status quo.

THE VARIOUS RAIL ROUTES that would become the Southern Railway had a long and tangled history before the rise of the Southern in the 1890s. In fact, the Southern Railway was not even the first corporation dubbed the "Southern Railway." Attempts to forge a region-wide rail system dated back to the Civil War, when the Confederate government physically patched together roads that were originally built to serve states and localities, not a wider region. The Richmond & Danville was perhaps the most essential line of this Confederate system. This road at first served simply its eponymous cities in Virginia, but it gained immense importance after the Confederate government built a connecting line between Danville and Greensboro, which allowed access to the state-owned NC RR and a whole chain of lines connecting Richmond and Atlanta.[11] The system splintered when the Confederate government that operated this system fell, and during Reconstruction, the struggle to control these lines continued between southern state governments and northern capitalists. Tom Scott, president of the Pennsylvania Railroad, saw in this corridor an opportunity to create a southern railroad empire, and in 1873 he created the Southern Railway Security Company, a holding company he used to purchase the various pieces of his system. The SRSC lasted only until 1876, when it sold off most of its holdings, but before its demise it succeeded in forging a unified rail corridor between Atlanta and Richmond.[12]

After the SRSC fell apart, the next major attempt to consolidate this corridor into a single system came from the Richmond & West Point Terminal. Like the SRSC, the Richmond Terminal did not actually buy railroads, opting instead to simply purchase majorities of their stock. The core of the Richmond

Terminal was the R&D company, but the end of the 1880s the company also controlled two other major systems, the East Tennessee, Virginia & Georgia and the Central of Georgia. The terminal holding company epitomized the problems with the increasing control of southern railroads by distant financiers. Investors were more interested in using the railroad properties for short-term profits than for a long-term strategy, and the stock prices of these bonds held little relation to the actual condition of the lines they represented. This complicated system collapsed in 1892, and by the end of the year, the Richmond Terminal system and all the lines it owned were in receivership awaiting some sort of financial reorganization.[13] A year later, the Panic of 1893 further compounded the chaos in southern railroading. Southern rail lines outside the purview of the fallen Richmond Terminal suffered as investors became newly suspicious of high railroad stock prices. For the nation as a whole, 128 lines with over 100 miles fell into receivership during the 1890s, and thirty-three of these were southern roads. Fifteen of these southern receiverships were associated with the collapse of the Richmond Terminal system.[14]

The hard times of the 1890s set in motion a wave of receiverships in the South that spoke to a serious flaw with the boom of the 1880s. Simply too many railroads had been built, and this overconstruction made it nearly impossible to operate these lines at a profit. In seeking to explain the calamity that had befallen the state's railroad corporations, the Georgia Railroad Commission noted how the five years before 1891 "stimulated railway construction to an abnormal extent in the state." Eight hundred miles' worth of new road led to intense expenditures from existing roads to match the new competition, which piled up indebtedness and helped usher in receiverships.[15] Residents of southern towns along recently built railroad corridors experienced the shock waves of the panic as their local railroad dreams went up in smoke. The GS&F collapsed in 1891 after President W. B. Sparks's ambitious attempt to build what he called another road out of Macon failed to attract the attention of outside conglomerates.[16] As the CF&YV, a road stretching through largely unpopulated swathes of North Carolina countryside on its way from Greensboro to Wilmington, tumbled into debt in 1893, the road's financial officer, William A. Lash, was besieged with letters from widows in Baltimore, bankers in New York, and prospective investors, demanding answers and information. The sad fate of the CF&YV demonstrated some hard truths about the tough times of the 1890s. Lines that already were in a precarious position had little hope of surviving the crippling depression of the 1890s, and the failure of southern railroad properties hurt bondholders of all stripes.[17]

By 1893, the landscape of the South was littered with railroads that were for the most part physically intact (and still operating) but financially ruined. Ultimately the task of picking up the pieces of the Richmond Terminal and the other indebted roads fell to the only entities with enough capital to build a regional network of railroads in the South—the various firms and holding companies controlled by J. P. Morgan, America's richest man. On May 1, 1893, Morgan's firm issued its first plan to reorganize southern railroads. The challenge was immense. Beyond the necessary financial wizardry needed to render the roads solvent, the proposed new system faced serious physical issues. Roads struggling to pay debts also had trouble keeping up a solid record of maintenance, and the report noted that while most other American railroads had been implementing improvements to the roadbeds and equipment, the Richmond Terminal lines could not due to debt obligations. The report suggested an emphasis on through traffic and building up the region, as opposed to small local business. The region and the system would take priority over local development and the wishes of individual towns. The best way to solve these issues was to create an entirely new railroad company that united all the lines that previously were under the purview of the Richmond Terminal. The report argued, "The present disjoined and complicated system shall give place to one solid and permanent organization."[18]

In addition to the financial reconstitution of the company, Morgan and the reorganization committee needed to rehabilitate the image of the corporation in the eyes of both southern consumers and stockholders. Accusations of carpetbag influence and fear mongering about Yankee control helped doom Tom Scott's SRSC back in the 1870s, and the men behind the Southern Railway were even more explicitly connected with Wall Street and northern influence.[19] So in contrast with the corporation's northern ownership, the road's founders marketed the Southern Railway as an explicitly "southern" company and packaged with a message of regional restoration. The rebranding of the road started at the very top, and Morgan and his associates tapped Samuel Spencer, a man uniquely suited to play the role of president of the Southern Railway. In addition to his talents at railroad management, Spencer's biography perfectly fit the bill for these rebranding efforts. He was a native southerner, born in 1847 in Columbus, Georgia. He served under Nathan Bedford Forrest's cavalry unit during the Civil War, and then received degrees at the University of Georgia and the University of Virginia before rising through the ranks of a number of railroad companies. Spencer then became president of the Baltimore & Ohio Railroad, but after resigning this office he worked for Morgan as a railway expert.[20] The sentiments of an Atlanta lawyer, who wrote to Spencer after his appointment, "All of our people will be delighted to know that a southern man is at the head of this great enterprise, upon which the future prosperity of the South is so greatly dependent," were common.[21]

The location of the new corporation's headquarters also reflected these desires to brand the road as "southern." In 1894, W. H. Green pondered different options in a letter to Spencer. Green worried that if the headquarters were located in Richmond, people "would likely say, while we call our property the 'Southern Railway,' we are still a Virginia concern, and operating the property in the interest of Richmond." Atlanta would be a great option, as the new system would control at least four of the nine lines entering Atlanta, but of course placing the headquarters in Atlanta would "dissatisfy the whole state of Virginia." Ultimately they chose Washington for the corporate headquarters, but the tough nature of the decision speaks to how the new corporation tried every avenue to establish itself as a railroad for the entire South.[22] The iconography of the line also reflected the break with the past the leadership hoped to represent. The road picked a new trademark in July 1894, an S and R with an arrow running through it, which the *Atlanta Constitution* celebrated as a "striking emblem, representing the swift flight of the trains" and the "directness of the route" and noted the company could not retain the old logos, "for they were of companies that are now dead."[23] These discussions even extended to the names of routes. Letters between Finley and Spencer centered on the need to affix the name of the new corporation firmly in consumers' minds. Spencer wrote Finley to suggest that they do away with the old trademark of the Piedmont Air Line, the previous name for the route between Atlanta and Richmond. Spencer argued, "I want to get down as soon as possible to the Southern Railway being known as but one thing."[24] Spencer also wanted to do away with the old "Richmond & Danville" name. As late as 1897 he wrote to Finley to ask why some boxcars still were marked "Richmond and Danville Dispatch," as it was "rather undesirable to keep alive in this way the name of a railroad company which has ceased to own any property, has gone out of business and whose insolvency was very conspicuous."[25]

When the Southern Railway came into existence on July 1, 1894, the road's boosters declared the new company's birth a turning point for the entire region. To the men behind the company's formation, the consolidation was an economic necessity for the South. Spencer himself later argued, "The Southern Railway company is probably as good an illustration of consolidation as exists in this or any other country," and a biographer of Morgan would call this act of corporate wizardry one of the banker's greatest achievements.[26]

Celebrants of the new system used metaphors of nature to describe the system's birth. The *Raleigh News-Observer*, which later became a steadfast critic of the Southern, lauded the creation of the corporation and hoped it would cause a "notable reawakening of industrial enterprise throughout the South." As the *Observer* noted, "a reconstruction of nature supplies life and new growth in place of death and decay."[27] In the annual report announcing the road's surrender to the Richmond Terminal, the board of the Central of Georgia argued, "It has become inevitable, that consolidation of many of the most important Southern roads into large systems and trunk lines, shall take place." The board concluded that it would opt to "be in the consolidation rather than out of it."[28]

The influential booster publication the *Manufacturers' Record* was full of effusive praise for the new system that spoke to how the company represented an alliance between northern capital and southern railroads. The entrance of Morgan into southern railroading represented "the greatest combination of financial and railroad power and constructive, rather than destructive influences in the financial world," argued one editorial. The Vanderbilts "have placed their faith and money in the South," which would lead to "the investment of many millions by others who follow their lead."[29] London investors loved buying Southern Railway stock, noted one man, and another declared that the company gave "evidence to the outside world of a faith in the future of the South by the stronger financial interests in this and other countries." As a president of an Atlanta bank concluded, "no other recent event in this section" held this much importance.[30]

The company fully embraced this role as New South talisman. An interview with the company's vice president, A. B. Andrews, in February 1895 hit all the usual notes seen in booster rhetoric. He touted the South's resources, low prices for land, and favorable laws for business, and he invited outside investment.[31] The road also began producing yearly publications like *The Southland* in 1898, which provided extensive information about the resources and major industries of each southern state, as well as a discussion of the various ways in which the Southern Railway was aiding the project of regional industrial growth. As *The Southland* crowed in its opening pages, the "advance of the Empire of the South has been one of the more noteworthy movements in the industrial and commercial history of the world," and a comparison of the South with other sections of the nation "brings out with startling clearness and in incontrovertible figures the majesty and rapidity of its unparalleled progress."[32] These publications represented nothing less than a full-hearted embrace of the New South mythology first crafted by boosters in the 1880s, and they placed the Southern Railway at the heart of the project of regional redemption.

But while the Southern's backers saw the road as the South's economic savior, and the natural result of reckless railroad construction, plenty of southerners contested the rise of this new corporate monstrosity, especially as the new company began to grow. The southern railroad landscape was full of insolvent roads, as eighteen other southern railroads unrelated to the Richmond Terminal system also fell into receivership in the 1890s.[33] So the well-funded Southern had ample opportunity to expand and grow. Existing railroad companies quickly realized the threat the new company would pose to their business. In a special report to the L&N's president, Milton Smith warned management that the L&N could expect "merciless competition" from the new system, which was poised to snatch up many of the orphaned southern roads that lingered in receivership.[34] But as the new company began to expand its territory through acquisitions, more and more communities fell under its influence. As opposed to the institutional murkiness of previous conglomerates like the Richmond Terminal, a collection of lines so confusing that even investors had trouble understanding, or the Southern Railway Security Company, an ephemeral holding company that lasted only a few years, the Southern Railway constituted a clear target for foes of railroad corporations (figure 7). The Southern Railway put a tangible face on railroad consolidation in the South, and it gave clear evidence of the increasing power of transportation monopolies and the control of the South's roads by Wall Street bankers. The fact that this face was cloaked in a message of southern salvation mattered little to the road's foes.

THE CONFLICTING PUBLIC images of the Southern Railway—regional savior and grasping octopus—clashed first in Samuel Spencer's home state of Georgia, which by 1895 boasted over 5,000 miles of railroad, the largest network in the South. The Southern's efforts to expand had to overcome legal barriers in Georgia, specifically the state's 1877 constitution, which included an antimonopoly clause that barred the general assembly from authorizing any purchase of shares or stock that would "lessen competition in their respective businesses or to encourage monopoly."[35] There was even precedent for use of this clause when it came to railroad consolidation. When the Richmond Terminal's organizers secured a lease of the Central of Georgia, they had to take complicated steps to skirt the constitution. The Richmond Terminal leased the Central to the Georgia Pacific, which in turn was leased to the R&D, which itself was directly owned by the Richmond Terminal

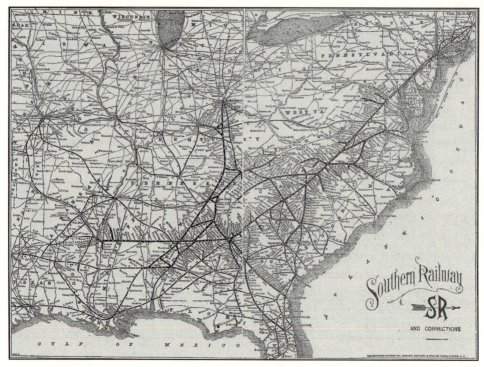

FIGURE 7 The Southern Railway system in 1895. When the company was born in 1894 it was the largest railroad in the South, and the system quickly reached monopoly status in North Carolina and Georgia.

holding company.[36] These maneuvers were not enough to stave off an 1892 lawsuit, which invoked the antimonopoly clause and successfully blocked the outside ownership of the Central of Georgia Railroad for a short period of time.[37]

In 1895, the Southern began a buying spree in Georgia that started small, with the acquisition of the insolvent Atlanta & Florida Railroad (A&F), a line extending south of Atlanta that despite its ambitious name actually terminated in Fort Valley, nowhere near Florida. When the L&N president and Samuel Spencer met in Kennesaw, Georgia, on October 28, 1894, to discuss the status of the indebted roads in their territory, both had agreed to let the A&F "eke out a miserable existence." But on June 22 1895, the Southern acquired control of this line for $275,000.[38] Along the line of the purchased road, the *Houston County Home Journal* rued the fact that Southern ownership spelled the end of the town's plan to extend the line, noting, "There is little hope that the road will be extended south of Fort Valley."[39] The *Tifton*

Gazette noted that "the Southern Railway has gobbled up the Atlanta and Florida, and some of the exchanges fear that it may get a corner on the Atlantic Ocean. If that could be accomplished the editors might then travel on a pass to Europe."[40] But jokes about the purchase obscured an important truth about this acquisition, that even a seemingly insignificant purchase of a small unprofitable road like the A&F had an impact on competition. After the road was "gobbled," an L&N traffic agent in Atlanta asked officials with the A&F to furnish them some cars to ship melons, but the road responded that this lenient arrangement of car-sharing was only viable "until the Southern Railway gobbled them." Melon shippers along the territory of the purchased line now had no choice but to use Southern Railway cars.[41]

When the Southern bought another small and insolvent line, the Georgia Midland, in 1896, the *Atlanta Constitution* joked, "There was not any great amount of formality about the matter, as to take possession of a railroad is not entirely a new experience with the Southern."[42] From the perspective of Atlantans, this consolidation brought benefits only to communities along this line. When the first train went down this line, it carried a "big bundle of *Constitutions*" and at "all points good crowds were out to meet this train." In Griffin, people had previously waited until 10 A.M. to get their papers, and now they could have it "with their rolls and coffee." In this day, argued the paper, "time is everything, and if a man were in the midst of an African desert and could get his morning papers on time he would be almost as well up as if he were in the heart of a city." The *Constitution* argued consolidation was a boon to hinterland residents, but for some, especially merchants in Griffin, the monopoly control of the Southern was a mighty steep price to pay for faster *Constitutions*.[43] Merchants in Griffin later challenged the rates their Southern Railway charged. In April 1897, M. H. Brewer, a wholesale grain merchant in Griffin, presented a case to the Georgia Railroad Commission and argued that since the "expenses of the operation of the various railroad lines in this state have been largely reduced by consolidation," the commission should reduce freight rates in the state by a third. His petition continued to blame excessive "capitalization and bonded indebtedness" of the Southern for high rates.[44] At one point Brewer even threatened that "every station between Atlanta and Macon on the Central and every one between Atlanta and Columbus" would file bills against the Southern.[45] Brewer's petition tapped into a powerful argument that resonated across Georgia and the South at large: where were the benefits of consolidation in towns like Griffin?

The purchase of these small roads caused minor controversies, but the Southern's acquisition of the Macon-based Georgia Southern & Florida touched off a full-blown crisis for the conglomerate. After the GS&F tumbled into debt in 1891, it was subsequently managed by W. B. Sparks, one of its original planners, as a receiver. The road's ultimate fate awaited the conclusion of various legal battles among bondholders, but by 1895, these battles began to wind down and rumors swirled as to who would purchase the road, which despite its financial troubles still tapped a productive territory. A paper in Tifton floated the Plant System, the Seaboard Air Line, a committee of bondholders, and a "syndicate of workingmen" as potential suitors.[46] But unbeknownst to these observers, the Southern had been slowly purchasing bonds of the road, and on June 6, 1895, the Southern officially announced that it had purchased a majority of the GS&F's bonds. Sparks himself was surprised, noting that he had assumed H. B. Plant, head of a system that formed a regional rival to the Southern, would buy the road. From the start, this purchase raised red flags with regard to its constitutionality. Even the railroad-friendly *Macon Telegraph* warned of a legal fight and noted, "In the opinion of Macon railroad men, the Southern and Georgia Southern roads have been operating as competing lines, and therefore one cannot be purchased by the other."[47] To work around legal barriers and calm public anger, Spencer directed a mapmaker to not show the GS&F like the system's other recently acquired roads, and he sent his vice president, A. B. Andrews, to Macon to counteract negative sentiment from employees during what he called the "general gobbling up process." In light of the public hostility, Spencer concluded, "The Southern Railway cannot operate GSF as part of its system. It must be operated independently under its own board of directors and officers and the Southern Railway will simply be a majority stock holder."[48]

From the start W. B. Sparks led the campaign against the Southern in Macon. The original mastermind behind the project, he had lost his position in a bitter struggle after the Southern took indirect control of the GS&F. A new board planted with Southern Railway men officially kicked him out of his position in favor of William Shaw, a new vice president shipped in from Baltimore, and later elected Samuel Spencer as president, a distinction Spencer would hold every year until his death.[49] In letters, Spencer privately argued against keeping on Sparks, noting he would be against having Sparks on the payroll due to his litigation with the company, his botched management of a model farm, and his ties to the bankrupt Macon & Birmingham railroad project.[50] But whatever the reason for the dismissal, this would not be the last they heard of the disgruntled former receiver.

Sparks's crusade against the Southern could be dismissed as mere sour grapes were it not for the fact that his arguments tapped into sentiments that were common in Macon. Macon boosters had desperately built railroads like the GS&F in the 1880s in an attempt to spur competition, bring down freight rates, and induce economic growth. But by 1895, Macon was clearly losing its struggle for primacy to Atlanta, and the Southern's moves in the city threatened to further stifle growth. Spencer corresponded with N. E. Harris, the system's division counsel in Macon, as his plans took shape, asking him to keep him informed of potential challenges, and to "shape the newspapers of Macon in such way as to indicate the advantages" of Southern Railway control.[51] Harris was at first dismissive of the gathering opposition to the road's control of the GS&F. In a June 10 letter, he attributed the unrest to two sources: officers of the GS&F anxious to maintain their positions with the line, and bondholders who had not yet sold their bonds.[52] However, in a second letter, Harris agreed with Spencer's plan to operate the road independently. Many citizens had feared "shops, etc would be moved away from the city at once and the large retinue of employees and officers would be turned off and their livelihood stopped without notice."[53] Farther down the line in Tifton, the local paper noted how employees of the GS&F had "visions of a general re-organization and the instatement of new men in all the important places."[54]

Reshuffling the company's attorneys also provoked anger from prominent Macon citizens like lawyer Joseph Hall, who served as general counsel for the GS&F. For small-town lawyers like Hall, railroad business was typically the most lucrative field of work available, but unfortunately for Hall, the new management began to shove him out the door after the purchase of the GS&F. First the Southern lowered his salary to $4,000, and then an attorney with the Southern directly informed him his services were no longer needed.[55] Hall pointed out that his firm represented the road through its troubled period of receivership, when the line faced "suits for very large amounts for personal injuries, for lost freight, for rights of way, for damages to property."[56] Hall sought to use his past loyalty and service as an argument for keeping his job, but from the perspective of the Southern system, Hall's past service with the GS&F may have been precisely the reason why he was let go. A man with such intimate knowledge of the predecessor company's dealings could form a serious impediment to the new leadership. Later Hall would frame his conversion from railroad lawyer to antirailroad agitator in more moral terms, noting in 1901 that rather than being fired, he had "abandoned the representation of the railroad co because no honest man could do much work as was required by railroad companies."[57]

And in a final testament to the widespread hostility to the purchase of the GS&F, the local business community also got involved in the opposition to the Southern. The chairman of the transportation committee of the Macon Chamber of Commerce wrote to Spencer and rued how "the consolidation of your company and its control of the traffic of the principal lines entering and centering in Macon is viewed with some degree of apprehension by some of our people." He hoped the Southern Railway would "recognize the importance of Macon as a distributing center for your lines, and that you will see that in building up its interests." And he wished that the reorganization would do little to disturb local employees, as some of Macon's "best and most conservative citizens" were railroad employees.[58]

Spencer responded in a lengthy letter that resonated across the country, as it spoke to both local and national concerns over railroad consolidation. He started with a discussion of Macon's concerns, noting that the Southern would operate the Central of Georgia independently, and claiming the road did not fully own the GS&F. But he quickly pivoted to a discussion of the larger issue at play, namely, the rapid consolidation of southern railroad companies. The trend toward large systems was "the legitimate and inevitable result of reckless and speculative construction of needless railroads throughout the South and the hopeless struggles to sustain them when built." After the "widespread ruin and bankruptcy" that befell the South's railroads in the aftermath of the Panic of 1893, only two options remained: to consolidate these roads or let them "starve separately." On their own, the destitute lines would degenerate below reasonable standards of service.[59]

Spencer continued his argument with a pivot to the broader issue of the size of railroad companies. He noted that unlike an individual, a railroad "is not permitted to die," so "the inevitable end for them" was to be "attached to some larger system and be nursed and supported in return for the small traffic they can contribute."[60] Large, rationally managed companies were the only natural result of the churn of capitalist competition. The letter was a rare moment of ideological clarity from a man whose political opinions often took a backseat to the more mundane operations of a railroad corporation, and it struck like a lightning bolt. Letters of support poured in not just from Macon, where a chamber of commerce member lauded the "clean cut, strong and manly document," but also from other railroad presidents across the country facing similar issues. The *Railway Gazette* printed the letter in full, and Spencer later directed a subordinate to send copies to every single member of the Georgia legislature.[61]

The clash in Macon clearly spoke to a larger issue in both the South and the rest of the nation at this hinge point between two drastically divergent visions of political economy. Spencer advocated for the big-picture view of the large railroad systems, which in his eyes would deliver growth for all. Improving the system, even if this meant near-monopoly power for the rising conglomerates, was the only way to fix indebted railroads and continue the New South railroad revival. Businessmen in Macon and other towns who found themselves unexpectedly under the Southern Railway umbrella clung to an older vision of what a railroad company, and the forces of capitalism, could do for their communities. A railroad built and funded by a community should be devoted first and foremost to building up that town's business and industry, by increasing competition and lowering rates. As lines like the GS&F, which was planned by local elites and largely funded with local backing, were gobbled up by the South, residents in these towns felt like their economic futures were being torn away by the consolidation process.

SPENCER'S LETTER MAY HAVE swayed some skeptics in Macon, but the Southern's complicated acquisition of the Central of Georgia only added to pressure to break up the company. The Central, based in Savannah, was an old system originally built before the Civil War by the state, and the road held great sentimental significance for Georgians. In an 1894 speech in Atlanta, Tom Watson called the line "the great Central Railroad—the pride of Georgia—built with Georgia courage, with Georgia labor, with Georgia capital."[62] In fall of 1895, at the same time the Southern was reorganizing the leadership of the GS&F, the system also took steps to exert control over the reorganized shell of the Central of Georgia. As a key element of the Richmond Terminal, the final piece of Samuel Spencer's Georgia rail empire would be the trickiest to attain. The Southern took control of this road by purchasing it at a foreclosure sale, but as an attorney with the road later admitted, the property was not directly delivered to the company, the reason being "the law of Georgia with respect to competition." Instead the Richmond Terminal Organization Committee, a body temporarily organized to facilitate the complex reorganization and that remained intact, took the majority of stock, a technical difference that ensured protection from Georgia's anticompetition clause.[63] But behind these cloaking maneuvers, it seemed clear to observers in Georgia that the Southern was behind these ownership changes. On October 30, Samuel Spencer himself showed up in Savannah to represent the Southern during the official transfer from the old receivers to its new owners. At a dinner the next day, the Central's officials and various Savannah businessmen toasted the new ownership and Spencer attempted to assuage the fears of Savannah residents. He claimed that "the Central shall be operated in its own interests" and noted that "the Southern does not reach Savannah, but the Central does and the Central is as free now as it ever was to build up your city."[64]

The Georgia Railroad Commission did not agree with this assessment, and it saw the Central's purchase as proof that the Southern had acquired an effective monopoly over Georgia's railroads. Although the commission was closely monitoring the Southern's actions, its powers to act were quite limited. The 1895 annual report described the Southern's buying spree, detailed the purchase of the A&F and the GS&F roads, and noted that it "is understood that the Southern Railway company is the real owner of all the stock of the Central Railway and Banking Company." The report was explicit in noting the "tendency towards consolidation" in both Georgia and the United States at large, but could only recommend legislation, as the body had no jurisdiction to do so.[65] In 1896 the commission noted that with all these direct and indirect purchases, "it makes the mileage of said Southern Railway system in Georgia, with its allied lines, 2,135.48 miles." The Plant System, the next largest competitor for the Southern, had only 616.25 miles. The state had a total of 5,291.41 miles at this point, so by 1896 the Southern had control of over 40 percent of the state's rail mileage.[66]

To prosecute this case against the Southern, the commission did its best to untangle the webs controlling the state's roads, but it struggled to unmask the real owner of Georgia's properties to the public. The commission needed to decide whether to treat these roads as independent or as part of a system in order to exercise its most important power, to set freight rates. Proof that the Central and GS&F were owned by the Southern would allow the commission to indict the system as monopolistic and lower freight rates throughout the state. The *Savannah Morning News* noted this would be a "full showdown by the Central for the purpose of ascertaining whether or not it is owned or controlled by the Southern Railway Company."[67] In a series of hearings held in the summer of 1896, officials with the two roads were intransigent, even outright hostile, to the commission's inquiries. H. M. Comer, the president of the Central, told a reporter in April, "The road's there, and we're running it. Isn't that enough?" and the reporter noted, "The fact that the two lines are managed by different directories is the technical point that is giving the railroad commissioners some trouble."[68] By July, the commission still could not figure out who owned the Central of Georgia. An official with the Central claimed the stock was owned by "Messrs. Thomas and Ryan, who do not constitute the Southern Railway Company," and the lawyer representing the GS&F argued that the stock of that road was held by "Parsons & Edwards of Boston." No one seemed to actually know who these men were, or what interest they represented, and the commission wondered why these men were not the ones testifying before the body.[69]

Finally, in October 1896, the commission got Samuel Spencer himself to testify before the commission. The *Savannah Morning News* summarized these confusing findings by simply stating, "The Southern Railway owns the Central of Georgia, and then again it does not own it" and arguing that the actual relationship between the Southern and the Central was "Now you see it—now you don't."[70] In the end, the commission could not figure out who controlled these lines, so the body had to alter its own rules in order to exert its rate-setting powers over the Southern. Instead of requiring explicit control of the roads at stake, the new rule treated connecting roads under direct *or* indirect control by another company as the same entity for the purposes of calculating the tariff. Subsequently, the GS&F was moved from the higher-class No. 6 to the lower-class No. 4 rates that the body applied to the rest of the Southern.[71] Later William Shaw wrote to Spencer to complain that the change of class cost the company about $12,000 a year.[72] Shaw griped about the commission's investigations to Spencer in private, writing, "I have become impressed with the strong undertone of continued bad feeling in this state towards the railroads," and lamented the body's continued efforts to lower rates.[73] In the end, the Central would retain independence in name—indeed, the Southern would not officially take possession of the Central until 1963.[74] Yet, the entire episode pointed to a problem typical among regulatory bodies that hoped to sort out railroad purchases: consolidation was a deliberately complicated process, so much that for a few years, Georgians had no idea who actually controlled their most cherished state-funded project.

Beyond rate-setting, the commission did not have any other powers to act against the Southern. The commission's 1896 report stated, "The declared policy of the state is against consolidation and combinations which promote monopoly and stifle competition," and it directed the legislature to note "the steady progress and growth of these combinations in the state."[75] The ineffectual commission's warning to lawmakers meant the Georgia statehouse would likely be the next venue for battles over consolidation. In the fall of 1895, an employee with the Southern's law department wrote to A. B. Andrews that he "learned today that an organized effort will be made at the approaching session of the legislature to attack the Southern's control of the Central and GSF railways."[76] On November 22, the first antirailroad legislation of the session appeared from a Mr. Johnson from Hall County, who presented a bill that referred to the recent commission report and "to the tendency of the railroads to consolidate, and expresses doubt as to the effect of this tendency upon the interests of the public." Johnson wanted the attorney general to investigate matters, but the reporter described the prospects of this bill passing through the assembly as "doubtful."[77]

Political support for measures like this came largely from the Georgia Populist Party, which reached its apex at about the same time as the consolidation of the Southern. Populists articulated a vision of political economy of smaller and farmer-owned cooperatives and corporations that aligned with the locally oriented goals of Macon businessmen. Populists already upset about concentrations of power and wealth in Wall Street were understandably aggrieved about the rapid rise of a J. P. Morgan–backed corporate behemoth in the South. Georgia Populist Tom Watson's *People's Party Paper* found in the Southern a ready foil for his editorial rage. In response to the Southern's buying spree, Watson argued, "The Southern Railway system has bought all the competing lines in Georgia, with three exceptions and is today the most daring and conspicuous criminal in Georgia." However, "the newspapers are muzzled, the Democratic leaders subsidized, the Populist leaders powerless and the public helpless." Watson rued how "Governor Atkinson, with all his will power and pluck, does not dare to raise his finger against the Democratic millionaires who are wiping their feet upon the fundamental laws of the state."[78]

But the actual impact of Watson's rage and the Populist critique of the Southern was blunted by the fact that the Southern was hard at work filling the 1894 legislature with friends and allies. In March 1894, before the Southern even legally existed, A. B. Andrews furnished Spencer with a list of reliable attorneys with railroad experience in Atlanta who should be retained by the new corporation and who could potentially serve the company as allies in Georgia's legislature.[79] The goal was, in the words of H. M. Comer, to secure "in the next Legislature a sufficient number of votes to at least modify the objectionable railroads laws."[80] The main target of the Southern's backers was a law from the 1892 session that allowed railroads to consolidate but gave the caveat that "no railroad shall purchase a competing line of railroad or enter into any contract with a competing line of railroad calculated to defeat or lessen competition in this State."[81] The Southern's shadowy campaign to control the legislature in 1894 was aided by the distractions of an unusually contentious gubernatorial campaign. Much of the attention in Georgia politics was focused on a hotly contested gubernatorial race between George Atkinson, a younger reform-minded Democratic politician, and Clement Evans, a Civil War veteran allied with the older Bourbon faction of the party. The Southern's allies noticed this conflict, and hoped to use it to their advantage. As W. A. Henderson argued that this race and the election of two senators "swallow up all issues" in the state, which would "keep any issue concerning our interests in the background."[82] H. M. Comer argued in a letter that "the more important matter for us is to control the legislature," as domination of the legislature would in essence give the railroads control of the governor, and Comer advocated a "quiet canvass" to elect a favorable legislature as opposed to a risky and open play for one of the governor candidates.[83]

It was up to W. A. Henderson to undertake this "quiet canvass" in the spring of 1894, when he traveled around the state to points along the Southern. In his report to Spencer he wrote, "Not a soul knows the real object of my visit." He had "tangible business at every point" and brought up railroad matters "quite casually." In his report he laid out each district and its candidates, noting which ones would be friendly to the company and which would be their foes. Many of the Southern's preferred candidates were railroad lawyers, already on the payroll of the road. In Macon, the road backed their local counsel N. E. Harris for Senate, as he "would be of infinite service" to the railroads in that body.[84] Out in the hustings, the 1894 campaign was one of the most violent Georgia had seen. With the Populist Party threatening to break Democratic control of the state, the race was characterized by race-baiting, violence, voter intimidation, and outright fraud. Tom Watson lost his congressional seat in a race marked with irregularities and then launched a vigorous challenge to contest the results. In the race for governor, Populists were incredulous that their candidate James K. Hines had lost to Atkinson. The election of 1894 has thus understandably received attention from historians of Populism, as a high water mark when the Populist protagonists were beaten back by the race card, or as a missed opportunity for a third-party victory. But an overlooked facet of this contest is that it also helped fill the legislature with a slate of pro-railroad men, like N. E. Harris, who won his seat in Macon.[85] At the same time that violent disruptions, nighttime raids, and political appeals to white supremacy dented Populist support, behind-the-scenes payments and machinations from the Southern Railway helped defeat antirailroad candidates and secure a friendly legislature for the corporation, just before a major move into Georgia.

The Populists who did make it into the legislature lacked the clout to impact the legislative agenda during the Southern's period of growth and consolidation. At its high point in 1894, the Georgia Populist Party controlled only 21 percent of the seats in the General Assembly, and these members hardly made any challenges to the state's economic order. Mell Branch, one legislator, issued a number of resolutions demanding that the governor enforce state laws against railroad monopolies, but otherwise, the crest of Populist power in the state saw little action on monopolies in the legislature. From their high point in 1894, the Georgia Populist Party collapsed quickly. The rapid downfall was aided by the national defeat of William Jennings Bryan's fusion campaign, and the ultimate death knell was a futile attempt to fuse with Republicans in an 1898 state election.[86] The Southern's foes found the road an implacable enemy in the legislature. After an antirailroad bill was defeated in 1895, the legislator who introduced it complained, "He had fifteen of the committee pledged to him, but when he left the room for two minutes, the octopus swallowed seven of them."[87]

The metaphor of the railroad as a grasping octopus swallowing all in its path was common in the West, where the Southern Pacific seemed to control all aspects of life, but now the octopus had come to Georgia's legislature in the shape of the Southern Railway. Indeed a survey of the actual laws passed by the Georgia legislature between 1894 and 1896, the years of the Southern's "gobbling," demonstrates the lack of action in the legislature. An 1894 act allowed railroads to run cars with perishable goods on Sundays, and one clarified the process of fixing liens on railroads.[88] The 1895 session contained few laws relating to railroads, the only notable act being one that defined the rights of purchasers of railroads, an act extremely favorable to the Southern.[89] The only adverse legislation coming out of the 1896 session was a law that let the Railroad Commission compel testimony and one that held receivers liable for damages caused by the operation of their roads.[90]

With a pro-railroad legislature and governor in place, it is no surprise that Sparks's 1897 petition, which called for the Atkinson to place the company in a receivership, ultimately did not succeed. Spencer wrote to a friend that while the "suit may annoy," it was not dangerous, and the signers were merely "malcontents" who lost positions with the GS&F during consolidation.[91] The *Savannah Morning News* agreed that the whole scheme was nothing more than a ploy on the part of Sparks to become receiver of the Southern.[92] But Sparks's effort clearly tapped into larger currents of discontent with the company. N. E. Harris, the Southern's head lawyer in Macon, later recalled that the suit had "the best local attorneys that the city afforded" and "some of the best citizens in the town for complainants."[93] The *Telegraph*, the newspaper in Macon adamantly opposed to this effort, printed a series of interviews with prominent businessmen in the city. A cotton merchant noted that the present rate discrimination kept Macon's merchants from expanding their trade much beyond the city, and that many towns that should have been within Macon's territory were carving out niches of their own. A grocer who was "totally opposed to monopolies" agreed that Macon was losing trade to other Georgia towns, and another businessman admitted that while he did not know who owned the roads in the city, he thought it would be "ill-advised" and a "positive disaster" to Macon's business interests to put the Southern in the hands of a receiver.[94] Even the pro-railroad *Savannah Morning News* admitted that in the early days, Georgia's roads were "controlled by the citizens of the state, and their managers were within reach of home public sentiment," but now "the people of Georgia are no longer the owners of the railroads" and the roads were now "soulless corporations" whose owners had no local or state interests.[95]

The additional power of the petition can be seen in how, for a brief period of time, it made railroad consolidation, or the "railroad question," a hotly debated topic on the pages of Georgia's newspapers. Here the Southern also had well-placed friends. At the state's most influential paper, the *Atlanta Constitution*, the roads had essentially what amounted to a paid employee. A letter to Spencer revealed that the Southern paid Frank Weldon $150 a month to write articles in the *Constitution* that "will tend to give the public in Georgia a better understanding of such matters and thereby create a more kindly feeling towards corporations."[96] The antirailroad *Macon News* also attacked the *Savannah Morning News*, noting "the interests of its owner are so identified with those of the Southern railway consolidators that it will even stultify itself in order to aid in carrying out the scheme."[97] A paper in one of Macon's commercial rivals, Hawkinsville, noted in October how "the *Macon Telegraph*, had to consistently deny that it was directly owned by the Southern."[98] Even though the Southern itself may not have controlled the *Telegraph*, a good friend of the railroads clearly did. N. E. Harris later wrote that Major J. F. Hanson, the paper's owner, became owner "through his connection with the railroads," specifically H. M. Comer of the Central. Later Harris would use his influence with Spencer to get Hanson appointed as chairman of the board of the Central.[99] Georgia newspapers had to choose a side between the pro-railroad and antirailroad camps in this dispute, but the money and power in this fight were largely on the side of the Southern.

The Sparks petition was eventually withdrawn after its supporters realized Governor Atkinson would not act on it and it was doomed to fail.[100] Though he celebrated the petition's failure, N. E. Harris, the Southern's division counsel in Macon, warned the road's officials that they needed "a little more discretion about passes and the courtesies of the road here," as "every blunder in any railway in this city is charged to us." Harris also noted how Sparks bitterly complained to him that the people of Macon were "in love with their chains."[101] From there the issue moved into the courts, where H. M. Comer talked to Judge Speer and reported that though there is no ground to fear any action from this judge, "there are some very bitter people in Macon."[102] It is no surprise that the corporation had little to fear from Judge Speer. When the Southern Railway was formed in 1894, Speer wrote to Spencer to assure him of his support, noting that while he had been a judge for nine years, he did "not recall a single instance in my court where there has been a failure to protect the rights of northern or non-resident investors."[103] In the end, a judge dismissed the remnants of the case in 1901, and the *Constitution* remarked on the death of litigation which "at one time threatened to prove one of the most sensational cases of railway litigation known to the courts."[104] Georgia's efforts to splinter the Southern octopus reached their unceremonious conclusion with this court case. But despite its failure, the Sparks petition and subsequent debate gave voice, however muffled by the railroad-friendly press, to an alternate vision of corporate consolidation in Georgia and a contrary view of what the Southern represented.

THESE EFFORTS IN GEORGIA moved in tandem with a vigorous attempt to break the Southern Railway's main line in North Carolina. The North Carolina Railroad, which stretched from Goldsboro to Charlotte through the middle of the state, was, like the Central of Georgia, an antebellum state project that held sentimental value to many North Carolinians. The road was first linked into a larger southern system during the Civil War, when the Confederate government connected it to the R&D system. These ties continued after the war, and in 1871 the R&D leased the road for thirty years to solidify the system's corridor between Atlanta and Richmond. In 1895, the newly created Southern Railway inherited this lease from the R&D, and officials quickly moved to shore up control of the line. The Southern hoped to build up Norfolk as a port and wanted to be sure it could rely on the NC RR corridor before making heavy investments there.[105] After brief negotiations, North Carolina's governor, Elias Carr, offered the road a ninety-nine-year lease, which went into effect August 16, 1895. For the directors of the NC RR, the lease seemed like an obvious response to the South's competitive railroad climate, and their arguments typically focused on the benefits of systemization. In the lease document they argued, "In this day of railroad systems, an independent railroad (no longer than ours) running between two interior towns cannot exist, if those who control the railroad that has occupied its territory, want it."[106] A paper in Greensboro, a town along the line, agreed that "when this line is transformed into the great artery through which must pass the bulk of the products of the great South and West," the wisdom of the lease would make sense.[107] In case these positive benefits were not enough, the Southern also wielded a big stick in negotiations by threatening to build a parallel line from Mocksville to Mooresville that would render the NC RR irrelevant if the lease was not made.[108]

While the lease seemed to make sense from an economic standpoint in the environment of rapid consolidation, opposition began to build as soon as the deal was signed. The state's Populist Party, a group naturally predisposed to loathe large corporate combinations, immediately came out against the lease. In Marion Butler's *Caucasian*, an editorialist wrote, "Thunderous disapproval is ringing from the mountains to the sea" of the "secret ninety-nine-year deal." The writer suggested that the Southern wanted to secure a deal before "great political changes" in the next year would elect a new legislature more hostile to railroads.[109] A July 1896 letter to the *Caucasian* expressed similar outrage that roads built by North Carolinians should fall to outside control and proclaimed that if the ninety-nine-year lease could stand, "it is but a question of time when the Southern Railway will control all the railroads in North Carolina."[110] For Populists the secrecy and corruption of the lease seemed to embody everything wrong with the way railroads and corporate power operated.

Populists were expected foes of this consolidation, but momentum against the lease also came from unexpected sources. David Schenck, a former employee of the Southern's predecessor, the R&D system, blended personal grievances with systemic critiques when he spearheaded a campaign against the Southern's lease. Schenck had made a remarkably adept journey through many of the profitable enterprises the late-nineteenth-century South had to offer. During the Civil War, he got a plum commission as a sequestration receiver, which he used to punish suspected Unionists and greatly enrich his personal finances.[111] In 1882, Schenck first signed on as a lawyer with the R&D, an appointment that was both more lucrative and more secure than his former politicized spot in the state judiciary. Though he welcomed this work at first, he had many personal disagreements with the railroad's management, and slowly became more disillusioned with the railroad's machinations.[112] We have seen how in the aftermath of the Bostian Bridge train wreck, Schenck refused to sign petitions removing the damage lawsuits to Charlotte because in his words, they "contained falsehoods."[113]

Perhaps because of Schenck's age or failure to follow the company line, Leslie Ryan, assistant counsel for the Southern, informed Schenck in May 1895 that he would be fired "under the plan of reorganization of the legal department."[114] A look at Schenck's diary entries from previous years revealed a few reasons why the Southern Railway may have shoved the lawyer out the door. In 1893 he noted that while he was getting a salary of $2,500 from the railroad, the job had "not required scarcely any work" and he was spending half his time establishing a battlefield park at the site of the Battle of Guilford Court House in Greensboro.[115] From the perspective of the Southern Railway, Schenck was an aging and increasingly unreliable employee, and the corporate reorganization seemed like a good excuse to quickly cut ties with him. A personal feud with the Southern's vice president, A. B. Andrews, may also have contributed to Schenck's falling out with the company. As the railroad tried to fire Schenck, he sent a letter to Andrews that threatened to expose various misdeeds of the R&D if he was not retained. Spencer directed a subordinate to save this incendiary letter in case it was someday necessary to publish it and publicly expose Schenck.[116] Schenck blamed Andrews personally for his firing in a later letter to Southern officials, accusing him of "maligning me secretly to the officials of the road while professing friendship for me." As Schenck lamented, "it is a great misfortune that railroad officials lose conscience and humanity in proportion to their rise and success in corporate life."[117]

Whatever the root cause of Schenck's disgruntlement, in late 1895, he ripped into the Southern in a series of letters printed in the *Caucasian*. Though his grievances may have been personal, he framed the attack on the Southern in the broader language of antimonopolism. He assailed the Southern as a "foreign corporation," chartered in Virginia, and with no right to acquire a line in North Carolina. Schenck pushed the legislature to pass an act that would keep the Southern from removing any legal challenges to federal court, and suggested giving more power to state railroad commissioners. The plan of the Southern was to "swallow up all smaller roads, and where that job is too large, to destroy them by unfair competition."[118] In another letter Schenck attacked the "methods of corporations," who always have men to "do their dirty work," and the salaried officials "whose greed for gain sears their consciences and destroys their power to discriminate between right and wrong." He warned that the Southern was "stretching out its octopus hands to gather in the Cape Fear and Yadkin Valley Railroad—about the only distinctly North Carolina railroad remaining out of their grasp." He also lauded the efforts of the Railroad Commission to improve safety on the Western

North Carolina Railroad. Though the R&D had made the road "the dumping ground for all the old worn out rails in their system," a fact tragically seen in the Bostian Bridge wreck, the commission's mandates had rendered the Western North Carolina a "fine, safe road." So for Schenck, his experience working for the R&D—in personal dealings with executives, and in dealing with a horrific train wreck—meshed with a systemic critique of the Southern's corporate power. Schenck also kept up private correspondence with Populist leader Marion Butler as his attacks continued in public. He wrote to Butler that his heart ached to "think of the slavery that awaits our children" who would become "hewers of wood and drawers of water for millionaires," and he expressed outrage at the "absolute control the Southern RR" exercised over the state.[119] Schenck spent much of his time in 1896 preparing anti-railroad bills for Butler's consideration, and he hoped that a platform "declaring for corporation reform" would be a "talking plank with the common people."[120]

Along with the cooperation between Schenck and Butler, the issue also attracted attention from the other side of the political spectrum. In 1895, Josephus Daniels was a newspaperman on the rise in North Carolina Democratic politics. After Daniels took control of the *Raleigh News-Observer* in 1894, the paper quickly became one of the most influential Democratic papers in the state. The party was in some disarray in the mid-1890s, and Daniels took charge of a reform-minded group of Democrats that would eventually seize control from the party's old Bourbon faction. In the minds of Daniels and other Democrats, Bourbons like Governor Carr were in the pocket of the railroads. Daniels's hatred of the Southern was also partly motivated by the fact that the Southern was paying off the editor of his paper's main competitor, the *Raleigh Times*.[121] The *News-Observer* attacked the lease as "a crime of a century" and a "blunder without excuse" when it was made. The paper agreed with the governor's attack on the lease as "a rental for so long a term is unwise," and it should not have been hastily made six years before the old lease expired. Why not wait another six years, and then lease the road to the highest bidder, the paper asked?[122] As the *Statesville Landmark* noted, "nearly all the newspapers of the State opposed the lease" when it was made, "especially for so long a term of years and for such a slight advance over" the earlier rate.[123]

The other attack from the *Observer* centered on the undemocratic way the lease was negotiated and settled in closed-door meetings between the state railroad's board of directors and Southern Railway leadership. Before the lease was made, the paper had warned that the railroad's directors would make a blunder if they made a new lease "without first submitting it to the representatives of the people." As the *Observer* argued, "The road belongs to the State, and the tax-payers, who built the road, had a right to be permitted to pass upon the question." And just like the Populists and Schenck, many Democrats saw grand conspiracies behind the Southern's actions. A Morganton paper fretted that "everything now points to the consolidation of the ownership and control of the railroad lines of the South in the hands of a New York syndicate that is the representative of the Rothschilds in America," and in these dire times "it will be of the greatest importance to North Carolina to own and operate her own line of railroad from the mountains to the sea."[124]

The unusual nature of North Carolina's electoral politics, namely, the strength of opposition parties—both Populist and Republican—and the divisions among Democrats ensured that these various critiques of the lease could find more of a political platform than they did in Georgia. North Carolina Republicans attracted votes both from African American voters, who continued to vote in large numbers in North Carolina through the 1890s, and from white Republicans in mountain counties. Similarly, the state's Populist movement, buoyed first by leaders like Leonidas Polk and later Marion Butler, was one of the stronger third-party insurgencies in the South. Though on a national level Democrats and Populists fused in 1896 to present a united front on the issue of coining silver, North Carolina's Populists allied with Republicans to challenge the Democratic status quo. This was a risky choice for the Populists. As Schenck warned Marion Butler in a letter, fusing with Republicans would threaten to bring back the "horrors of Reconstruction," which to Schenck meant African American office holding and political power, but he saw the fusion as necessary as a way to "redeem our state from corporations whose insidious hands are even undermining the republic and corrupting its officeholders with money."[125]

This fusion gamble worked, and in 1896 North Carolina elected a Republican governor and swept Populists and Republicans into power in the state legislature. This new progressive state government took important steps in terms of African American voting rights and education funding, and it formed a rare and remarkable rebuke to one-party rule in the post-Reconstruction South. But one of its first and most pressing priorities was to annul the Southern's lease. As soon as he was elected, the new Republican governor, Daniel Russell, seized on the lease as an issue to unite North Carolinians of all partisan persuasions. In a detailed interview a month after his election, Russell noted the great wealth and effort that North Carolina had put into the building of the NC RR, and attacked the Southern as a company run by "princes of plutocracy," and noted "hundreds of millions of its securities are held by millionaires in New York and London." He argued that his Democratic predecessors should have driven a harder bargain for the lease of the NC RR, which Russell called a "golden link" in the Southern's "great chain extending from the waters of the gulf to the Potomac and the Chesapeake."[126] In his inaugural address he similarly devoted a whole section to railroad matters and called the deal "not a lease but an attempted purchase" of a North Carolina road by a "foreign corporation," and he called on the legislature to bar outside corporations from holding or operating railroads in North Carolina without proper examination to ensure the consolidation is "not prejudicial to the interests of the state."[127] The stakes were nothing less than keeping the state "safe from Railroad Domination," wrote John Graham in a letter celebrating the governor's strong stance.[128]

The first main push of his administration would thus be a legislative attack on the ninety-nine-year lease. And as Russell's fight proceeded, there was at least some awareness that the antilease effort was linked to battles against Southern Railway consolidation in other states. A report in Russell's files argued that J. P. Morgan dictated the policy of the Southern, Chesapeake & Ohio, and Norfolk & Western systems, giving Morgan 11,000 miles under his command. Cities like Macon, Asheville, and Knoxville had found themselves "bottled up" by Morgan-backed railroads, and if Morgan could secure the NC RR and the Seaboard Air Line, he would have all of the southern states in his grip. The report concluded with a hopeful note that Morgan had "stirred the legislatures of North Carolina, South Carolina, and Georgia" to action.[129] When Georgia's Railroad Commission failed to reduce rates in 1897, North Carolina Populists noted the similarities between the two states, arguing that railroads owned the commission in both states, and "it looks like the Southern Railroad has a prior lien in both States."[130] As the lease bill wound through the state legislature, the *Raleigh News-Observer* referenced the Georgia Railroad Commission's attempts to determine the Southern's control of the Central of Georgia and pointed out that "the people of Georgia are having a fight against corporation domination somewhat similar" to what was transpiring in North Carolina.[131] North Carolina Populists also tapped into currents in the national third-party movement. Butler wrote to William Jennings Bryan in December 1896 urging him to place the "transportation question" on the same level as financial issues in the next campaign, due to the "pernicious activity of the railroad companies in the last campaign in the interest of the gold standard."[132]

So when the 1897 legislative session began, a coalition of strange bedfellows pushed for the annulment of the lease, including Republican governor Russell, his Populist allies in the legislature, and influential Democrats like David Schenck and Josephus Daniels, editor of the largest paper in the state. From the start, the lease fight was about two distinct visions of political economy—the benefits of systemization versus the narrower, state-focused mission of the old NC RR. The minority report in one antilease bill expressed worry about the impact on the Western North Carolina Railroad, which would lose its connections to a broader system if its feeder line, the NC RR, became independent. Annulling the lease would "turn back the hands of the clock of progress fifteen years" and mean slow local trains, "instead of safe, swift, and well equipped through trains, running upon through schedules northward to the metropolitan cities."[133] Industrialist Julian Carr argued in the *Manufacturers' Record* that annulling the lease would "bring upon the great state of North Carolina the taint of repudiation," and he warned that "capital is not coming here" if North Carolinians kept up this fight.[134] The *Greensboro Patriot* expressed displeasure that "our esteemed townsman," David Schenck, was on board with the antilease push, and noted that while the road was "valuable as part of a great railroad system," it would fail to pay its operating expenses and go bankrupt on its own. These sentiments were not surprising, as Greensboro was experiencing the first benefits of this system at this point. The same day this editorial was published, the paper also noted that the first Southern Railway freight train on the new Norfolk route arrived in town.[135]

Lease opponents assailed the loss of sovereignty the deal represented, and invoked state pride. At the height of the battle, North Carolina tobacco magnate R. J. Reynolds went so far as to mail a $100 check to Daniels, to defray the travel costs Daniels would incur with the loss of his free pass over the Southern lines. Daniels printed a facsimile of the check in his paper along with a note from Reynolds that expressed hope that "this great break-water between the people of North Carolina and grasping monopoly may be restored to its rightful owners."[136] Critics also pointed out the unfairness in the bidding process. In February, the Southern's main competitor in North Carolina, the Seaboard Air Line, offered to lease the road at a price of $400,000 a year, almost twice what the Southern was paying.[137] When Russell released this information, including his correspondence with Seaboard officials, in a special message to the legislature, it created a "sensation in Raleigh" and threatened to render the lease, in Russell's words, "fraudulent in law and morals."[138]

In the end, legislative chicanery and heavy railroad lobbying efforts defeated the attacks on the lease in the North Carolina legislature. After Populist legislators first introduced a bill to break the lease, it ended up in committee, where the *Caucasian* lamented "high salaried railroad attorneys" irrevocably altered and weakened the bill. The railroad then looked for a compromise in which the Southern would only lease the road for thirty years. On a number of key votes, the railroad position won by one vote, which reeked of corruption to the Populists.[139] "Every body here does not hesitate to say they believe great quantities of money is [*sic*] being used here on the RR lease question," argued a Populist in a letter to Butler.[140] The Populists were also weakened by a factional dispute over whom to support for the U.S. senatorship.[141] The Southern Railway secretly established a new paper, the *Daily Tribune*, to attack the lease from the Republican standpoint, but as Daniels recalled in his memoir, the company was embarrassed when the *Raleigh News-Observer* bought the paper's books and revealed both that the company's vice president A. B. Andrews owned a huge block of stock in the paper and that the Southern was giving it favorable freight rates.[142]

As the fight reached a fever pitch and railroad lobbyists tried to stop any further action on the bill, yells of protest rang out and order broke down, leading at least one legislator to compare the scenes to the disorder of the Reconstruction-era 1868 statehouse. Daniels recalled that the "rioting in the House of Representatives was so disgraceful that the speaker made an appeal to the police force of Raleigh to come to the capitol." Daniels blamed the mess on a breach in the fusion movement's unstable coalition between Republicans and Populists and later remarked, "The Populists who were fighting the lease believed that most of those who had bolted were in the pay of the railroads and did not hesitate to say so."[143] With the legislative bullet dodged, the Southern looked to other venues to prevent future attacks, and the battle went to the courts. The lease fight ended in March 1897 with a court injunction that barred any further attempts to modify the deal. The *Atlanta Constitution* reported that the issue of the NC RR "has been attracting a great deal of attention throughout the country recently, owing to the important part which the road plays in the Southern's through line between Washington and Atlanta."[144]

After the failure of the various antilease bills in the legislature, North Carolina Populists hoped to make the 1898 election a referendum on the Southern Railway's domination of the state. "The people will have a chance to elect a Legislature next time, the members of which will not be subject to the commands of a big railroad magnate," argued the *Caucasian*.[145] "Beware of the year 1898," warned Russell in a blistering letter after the bill went down in flames. The people of North Carolina were aroused, he claimed, and "will settle with these alien money nabobs in 1898," and he hoped that the state courts would also chime in and "not wear the collar of the monarchs and ma-neaters of Wall and Lombard Street[s]."[146] A letter to Marion Butler urged the Populists to make the railroad issue central to the campaign, as it would give the party a "moral element to the campaign which could not be over-come by the Democrats."[147] Butler's paper, the *Caucasian*, warned of a "scheme of the North Carolina overseer or J. Pierpont Morgan and the Rothschilds to capture the next legislature of this State." As early as September 1897, the pa-per ominously noted that the "one hope for the railroad to capture the next legislature" was for the "nigger to be made the issue to draw the attention of the people away from the schemes that are being laid by the 'overseer and his help.'"[148]

Would the campaign be fought to redeem the state and its railroads from corporate overlords? The Populist Party thought it had a winning issue to take to the people, and the party's 1898 platform devoted an entire page to railroad issues, as it called for an end to the free pass system, election of rail-road commissioners by direct vote, reduced freight and passenger rates, and an end to the NC RR lease, which the platform argued was preserved in the last session only by "the mysterious power of a strong railroad lobby."[149] But it was the reaction of the Democrats, torn between pro- and antilease fac-tions, that would prove more critical. The Southern's most vociferous foe in the 1897 fight, Josephus Daniels, best epitomized the tension within the party. Despite his partisan distaste for the governor, he began to shift tactics after the legislative defeat, linking Southern Railway domination to "Negro rule," and in an editorial bluntly entitled "Anglo Saxons Must Rule North Carolina," he attacked Populists and Republicans who had "sold out to the gold-bugs, to the Southern Railway, to the trusts, and to everything else that had the money to pay for them."[150] Another Daniels editorial noted the Southern Railway would "regret above all things to see the white men come together and control the state" and argued that "political railroads" like the Southern "thrive better when the Negro and his corrupt and ignorant white allies are in control."[151] In a total reversal, Daniels was able to merge his critique of the Southern's mono-poly power with an attack on the corruption and racial amalgamation of the biracial state government and the railroads it owned.

In light of their strong antirailroad platform, the Populists offered to aban-don their Republican allies, who on a national level were intimately tied with big business, especially after William McKinley's win in 1896, and fuse with the Democrats. The Populists hoped that cooperation with Democrats could secure an "anti-monopoly Legislature" that would oppose the gold standard, prohibit the use of free passes, strengthen the railroad commission, and use "all lawful and legitimate means" to set aside the ninety-nine-year lease. But at the Democratic Party convention the Democrats declined this offer for an antimonopoly coalition, leaving the Populists twisting in the wind. In the aftermath of this rebuttal, Populists attacked the Democrats as captured by "gold-bugs and railroad lawyers."[152] A report from the *Caucasian* counted twenty-three railroad lawyers on various committees in the convention, and it rued that the Populist fusion proposal was met with "jeers, howls and hisses and all sorts of pandemonium antics" from the Democratic Party's "railroad contingent."[153] The Populists were forced, once again, to cast their lot with the Republicans.

The battle lines for the 1898 campaign were thus drawn. A tenuous fusion between Populists and Republicans with a strong antimonopoly platform arrayed against a Democratic Party desperate to regain power. The mobilizations for the Spanish-American War, which lasted from April to August, only added to the martial atmosphere and racial anxieties in the state. In these months, white and black men flowed through North Carolina on the state's rail lines on the way to Florida and deployments in Cuba.[154] The campaign rhetoric also spoke to the high stakes of the contest, as the Populist campaign spoke of the Southern Railway and its lieutenants in conspiratorial tones. The *Caucasian* labeled Southern vice president A. B. Andrews as "the most active and influential of Rothschild's agents in the State" with "railroad attorneys in every corner of the state, if not in every county," and it warned that Andrews was ready to "distribute mileage books or free passes and no doubt go to the extent of furnishing cold cash to accomplish his purpose." It further warned that at every state or local convention, "there will be some agent of corporation influence standing by attempting to get himself elected a delegate."[155] Josephus Daniels later recalled how Andrews used free passes to buy off lawyers. Free travel anywhere between New Orleans and Washington, the distance of the Southern's lines, was a powerful incentive to support the company's policies.[156] A South Carolina man wrote Butler to "permit a plain citizen to thank you for your noble fight in Raleigh against the money power" and hoped that the effort would be "endorsed by every true North Carolinian who pray[s] deliverance from the clutches of the shylocks of New York and New England."[157]

Whether or not these accusations of railroad bribery were true, it was clear that the Democrats' reluctance to latch onto the Populist anti-Southern crusade

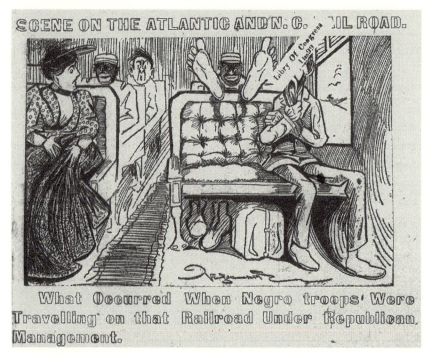

FIGURE 8 The Democratic-controlled *Raleigh News-Observer* linked white supremacy with allegedly corrupt Republican control of North Carolina railroads, reversing the paper's earlier critiques of the Southern Railway. The party ran a daily drumbeat of racist cartoons like this one in the run-up to the 1898 election. *Raleigh News-Observer*, October 5, 1898.

was due to the fact that they already had a winning issue: white supremacy. In the eastern half of the state, home rule laws passed by the biracial fusion government had put African Americans into office, and the white Democratic press reported constantly on the alleged racial outrages that ensued from this situation, such as black postmasters collecting mail from white women, or black men in charge of white men in chain gangs. Front-page editorial cartoons in Daniels's *News-Observer* were especially crucial, and emblematic of the way the party harnessed modern mass media to the cause of white supremacy. The monster of black domination, portrayed in one cartoon as a clawed vampire descending on the white citizens of North Carolina, replaced J. P. Morgan and his railroad octopus as the most dire threat to the state. One cartoon provided a direct link between the Republican government's state-owned railroads and the upending of the racial order that the fusion government represented. It showed black men riding on the Atlantic & North Carolina, a state-owned railroad in eastern North Carolina, with their feet up, to the dismay of the white woman on the train (figure 8).[158]

With such rhetoric, it was no surprise that the campaign soon escalated to violence. After Alex Manly, publisher of a black paper in Wilmington, published an inflammatory editorial that attacked the "black rapist" justification for lynching and that insinuated that white women enjoyed the company of black men, outraged white men took their anger to a whole other level on Election Day. Violence instigated by paramilitary, white supremacist "red shirts" reverberated across the state, including an outright coup in Wilmington that killed dozens of black residents, and the Democrats took power after an election that hardly could be considered fair. The message of white supremacy, backed by the barrel of a gun and widespread voting irregularities, carried the day in November.[159] In the aftermath of the election, victorious Democrats quickly moved to disenfranchise black voters, crushing Republican strength in the state, and the Populists disintegrated as they did on a national level. The Southern's reign was also secure in North Carolina. The ninety-nine-year lease stood, and though the Southern no longer exists, its successor company, the Norfolk Southern, continues to lease the NC RR from the state.

THE RISE OF THE Southern Railway brought residents in states along the line in touch with a key element of modern capitalism, the large corporation. Its sheer size marked it as the largest company the region had ever seen, and it served as the corporate embodiment of a number of key factors of the capitalist system. The Southern provided southerners with a concrete example of how railroad companies exhibited a tendency toward consolidation and increasing levels of outside control, a prioritization of the needs of the system over the desires of local or state interests, and an aggressive interest in influencing political debates. The diverse array of actors that challenged the consolidation of the Southern spoke to the anxieties this new corporate octopus produced, and though the antimonopolists lost, their arguments constituted a powerful counternarrative to the story of New South railroad revival.

Moreover, the Southern Railway's victory highlights important lessons that explain the ultimate defeat of southern Populism. The role of race in the Populist downfall is a well-told story in southern history, and it is a story that fits into broader themes of the region's political history. White southern elites, whether they be plantation owners or New South businessmen, have always proved adept at mobilizing lower-class whites around the banner of white supremacy.[160] The rapid collapse of Populism and the defeat of antimonopoly movements in North Carolina and Georgia fit this same pattern but add a twist: the central role of outside capital and railroad corporations like the Southern Railway. Southern Railway lawyers were certainly not at the front of the mobs, shouting down Tom Watson's speeches or leading nighttime raids to intimidate black voters, but their behind-the-scenes work in terms of funding and influence was just as helpful in swaying key elections and defeating hostile legislation. Protecting the railroad's new consolidation and upholding the racial order challenged by Populism went hand in hand in North Carolina and Georgia, and the defeat of Populism meant the death of a specific type of antimonopoly politics.

The piece-by-piece construction of the Southern Railway system thus marked a crucial turning point in southern railroading. More so than any corporation, the Southern Railway embodied the tensions in New South railroading. Was the company the agent of the South's economic redemption or a monopolistic octopus that strangled the region? The company's southern branding was not enough to deflect criticism of its Wall Street backing and monopoly power. But beyond these implications for the New South dream, this was also a moment that clarified a specific version of capitalism. Much of the 1880s railroad growth in the South was motivated by an impulse to develop local areas, increase competition, and challenge growing railroad systems. Lines like the GS&F supported an ecosystem of smaller railroad lines owned by local businessmen that would crisscross the region, provide adequate transportation for passengers, compete for business, and keep shipping rates low. In the next decade, politicians, particularly those aligned with the Progressive movement, continued to use railroad power as a foil and sought to regulate companies like the Southern with railroad commissions and other rules, but their attacks lacked the edge of the antimonopoly politics of the 1890s, which sought to break up large systems. The 1890s octopus attacks directly challenged the notion that bigger is better, and that the needs of the system should take precedence over the needs of the local.[161] Though railroad critics tried to harness the image of the octopus to challenge both the Southern and the Democratic governments that supported it, another horrifying monster, the vampire of black rule, proved more of a threat to the white South and the Southern.

Conclusion

A Procession of Spectres

We have lost fewer lives to the invading host of Sherman's army
than we have lost to the railroads.
—Tom Watson, 1906

As his train cut through the mountains of Virginia, on his way back from a hunting trip in 1906, Samuel Spencer likely had much to ponder. As president of the Southern Railway, he was in command of a company that controlled 7,250 miles of railroad stretching from Washington, D.C., and Cincinnati in the north to Atlanta and New Orleans in the south. Maybe his thoughts were on his recent campaign fighting against new federal railroad regulation.[1] Or perhaps Spencer took time to consider the incredible amounts of power he could wield. A stroke of his pen, to readjust a freight rate or approve a new extension, could condemn a town to irrelevancy, spur an industrial boom, or transform a primeval stand of pine into lumber. In the decades before his journey, the South's political economy had been decisively reordered in favor of men like Spencer and large corporations like his Southern Railway. After two decades of rapid expansion, standardization, and systemization, the southern railroad industry entered the twentieth century constituted in what is essentially its modern form, and five major northern-backed corporations controlled the majority of the South's rail mileage.[2] We will never know whether Spencer's mind lingered on business topics like these, or simply on his various victories or defeats on the hunting excursion, but whatever ruminations Spencer had were cut short when another Southern Railway train following faulty signals slammed into Spencer's private car outside Lynchburg, Virginia.

Spencer was killed instantly, and an outpouring of grief greeted the news of his unexpected death. On Sunday, December 2, every single train on the Southern Railway system stopped and stood still for five minutes, and condolence messages poured into Southern headquarters from around the nation. In these laments, writers typically framed Spencer's demise not just as a personal or corporate tragedy but also as a blow to the South at large. Expressing a sentiment evident throughout the southern press, a Charleston paper rued that the South "has lost one of its best and most loyal friends."[3] "Out of a tangled mass of scrap iron he constructed a grand system of railroads and helped to rehabilitate the whole South," argued the *Atlanta Constitution*.[4] An Atlanta railroad contractor went so far as to call Spencer's death the worst loss to the South since the Civil War.[5] Connections to his Civil War service abounded. One paper compared his demise at the hands of his own system to Stonewall Jackson's death by friendly fire, and a New Orleans editorial remarked that "the same courageous spirit that actuated Private Spencer in his little gray jacket" was seen in "the councils of the largest and most powerful railroad corporations."[6] Northern papers agreed. The *Boston Globe* called him a "strong type . . . of the real New South, to which slavery, secession and the passions of the Civil War are as much ancient history as they are to us of the New North."[7] When he was told of Spencer's sudden passing, J. P. Morgan's "frame stiffened and shook as if a powerful current of electricity had passed through his body," and then the millionaire began openly weeping in public.[8] Spencer's death had revealed an intertwined relationship that, in the minds of both northern and southern elites, had come to define the South at the dawn of the twentieth century. The region's redemption from the nadir of the Civil War, in both an economic and a cultural sense, was linked to railroad connections and the forces of unbridled capitalism represented by the Southern Railway.

Of course, the very accident that killed Spencer, a deadly breakdown of corporate policy, would seem to cast some doubt on the success of this link. At least one paper observed, "The manner of his death is a most tragic commentary upon the railroad situation in the South today."[9] And another pointed out the "grim sarcasm" in the fact that "the death-roll of the Southern has been one of the most terrible in the history of America's railways."[10] As always, cataclysm kept pace with the various glories of the southern railroad. Months before the collision near Lynchburg, Georgia Populist leader Tom Watson had read Spencer's report of how the Southern increased its earnings by 525 percent in its eleven years of existence, and he responded with rage. Watson argued that a "procession of spectres" stalked the means by which these profits were made, and quipped, "We have lost fewer lives to the invading host of Sherman's army than we have lost to the railroads" (figure 9). Watson pointed out the northern ties behind the Southern Railway and called Spencer a "sepoy, the hireling of a foreign master, trained, uniformed, armed and paid to conquer and plunder his own people."[11]

Watson's "procession of spectres" purportedly haunting the Southern Railway was an apt metaphor to describe the anxieties that greeted the expansion of railroads and capitalism in the New South. As we have seen, the rapid spread of rail lines, improved speed of transit, increased connection and

"We lost fewer lives to the invading host of Sherman than we have lost to the railroads under Sam Spencer."

FIGURE 9
Tom Watson raged against Samuel Spencer's Southern Railway and claimed a "procession of spectres" haunted Spencer's wealth. In *Tom Watson's Magazine*, April 1906, 164. Courtesy of Perkins and Bostock Libraries, Duke University.

circulation, and proliferation of new modes of thought in the 1880s and '90s produced new forms of enchantment in southern life, and this magic veered wildly between the emotional extremes of joy and terror. In an attempt to harness the power of the railroad, boosters drew a clear link between this network of iron rails and the idea that a New South had emerged. But like Marx's metaphorical sorcerer who failed to control his spells, the forces of capitalism could easily turn against their masters, and these decades were replete with evidence of the dark magic of the southern railroad network. The pell-mell pace of industrial development claimed countless lives of workers in collapsed tunnels and lonely work camps, and endangered passengers on shoddily built bridges and broken-down sections of track. Circulation and connection brought yellow fever deep into the southern interior, and though public health officials, railroad companies, and regional boosters sought to downplay the threat, the continued use of the shotgun quarantine served as a clear expression of southerners' lack of confidence in authorities and the railroads. Railroad Bill and Rube Burrow's careers gave visceral evidence of how the magic of the railroad could be turned to violence and plunder by both black and white criminals. As large systems like the Southern Railway, Atlantic Coast Line, and Seaboard Air Line took shape, small towns, embittered merchants, and politicians across the region invoked the monstrous octopus to contest the constriction of consolidating rail lines.

As the forces of circulation and connection rapidly reordered southern life, the very same white southerners who eagerly anticipated the arrival of this network expressed horror at the spectres that seemed to emerge from the region's African American population. Black southerners rode the rails for business or pleasure and took jobs building, maintaining, and working on railroads, and they claimed railroad magic as their own. White accounts reveal how the rail network functioned as a funhouse mirror of sorts, distorting and exaggerating what one saw or witnessed. The railroad's phantasmagoria enlivened descriptions of commodities, birthed cities out of nothing, and enriched investors, but for the white South, applying these powers to black southerners threatened the reestablishment of the racial order. Anonymous black faces circulating through the network coded as criminal to fearful whites, leading to imagined stock characters like the black rapist, the train wrecker, and the rambling bad man. From the vantage point of speeding trains, white boosters pointed out black idleness and misdirection, and saw aimless wandering in the black travelers who did ride the rails. Groups of African Americans appeared as aimless mobs, disconnected from progress. Other figures like the upwardly mobile or middle-class black man, respectable black woman, or mixed-race passenger directly challenged the emerging black and white divisions in rail cars and throughout the region. As white politicians worked to redeem the region from Reconstruction's alleged horrors, these new troubling archetypes, fueled by the railroad network, posed a serious challenge.

This "procession of spectres" traced the rise of the southern railroad network, but why did this matter? The 1890s were a clear turning point in the history of the South. Insurgencies like the Farmers Alliance, Knights of Labor, and the Populist Party threatened to unravel the South's ruling coalition of northern capital, business-minded "New South" men, and conservative white Democrats. African Americans similarly resisted the rise of Jim Crow laws and attempted to harness and claim the mobility of the railroad and the empowerment of consumer capitalism. This was a clear opportunity for the region's political economy to break out of its "colonial" relationship with the North and shift in a more favorable direction for blacks, workers, yeoman farmers, and other marginalized groups.[12] The decade also marked a transitional period for American capitalism. Would the interstate, networked vision of the Southern Railway and its competitors triumph over a more locally oriented mode of development? Would regulation or even nationalization curtail the power of railroads? And would large monopolistic corporations rule the American economy?[13] The symbolism of the railroad had brought the values of capitalism to the South, and critiques of the railroad and moments that shattered the railroad phantasmagoria could easily have spiraled into more systemic attacks. Yet these counternarratives to the railroad's glory never were able to shatter the railroad's symbolic power, as evidenced by the continued linkage between the Southern Railway and the South's salvation that greeted Spencer's passing.

To make the railroad and capitalism's magical powers palatable for the region, white southerners had to circumscribe black power and mobility. As boosters wrote the story of capitalism through interactions with railroads, the definition that emerged was selective. Black men and black women's contributions were marginalized at expositions, and their labors were ignored, violently attacked, or constrained by the widespread use of convict leasing. Free labor is often considered key to the operation of capitalism, but the racialized system of convict labor that built southern railroads echoed the forced labor of slavery, limited the advancement of workers, and provided justification for horrific working conditions in southern rail camps. The impulse to harness the railroad's power also meant that the railroad became the number one battleground for fights over segregation laws, which used race to define who could and could not fully enjoy the benefits of rail transportation. Solutions to yellow fever epidemics—to entrap and isolate black populations—were an especially stark and callous version of the segregation regimes that took root in the 1880s and '90s. Black southerners attempted to claim railroad magic as their own, but the arrival of a strict black-and-white color line in rail travel limited the power of the upwardly mobile black traveler.

More seriously, white elites were adept at using racism and the white fear of black criminality to distract from the railroad's calamities. The use of race and appeals to whiteness to defeat class-based organizing and mobilize lower-class whites on the side of the region's white leadership is in some respects a continuity in southern history that can be traced from Bacon's Rebellion to the formation of the Confederacy to George Wallace's political career. But it is clear that the 1880s and '90s were an exceptional time period in this regard. The violent defeat of southern Populism, and the ways in which the monster of black rule proved more fearful to white voters than the entangling Southern railway octopus, forms the most prominent example in the New South era. Beyond this, elites consciously deployed the new terrifying stereotypes of African Americans to help defeat challenges to the status quo and to normalize the anxieties of capitalism. As a red herring to distract from their horrific safety record, railroad companies used the black train wrecker, an analogue to other bogeymen spawned by the increasing circulation of "strange negroes" like the black rapist. The same dynamic led to community rituals like spectacle lynchings and the commodification of black bodies, seen in Railroad Bill's death, which also served to ameliorate white anxieties. Similarly, "White Man's Burden" imperialism—the occupation or "cleansing" of Cuba—decisively ended the threat of yellow fever, and not enhanced quarantine regulations. Redirecting white anger and outrage toward anonymous black travelers and workers protected outside corporations and deflected serious critiques of capitalism. New South elites and corporations used race to normalize the counternarratives of progress produced by the railroad, and the ultimate defeat of these critiques of the railroad ensured the survival of the New South project.

Spencer's death marked the end of an era, as a period of flux and contestation in southern railroading drew to a close. The passage of time only helped the monsters of the 1890s recede into myth and memory. The last southern state to officially segregate travel, North Carolina, did so after the 1898 election had violently ended the reign of the Populist-Republican fusion coalition. *Plessy v. Ferguson*, the Court case that ordained the fiction of separate but equal accommodations, began when Homer Plessy challenged Louisiana's segregation law by riding in the white car of a New Orleans railroad. After this case, a system of Jim Crow cars and waiting-room areas provided structure and clarity to southern travel for whites, and though African Americans would continue to resist Jim Crow, segregation would remain standard on southern railroads until the 1960s.[14] Yellow Jack paid his last visit to the southern railroad network in 1905, and once again legal and illegal quarantines popped up to stop the spread of the disease on southern rail lines.[15] But in 1905, the more important developments to control yellow fever occurred within cities, where public health officials waged a vigorous effort to exterminate mosquitoes, which by this point had been firmly established as the fever's method of transmission. These methods worked, and after decades of fear, southerners along rail corridors could finally trust that the next train would not bring a shipment of death and the dreaded black vomit along with its usual freight.[16]

Though the South would continue to bear witness to horrible train wrecks, the numbers fell from the peak of the 1890s as companies repaired broken-down track and instituted more safety measures. Train wreck ballads recording details of these disasters, like "Wreck of the Old 97," continued to haunt the airwaves, but the menace of train wrecking would never again frighten the

South as it did in the 1890s.[17] The South's most notorious train robbers lost their lives in gunfire and drifted into legend as foes of the system, rather than personifications of capitalism's power. Train robbers thrived on transitional periods, and improved security methods made the crime increasingly difficult and unprofitable. As angry as Tom Watson's words were, the outpouring of commemoration after Spencer's death suggests that Watson, and the anti-railroad critique he gave voice to, was in the minority. In the aftermath of the 1896 presidential election, and various setbacks on a state level, Watson's Populists crumbled into irrelevancy, and Watson himself gained notoriety not as an antimonopoly crusader, but as a race-baiting demagogue. Though antirailroad politicians still made hay battling the railroads, Progressive-era attacks on the railroad lacked the vision and venom of the 1890s critique.[18]

The New South story of the railroad survived, obscuring a darker relationship between capitalism and white supremacy, two intertwined forces that moved in tandem and strengthened in the 1880s and '90s. This is not a portrait of capitalism that squares with most mid-twentieth-century Americans' perceptions of the system. In a Cold War world threatened by Soviet Communism, American capitalism was supposed to be a beacon of freedom and democracy, and the large corporation was hailed as a source of stability and order. But the South has always posed a particular challenge to these whiggish narratives of the history of American capitalism. So for much of the twentieth century, the false dichotomy of a premodern, anticapitalist Old South and a progressive New South redeemed by capital helped reconcile the nation to a part of the country where capitalism took on a warped form. Both of these mythic Souths were inextricably linked. The creation of a pastoral Old South distinct from capitalism was predicated on a New South where the forces of capitalism operated cleanly.[19] No wonder historians throughout the twentieth century continued to sever both the horrors of slavery and the disasters of the railroad from the history of capitalism. With a more critical eye, we can see both that the Old South was far more capitalist than we liked to admit and that the New South was by no means rescued by the railroad and the unleashed forces of capitalism.[20]

The importance of storytelling and narrative to capitalism's success has only continued in the twentieth and twenty-first centuries. Long-haul trucking, an economic force that led directly to the rise of industrialized agriculture, the Wal-Mart economy of big-box stores, centralized distribution, and the death of local business, lingers in the cultural imagination as a venue for manly independence. Wal-Mart, the quintessential model of late-twentieth-century capitalism, itself emerged from a hinterland region with a history of anticorporate Populism, cloaking its spread in a heartland-friendly message of Christian family values.[21] For defenders of Wall Street institutions, the devastating crash of the economy in 2008 was the fault of reckless lenders or overgenerous government programs, and not the inherent result of a financial system that incentives risk-taking and offers bailouts as a backup plan.[22] Modern prophets of neoliberalism tout the alleged naturalness of capitalism and preach devotion to the alleged infallibility of the free market. Social media companies like Facebook, which have a clear financial incentive to add membership and sell advertisements, whatever the costs to communities, preach about the benefits of connecting the world in a messianic tone. If capitalism is predicated on cycles of boom and bust, the mythmaking that accompanies these busts, whether authored by economic panics, factory closures, or train wrecks, is critical to the operation of the system. Wracked with war, political turmoil, and racial upheaval, the postwar South needed a story to fully embrace capitalism after the Civil War, and the railroad provided the means to tell this tale.

> The old high rolling days of steam have faded and a little of the old rich glamor has worn off now, but some of us still wake up and find ourselves listening for that long lonesome whistle in the night. That's the sound America's dreams are made of.
>
> —Johnny Cash, in *Ridin' the Rails* (1974)[23]

Broken-down and rusted engines, decrepit depots, crumbling trestles, fading murals of trains, and derelict rail corridors overgrown with kudzu litter the modern landscape of the South. The railroad was a powerful emblem of capitalism's transformations in the late nineteenth century, but railroads today evoke nostalgia and sadness over the decline of a once vital American industry. In this age of globalization and neoliberalism, the Illinois Central rail corridor, which was the site of Civil War raids, a vector for yellow fever in 1878, the inspiration for William Faulkner's fictional railroads, the location of Casey Jones's famous wreck, and the track of the iconic City of New Orleans passenger train, is actually now controlled by a Canadian corporation. Some of the Mississippi towns along this iconic route lack rail service entirely now, with a faded or worn right-of-way all that remains of an old connection to the outside world. Indeed, in much of the nation, the options for rail travel in the 1880s far outstrip those in the 2010s. In many of the southern towns first built by the railroad, it takes an astute observer to find an old abandoned right-of-way. Cycling on one of the nation's many rails-to-trails projects is now the best way to view many of the landscapes the railroads molded in the nineteenth century. If the 1880s and '90s constituted a golden age for southern railroading, the twentieth century marked the industry's slow and steady decline. Free market advocates blame heavy government regulation of railroads and the meddling of the Interstate Commerce Commission, but the more tangible culprit was the proliferation of roads, interstates, automobiles, and trucks and America's embrace of car culture.[24]

Perhaps the most prominent purveyor of mid-twentieth-century railroad nostalgia was Johnny Cash, who sang more songs about the railroad than perhaps any other artist. In the 1970s, as passenger rail lines across the country shut down under the crush of Amtrak regulation and the competition posed by airlines and interstates, Cash filmed a TV movie, Ridin' the Rails, that took viewers on a tour through American railroad history by song. He retells (and sings) the stories of John Henry, Casey Jones, and the Wreck of the Old 97. His cover of Steve Goodman's "The City of New Orleans" recounts a trip on the Illinois Central corridor between Chicago and New Orleans, "The L&N Don't Stop Here Anymore" mourns the end of an iconic southern company's service to coal country, and "The Night They Drove Old Dixie Down" notes the role of the railroad in the fall of the Confederacy.[25] Rosy images of a past era of railroading appear across musical genres, but as Cash's career demonstrates, such laments are most often sung with a southern accent. On "Texas Eagle," Steve Earle reminisces about childhood rides on the Texas Eagle, and laments that "nowaday's they don't make no trains . . . they shut the eagle down awhile ago, sold it to the railroad down in Mexico." On R.E.M.'s most explicitly "southern" record, Fables of the Reconstruction, the band included "Driver 8," a dark and driving train song in which lead vocalist Michael Stipe invokes southern imagery: divided fields, revival tents, and the iconic Southern Railway passenger train the Southern Crescent. Gillian Welch similarly pairs southern scenes with passing fireball trains in "Down along the Dixie Line." Musical trains almost invariably take journeys to romanticized landscapes in Georgia, Tennessee, the Carolinas, and other southern locales, and the most prominent legends of the railroad enshrined in song, such as John Henry, Casey Jones, Railroad Bill, and Steve Brady, the doomed conductor of the Old 97, all met their demise along southern rail lines.[26]

This thick haze of nostalgia makes it a challenge to recapture the intensity of the nineteenth century's embrace of the railroad and the visceral thrill that Americans had from riding the rails or seeing a smoke-bellowing locomotive. But there are flickers of this old phantasmagoria today. Rail fans cluster to sites like the Folkston Funnel in southern Georgia, a bottleneck of sorts where dozens of freight trains roar past a viewing platform daily on their way to and from Florida. Hobbyists assiduously assemble small-scale models of routes, towns, and other rail infrastructure, and the glamour of passenger trains like the Dixie Limited, City of New Orleans, and Southern Crescent still lives on in memory for those old enough to have ridden these trains in their heyday.[27] Railroads remain essential to the American economy and the symbolism of the railroad endures, albeit with more advanced technology. Barack Obama spoke to the symbolic power of high-speed rail in his 2011 State of the Union address, pushing for new development to help pull the nation out of the Great Recession and connect the nation for the new century. He set a goal of giving 80 percent of all Americans access to high-speed rail within twenty-five years, promising travel speeds comparable to air travel, and half that of car travel.[28] The American high-speed rail renaissance largely remains stuck at the station, but high-speed rail *has* taken root in China, where a massive investment project is connecting the nation, though of course, the rapid drive to build these new railroads has not been without lapses in safety and high levels of corruption.[29]

The blowing of a locomotive whistle remains, despite these decades of decline, a powerful yet ambivalent image in American culture. For those living near train tracks, the sound is an annoyance, or a warning of the tangled traffic and disruption engendered by the passing train. While older generations may look backward upon the blowing of the whistle to an age of railroad glory of their youth, perhaps to a time when they rode the Southern Crescent or another glamorous streamliner, others look to the future, to the hope of shimmering new high-speed rail lines. The shrill blast of a train's whistle can symbolize a dramatic shift in a narrative, as an arriving train could bring anything—new characters, fresh dangers, freedom from the drudgery of one's routine life. But if the train whistle brings excitement, it also can evoke sadness and desperation, as do the lonesome whistles in blues and country songs that mourn departed family members, companions, or lovers. Rail lines also stand as a common marker for a life on the road, and the isolated life and miseries of a traveling rambler. Yet through all these diverse meanings there is one commonality: the whistle is a moment when one takes notice and the action stops. As R.E.M.'s Michael Stipe sings in "Driver 8," "Bells are ringing through the town again / The children look up / All they hear is sky blue bells ringing."[30] The blowing of a whistle remains a window into the history of the southern railroad and capitalism, a history that is simultaneously exhilarating and terrifying, routine and extraordinary, celebratory and tragic.

Notes

Introduction

1. "A Ride on an Engine," *New Orleans Daily Picayune*, April 24, 1892.

2. These works all make a similar point about how rail travel was an encounter with capitalism: Schivelbusch, *Railway Journey*; L. Marx, *Machine in the Garden*; Richter, *Home on the Rails*, 11.

3. On the antebellum southern railroad's history, see Marrs, *Railroads in the Old South*. The link between 1850s railroads and secession is seen in Ford Jr., *Origins of Southern Radicalism*; Link, *Roots of Secession*; Noe, *Southwest Virginia's Railroad*.

4. There is a robust debate on the influence and strength of the antebellum southern railroad network. Majewski, *House Dividing*, 9–11; Majewski, *Modernizing a Slave Economy*; and S. R. Nelson, *Iron Confederacies*, 26, highlight how slavery hampered southern railroad

development and downplay the connectivity of the antebellum network. William Thomas has argued precisely the opposite, that the Old South had levels of connectivity and railroad penetration that matched or even exceeded those seen in the North. Thomas, *Iron Way*, 28; Thomas, "Swerve Me?," 166–88. The Civil War also constituted a test of this network, and there are mixed conclusions as to whether the Confederacy's railroads helped or hindered the Southern cause. See Clark Jr., *Railroads in the Civil War*. Whether one sees the Old South as an era of railroad underdevelopment or intense connection, it is still clear that the developments in southern railroading in the 1880s and '90s were significant in either intensifying already existing connections or forging a cohesive network out of an underdeveloped one. The disruptions and disconnections of the Civil War and Reconstruction eras also make the connectivity of the 1880s and '90s especially significant.

5. Ayers, *Promise of the New South*, 9–12; Stover, *Railroads of the South*, 3–4; Klein, *Great Richmond Terminal*.

6. "Among the Kings," *Atlanta Constitution*, February 13, 1880.

7. Scholars have used the railroad to weigh into the question of whether the region experienced change or continuity over the tumultuous second half of the nineteenth century. While some aspects of the New South political economy like land ownership, low wage levels, a coercive form of racialized agricultural labor, and dominance of cotton culture may have persisted, it is clear that the new railroad network touched off dynamic change. The continuity argument is most strongly voiced by Weiner, *Social Origins of the New South*, and Billings Jr., *Planters and the Making of a "New South,"* who both emphasize the planter class's persistence, but other works emphasize key elements of continuity. Marler, *Merchants' Capital*, traces the continuities of "merchant capital," and Gavin Wright, *Old South, New South*, 12, 39, notes the continued low-wage nature of the southern economy but highlights the changes in the railroad network after Reconstruction. Lines built during Reconstruction were mostly local and regional, he notes. On these transformations and changes wrought by the railroad, see Woodward, *Origins of the New South*; Woodman, *King Cotton and His Retainers*; Ayers, *Promise of the New South*; Stover, *Railroads of the South, 1865–1900*, 275. And on changes in the countryside and in the situation of yeoman farmers along new rail lines, see Hahn, *Roots of Southern Populism*. Textile industrialization also speaks to the change side of this argument, as detailed in Carlton, *Mill and Town in South Carolina*, and Hall, *Like a Family*.

8. Woodward, *Strange Career of Jim Crow*; Rabinowitz, *Race Relations in the Urban South*; and Ayers, *Promise of the New South*, differ slightly on their interpretation of how integrated pre–Jim Crow rail cars were, but all highlight the railroad as central in the formation of these laws.

9. On the continuity of black protest on the railroad, this work is particularly indebted to Kelley, *Right to Ride*; Pryor, *Colored Travelers*. And on the railroad's impact on black culture, see Kornweibel, *Railroads in the African American Experience*, and Dinerstein, *Swinging the Machine*.

10. This emphasis on the railroad as a network and a broader agent and symbol of economic and cultural change is inspired by these landmark works in railroad history: Schivelbusch, *Railway Journey*; Stilgoe, *Metropolitan Corridors*; Cronon, *Nature's Metropolis*.

11. As H. G. Wells once remarked, "the nineteenth century, when it takes its place with the other centuries in the chronological charts of the future, will, if it needs a symbol,

almost inevitably have as that symbol a steam engine running upon a railway." Quote in M. Matthews, *Civilizing Machine*, 1. Examining capitalism's persistence as an idea and a culture is a major thrust of the "new history of capitalism" embodied in Zakim and Kornblith, *Capitalism Takes Command*, 1–4, and Beckert and Desan, *American Capitalism*, 9–12.

12. Journalist Tom Zoellner calls the magic of rail travel the "Train Sublime" in his narrative of modern-day rail travel: Zoellner, *Train*, xi. Stilgoe, *Metropolitan Corridors*, 4, also notes the "magic of railroading." On train songs, see Cohen, *Long Steel Rail*.

13. Johnson, *River of Dark Dreams*; Beckert, *Empire of Cotton*; Baptist, *Half Has Never Been Told*; Rothman, *Flush Times and Fever Dreams*; Beckert and Rockman, *Slavery's Capitalism*. Beyond these works, a whole host of scholars have drawn attention to aspects of modernization in the Old South. The Old South was more industrialized, more capitalistic, and more modern than we had thought. See the two edited collections Barnes, Schoen, and Towers, *Old South's Modern Worlds*, and Delfino, Gillespie, and Kyriakoudes, *Southern Society and Its Transformations*; and Majewski, *Modernizing a Slave Economy*.

14. Assessing the nature of the New South's political economy has been a fervent field of debate. Woodward focuses attention on the bourgeois class of business-oriented New South men, who allied with northern capitalists to modernize the region. Yet he also laments the colonial nature of the economy that developed and the ultimate defeat of the Populist revolt of South and West. Other works use modernization theory models to argue that the New South followed a deviant path, the so-called Prussian Road. Modernization of the economy proceeded without a more equitable distribution of resources, and these historians de-emphasize the New South's links to capitalism. See Weiner, *Social Origins of the New South*, and Billings Jr., *Planters and the Making of a "New South."* Wright, *Old South, New South*, 13, contests Woodward's colonial economy model. The most recent synthesis of the region, Ayers's *Promise of the New South*, largely sidesteps these debates, opting for a decentralized and postmodern approach that privileges voices from the ground. The dynamic energy of the railroad pulses through this work (and appears on the cover), yet many key railroad crises and disasters besides the segregation debate go unexamined.

15. This project is partial to the definition of capitalism presented by Michael Zakim, who notes that it is "a system of profitmaking based on the perpetual movement of goods and persons," and by Joyce Appleby, who notes that capitalism is both an economic and a cultural system. Quote from Zakim and Kornblith, *Capitalism Takes Command*, 1. As a symbol and a network, the New South railroad perfectly combines these economic and cultural functions of capitalism. "Economic practices are imbedded in culture," remind the authors of Haskell and Teichgraeber III, *Culture of the Market*, 2. In light of the "unnatural" nature of capitalism, works that examine the culture of capitalism are crucial to recover the anxieties of transitional moments in capitalism's history. Addressing this question of how capitalism spreads is a key thrust of the edited volume by Zakim and Kornblith, *Capitalism Takes Command*, but other works have taken up similar arguments on the cultural history of capitalism. Of particular inspiration is Agnew, *Worlds Apart*. This formulation of "capitalism in action" is taken from Beckert and Desan, *American Capitalism*, 11.

16. Recent works have sought to expand the bounds of Reconstruction beyond the political and military developments of 1865 to 1877 and taking a broader view of the process of reconstructing southern capitalism squares with these works. Tracing sectional reconciliation

is one way this has happened, as in Blight, *Race and Reunion*. Prince, *Stories of the South*, also uses a longer periodization to discuss the reconstruction of southern identity. And this thrust is also found in works that emphasize the lingering destruction of the war on bodies, minds, structures, and landscapes, such as M. K. Nelson, *Ruin Nation*, and Berry, *All That Makes a Man*, or in the process of reconstituting white supremacy. Kantrowitz, *Ben Tillman*; Hale, *Making Whiteness*.

17. Beckert, *Empire of Cotton*, 241, 275, details the importance of the Civil War to the global capitalist system. Also see Beckert, *Monied Metropolis*, and Adams, "Soulless Monsters and Iron Horses."

18. On the shift to sharecropping, see O'Donovan, *Becoming Free in the Cotton South*, and Wright, *Old South, New South*, 84–86. Mitchell, *Rise of Cotton Mills in the South*, 56–72, also notes the long persistence of white characterizations of regional economic malaise and the importance of 1880 as a jumping-off point for southern industry.

19. Hillyard, *New South*, 37–38; Edmonds, *South's Redemption*, 35.

20. Goodwyn, *Populist Moment*; Hahn, *Roots of Southern Populism*; Postel, *Populist Vision*; McLaurin, *Knights of Labor in the South*; Shapiro, *New South Rebellion*; Kelley, *Right to Ride*.

21. Woodward, *Origins of the New South*; Gaston, *New South Creed*.

22. Blight, *Race and Reunion*; Hale, *Making Whiteness*, 43.

23. Kantrowitz, *Ben Tillman*; Blum, *Reforging the White Republic*; Prince, *Stories of the South*, 119. On the defeat of the southern Knights of Labor, see McLaurin, *Knights of Labor in the South*, 4, 22–25.

24. On financial panics, see Nelson, *Nation of Deadbeats*; Baptist, "Toxic Debt, Liar Loans," 69–92; Rothman, *Flush Times and Fever Dreams*, 290–301. An earlier era of capitalism's crises is discussed in Linebaugh and Rediker, *Many-Headed Hydra*; Piketty, *Capital in the Twenty-First Century*.

25. Benjamin, *Arcades Project*, 390; Toews, *Communist Manifesto by Karl Marx and Frederick Engels*, 70–71.

26. Benjamin, *Arcades Project*, 391; Zakim and Kornblith, *Capitalism Takes Command*, 5, 284.

27. For the concept of monstrosity as emblematic of the anxieties of the expansion of capitalism, see McNally, *Monsters of the Market*; Linebaugh and Rediker, *Many-Headed Hydra*; Rothman, *Flush Times and Fever Dreams*. The "Octopus" branch of historiography is best epitomized by the plot of the muckraking novel by Norris, *The Octopus*, and this idea is challenged in Orsi, *Sunset Limited*, xiv, 92–93. These examples, and this book, also challenge the notion that modernity is "disenchanted" of superstition and myth. Saler, "Modernity and Enchantment," 692–716.

28. Zakim and Kornblith, *Capitalism Takes Command*, 281. One way the inherent turbulence of nineteenth-century capitalism was ameliorated was through insurance companies, as detailed in Levy, *Freaks of Fortune*.

29. Chandler, *Visible Hand*. The railroad was the essential web that knitted together Robert Wiebe's "island communities" in Wiebe, *Search for Order*. Two older examples of this "colonizer" literature include Overton, *Burlington Route*, and Gates, *Illinois Central Railroad*. Orsi, *Sunset Limited*, xiv, is a modern work that harkens back to this branch of the literature. This book aligns with recent trends in business history that "reject any notion that business . . . has or had a 'civilizing mission'—to bring efficiency, order, growth or rationality to society"; Scranton and Fridenson, *Reimagining Business History*, 5–6.

30. This is a conclusion that this book shares with White, *Railroaded*, xxxi, 539. As White notes in his history of western transcontinental, the railroad corporation led to environmental devastation, obscene levels of corruption, illogical overconstruction, and economic ruination.

31. There is an admittedly vast literature on global railroad development, but the most influential studies for this work are Weber, *Peasants into Frenchmen*; Freedman, *Tokyo in Transit*, 1–12; Clark, *Redemptive Work*, 6; M. Matthews, *Civilizing Machine*; Payne, *Stalin's Railroad*; Headrick, *Tools of Empire*. Christian Wolmar, *Blood, Iron, and Gold*, provides a solid synthesis of the story of global railroad development.

32. In many of the more recent works on the New South, corporate power is absent or in the background of the narrative. This is particularly true in the most influential recent synthesis of the era, Ayers, *Promise of the New South*. Accounts of the rise of Jim Crow similarly place a heavy focus on gender and "on-the-ground" interactions in rail cars while not focusing on the incentives and motives of railroad officials and elites. For example, Gilmore, *Gender and Jim Crow*, does a masterful job of inserting women into the story of the 1898 campaign, but it does not mention the Southern Railway, which was also a prime beneficiary of the coup in Wilmington.

33. The source base of this project is aligned with that of works in the "new history of capitalism" which marks a deliberate shift away from social history and which seeks to "re-insert political economy as a category of analysis"; Beckert and Desan, *American Capitalism*, 10–13. As a field, business history also is, by its nature, concerned with a top-down approach to archival research. For more on the centrality of the railroad to new works in business history, see Scranton and Fridenson, *Reimagining Business History*, 227–37.

34. *Engines of Redemption* echoes the approach of works that look at how elites supported the construction of white supremacy, such as Stephen Kantrowitz's biography of Ben Tillman and Glenda Gilmore's analysis of political messaging in the 1898 White Supremacy Campaign. Kantrowitz, *Ben Tillman*; Gilmore, *Gender and Jim Crow*.

35. In a broad sense, this manuscript agrees with the findings in Saler, "Modernity and Enchantment," 692–716.

Chapter One

1. Field, *Blood Is Thicker than Water*, 11.

2. Field, 16, 45, 137.

3. Schivelbusch, *Railway Journey*, 34–37.

4. Schivelbusch, 10–29. Lears, *Rebirth of a Nation*, 1, characterizes the decades between the Civil War and World War I as marked by a "widespread yearning for regeneration—for rebirth that was variously spiritual, moral, and physical."

5. Majewski, *Modernizing a Slave Economy*, 146–48. My focus on the lingering traumas of the Civil War is inspired by newer works that emphasize the brutality of the conflict and its aftermath, namely, M. K. Nelson, *Ruin Nation*, and Downs, *Sick from Freedom*.

6. Thomas, *Iron Way*, chaps. 5 and 7.

7. Thomas, 28, 98; J. Davis, *Rise and Fall*.

8. The best comprehensive bibliography of these postwar travel narratives is Clark, *Travels in the New South*.

9. Reid, *After the War*, 28, 330, 339, 350, 425.

10. Andrews, *South since the War*, 108–9, 201.

11. Andrews, 29, 31, 214.

12. Trowbridge, *Picture of the Devastated States*, 501, 511.

13. Kennaway, *On Sherman's Track*, 104, 155, 162, 193.

14. Gaston, *New South Creed*, 45.

15. W. D. Kelley, *Old South and the New*, 1–4.

16. McClure, *South*, 19.

17. "Notes in the South," *Railway Gazette*, April 15, 1887.

18. "Southern Railroads," *Railway Gazette*, September 7, 1888.

19. Hardy, *Down South*, 14, 100–104.

20. Ingersoll, *To the Shenandoah and Beyond*, 16, 42–46, 56, 82, 89, 113.

21. Cowan, *New Invasion of the South*, 10, 34, 38, 43.

22. Cowan, 41, 86.

23. Blight, *Race and Reunion*, 209.

24. Rebecca Harding Davis, "Here and There in the South. I—Old and New," *Harper's New Monthly Magazine*, July 1887, 238, 243. The trope of northerners being awakened to the wonders of the New South is a common one. See Prince, *Stories of the South*, 119.

25. Mullen, *Dream of "Ellen N,"* 36.

26. McClure, *South*, 97.

27. Bruce, *Southwest Virginia and Shenandoah Valley*, 76, 136.

28. Raymond's Vacation Excursions, *Twenty Days' Tour through the New South*.

29. Edmonds, *South's Redemption*, 5.

30. Sylvester L. Cary Scrapbook, 245, LSU.

31. Sylvester L. Cary Scrapbook, 547, LSU.

32. T. D. Clark, *Pioneer Southern Railroad*, 76, 96, 111; Stover, *Railroads of the South*, 155–85.

33. "E. D. Frost to Henry McComb," October 31, 1875, ser. 22.2, box 35, folder 891, ICRR.

34. "E. D. Frost to Henry McComb," November 24, 1875, ser. 22.2, box 35, folder 891, ICRR.

35. "E. D. Frost to Henry McComb," January 3, 1876, ser. 22.2, box 35, folder 891, ICRR.

36. "E. D. Frost to Henry McComb," January 28, 1876, ser. 22.2, box 35, folder 891, ICRR.

37. Poor, *Manual of the Railroads*, 812.

38. Corliss, *Main Line of Mid-America*, 172–73.

39. "William K. Ackerman to Constantine Melenas," January 12, 1878, ser. 1.1, box 1, folder 2, ICRR; "William K. Ackerman to Ernest Dichman," July 25, 1878, series 1.1, box 1, folder 2, ICRR.

40. Annual Reports to Stockholders, 1878, Record Group IC 2, ser. 2, vol. 4, 1871–97, ICRR; Annual Reports to Stockholders, 1879, Record Group IC 2, ser. 2, vol. 4, 1871–97, ICRR; Annual Reports to Stockholders, 1881, Record Group IC 2, ser. 2, vol. 4, 1871–97, ICRR; Corliss, *Main Line of Mid-America*, 226; Annual Reports to Stockholders, 1889, Record Group IC 2, ser. 2, vol. 4, 1871–97, ICRR.

41. "Railroad Progress in the South," *DeBow's Review*, July–August 1867, 117.

42. Adams, "Soulless Monsters and Iron Horses," 249–76.

43. Summers, *Railroads, Reconstruction*, 5.

44. Stover, *Railroads of the South*, 61.

45. Summers, *Railroads, Reconstruction*, xi.

46. Stover, *Railroads of the South*, 71; Brown, *State Movement in Railroad Development*, 192–202; King, *Great South*, 506.

47. G. P. Downs, *After Appomattox*, 25.

48. S. R. Nelson, *Iron Confederacies*, chaps. 5 and 6.

49. Churella, *Pennsylvania Railroad*, 438–46.

50. S. R. Nelson, *Iron Confederacies*, 163–69.

51. Woodward, *Origins of the New South*, 30–39.

52. Williamson, *Florida Politics in the Gilded Age*, 89, 97.

53. Woodward, *Origins of the New South*, 113, 120.

54. "The War of the Rail," *Atlanta Constitution*, January 18, 1880.

55. Klein, *History of the Louisville & Nashville Railroad*, chap. 7.

56. "War of the Rail."

57. Nixon, *Henry Grady*, 168.

58. Link, *Atlanta*, 145–46.

59. Nixon, *Henry Grady*, 168.

60. Klein, *Great Richmond Terminal*, 8–17.

61. Adams, "Soulless Monsters and Iron Horses," 249–76.

62. Klein, *History of the Louisville & Nashville Railroad*, 126–70.

63. "Among the Kings," *Atlanta Constitution*, February 13, 1880.

64. Klein, *Great Richmond Terminal*, chap. 3.

65. Eckert, *John Brown Gordon*, 36, 39, 106.

66. The details of this deal are sketched out, and a look at the spotty surviving correspondence is in Eckert, *John Brown Gordon*, 225–35.

67. Gordon, *Reminiscences of the Civil War*, 90, 448.

68. Blake, *William Mahone of Virginia*, 40, 59, 67, 83, 274.

69. "It was a poor subsidiary of an Eastern railroad that could not find some impoverished brigadier general to lend his name to a letterhead," argues C. Vann Woodward. Woodward, *Origins of the New South*, 14, 34.

70. "Changing the Gauge," *Atlanta Constitution*, June 1, 1886.

71. Puffert, *Tracks across Continents*, 7, 105–7.

72. Trelease, *North Carolina Railroad*, 190–91, 252, 321–24.

73. Field, *Blood Is Thicker than Water*, 16.

74. William Ackerman to Randolph, October 8, 1880, William K. Ackerman Out-Letters, ICRR.

75. *Annual Reports to Stockholders*, bound volumes, 1852–1960, 1880, ICRR.

76. J. F. White to H. A. Wim, June 1, 1885 and J. F. White to John Cook, November 15, 1885, in White, J. F. Out-Letters, March 1884–November 1885, ICRR.

77. "The Disappearance of the 5 ft. Gauge," *Railway Gazette*, July 15, 1881.

78. *Annual Report of the President and Directors of the Louisville and Nashville Railroad Company*, 1883.

79. *Reports of the General Manager of the Georgia Railroad from April 1st, 1881 to June 30th 1892*, 133.

80. *Fiftieth Report of the President and Directors of the Central Rail Road and Banking Company of Georgia to the Stockholders*, 13.

81. "Change of Gauge," *L&N Employes' Magazine*, May 1932, 31.

82. "Our Birmingham Letter," *Manufacturers' Record*, June 5, 1886.

83. "Once upon a Time., *L&N Employes' Magazine*, June 1955, 20–21.

84. "Resetting the Rails," *Louisville Commercial*, May 31, 1886.

85. "Preparing for Quick Work," *Atlanta Constitution*, May 14, 1886.

86. "Changing the Gauge," *Atlanta Constitution*, June 1, 1886.

87. "Chattanooga," *NOP*, May 31, 1886.

88. "Our Standard (Gauge) Adopted all over Union," *Harpers Weekly* 30 (1886): 364.

89. Editorial, *SMN*, June 7, 1886.

90. Field, *Blood Is Thicker than Water*, 16.

91. "Recent Accidents," *Atlanta Constitution*, June 10, 1886.

92. "Results of the Change," *Atlanta Constitution*, June 12, 1886.

93. Foster, *Ghosts of the Confederacy*; Blight, *Race and Reunion*.

Chapter Two

1. Sala, *America Revisited*, 10; *Along the Gulf*.

2. *Our Great All Around Tour for the Winter of '84–'85*, 22.

3. Cowan, *New Invasion of the South*, 43; *World's Industrial and Cotton Centennial Exposition New Orleans*, 3–5.

4. *Official Catalogue of the World's Industrial and Cotton Centennial Exposition*, 2.

5. *World's Exposition Catalogue and Guide*, 15–20; "The Exposition," *Manufacturers' Record*, March 11, 1885.

6. *World's Industrial and Cotton Centennial Exposition New Orleans*, 13.

7. Zacharie, *New Orleans Guide*, 3.

8. "The Exposition," *Manufacturers' Record*, March 21, 1885.

9. Benjamin, *Arcades Project*, 7, 201. Historians have examined expositions as valuable windows into the culture of capitalism. Cronon, *Nature's Metropolis*, chap. 8, does this for Chicago. Richards, *Commodity Culture of Victorian England*, describes the significance of the 1851 event in ushering in a new age of advertising in England. Also see Zakim, "Importing the Crystal Palace"; Williams, *Dream Worlds*; Osterhammel, *Transformation of the World*, 14–15; For the New South expositions, see Rydell, *All the World's a Fair*; Beezley, "Exhibiting Visions of a New South," 26–65.

10. Warner, *Studies in the South and West*, 44.

11. Miscellaneous Newspaper Clippings, Vertical Files, Fairs, Festivals, World's Fair (1884) folder 3, Tulane University Special Collections, New Orleans, Louisiana.

12. Beckert, *Empire of Cotton*, 67, 121, 200; Baptist, *Half Has Never Been Told*, chap. 3.

13. *Visitors Guide to the World's Exposition*, 4; Zacharie, *New Orleans Guide*, 5, 15.

14. *Official Catalogue of the World's Industrial and Cotton Centennial Exposition*, 100.

15. "The Exposition," *Manufacturers' Record*, April 25, 1884.

16. K. Marx, *Capital: Volume 1*, 125–32, 163–77.

17. "The Richmond & Danville's Fine Display at New Orleans," *Manufacturers' Record*, March 28, 1885.

18. Perkins, *Practical Common Sense Guide Book*, 9.

19. "The New Orleans Exposition," *Railway Gazette*, February 20, 1885.

20. *Official Catalogue of the World's Industrial and Cotton Centennial Exposition*, 42.

21. *Visitors' Guide to the World's Industrial and Cotton Centennial Exposition*, 10.

22. Perkins, *Practical Common Sense Guide Book*, 6, 32, 46.

23. Benjamin, *Arcades Project*, 14; Schivelbusch, *Railway Journey*, 191, 197.

24. Harvey, "World's Industrial and Cotton Centennial Exposition."

25. "The New Orleans Exposition," *Manufacturers' Record*, May 16, 1885.

26. Marler, *Merchants' Capital*, 220–30.

27. Hale, *Making Whiteness*, 147–51; Perkins, *Practical Common Sense Guide*, 44.

28. Cardon, "South's New Negroes," 287–326.

29. "The Georgia Southern," *MWT*, December 15, 1888.

30. Carlton, *Mill and Town in South Carolina*, 13.

31. Stover, *Railroads of the South*, 196. One can see these lines as a prime example of Gerald Berk's "regional republicanism," an alternate vision of American political economy centered on smaller, more decentralized corporations. Berk, *Alternative Tracks*, 4.

32. *Cape Fear and Yadkin Valley Railway*, 10.

33. *Troy (Ala.) Messenger*, February 28, 1889.

34. "The Macon and Florida Air-Line," *MWT*, October 7, 1883.

35. "The Macon and Florida Air-Line Railroad," *MWT*, November 21, 1883.

36. "A Rich Country," *MWT*, October 7, 1888.

37. *Greensboro Patriot*, May 18, 1883; *Fayetteville Observer*, March 19, 1884.

38. *Proceedings of the Annual Meeting of Stockholders of the Cape Fear and Yadkin Valley Railway*, 10.

39. Carlton and Coclanis, *South, Nation, and the World*, 82.

40. "The Cape Fear and Yadkin Valley Railway," *Greensboro Patriot*, May 18, 1881.

41. *Palatka (Fla.) Daily News*, January 24, 1888.

42. "The New Florida Road," *MWT*, November 22, 1887.

43. "The Midland R.R.," *MTDA*, August 4, 1889.

44. "The Alabama Midland," *MTDA*, March 2, 1888.

45. Editorial, *Greensboro Patriot*, January 26, 1883.

46. "The Georgia Southern," *MWT*, February 21, 1888.

47. Klein, "Competition and Regulation," 324; White, *Railroaded*, 179.

48. "Railroad Rumbles," *Andalusia (Ala.) Covington Times*, December 20, 1895.

49. Editorial, *Andalusia (Ala.) Covington Times*, December 27, 1895.

50. Editorial, *Andalusia (Ala.) Covington Times*, November 6, 1896.

51. From Charles Iverson Graves, August 18, 1882, in the Charles Iverson Graves Papers no. 2606, SHC.

52. From Charles Iverson Graves, August 20, 1882, in the Charles Iverson Graves Papers no. 2606, SHC.

53. "The South's Awakening," *Manufacturers' Record*, May 8, 1886.

54. Hardy, *Down South*, 14, 100–104.

55. "The War of the Rail," *Atlanta Constitution*, January 18, 1880.

56. Corliss, *Main Line of Mid-America*, 201–5.

57. "Not Badly Balked," *Troy (Ala.) Messenger*, July 25, 1889.

58. "From Macon to the Sea," *MWT*, April 10, 1890.

59. Willis, *Forgotten Time*, 90–94.

60. J. C. Clarke to Stuyvesant Fish, April 6, 1885, J. C. Clarke Out-Letters, 1874–1891, ICRR.

61. J. C. Clarke to Stuyvesant Fish, April 6, 1885, J. C. Clarke Out-Letters, 1874–1891, ICRR.

62. J. C. Clarke to Stuyvesant Fish, December 13, 1886, J. C. Clarke Out-Letters, 1874–1891, ICRR.

63. To J. C. Clarke, February 4, 1885, In-Letters, President's Office, ICRR.

64. From Charles Iverson Graves, May 7, 1882, in the Charles Iverson Graves Papers no. 2606, SHC.

65. From Charles Iverson Graves, May 21, 1882, in the Charles Iverson Graves Papers no. 2606, SHC.

66. "Election of Officers," *MWT*, June 14, 1888.

67. "Wenona," *MWT*, October 10, 1888.

68. *Cape Fear and Yadkin Valley Railway*, 14, 43 49.

69. Editorial, *MTDA*, February 6, 1888; *MTDA*, July 14, 1889.

70. Stilgoe, *Metropolitan Corridors*, 199, 203, 221.

71. Corliss, *Main Line of Mid-America*, 238–39.

72. "Another Railroad Pointing toward Thomasville," *MWT*, May 4, 1888.

73. "Crawling Earth," *MWT*, October 27, 1888.

74. *Illustrated Guide Book of the Western North Carolina Railroad*.

75. Kirby, *Mockingbird Song*, 113–17, 121.

76. Hahn, *Roots of Southern Populism*, 166–69; Grant, *Rails through the Wiregrass*, 111–15.

77. Outland, *Tapping the Pines*; Cronon, *Nature's Metropolis*, chap. 4.

78. "The Richmond & Danville's Fine Display at New Orleans," *Manufacturers' Record*, March 28, 1885.

79. Georgia Railroad Collection, MS 2517, folder 1, p. 102, UGA; Cronon, *Nature's Metropolis*, 213–18.

80. To H. Waters Esq, October 23, 1905, box 253, Chairman's Correspondence File, L&NRR.

81. Linebaugh and Rediker, 50–60.

82. Faulkner, *Go Down, Moses*, 320–21.

83. Cronon, *Changes in the Land*, 5, 12.

84. "Calhoun's Railroad Speech," *Manufacturers' Record*, February 22, 1890.

85. Nash, *Wilderness and the American Mind*, 1.

86. Faulkner, *Unvanquished*, 260.

87. Millichap, *Dixie Limited*, 24–35.

88. "Banquet," *Troy (Ala.) Messenger*, January 2, 1890.

89. "Railroad Celebration," *Greensboro Patriot*, June 19, 1884.

90. *Cape Fear and Yadkin Valley Railway*, 13.

91. "Culloden Celebration," *MWT*, July 5, 1890.

92. "The First Ride," *MWT*, December 1, 1887.

93. "A Beautiful Train," *MWT*, November 6, 1888.

94. "About the Midland," *Troy (Ala.) Messenger,* January 8, 1889.

95. "Growing South Georgia Towns," *MWT,* March 6, 1889.

96. "Culloden Celebration," *MWT,* July 5, 1890.

97. "Sale of Georgia Southern Bonds," *MWT,* March 16, 1889.

98. "Rich Country."

99. "The Georgia Southern," *MWT,* December 15, 1888.

100. "The Cape Fear and Yadkin Valley Railway," *Fayetteville Observer,* April 30, 1884.

101. "The Sick Man of East Carolina," *Fayetteville Observer,* February 27, 1884.

102. "The Midland," *Troy (Ala.) Messenger,* February 27, 1890.

103. "Six Railroads," *Wilmington Messenger,* March 22, 1890.

Chapter Three

1. Dinerstein, *Swinging the Machine,* 120; Nelson, *Steel Drivin' Man,* 126–27.

2. Odum, *Rainbow Round My Shoulder,* 269–75.

3. Odum.

4. Plenty of subsequent observers have pointed out the flaws in Odum's Black Ulysses archetype and in his scholarship in general. W. P. Jones, *Tribe of Black Ulysses,* 2–8; Nelson, *Steel Drivin' Man,* 115–16.

5. Odum, *Rainbow Round My Shoulder,* 271.

6. Dinerstein, *Swinging the Machine,* 120; Nelson, *Steel Drivin' Man,* 126–27.

7. Baptist, *Half Has Never Been Told,* chap. 4.

8. Odum, *Negro Workaday Songs,* 11.

9. Nelson, *Steel Drivin' Man,* chap. 6, refers this communication network as the "Southern Railway Octopus."

10. Linebaugh and Rediker, *Many-Headed Hydra,* 174–210.

11. Quote from Filene, *Romancing the Folk,* 17.

12. *Illustrated Guide Book of the Western North Carolina Railroad,* 13.

13. McKinney, "Zeb Vance," 58–67.

14. *Illustrated Guide Book of the Western North Carolina Railroad,* 1, 4.

15. L. Jones, *Minstrel of the Appalachians,* 235.

16. Lichtenstein, *Twice the Work of Free Labor,* 1–9, 46; Nelson, *Steel Drivin' Man,* chaps. 4 and 5.

17. LeFlouria, *Chained in Silence,* 44–48.

18. "The C.F. & Y.V. R.R.," *Greensboro Patriot,* December 1, 1882.

19. Cape Fear and Yadkin Valley Railroad," *Greensboro Patriot,* June 8, 1881.

20. *Greensboro Patriot,* April 24, 1884,

21. "Coming from Palatka," *MWT,* May 4, 1888.

22. "The Georgia Southern and Florida Railroad Company," *MWT,* September 4, 1887.

23. White, *Railroaded,* 225–29, notes a similar process of erasing labor from western railroad construction.

24. Dooley Smith to Charles Iverson Graves, February 26, 1883, in the Charles Iverson Graves Papers, no. 2606, SHC.

25. From H. A. Grady, November 5, 1884, in the Grady Family Papers, no. 3486-z, SHC.

26. Powell, *American Siberia,* 9–13, 150–60.

27. Lichtenstein, *Twice the Work of Free Labor*, 51–60; LeFlouria, *Chained in Silence*, 67–72.

28. Virginia and North Carolina Construction Company Record Book, pp. 5, 30, 66, 102, 112, no. 5030, SHC.

29. Nitze, *Report of the Mineral Resources along the Route of the Roanoke & Southern Railroad*, 4.

30. "Southern Railroad News," *Manufacturers' Record*, June 28, 1890; Editorial, *Manufacturers' Record*, March 5, 1892.

31. Two recent works that most explicitly make the case for the capitalist nature of the Old South are Beckert, *Empire of Cotton* and Baptist, *Half Has Never Been Told*. The debate over continuity and change in nineteenth-century southern history largely has responded to Woodward, *Origins of the New South*. Works that emphasize continuity over Woodward's change—books like Weiner, *Social Origins of the New South* and Billings Jr., *Planters and the Making of a "New South"*—come at this argument by mainly looking at the planter class.

32. Green and Woodson, *Negro Wage Earner*, 100–4.

33. Nelson, *Iron Confederacies*, 103–7; Green and Woodson, *Negro Wage Earner*, 105–6; Arnesen, *Brotherhoods of Color*, 30–31, 36.

34. Arnesen, *Brotherhoods of Color*, 25–28; Cohen, *Long Steel Rail*, 132–37, 197–200.

35. Arnesen, *Brotherhoods of Color*, 17–23. Grace Hale notes similarities between the Porter and the mammy. See Hale, *Making Whiteness*, 74. On the key role of black Pullman porters in African American racial progress, see Tye, *Rising from the Rails* and Bates, *Pullman Porters and the Rise of Protest Politics in Black America*.

36. Hall, *Like a Family*, 65–67.

37. McLaurin, *Knights of Labor in the South*, 4.

38. Bruce, *1877*, 261–65.

39. Some works that seek to recover these fleeting moments of interracial cooperation are Arnesen, *Waterfront Workers of New Orleans*; Letwin, *Challenge of Interracial Unionism*; Shapiro, *New South Rebellion*.

40. White, *Railroaded*, 336–40.

41. Nelson, *Steel Drivin' Man*, 58, 91.

42. Nelson.

43. Wells, *Crusade for Justice*, 18–20; Decosta-Willis, *Memphis Diary of Ida B. Wells*, 140.

44. Wells, *Crusade for Justice*, 18–20; Decosta-Willis, *Memphis Diary of Ida B. Wells*, 140.

45. For the link between geography and movement and freedom, see Camp, *Closer to Freedom*, and Welkie, *Recasting American Liberty*, 280–81. On antebellum protests against segregation, see Pryor, *Colored Travelers*, 1–4, 46, 56, and Kelley, *Right to Ride*, 15–32.

46. Pryor, *Colored Travelers*, 2–5; Kornweibel, *Railroads in the African American Experience*, 354–55; Hahn, *Nation under Our Feet*, chap. 7.

47. Hale, *Making Whiteness*, 125; Oldfield, "State Politics, Railroads," 71–91.

48. On antebellum protests against segregation, see Pryor, *Colored Travelers*, 1–4, 19, 46, 56, 78, 102, and Kelley, *Right to Ride*, 15–32.

49. Woodward, *Strange Career of Jim Crow*, 23–37; Rabinowitz, *Race Relations in the Urban South*, 182–92; Kelley, *Right to Ride*, 33–35.

50. W. L. Bragg to G. Jordan, December 21, 1883, Alabama Railroad Commission Letterbook, ADAH.

51. Welkie, *Recasting American Liberty*, 286–87; King, *Great South*, 782.

52. Field, *Bright Skies and Dark Shadows*, 152.

53. Kelley, *Right to Ride*, chap. 3.

54. On the exceptional nature of the New South push for white supremacy, see Kantrowitz, *Ben Tillman* and Hale, *Making Whiteness*.

55. Schivelbusch, *Railway Journey*, 53–64.

56. Field, *Bright Skies and Dark Shadows*, 99; Ralph, *Dixie*, 379.

57. Harley, *Southward Ho!*, 3.

58. Mullen, *Dream of "Ellen N,"* 49.

59. Harding, "Here and There in the South," 242.

60. Field, *Bright Skies and Dark Shadows*, 100.

61. Sala, *America Revisited*, 223.

62. Field, *Blood Is Thicker than Water*, 17; Sala, *America Revisited*, 223–27; Cohen, *At Freedom's Edge*, 4.

63. Kornweibel, *Railroads in the African American Experience*, 354–55; Hahn, *Nation under Our Feet*, chap. 7.

64. Cohen, *At Freedom's Edge*, 4.

65. Sala, *America Revisited*, 2.

66. Richter, *Home on the Rails*; Schivelbusch, *Railway Journey*, 82–88.

67. Ayers, *Vengeance and Justice*, 238–45; Ayers, *Promise of the New South*, 137–46.

68. Brundage, *Lynching in the New South*, 13–14, tracks this surge in lynching and connects this growth to newly opened rail corridors.

69. Hardy, *Down South*, 85. For more on this stereotype, see Pryor, *Colored Travelers*, 68.

70. To the Alabama Railroad Commission, September 21, 1891, Alabama Railroad Commission Letterbook, ADAH.

71. E. T. Jeffrey to J. G. Mann, September 3, 1888, E. T. Jeffrey Out-Letters, ICRR.

72. Cohen, *At Freedom's Edge*, 218–19; Oldfield, "State Politics, Railroads," 71–91.

73. On the importance of these various Old South archetypes, see Hale, *Making Whiteness*, 60–61, 74, 100, and on the broader phenomenon of romanticizing the Old South, see Cox, *Dreaming of Dixie*.

74. Hale, *Making Whiteness*, 44.

75. Welkie, *Recasting American Liberty*, 293; Pryor, *Colored Travelers*, 68. Hale, *Making Whiteness*, 128–29, especially highlights the challenge that the middle-class black traveler posed to whiteness.

76. James Fentress to the Mississippi Railroad Commission, June 29, 1889, In-Letters: President's Office, ICRR.

77. Mississippi State Railroad Commission, Minute Book, p. 219, MDAH.

78. Welkie, *Recasting American Liberty*, 274–76; Stilgoe, *Metropolitan Corridors*, 199–203.

79. The best works that deal with segregation on southern railroads include Rabinowitz, *Race Relations in the Urban South*, 182–92; Ayers, *Promise of the New South*, 136–46; Hale, *Making Whiteness*, 123–29; Kornweibel, *Railroads in the African American Experience*, chap. 10. All agree that railroads were the most charged public space when it came to the debate over segregation, and they all note the uncertainty that characterized rail travel for African Americans.

80. Inscoe, *Writing through the Self*, chap. 4.

81. J. W. Johnson, *Along This Way*, 63–65.

82. J. W. Johnson, 84–87.

83. J. W. Johnson, 87–89.

84. H. Walters to M. H. Smith, July 28, 1904, folder 238, Chairman's Correspondence file, L&NRR.

85. Du Bois, *Darkwater*, 227–31.

86. J. W. Johnson, *Along This Way*, 86–87.

87. Odum, *Negro and His Songs*, 161–68; Odum, *Rainbow Round My Shoulder*.

88. Odum, *Negro Workaday Songs*, 37; Odum, *Rainbow Round My Shoulder*, 4, 68–71.

89. Odum, *Negro and His Songs*, 171, 220–22.

90. Odum, *Negro Workaday Songs*, 132.

91. Odum, *Negro and His Songs*, 158, 275.

92. Odum, 112–15.

93. Giggie, *After Redemption*, 51–53. An excellent description of some African American train songs can be found in Kornweibel, *Railroads in the African American Experience*, chap. 11.

94. Giggie, *After Redemption*, 25–26, 37–46; Kelley, *Right to Ride*, 48, discusses all-black excursions as a popular way to overcome white oppression.

95. Cohen, *At Freedom's Edge*, 248, 251.

96. Dinerstein, *Swinging the Machine*, 69–71, 87–89; Kornweibel, *Railroads in the African American Experience*, 288.

97. The argument that segregation was modern has been echoed by other scholars who point out the modern nature of the phenomenon. See Hale, *Making Whiteness*, 126–35, and Ayers, *Promise of the New South*, 145.

Chapter Four

1. *Report of the Mississippi State Board of Health, for the Years 1878–'79*, 42.

2. Dromgoole, *Dr. Dromgoole's Yellow Fever Heroes*, 114.

3. "Condition of Grenada," *New Orleans Times*, August 28, 1878.

4. *The Epidemic of 1878, in Mississippi*, 160–62; *Report of the Mississippi State Board of Health*, 42–44.

5. Centers for Disease Control, "Yellow Fever."

6. McNeill, *Mosquito Empires*.

7. Humphreys, *Yellow Fever and the South*, 17–44, provides the definitive discussion of the evolving research on the disease. This distillation of the various theories of transmission comes from Nuwer, *Plague among the Magnolias*, 15. Duffy, *Sword of Pestilence*; Kelman, *River and Its City*, 88–89, cover the 1853 epidemic.

8. Nuwer, *Plague among the Magnolias*, 22.

9. "The Fever at New Orleans," *Atlanta Constitution*, July 28, 1878.

10. Bruton, "National Board of Health," 122.

11. "Their Idea of It," *NOP*, August 9, 1878.

12. "The Mobile Blockade" *Atlanta Constitution*, August 1, 1878.

13. Editorial, *NOP*, August 3, 1878.

14. F. Chandler to J. C. Clarke, July 31, 1878, New York Office In-Telegrams, ICRR.

15. *Epidemic of 1878, Report of the Yellow Fever Relief Work*, 136.

16. Keating, *History of the Yellow Fever*, 134.

17. "Quarantines and Yellow Fever," *Louisville Commercial*, August 18, 1878.

18. "Local Paragraphs," *Memphis Daily Appeal*, August 7, 1878.

19. Kate Simpson Letter, no. 1187, SHC.

20. Keating, *History of the Yellow Fever*, 95.

21. Nuwer, *Plague among the Magnolias*, 117.

22. Editorial, *Raymond (Miss.) Hinds County Gazette*, November 20, 1878.

23. "Mississippi—Onward!," *Raymond (Miss.) Hinds County Gazette*, May 1, 1878.

24. Dromgoole, *Dr. Dromgoole's Yellow Fever Heroes*, 113.

25. Willis, *Forgotten Time*, 210.

26. J. C. Clarke to W. H. Osborn, August 16, 1878, New York Office In-Telegrams, ICRR.

27. William Ackerman to Randolph, October 7, 1878 and William Ackerman to J. A. Beck, October 7, 1878, ICRR.

28. William K. Ackerman to Osborn, August 25, 1878, William K. Ackerman Out-Letters, ICRR.

29. Dromgoole, *Dr. Dromgoole's Yellow Fever Heroes*, 117.

30. "The Proposed Stoppage of Trains," *Vicksburg Daily Herald*, September 15, 1878, and "The Epidemic," *New Orleans Times*, September 10, 1878.

31. Dromgoole, *Dr. Dromgoole's Yellow Fever Heroes*, 120.

32. *Epidemic of 1878, Report of the Yellow Fever Relief Work*, 179.

33. *Eighteenth Annual Report of the President and Board of Managers*, 17.

34. "The Fever Abroad," *MDA*, October 12, 1878.

35. Keating, *History of the Yellow Fever*, 179.

36. Keating, 378.

37. "The Yellow Fever," *Atlanta Constitution*, August 30, 1878.

38. J. C. Clarke to W. H. Osborn, August 28, 1878, New York Office In-Telegrams, ICRR.

39. J. C. Clarke to R. Colquhoun, August 28, 1878, J. C. Clarke Out-Letters, ICRR.

40. Wells, *Crusade for Justice*, 10–13.

41. "An Unlucky Town," *NOP*, September 26, 1878.

42. "A Physician's Experience," *NOP*, October 10, 1878.

43. "Nesbitt, Miss.," *MDA*, October 22, 1878.

44. Keating, *History of the Yellow Fever*, 13.

45. Bruton, "National Board of Health," 103.

46. Dromgoole, *Dr. Dromgoole's Yellow Fever Heroes*, 71. Blum, *Reforging the White Republic*, 148, also cites this quote, providing it an as example of a "genocidal" vision promoted by the epidemic.

47. John Stone Marshall Papers (correspondence), September 18, 1878, MDAH.

48. Blum, *Reforging the White Republic*, 145–47.

49. *Epidemic of 1878, Report of the Yellow Fever Relief Work*, 165.

50. J. C. Clarke to L. T. Brien, September 5, 1878, Out-Letters: President's office, November 1874–October 1891, ICRR.

51. *Twenty-Second Annual Report of the President, Vice-President and Directors of the Mississippi and Tennessee Railroad Company*, 14.

52. Nuwer, *Plague among the Magnolias*, 115.

53. *Report of the Mississippi State Board of Health, for the Years 1878–'79*, 7, 91.

54. Dromgoole, *Dr. Dromgoole's Yellow Fever Heroes*, 21.

55. "The Quarantine Question," *NOP*, November 22, 1878.

56. "Protect the Public Health," *MDA*, November 23, 1878.

57. *Raymond (Miss.) Hinds County Gazette*, December 25, 1878.

58. Humphreys, *Yellow Fever and the South*, 56–57. Chap. 3 discusses how businessmen influenced public health legislation. As Humphreys argues, yellow fever's threat to the economy meant commercial interests began to shape southern public health directives.

59. National Board of Health, *Annual Report of the National Board of Health, 1879*, 303–4.

60. National Board of Health, 303–4.

61. Bruton, "National Board of Health," 217, 367.

62. Baker, "Sneaky, Cowardly Enemy," 18.

63. Davis, *History of Jacksonville, Florida*, 160–61.

64. Campbell, *Winter Cities in Summer Lands*, 8.

65. Hardy, *Down South*, 130.

66. Stover, *Railroads of the South*, 94, 186–206.

67. Department of the Interior, Census Office, *Report on Transportation Business in the United States at the Eleventh Census: 1890*, 4.

68. Baker, "'Sneaky, Cowardly Enemy,'" 18.

69. *Report of the State Board of Health for 1892*, 27.

70. Fairlie, "Yellow Fever Epidemic of 1888 in Jacksonville," 95–108.

71. Edwin Rennolds Diary, August 12, 1888, UF.

72. Adams, *Report of the Jacksonville Auxiliary Sanitation Association*, 197.

73. "Shotguns at Hampton," *SMN*, August 22, 1888, "Saint Augustine," *SMN*, September 27, 1888.

74. "Jacksonville," *Ocala Banner*, August 24, 1888.

75. Editorial, *SMN*, August 15, 1888.

76. "An Impromptu Sanitary Citizen's Meeting," *Ocala Banner*, August 17, 1888.

77. "Jacksonville Shut Out," *SMN*, August 11, 1888.

78. "Precautions at Waycross," *Jacksonville Times-Union*, August 14, 1888.

79. "Waycross Quarantines," *SMN*, August 25, 1888.

80. "Callahan Means Business," *SMN*, August 13, 1888; "Fernandina's Quarantine," *Jacksonville Times-Union*, August 19, 1888; "There Is No Increase," *Atlanta Constitution*, August 12, 1888.

81. "Savannah, Florida & Western Railway," *SMN*, September 6, 1888.

82. "Callahan's Shotgun Quarantine," *SMN*, August 17, 1888.

83. "To Put Back One Train," *SMN*, August 29, 1888.

84. "A Trifle Uncomfortable," *Jacksonville Times-Union*, August 27, 1888.

85. "To Visit Governor Perry," *Atlanta Constitution*, August 29, 1888.

86. Adams, *Report of the Jacksonville Auxiliary Sanitation Association*, 212.

87. "The Fever Train," *Atlanta Constitution*, September 15, 1888.

88. Adams, *Report of the Jacksonville Auxiliary Sanitation Association*, 216–17.

89. "Fever Train."

90. "The Quarantine at Jesup," *SMN*, September 14, 1888.

91. Editorial, *Atlanta Constitution*, September 19, 1888.

92. "Fever Train."

93. Adams, *Report of the Jacksonville Auxiliary Sanitation Association*, 216–17.

94. Adams, 214.

95. Cohen, *At Freedom's Edge*, 217–20, provides a helpful chart of when various southern states passed segregation laws.

96. Adams, *Report of the Jacksonville Auxiliary Sanitation Association*, 13, 19, 24, 129; Ortiz, *Emancipation Betrayed*, 50–52; McLaurin, *Knights of Labor in the South*, 92–97.

97. Letter from Armour Company to Edwin Smith, October 10, 1888, Edwin Smith Papers 1884–1896, UF.

98. Wilkinson and Co. Bone Fertilizers, October 8, 1888, Edwin Smith Papers 1884–1896, UF.

99. "The Effect on Trade," *SMN*, August 15, 1888.

100. "Gainesville Shut Out," *SMN*, September 18, 1888.

101. Adams, *Report of the Jacksonville Auxiliary Sanitation Association*, 201–4.

102. Adams, 202–3.

103. Adams, 206–7.

104. Letter to Edwin Smith, November 5, 1888, Edwin Smith Papers 1884–1896, UF.

105. E. T. Jeffrey to Stuyvesant Fish, September 25, 1888, E. T. Jeffrey Out-Letters, ICRR.

106. Editorial, *Grenada (Miss.) Sentinel*, September 29, 1888.

107. "Jackson," *NOP*, September 28, 1888.

108. M. F. Surghnor Diary, September 23, 1888, MS 647, LSU.

109. Editorial, *Atlanta Constitution*, September 17, 1888.

110. "Will Tear Up Tracks," *Louisville Commercial*, September 25, 1888.

111. "Sustain the Officers and Maintain the Quarantine," *Jackson New Mississippian*, September 5, 1888.

112. "The Fever in Jackson, Miss.," *Grenada (Miss.) Sentinel*, October 13, 1888.

113. E. T. Jeffrey to Morey, September 27, 1888, E. T. Jeffrey Out-Letters, ICRR.

114. E. T. Jeffrey to James Fentress, October 1, 1888, E. T. Jeffrey Out-Letters, ICRR.

115. "Shotgun Quarantines," *SMN*, October 7, 1888.

116. "Gunning for Refugees," *Atlanta Constitution*, September 25, 1888.

117. "Birmingham," *NOP*, September 19, 1888.

118. "The Panic Widespread," *Grenada Sentinel*, September 29, 1888.

119. "Railroads Resuming," *Louisville Commercial*, September 29, 1888.

120. E. T. Jeffrey to Stuyvesant Fish, September 29, 1888, In-Letters, President's Office, ICRR.

121. Stuyvesant Fish to James Fentress, October 13, 1888, Out-Letters: President's Office, ICRR.

122. E. T. Jeffrey to Stuyvesant Fish, October 19, 1888, In-Letters: President's Office, ICRR.

123. Humphreys, *Yellow Fever and the South*, 114.

124. J. T. Harahan to James Dunn, September 7, 1897, In-Letters: President's Office, ICRR.

125. "An Old Inhabitant on Yellow Fever in Mississippi," *NOP*, October 18, 1888.

126. W. S. King to All Concerned, September 16, 1897, E. P. Skene In-Telegrams, A. J. Greif to E. P. Skene, September 18, 1897, E. P. Skene In-Telegrams, ICRR.

127. Editorial, *Jackson Daily Bulletin*, September 18, 1897.

128. A. A. Sharp to E. P. Skene, October 28, 1897, E. P. Skene In-Telegrams, ICRR.

129. M. Gileas to E. P. Skene, October 30, 1897, E. P. Skene, In-Telegrams, ICRR.

130. James Fentress to Stuyvesant Fish, January 31, 1898, In-Letters, President's Office, ICRR.

131. Humphreys, *Yellow Fever and the South*, 142–46.

132. Espinosa, *Epidemic Invasions*, 2.

133. Humphreys, *Yellow Fever and the South*, chap. 5.

134. Correspondence to the Mississippi Board of Health 1905–07, MS 782, Letter from Dr. W. H. Saunders, August 5, 1905, LRC.

135. Zacharie, *New Orleans Guide*, 92–93, Illinois Central Railroad, *The Great South*, 42.

136. Examples of the isolation of works on yellow fever include Ellis, *Yellow Fever and Public Health in the South*, and Bloom, *Mississippi Valley's Great Yellow Fever Epidemic of 1878*. A recent work that corrects this oversight, at least for the history of the Civil War era, is J. Downs, *Sick from Freedom*.

137. The long-established model for using an epidemic as a window into society is Rosenberg, *Cholera Years*. Another inspiration is Fenn, *Pox Americana*.

Chapter Five

1. This narrative is drawn from "The Story of the Wreck," *Statesville Landmark*, September 3, 1891; "At Bostian's Bridge," *Raleigh News-Observer*, August 30, 1891; "Aroused From Sleep to Death," *Hickory (N.C.) Press and Carolinian*, September 3, 1891; "Frightful Accident on the Western N.C. Railroad," *Salisbury (N.C.) North Carolina Herald*, September 2, 1891.

2. "Through Cahaba Bridge," *Birmingham State-Herald*, December 29, 1896.

3. Schivelbusch, *Railway Journey*, 131–34.

4. Editorial, *Morganton (N.C.) Herald*, September 3, 1891.

5. "Awful Accident!," *Birmingham News*, December 28, 1896.

6. Editorial, *Atlanta Constitution*, January 26, 1897.

7. One analogue to train wrecking would be the machine breaking of the Luddites, as discussed in Reddy, *Rise of Market Culture*; Randall, *Before the Luddites*. Agnew, *Worlds Apart*, and Linebaugh and Rediker, *Many-Headed Hydra*, provide similar arguments about natural resistance engendered by capitalism more generally. Deliberate attacks on trains are largely absent from this historiography of resistance, one exception being Stowell, *Streets, Railroads and the Great Strike of 1877*, which examines antirailroad violence in the context of the strikes of 1877.

8. Aldrich, *Death Rode the Rails*, 43. Mark Aldrich, a historian who charts rail disasters, blames the rise specifically on "the construction of flimsy railroads in the South and West," as well as on efficiency demands that drove up the weight of trains and placed additional burdens on tracks.

9. The most definitive recent study of railroad accidents, Aldrich, *Death Rode the Rails* reminds us of the need to look at regional differences in railroad safety. For the structural problems with southern industrialization, see Wright, *Old South, New South*.

10. Aldrich, *Death Rode the Rails*, 131–41.

11. Stover, *Railroads of the South*, 257.

12. Baldwin to Samuel Spencer, December 28, 1895, in the Samuel Spencer Files, box 26B, file 50, SRHAC.

13. Interstate Commerce Commission, *Statistics of Railways in the United States* (1891), 96.

14. Data drawn from Interstate Commerce Commission, *Statistics of Railways in the United States* (1893) 74–75, (1894) 84–85, (1895) 93–94, (1896) 96–97, (1897) 94–95, (1898) 106–7, (1899) 107, (1900) 108.

15. "Hurled to Death," *Charlotte Chronicle*, August 28, 1891.

16. The account of Raleigh is from a Wilmington correspondent in "The News at Raleigh," *Wilmington Messenger*, August 29, 1891; "The Terrible Disaster," *Wilmington Messenger*, August 28, 1891.

17. Ayers, *Vengeance and Justice*, 243, argues that new forms of communication in the 1880s and '90s allowed for the more rapid spread of news about lynchings, amplifying the impact of isolated crimes and fueling the "crisis of the New South."

18. "A Fatal Error," *The Sunny South* (Atlanta), September 3, 1892.

19. "The Fatal Disaster on the Western N.C.," *Charlotte Chronicle*, August 28, 1891.

20. Letter from P. Hillard to Bennehan Cameron, August 31, 1891, in the Bennehan Cameron Papers no. 3623, subser. 1.2, folder 155, SHC.

21. Letter from Sallie Mays to Bennehan Cameron August 28, 1891, in the Bennehan Cameron Papers no. 3623, subser. 1.2, folder 155, SHC.

22. Letter from P. D. Cameron to Benneham Cameron, August 28, 1891, in the Bennehan Cameron Papers no. 3623, subser. 1.2, folder 155, SHC.

23. Letter from W. H. Williams to Bennehan Cameron, August 29, 1891, in the Bennehan Cameron Papers no. 3623, subser. 1.2, folder 155, SHC.

24. "Through Cahaba Bridge," *Birmingham State-Herald*, December 29, 1896.

25. "'Ghost Train' Hunter Killed by Train in North Carolina," CNN; "Bostian Bridge Legend Drew Ghost Hunters," *Statesville Record & Landmark*, August 30, 2010.

26. Letter from S. P. Read to Bennehan Cameron, September 9, 1891, in the Bennehan Cameron Papers no. 3623, subser. 1.2, folder 157, SHC.

27. Faust, *This Republic of Suffering*, 6–17.

28. Letter from Naci Moore to Dr. Hill, undated, in the B. F. Long Papers, no. 4071, SHC.

29. Letter from M. A. Kirkland to Bennehan Cameron, August 28, 1891, in the Bennehan Cameron Papers no. 3623, subser. 1.2, folder 155, SHC.

30. Quote from Alvarez, *Travel in Antebellum Southern Railroads*, 127.

31. "Latest from the Wreck," *Asheville Daily Citizen*, August 28, 1891. A similar result could be seen in the Hamlet, North Carolina, wreck in 1911, in which old wooden cars reserved for blacks crushed on impact, killing nearly a dozen. Kornweibel, *Railroads in the African American Experience*, 166.

32. The "Crash at Crush" made headlines across the region. This account is drawn from "The Collision," *Brewton (Ala.) Standard Gauge*, September 24, 1896.

33. "The Statesville Wreck," *Atlanta Constitution*, August 30, 1891.

34. "Local Department," *Statesville Landmark*, November 5, 1891.

35. Wood, *Lynching and Spectacle*, 10–13. Wood argues that intense interest in lynchings and other scenes of violence (such as train wrecks) comes from the increasing insulation Americans had from violence in the late nineteenth century. Just as lynching spectacles

"could alleviate many of the anxieties that modern life generated," train wreck spectacles served a similar function for traumatized communities.

36. *RNO*, October 25, 1887.

37. "Responsibility in Railway Accidents," *NOP*, March 9, 1891.

38. Editorial, *Greensboro Patriot*, September 3, 1891; "They Are Censured," *Concord (N.C.) Weekly Standard*, November 3, 1891.

39. W. H. Baldwin to Samuel Spencer, November 20, 1897, in the Samuel Spencer Files, box 30, file 952, SRHAC.

40. Newspaper Clipping, March 6, 1896, in the Southern Railway Executive Files, box C, file 34, SRHAC.

41. N. E. Harris to W. H. Baldwin, March 6, 1896, in the Southern Railway Executive Files, box C, file 34, SRHAC.

42. McCombs, *Stone Creek Wreck*, 111, 159.

43. "Regular Record of Railway Slaughter," *NOP*, August 8, 1891.

44. Usselman, *Regulating Railroad Innovation*, 121–31.

45. Aldrich, *Death Rode the Rails*, 90.

46. Beeby, *Revolt of the Tar Heels*, 15, 20–21.

47. Stover, *Railroads of the South*, 190.

48. Historians examining the struggles of working peoples in the New South era have questioned the notion of a quiescent southern working class, and demonstrated that the South was indeed fertile ground for labor radicalism; see McLaurin, *Knights of Labor in the South*; Letwin, *Challenge of Interracial Unionism*; and Shapiro, *New South Rebellion*. The wide spread of Populism in the South similarly shows the many grievances held against the railroad-dominated New South political economy. See chap. 7 of this book; Ayers, *Promise of the New South*, chap. 10; Postel, *Populist Vision*.

49. Stowell, *Streets, Railroads*, makes such an argument for northern cities afflicted with riots during the 1877 strike. He contends that violence against trains and railroad property was a manifestation of long-held grievances against railroad corporations.

50. "Train Wrecking," *Railway Gazette*, May 30, 1884.

51. "Train Wrecking," *NOP*, January 11, 1893.

52. "Vicksburg," *NOP*, September 9, 1890.

53. Letter from C. E. Goodman to G. E. Goodman, June 11, 1894, in William Stevens Powell Material for Iredell and Adjacent Counties, N.C. no. 3300, SHC.

54. Stiles, *Jesse James*; also chap. 6 of this book.

55. William Pinkerton, "Highwaymen of the Railroad," *The North American Review* 157 November 1893): 530–41.

56. Thomas, *Lawyering for the Railroad*, 113–17.

57. "About the Western N.C. Road," *Charlotte Chronicle*, August 30, 1891.

58. "A Sensational Letter," *MWT*, December 4, 1896.

59. "Is He The Wrecker?," *Atlanta Constitution*, March 23, 1895.

60. "Reed Solicitous for Miss Rush," *Atlanta Constitution*, May 21, 1897.

61. A more cohesive retelling of the story of the Bostian's Bridge wreck can be found in Huffard, "Ghosts, Wreckers and Rotten Ties."

62. This testimony is printed in full in "The Story of the Wreck," *Statesville Landmark*, September 3, 1891.

63. "Story of the Wreck."

64. "Story of the Wreck."

65. Letter from S. P. Read to Bennehan Cameron, August 31, 1891, in the Bennehan Cameron Papers, no. 3623, subser. 1.2, folder 155, SHC.

66. "Story of the Wreck."

67. A copy of this letter was reprinted in "The Narrative of the Wreck," *Statesville Landmark*, September 10, 1891.

68. "The Great Disaster," *Statesville Landmark*, September 10, 1891; "One Man Dissented," *Asheville Citizen*, September 12, 1891.

69. Thomas, *Lawyering for the Railroad*, 80; Diary, December 17, 1894, in the David Schenck Papers, no. 652, SHC.

70. *Statesville Landmark*, August 11, 1892; "Bostian Bridge Train Wreck in 1891 Is Considered Controversial," *Statesville Landmark*, August 25, 1966.

71. "That Terrible Wreck," *Progressive Farmer*, September 1, 1891; "The Bostian Bridge Disaster," *Progressive Farmer*, September 9, 1891; "A Diabolical Deed," *Richmond Dispatch*, August 29, 1891.

72. Samuel Spencer to W. W. Finley, December 28, 1896, in the Samuel Spencer President's Files, box 37, file 1454, SRHAC.

73. Samuel Spencer to W. A. Turk, December 28, 1896, in the Samuel Spencer President's Files, box 37, file 1454, SRHAC.

74. W. W. Finley to Samuel Spencer," December 30, 1896, in the Samuel Spencer President's Files, box 37, file 1454, SRHAC.

75. Letter to J. G. Metcalfe from R. Montfort, January 11, 1897, box 52, folder 11, L&NRR.

76. "Awful Accident!," *Birmingham News*, December 28, 1896.

77. Letter to J. G. Metcalfe from R. Montfort, January 13, 1897, box 52, folder 11, L&NRR.

78. Letter to J. G. Metcalfe from R. Montfort, January 20, 1897, box 52, folder 11, L&NRR.

79. Letter to J. G. Metcalfe from R. Montfort, January 14, 1897, box 52, folder 11, L&NRR.

80. Letter to J. G. Metcalfe from R. Montfort, January 14, 1897, box 52, folder 11, L&NRR.

81. Letter to W. W. Finley, December 30, 1896, in the Samuel Spencer President's Files, box 37, file 1454, SRHAC.

82. W.W. Finley to Samuel Spencer, December 31, 1896, in the Samuel Spencer President's Files, box 37, file 1454, SRHAC.

83. In his study of railroad legal departments, William Thomas reaches a similar conclusion about the Cahaba wreck. Thomas, *Lawyering for the Railroad*, 120–24.

84. W. H. Baldwin to Samuel Spencer, November 20, 1897, in the Samuel Spencer President's Files, box 30, file 952, SRHAC.

85. "Awful Accident!"

86. "Train Wreckers Take Twenty-Eight Lives," *Atlanta Constitution*, December 28, 1896.

87. "A Plunge to Death," *Greensboro Patriot*, December 30, 1896.

88. Editorials compiled in the article "The Cahaba Horror," *Atlanta Constitution*, January 2, 1897; Editorial, *Milledgeville Union and Recorder*, January 5, 1897.

89. "The Cahaba Wreck," *Birmingham State-Herald*, January 1, 1897.

90. "Two More Unfortunates," *Birmingham State-Herald*, January 2, 1897.

91. These data are gleaned from a search of the online *Atlanta Constitution* for "train" AND "wreck*" in the twenty-year period between January 1, 1878 and 1January 1, 1898. A

train-wrecking attempt could be something as innocent as a crosstie on a track, or a misplaced rail. As long as the paper suggested malicious intent or a deliberate effort to wreck a train, a case was tallied. Cases were tallied for attempted wrecks in all of the states of the former Confederacy except for Texas and West Virginia, which means the data set does include cases from ten states (Va., N.C., S.C., Ga., Fla., Ala., Miss., Tenn., Ark., La.).

92. Data from the *NOP* are from an online database (19th Century American Newspapers), with the same methodology as the search of the *Constitution*.

93. Data from the *RNO* are from an online database (19th Century American Newspapers), with the same methodology as the search of the *Constitution*. Years before 1880 are missing because the online database does not include them.

94. "Etched and Sketched," *Atlanta Constitution*, November 10, 1891.

95. "A Most Damnable Conspiracy," *Birmingham State-Herald*, January 10, 1897.

96. "Most Damnable Conspiracy."

97. Walter F. Jackson, "Hut by the Wateree," *Frank Leslie's Popular Monthly* (June 1885): 675–80.

98. "A Deadly Dilemma," *NOP*, January 15, 1893.

99. "A Railroad Medal," *Atlanta Constitution*, April 5, 1896.

100. "Columbus Toe Bluchers," *Atlanta Constitution*, October 29, 1893.

101. Advertisement, *RNO*, July 8, 1897.

102. Advertisment, *RNO*, July 7, 1898.

103. Data from the *NOP* are from an online database (19th Century American Newspapers), with the same methodology as the search of the *Constitution*. Data from the *RNO* are from an online database (19th Century American Newspapers), with the same methodology as the search of the *Constitution*. Years before 1880 are missing because the online database does not include them at this point.

104. Harlan, "Alabama Train Wreckers of 30 Years Ago," *L&N Employes' Magazine* 3 (September 1927): 37–39, 58–59.

105. Accident Record Book of the Nashville, Chattanooga, and St. Louis Railway, 1880–1894, p. 49, FHS.

106. Accident Record Book of the Nashville, Chattanooga, and St. Louis Railway, 1880–1894, pp. 72–74, FHS.

107. Letter to MR. A. D. Jones, General Superintendent, South Carolina and Georgia Railroad Co, October 24, 1894, South Carolina Railroads 1880–1920, USC.

108. Ayers, *Promise of the New South*, and Brundage, *Lynching in the New South*, track lynching violence, and both find peaks in the 1890s. Another influence would be the myth of "Black Ulysses," assumptions that blacks were incompatible with modernity and reduced to a permanent state of alienation (and thus criminality). Jones, *Tribe of Black Ulysses*, deconstructs this myth, at least in its relation to lumber workers. Ayers, *Vengeance and Justice in the New South*, 232, 250–53.

109. "The Ponchatoula Wreck," *NOP*, July 24, 1895.

110. "Attempt to Wreck a Train," *Atlanta Constitution*, August 1, 1899.

111. Ayers, *Vengeance and Justice in the New South*, 232.

112. "Riddled with Bullets," *NOP*, December 29, 1884.

113. "Riddled with Bullets."

114. "Vicksburg," *NOP*, July 26, 1888.

115. "Spaniards to Wreck Trains," *RNO*, April 29, 1898.

116. The Alabama legislature was in session when the Cahaba wreck occurred, but the first full session after the wreck began on November 13, 1898. *General Laws (and Joint Resolutions) of the General Assembly of Alabama, Passed at the Session of 1898–9*, 60, 153, 154, 157.

117. The railroad accident was in essence, as historian Wolfgang Schivelbusch states, the "result of management of industry on capitalist principles," a failure of technology left "subject to the dictates of the profit motive." Schivelbusch, *Railway Journey*, 132.

118. Train wrecking did occur in the North, though it is largely absent from the historiography. One exception, Stowell, *Streets, Railroads and the Great Strike of 1877*, reexamines the Great Strikes of 1877 by looking at violence against railroads.

119. This quote is taken from "The Great Disaster," *Statesville Landmark*, September 10, 1891.

120. N. Cohen, *Long Steel Rail*, the most comprehensive listing of American folk songs about trains, includes fifteen train wreck ballads, thirteen of which were set in the South. Cohen, 265, notes that Virginia's C&O Railway "surely holds a record for the number of train wreck songs it has inspired that have made some recoverable imprint on the hillbilly and folk traditions." Lyle, *Scalded to Death by the Steam*, 3, provides a map showing the locations of train wreck ballads that shows forty-three ballads, thirty-two of which were in the South.

121. These songs exist in many forms, so I have used the versions of the songs found in N. Cohen, *Long Steel Rail*, 132–57, 183–226.

122. Smith, *Mastered by the Clock*, discusses the spread of time discipline in the nineteenth-century South as a way to chart the spread of capitalism.

123. "Cause of Wreck Unknown Say Roads Officials," *Atlanta Constitution*, September 28, 1903.

124. "Speed of Travel," *Charlotte Chronicle*, September 3, 1891.

125. Two good narrative accounts of the wreck itself come from Corliss, *Main Line of Mid-America*, 301–11, and N. Cohen, *Long Steel Rail*, 132–57, 183–226.

Chapter Six

1. The spelling of "Burrow" is inconsistent in the contemporary source material. While most sources spell his last name "Burrow," some do refer to him as "Burrows." For the sake of consistency I am using "Burrow."

2. This narrative is drawn from "Train Robbery," *MDA*, December 17, 1888 and eyewitness accounts relayed in official reports to the Illinois Central, To E. T. Jeffrey, December 20, 1888, In-Letters: President's Office, ICRR.

3. "Redoubtable Railroad Bill," *MTDA*, August 6, 1895.

4. "Railroad Bill," *PDN*, August 5, 1895.

5. Agee, *Rube Burrow, King of Outlaws*, 20.

6. This basic account of Burrow's life is drawn from Agee, *Rube Burrow, King of Outlaws*, which is the most trustworthy of the dime novels detailing his exploits. Rube Burrow has not been the subject of much academic interest. Two exceptions are Rogers Jr., "Rube Burrow, 'King of Outlaws,'" 182–98, and Rogers Jr., "Violence and Outlawry in the New South."

7. Two recent narratives of Railroad Bill's life are Matthews, "Looking for Railroad Bill," 66–88, and Massey, *Life and Crimes of Railroad Bill*.

8. Eric Hobsbawm refers to this as "social banditry," and he traces the appearance of Robin Hood–esque figures in spots all across the world in Hobsbawm, *Bandits*, and Hobsbawm, *Primitive Rebels*.

9. Agee, *Rube Burrow, King of Outlaws*.

10. Outland, *Tapping the Pines*. Brundage, *Lynching in the New South*, similarly examines how railroad development led to the migration of large numbers of black laborers to the piney woods region.

11. Massey, *Life and Crimes of Railroad Bill*, 14–15; Polenberg, *Hear My Sad Story*, 130.

12. Penick, "Railroad Bill," 89.

13. "Railroad Bill," *PDN*, March 13, 1896.

14. "Held Up!," *MTDA*, September 2, 1890.

15. "Train Robbery," *NOP*, September 26, 1889.

16. "Train Robbed," *NOP*, December 16, 1888.

17. Summers, *Railroads, Reconstruction*, 91.

18. Turner, *Journey into Florida Railroad History*, 108–10; Klein, *History of the Louisville & Nashville Railroad*, 157–58, 181; Hildreth, "Railroads Out of Pensacola," 397–417.

19. "Good for Escambia," *Brewton (Ala.) Standard Gauge*, May 16, 1895; "The Rambler," *Brewton (Ala.) Standard Gauge*, August 8, 1895.

20. "Railroad Again Responsible," *MTDA*, July 10, 1895.

21. Stimson, *History of the Express Business*, 127; S. R. Nelson, *Iron Confederacies*, 42–44.

22. "A Heavy Haul," *NOP*, December 11, 1887; "Train Robbed," *NOP*, December 16, 1888.

23. "Where Was Rube?," *MTDA*, September 26, 1889.

24. "Goes Scott Free," *Birmingham Daily News*, September 3, 1890.

25. "Another Reward Offered," *MTDA*, April 10, 1895.

26. "Railroad Racket," *MTDA*, April 19, 1895.

27. Carmer, *Stars Fell on Alabama*, 122.

28. "Dare Devil Rube," *Birmingham Daily News*, October 17, 1889.

29. "Rube Burrows Heard From," *PDN*, September 19, 1890.

30. "Another One Bites the Dust," *MTDA*, April 9, 1895.

31. "The Revival of Train Robbery," *NOP*, November 14, 1888.

32. "Run Down at Last," *PDN*, November 9, 1889.

33. Stiles, *Jesse James*.

34. "The Industry of Train Robbing," *Railroad Gazette*, October 19, 1894.

35. "The Bottom Facts of It," *MDA*, December 18, 1888.

36. "Need of Train Police," *MDA*, December 17, 1888.

37. "Red Rube," *Atlanta Constitution*, November 3, 1889.

38. Editorial Comment, *Atlanta Constitution*, September 5, 1890.

39. "How to Stop Train Robbing," *Atlanta Constitution*, November 19, 1891.

40. "The Train-Robbing Industry," *NOP*, September 3, 1890.

41. These two deployments are discussed in letters in this file, Alabama Governor (1886–1890: Seay), Administrative Files, SG 8,415, reels 14–21, ADAH.

42. Letter to Thomas Seay from George Bartholomew, October 28, 1889, Alabama Governor (1886–1890: Seay), Administrative Files, SG 8,415, reels 14–21, ADAH.

43. "Negro Tramps," *PDN*, February 22, 1894.

44. Editorial, *PDN*, November 28, 1894.

45. "The Tramp Question," *PDN*, December 1, 1894.

46. "A Midnight Battle," *Atlanta Constitution*, April 8, 1895.

47. Carmer, *Stars Fell on Alabama*, 123.

48. "Betrayed and Shot!," *Brewton (Ala.) Standard Gauge*, July 4, 1895.

49. "Hot on His Trail," *Birmingham Age-Herald*, July 5, 1895.

50. "It Is Startling Anyway," *Birmingham Age-Herald*, July 7, 1895.

51. "Bowden Saw Him," *Birmingham Daily News*, November 5, 1889.

52. "Rube Again," *Birmingham Daily News*, November 6, 1889.

53. Editorial, *Blount County (Ala.) Herald*, November 14, 1889.

54. Editorial, *(Ala.) Messenger*, July 25, 1889.

55. Editorial, *MTDA*, September 3, 1890.

56. "Rube Did It," *Birmingham Daily News*, November 26, 1889.

57. A good summary of Bunch's career is found in "A Train Robber's Violent End," *Railway World*, August 27, 1892.

58. "Our Picayunes," *NOP*, December 5, 1890.

59. "Rube Burrows Had Sense," *Atlanta Constitution*, October 12, 1890.

60. Carmer, *Stars Fell on Alabama*, 136.

61. "Rufus Sanders on Rube Burrow," *MTDA*, October 19, 1890.

62. "Rufus Sanders on Rube Burrow."

63. "'Railroad' Seen Near Daphne," *Brewton (Ala.) Standard Gauge*, July 18, 1895.

64. "'Railroad' Bill Surrounded," *MTDA*, August 1, 1895.

65. "Has Given Them the Slip," *Birmingham Age-Herald*, August 5, 1895.

66. Editorial, *Pine Belt (Atmore, Ala.) News*, July 16, 1895.

67. "Demopolis," *Birmingham Age-Herald*, August 14, 1895.

68. "How Is This?," *MTDA*, August 10, 1895.

69. Carmer, *Stars Fell on Alabama*, 122–25.

70. Harlan, "Railroad Bill," *L&N Employes' Magazine*, May 1927, 30.

71. "More about Railroad," *MTDA*, August 7, 1895.

72. "Mississippi," *NOP*, December 21, 1888.

73. E. F. Jeffrey to Stuyvesant Fish, January 10, 1889, In-Letters: President's Office, ICRR.

74. Letter to Thomas Seay from W. A. Young, August 8, 1889, Alabama Governor (1886–1890: Seay), Administrative Files, SG 8,415, reels 14–21, ADAH.

75. "Rube Burrow," *Vernon (Ala.) Courier*, August 1, 1889.

76. "Citizens Meeting," *Vernon (Ala.) Courier*, August 8, 1889.

77. "The Rube Burrows Excitement," *Blount County (Ala.) News-Dispatch*, October 31, 1889.

78. Alabama Governor (1886–1890: Seay), Administrative Files, SG 8,415, reels 14–21, ADAH.

79. Editorial, *Blount County (Ala.) News-Dispatch*, November 7, 1889.

80. "Railroad Bill," *NOP*, July 10, 1895.

81. "Additional Reward Offered," *MTDA*, April 10, 1895.

82. "'Railroad' Bill Surrounded," *MTDA*, August 1, 1895.

83. "'Railroad' Bill,'" *Atlanta Constitution*, August 30, 1895.

84. "Is It the Wanted William?," *MDA*, August 17, 1895.

85. "Railroad Bill," *PDN*, September 18, 1895.

86. "Evergreen," *MTDA*, July 10, 1895.

87. "Is It Railroad Bill," *PDN*, July 13, 1895.

88. "Railroad Bill Dead," *MTDA*, March 8, 1896.

89. "Bill," *PDN*, July 16, 1895.

90. "Is Burrows Alive?," *PDN*, October 19, 1890.

91. "Canoe," *Brewton (Ala.) Standard Gauge*, March 12, 1896.

92. "More about Railroad," *MTDA*, August 7, 1895.

93. Carmer, *Stars Fell on Alabama*, 125.

94. Pinkerton, "Highwaymen of the Railroad," 530–41.

95. "A Plentiful Harvest of Train Robbers and Wreckers," *NOP*, December, 23, 1890.

96. "Responsibility for the Flomaton Robbery," *PDN*, September 5, 1890.

97. Editorial, *Railroad Gazette*, February 8, 1895.

98. "The Industry of Train Robbing," *Railroad Gazette*, October 19, 1894.

99. Agee, *Rube Burrow, King of Outlaws*, 7.

100. "Red Rube!," *Atlanta Constitution*, November 3, 1889; "He Talks!," *Atlanta Constitution*, November 10, 1889.

101. "Red Rube!"; "He Talks!"

102. "The Outlaw's Home," *Atlanta Constitution*, November 9, 1890.

103. "Citizens Meeting," *Vernon (Ala.) Courier*, August 8, 1889.

104. Turner III, "Badmen, Black and White," 171, 175.

105. *Abbeville (Ala.) Times*, October 17, 1890, cited in Rogers, "Violence and Outlawry in the New South," 4.

106. "He Talks!"

107. "The Burrow Boys," *MTDA*, February 6, 1888.

108. Stiles, *Jesse James*.

109. Letter to Thomas Seay, November 9, 1889, Alabama Governor (1886–1890: Seay), Administrative Files, SG 8,415, reels 14–21, ADAH.

110. Some examples of contemporary Rube Burrow literature include Ward, *Rube Burrow of Sunny Alabama*; W. B. Lawson, *Jesse James, Rube Burrows & Co*; Stout, *Rube Burrow*; Lawson, *Last of the Burrows Gang*.

111. Matthews, "Looking for Railroad Bill," 66–88.

112. "'Railroad Bill' Reward," *Brewton (Ala.) Standard Gauge*, March 19, 1896.

113. "Died with his Boots On," *Pine Belt (Atmore, Ala.) News*, March 10, 1896.

114. "Railroad Bill Dead," *MTDA*, March 8, 1896.

115. "The Outlaw Dead," *PDN*, March 13, 1896.

116. "The Outlaw's Body," *Atlanta Constitution*, March 10, 1896.

117. "Bill's Body Moved," *Atlanta Constitution*, March 19, 1896; *Brewton (Ala.) Standard Gauge*, March 26, 1896.

118. "Railroad Bill's Body Here," *PDN*, March 14, 1896.

119. Harlan, "Railroad Bill," 70.

120. "Railroad Bill Was Moved," *MTDA*, March 13, 1896.

121. "Notice," *Brewton (Ala.) Standard Gauge*, March 26, 1896.

122. "Burial of Railroad Bill," *PDN*, March 31, 1896.

123. Wood, *Lynching and Spectacle*, 10–13.

124. "She Sang Railroad Bill," *Atlanta Constitution*, October 13, 1898.

125. Carmer, *Stars Fell on Alabama*, 124.

126. S. R. Nelson, *Steel Drivin' Man*, makes a similar argument for the dissemination of the legend of John Henry through the work camps and mobile labor sites in what Nelson calls the southern railroad "Octopus." Also see chap. 3 of this book.

127. Odum, "Folk-Song and Folk-Poetry," 289–93.

128. N. Cohen, *Long Steel Rail*, 125–27.

129. Odum, *Negro and His Songs*, 204.

130. Odum, "Folk-Song and Folk-Poetry," 289–93.

131. The social bandit formulation is drawn from two books by Eric Hobsbawm. Hobsbawm, *Bandits*, and Hobsbawm, *Primitive Rebels*.

132. The political turn against railroads in Alabama is documented in Doster, *Railroads in Alabama Politics*.

Chapter Seven

1. "To Break the Big System," *Atlanta Constitution*, June 8, 1897.

2. "Macon Completely Bottled Up," *Macon News*, April 29, 1897.

3. "How Competition Has Been Wiped Out," *Macon News*, May 3, 1897.

4. "A Bold Demand," *MWT*, June 5, 1897.

5. Walter B. Hill to Samuel Spencer, June 5, 1897, Samuel Spencer President's Files, box 52, file 2032, SRHAC.

6. Austrian economist Joseph Schumpeter famously coined this term. Appleby, *Relentless Revolution*, 83.

7. Stover, *Railroads of the South*, 275.

8. Berk, *Alternative Tracks*, most persuasively makes the case that America's industrial order did not have to develop with large national systems and that railroads served national, not local, goals.

9. P. I. Welles to W. H. Barrett, November 2, 1898, Samuel Spencer President's Files, box 61, file 3112, SRHAC.

10. R. L. Vernon to W. A. Turk, October 3, 1898, Samuel Spencer President's Files, box 61, file 3112, SRHAC.

11. S. R. Nelson, *Iron Confederacies*, 41–45.

12. S. R. Nelson details this history and makes a strong case for the importance of the SRSC in setting the course of not only southern railroading but also the region's economic development at large. Other railroad historians have downplayed the importance of this holding company. Summers, "Iron Confederacies," 891–92. This review wonders about the "dubiousness of seeing Scott's security company, which was quickly liquidated, as so powerful past its own lifetime." Churella, *Pennsylvania Railroad*, 438–46, argues that unfair scapegoating of Tom Scott was the real long-term effect of the SRSC, and the region's reliance on cotton and tobacco was more the result of national economic trends than SRSC policy or conspiracy. At the very least it is clear that the SRSC laid the foundation for the *idea* of a southern railway conglomerate.

13. Klein, *Great Richmond Terminal*, 188–90, 235–37, 291; Campbell, *Reorganization of the American Railroad System*, 95.

14. Stover, *Railroads of the South*, 257–58.

15. Railroad Commission of Georgia, *Twenty-First Report of the Railroad Commission of Georgia*, 3.

16. "Like a Rocket," *Atlanta Constitution*, May 12, 1895; "The Macon Construction Company," *Columbus (Ga.) Daily Enquirer*, March 24, 1891.

17. Various letters in box 3 in the William A. Lash Papers, no. 3900, SHC.

18. From pages 4–9 from the Reorganization Plan found in Samuel Spencer President's Files, box 2, file 26, SRHAC.

19. S. R. Nelson, *Iron Confederacies*, chap. 4.

20. Campbell, *Reorganization of the American Railroad System*, 156–57.

21. John T. Glenn to Samuel Spencer, June 19, 1894, Samuel Spencer President's Files, box 4, file 56, SRHAC.

22. W. H. Green to Samuel Spencer, June 2, 1894, box 16, in the Samuel Spencer Papers, no. 3477, SHC.

23. "A New Trademark," *Atlanta Constitution*, July 22, 1894.

24. Samuel Spencer to W. W. Finley, December 3, 1895, W. W. Finley to Samuel Spencer, December 6 1895, Samuel Spencer President's Files, box 26C, file 65, SRHAC.

25. Samuel Spencer to W. W. Finley, March 20, 1897, W. W. Finley to Samuel Spencer, March 21, 1897, Samuel Spencer President's Files, box 43, file 1578, SRHAC.

26. Campbell, *Reorganization of the American Railroad System*, 158–59.

27. "A New Southern Railway," *RNO*, July 4, 1894.

28. *Fifty-Sixth Report of the President and Directors of the Central Rail Road*, 7.

29. "Vanderbilt Railroads South," *Manufacturers' Record*, September 7, 1894.

30. "Great Good for the South," *Manufacturers' Record*, September 14, 1894.

31. "Col. Andrews Talks," *RNO*, February 5, 1895.

32. Presbrey, *Southland*.

33. Stover, *Railroads of the South*, 257–58.

34. "Relations with the Southern," From Milton Smith to August Belmont, in *Louisville & Nashville Annual Reports: Special Report to the President, 1894–1895*, box 40, folder 19, L&NRR.

35. *Twenty-First Report of the Railroad Commission of Georgia*, 119.

36. Klein, *Great Richmond Terminal*, 225.

37. Stover, *Railroads of the South*, 251.

38. "A New Depot," *Atlanta Constitution*, June 22, 1895.

39. Editorial, *Houston County (Ga.) Home Journal*, June 27, 1895.

40. Editorial, *Tifton (Ga.) Gazette*, June 28, 1895.

41. To August Belmont, June 26, 1895, *Louisville & Nashville Annual Reports: Special Report to the President, 1894–1895*, box 40, folder 19, L&NRR.

42. "The Southern Takes Possession," *Atlanta Constitution*, July 3, 1896.

43. "News at Breakfast," *Atlanta Constitution*, July 20, 1896.

44. "Griffin Case Put Off a Month," *Atlanta Constitution*, April 21, 1897.

45. Quote found in Thomas, *Lawyering for the Railroad*, 208.

46. Editorial, *Tifton (Ga.) Gazette*, February 8, 1895; "A Sop to Cerberus," *Tifton (Ga.) Gazette*, March 29, 1895.

47. "The Big Railroad Deal," *MWT*, June 6, 1895.

48. Samuel Spencer to A. B. Andrews, June 12, 1895, Samuel Spencer President's Files, box 12, file 187, SRHAC; Samuel Spencer to J. M. Culp, June 11, 1895, Samuel Spencer President's Files, box 12, file 187, SRHAC.

49. "Shaw's Word Goes," *Atlanta Constitution*, September 10, 1895; "Each Goes His Way," *Atlanta Constitution*, September 11, 1895, Samuel Spencer President's Files, box 7, file 92, SRHAC.

50. Samuel Spencer to J. F. Hanson, October 1, 1895, Samuel Spencer President's Files, box 13, file 192, SRHAC.

51. Samuel Spencer to N. E. Harris, June 13, 1895, Samuel Spencer President's Files, box 12, file 187, SRHAC.

52. N. E. Harris to Samuel Spencer, June 10, 1895, Samuel Spencer President's Files, box 13, file 192, SRHAC.

53. N. E Harris to Samuel Spencer, June 12, 1895, Samuel Spencer President's Files, box 13, file 192, SRHAC.

54. Editorial, *Tifton (Ga.) Gazette*, June 21, 1895.

55. Guerry & Hall to Skipwith Wilmer, June 10, 1895 and June 14, 1895, Samuel Spencer President's Files, box 4, file 50A, SRHAC.

56. Guerry & Hall to Skipwith Wilmer, November 5, 1896, Samuel Spencer President's Files, box 4, file 50A, SRHAC.

57. To Spencer, January 31, 1901, Samuel Spencer President's Files, box 4, folder 50A, SRHAC.

58. S. R. Jacques to Samuel Spencer, June 12, 1895, Samuel Spencer President's Files, box 12, file 188, SRHAC.

59. Samuel Spencer to S. R. Jacques, July 10, 1895, Samuel Spencer President's Files, box 12, file 188, SRHAC.

60. Samuel Spencer to S. R. Jacques, July 10, 1895, Samuel Spencer President's Files, box 12, file 188, SRHAC.

61. "Consolidation and the Policy of the Southern Railway," *Railway Gazette*, August 2, 1895; Samuel Spencer to JSB Thompson, July 30, 1895, Samuel Spencer President's Files, box 12, file 188, SRHAC.

62. Editorial, *Atlanta People's Party Paper*, May 25, 1894.

63. Harrison, *History of the Legal Development of the Southern Railway*, 558.

64. "Free to Build up Savannah," *SMN*, November 1, 1895.

65. *Twenty-Third Report of the Railroad Commission of Georgia*, 7.

66. *Twenty-Fourth Report of the Railroad Commission of Georgia*, 12.

67. "Ownership of the Central," *SMN*, May 30, 1896.

68. "What the Commission Want," *SMN*, June 1, 1896.

69. "Who Owns the Central?," *SMN*, July 30, 1896.

70. "Ownership of the Central," *SMN*, October 22, 1896.

71. *Twenty-Fourth Report of the Railroad Commission of Georgia*, 37.

72. William Shaw to Samuel Spencer, November 25, 1897, Samuel Spencer President's Files, box 54B, file 14, SRHAC.

73. Shaw to Samuel Spencer, April 16, 1897, Samuel Spencer President's Files, box 52, file 2032, SRHAC.

74. Davis, *Southern Railway*, 236–38.

75. *Twenty-Fourth Report of the Railroad Commission of Georgia*, 13.

76. To A. B. Andrews, October 14, 1895, Samuel Spencer President's Files, box 24, file 740, SRHAC.

77. "A Fight on the Railroads," *SMN*, November 22, 1895.

78. On the Populist platform, see Postel, *Populist Vision*, 3–6, 9; *Atlanta People's Party Paper*, October 25, 1895.

79. A. B. Andrews to Samuel Spencer, March 19, 1894, box 15, in the Samuel Spencer Papers, no. 3477, SHC.

80. H. M. Comer to Samuel Spencer, May 4, 1894, box 16, in the Samuel Spencer Papers, no. 3477, SHC.

81. Georgia General Assembly, *Acts and Resolutions of the General Assembly of the State of Georgia* (1892), 49.

82. W. A. Henderson to Samuel Spencer, April 28, 1894, box 16, in the Samuel Spencer Papers, no. 3477, SHC.

83. H. M. Comer to Samuel Spencer, May 24, 1894, box 16, in the Samuel Spencer Papers, no. 3477, SHC.

84. W. A. Henderson to Samuel Spencer, May 3, 1894, box 16, in the Samuel Spencer Papers, no. 3477, SHC.

85. This election is detailed in Woodward, *Tom Watson*, 259–77; Shaw, *Wool-Hat Boys*, 102–23.

86. Shaw, *Wool-Hat Boys*, 126–34, 194. Shaw notes that one of the most surprising facts about the party's legislators was their "absence of any challenge to the economic order in Georgia."

87. To Samuel Spencer, December 7, 1895. Samuel Spencer President's Files, box 24, file 740, SRHAC.

88. Georgia General Assembly, *Acts and Resolutions of the General Assembly of the State of Georgia* (1894), 65–66.

89. Georgia General Assembly, *Acts and Resolutions of the General Assembly of the State of Georgia* (1895), 62.

90. Georgia General Assembly, *Acts and Resolutions of the General Assembly of the State of Georgia* (1896), 57, 63.

91. Samuel Spencer to G. W. Maslin, June 6, 1897, Samuel Spencer President's Files, box 52, file 2032, SRHAC.

92. "The Fight on the Southern," *SMN*, June 23, 1897.

93. Harris, *Autobiography*, 268–70.

94. "A Halt Called," *MWT*, June 6, 1897.

95. "Shut the Stable Door," *SMN*, June 24, 1897.

96. William Shaw to Samuel Spencer, June 10, 1897, Samuel Spencer President's Files, box 52, file 2032, SRHAC.

97. "Another Railroad Organ," *SMN*, June 13, 1897.

98. *Hawkinsville (Ga.) News and Dispatch*, October 21, 1897.

99. Harris, *Autobiography*, 270.

100. Glenn to Samuel Spencer, June 19, 1897, Samuel Spencer President's Files, box 52, 203, SRHAC.

101. N. E. Harris to Samuel Spencer, June 21, 1897, Samuel Spencer President's Files, box 52, file 2032, SRHAC.

102. H. M. Comer to Samuel Spencer, June 9, 1897, Samuel Spencer President's Files, box 52, file 2032, SRHAC.

103. Emory Speer to Samuel Spencer, July 27, 1894, Samuel Spencer President's Files, box 4, file 56, SRHAC.

104. N. E. Harris to Samuel Spencer, April 12, 1899, Samuel Spencer President's Files, box 54B, file 14, SRHAC; "An Old Case Is Dismissed," *Atlanta Constitution*, February 16, 1901.

105. "The North Carolina Railroad," *Greensboro Patriot*, July 31, 1895.

106. *Amendments Thereto of the North Carolina Railroad Co.*, 98.

107. "Renewal of the North Carolina Railroad Lease," *Greensboro Patriot*, August 21, 1895.

108. "History of the 99-Year Lease," *RNO*, January 31, 1897.

109. "That Railroad Lease," *Raleigh Caucasian*, August 29, 1895.

110. "That 99-Year Railroad Lease," *Raleigh Caucasian*, July 23, 1896.

111. Stewart, "Confederate Menace," 54–70.

112. Thomas, *Lawyering for the Railroad*, 47–51.

113. Diary, December 17, 1894, in the David Schenck Papers, no. 652, SHC.

114. Leslie Ryan to David Schenck, May 11, 1895, Samuel Spencer President's Files, box 10, file 141, SRHAC.

115. Diary, October 14, 1893, in the David Schenck Papers, no. 652, SHC.

116. Samuel Spencer to Francis Lynde Stetson, June 5, 1895, Samuel Spencer President's Files, box 10, file 141, SRHAC.

117. David Schenck to Francis Lynde Stetson, August 27, 1895, Samuel Spencer President's Files, box 10, file 141, SRHAC.

118. "That 99-Year R.R. Lease."

119. David Schenck to Marion Butler, March 10, 1896, in the Marion Butler Papers, no. 114, SHC.

120. David Schenck to Marion Butler, April 9, 1896, in the Marion Butler Papers, no. 114, SHC.

121. Craig, *Josephus Daniels*, 141, 146.

122. "The N.C. R.R. Lease," *RNO*, January 24, 1897; "History of the 99-Year Lease," *RNO*, January 31, 1897.

123. *Statesville Landmark*, August 23, 1895.

124. "History of the 99-Year Lease."

125. David Schenck to Marion Butler, April 4, 1896, in the Marion Butler Papers, no. 114, SHC.

126. "Gov. Russell on the 99 Year Lease," *Raleigh Caucasian*, December 10, 1896.

127. "Governor Russell's Inaugural Address," *RNO*, January 13, 1897.

128. John Graham to Daniel Russell, December 9, 1896 in the Daniel Russell Papers, no. 645, SHC.

129. Undated file in box 2, folder 19, in the Daniel Russell Papers, no. 645, SHC.

130. "Who Owns the State?," *Raleigh Caucasian*, August 12, 1897.

131. "The Fight Is On in Georgia, Too," *RNO*, February 25, 1897.

132. Marion Butler to William Jennings Bryan, December 18, 1896, in the Marion Butler Papers, no. 114, SHC.

133. From the text of the bill found in box 5, folder 54 of the Marion Butler Papers, no. 114, SHC.

134. "Capital and the South," *Manufacturers' Record,* March 5, 1897.

135. Editorial, *Greensboro Patriot,* January 1, 1896.

136. "Reduced Fac-Simile of Mr. Reynolds' Check," *RNO,* February 6, 1897.

137. "A Bomb in the 99 Year Lease," *Raleigh Caucasian,* February 11, 1897.

138. "Sensation at Raleigh," *Greensboro Patriot,* February 10, 1897; "Governor's Message on 99-Year Lease," *RNO,* February 6, 1897.

139. "More about the 99-Year Lease," *Raleigh Caucasian,* March 4, 1897.

140. J. H. Click to Marion Butler, February 23, 1897, in the Marion Butler Papers, no. 114, SHC.

141. Beeby, *Revolt of the Tar Heels,* 8, 156.

142. Daniels, *Editor in Politics,* 209, 213–15.

143. Daniels, 213–15.

144. "The Courts to Decide," *Atlanta Constitution,* March 22, 1897.

145. "The Story of the Fight," *Raleigh Caucasian,* March 11, 1897.

146. "Now the People Will Settle It," *RNO,* March 9, 1897.

147. J. J. Mott to Marion Butler, February 24, 1898, in the Marion Butler Papers, no. 114, SHC.

148. "The Kind of 'White Man's Party' Needed," *Raleigh Caucasian,* September 9, 1897.

149. Prepared by the State Democratic Executive Committee of North Carolina, *Democratic Hand Book: 1898,* 191–94.

150. "Anglo Saxons Must Control North Carolina," *RNO,* August 20, 1897.

151. "Concerning the Political Situation in the State," *RNO,* August 29, 1897.

152. State Democratic Executive Committee of North Carolina, *Democratic Hand Book: 1898,* 110–11.

153. "The Great Railroad Lawyer Convention," *Raleigh Caucasian,* June 9, 1898.

154. Gilmore, *Gender and Jim Crow,* 78–82.

155. "There Is Danger Ahead," *Raleigh Caucasian,* April 21, 1898.

156. Daniels, *Editor in Politics,* 211.

157. Edward Momses to Marion Butler, February 6, 1897 in the Marion Butler Papers, no. 114, SHC.

158. *RNO,* September 27, 1898; *RNO,* October 5, 1898; Gilmore, *Gender and Jim Crow.*

159. The best narrative of these events is in Gilmore, *Gender and Jim Crow.*

160. Woodward, *Origins of the New South,* 271; Ayers, *Promise of the New South,* chaps. 10–11; Goodwyn, *Populist Moment.*

161. The best study of the antirailroad issue in post-1900 southern politics is Doster, *Railroads in Alabama Politics.* Berk, *Alternative Tracks,* makes the case that the death of an alternative model of industrial development died with the consolidation of railroads into large conglomerates. The local development model of what a railroad corporation could be also fits neatly into Richard White's framework of a "utopian" version of capitalism, an idealized form of capitalism that diverged from the system that ultimately triumphed. White, "Utopian Capitalism," 119–39.

Conclusion

1. A collection of his writings and speeches on this subject (in the year before his death) is in the bound volume in the Samuel Spencer Papers, no. 3477, folder 369, vol. 11, SHC.

2. Stover, *Railroads of the South, 1865–1900*, 275.

3. Newspaper clipping from the *Charleston Courier*, November 30, 1906, in the Samuel Spencer Papers, no. 3477, folder 369, vol. 9, SHC.

4. Newspaper clipping from the *Atlanta Constitution*, December 2, 1906, in the Samuel Spencer Papers, no. 3477, folder 369, vol. 9, SHC.

5. Newspaper clipping from the *Atlanta Constitution*, November 30, 1906, in the Samuel Spencer Papers, no. 3477, folder 369, vol. 9, SHC.

6. Newspaper clipping from the *Charlotte Observer*, November 30, 1905, in the Samuel Spencer Papers, no. 3477, folder 369, vol. 9, SHC; newspaper clipping from the *New Orleans, La. Item*, November 30, 1905, in the Samuel Spencer Papers, no. 3477, folder 369, vol. 9, SHC.

7. Newspaper clipping from the *Wall Street Journal*, December 8, 1906, in the Samuel Spencer Papers, no. 3477, folder 369, vol. 9, SHC.

8. Newspaper clipping from the *New York City Globe*, November 29, 1906, in the Samuel Spencer Papers, no. 3477, folder 369, vol. 9, SHC.

9. Newspaper clipping from the *Atlanta Evening Journal*, November 29, 1906, in the Samuel Spencer Papers, no. 3477, folder 369, vol. 9, SHC.

10. Newspaper clipping from the *Atlanta Georgian*, November 30, 1906, in the Samuel Spencer Papers, no. 3477, folder 369, vol. 9, SHC.

11. Woodward, *Tom Watson*, 377–78; *Tom Watson's Magazine* 4 (April 1906): 164.

12. The importance of the 1890s in southern history was most famously stated by Woodward, *Origins of the New South*.

13. Berk, *Alternative Tracks*, and Postel, *Populist Vision*.

14. Hale, *Making Whiteness*, 125–38; Kelley, *Right to Ride*, chaps. 2 and 3.

15. Details on the quarantines associated with the 1905 epidemic can be found in Correspondence to the Mississippi Board of Health, 1905–1907, MS 782, LRC.

16. Espinosa, *Epidemic Invasions*, details the eradication campaign in Cuba. Humphreys, *Yellow Fever and the South*, chap. 5.

17. Aldrich, *Death Rode the Rails*, 70, 97, notes the decline in railroad accidents after the turn of the century.

18. The best work that traces the evolution to Progressive regulation of southern railroads is Doster, *Railroads in Alabama Politics*. On the import of the Populist defeat, see Goodwyn, *Populist Moment*, xiii.

19. Baptist, *Half Has Never Been Told*, xvi–xix.

20. Highlights of this so-called new history of capitalism include Baptist, *Half Has Never Been Told*; Beckert, *Empire of Cotton*; Beckert and Desan, *American Capitalism*; Beckert and Rockman, *Slavery's Capitalism*; Johnson, *River of Dark Dreams*.

21. Hamilton, *Trucking Country*; Moreton, *To Serve God and Wal-Mart*.

22. These arguments about the 2008 financial crisis are best summarized in Ferguson, *Inside Job*.

23. Cash, *Johnny Cash—Ridin' the Rails*.

24. Martin, *Railroads Triumphant*, vociferously makes the case that regulation is what killed the American railroad industry. A similar argument and an acknowledgment of the recent freight railroad revival are in Gallamore and Meyer, *American Railroads*.

25. Cash, *Johnny Cash—Ridin' the Rails*.

26. R.E.M., "Driver 8"; Steve Earle and the Del McCoury Band, "Texas Eagle"; Gillian Welch, "Down along the Dixie Line."

27. Millichap, *Dixie Limited*, chap. 10, captures some of the still-conflicted meanings of southern railroads in the late twentieth century.

28. For more on the potential twenty-first-century railroad revival, see Stilgoe, *Train Time*, and Zoellner, *Train*. White House Office of the Press Secretary, "Remarks by the President in State of the Union Address," January 25, 2011.

29. Osnos, "Letter from China, Boss Rail."

30. R.E.M., "Driver 8."

Bibliography

Primary Sources

MANUSCRIPT COLLECTIONS

Alabama Department of Archives and History, Montgomery, Alabama
    Alabama Governor (1886–1890: Seay), Administrative Files
    Alabama Railroad Commission Letterbook
Filson Historical Society, Louisville, Kentucky
    Accident Record Book of the Nashville, Chattanooga, and St. Louis Railway
Hargrett Rare Book and Manuscript Library, The University of Georgia Libraries, Athens,
    Georgia
    Georgia Railroad Collection
Louisiana and Lower Mississippi Valley Collections, LSU Libraries, Baton Rouge,
    Louisiana
    M. F. Surghnor Diary
    Sylvester L. Cary Scrapbook
Mississippi Department of Archives and History, Jackson, Mississippi
    Mississippi State Railroad Commission, Minute Book
    John Stone Marshall Papers (correspondence)
Newberry Library, Chicago, Illinois
    Illinois Central Railroad Collection
Southern Historical Collection, Wilson Library, University of North Carolina at
    Chapel Hill, Chapel Hill, North Carolina
    Bennehan Cameron Papers
    B. F. Long Papers
    Charles Iverson Graves Papers
    Daniel Russell Papers
    David Schenck Papers
    Grady Family Papers
    Kate Simpson Letter
    Marion Butler Papers
    Samuel Spencer Papers
    Virginia and North Carolina Construction Company Record Book
    William A. Lash Papers
    William Stevens Powell Material for Iredell and Adjacent Counties
Southern Railway Historical Collection, Kennesaw, Georgia
    Samuel Spencer President's Files
    Southern Railway Executive Files
Tulane University Special Collections, New Orleans, Louisiana

Correspondence to the Mississippi Board of Health, 1905–1907
Vertical Files
University Archives and Records Center, University of Louisville, Louisville, Kentucky
Louisville and Nashville Railroad Company Records, 1850–1982
University of Florida Special Collections, Smathers Library, Gainesville, Florida
Edwin Rennolds Diary
Edwin Smith Papers 1884–1896
University of South Carolina Special Collections, Columbia, South Carolina
South Carolina Railroads 1880–1920

NEWSPAPERS AND PERIODICALS

Andalusia (Ala.) Covington Times
Asheville Daily Citizen
Atlanta Constitution
Atlanta People's Party Paper
Atlanta The Sunny South
Birmingham Daily News
Birmingham Age-Herald
Birmingham State-Herald
Blount County (Ala.) Herald
Blount County (Ala.) News-Dispatch
Brewton (Ala.) Standard Gauge
Charlotte Chronicle
Columbus (Ga.) Daily Enquirer
Concord (N.C.) Weekly Standard
DeBow's Review
Fayetteville Observer
Frank Leslie's Popular Monthly
Greensboro Patriot
Grenada (Miss.) Sentinel
Harper's New Monthly Magazine
Harper's Weekly
Hawkinsville (Ga.) News and Dispatch
Hickory (N.C.) Press and Carolinian
Houston County (Ga.) Home Journal
Jackson Daily Bulletin
Jackson New Mississippian
Jacksonville Times-Union
L&N Employes' Magazine
Louisville Commercial
Macon News
Macon Telegraph
Manufacturers' Record
Memphis Daily Appeal
Milledgeville Union and Recorder

Montgomery Advertiser
Morganton (N.C.) Herald
New Orleans Daily Picayune
New Orleans Times
The North American Review
Ocala Banner
Palatka (Fla.) Daily News
Pensacola Daily News
Pine Belt (Atmore, Ala.) News
Progressive Farmer
Railroad Gazette
Railway World
Raleigh Caucasian
Raleigh News-Observer
Raymond (Miss.) Hinds County Gazette
Richmond Dispatch
Salisbury (N.C.) North Carolina Herald
Savannah Morning News
Statesville Landmark
Statesville Record & Landmark
Tifton (Ga.) Gazette
Tom Watson's Magazine
Troy (Ala.) Messenger
Vernon (Ala.) Courier
Vicksburg Daily Herald
Wilmington Messenger

GOVERNMENT REPORTS

Amendments Thereto of the North Carolina Railroad Co. with the By Laws, Mortgage and
    Lease. Raleigh: Edwards & Broughton, 1896.
Centers for Disease Control. "Yellow Fever." Available from http://www.cdc.gov/ncidod
    /dvbid/YellowFever/index.html; Internet; accessed October 25, 2011.
Department of the Interior, Census Office. Report on Transportation Business in the United
    States at the Eleventh Census: 1890, Part 1: Transportation by Land. Washington, D.C.:
    Government Printing Office, 1895.
General Laws (and Joint Resolutions) of the General Assembly of Alabama, Passed at the
    Session of 1898–9, Held in the Capitol in the City of Montgomery Commencing Tuesday,
    November 15, 1898. Jacksonville, Fla., 1899.
Georgia General Assembly. Acts and Resolutions of the General Assembly of the State of
    Georgia. Atlanta: James P. Harrison, state printers, 1892.
———. Acts and Resolutions of the General Assembly of the State of Georgia. Atlanta:
    James P. Harrison, state printers, 1894.
———. Acts and Resolutions of the General Assembly of the State of Georgia. Atlanta:
    James P. Harrison, state printers, 1895.

————. *Acts and Resolutions of the General Assembly of the State of Georgia*. Atlanta: James P. Harrison, state printers, 1896.

Interstate Commerce Commission. *Statistics of Railways in the United States*. Washington, D.C.: Government Printing Office, 1890.

————. *Statistics of Railways in the United States*. Washington, D.C.: Government Printing Office, 1891.

————. *Statistics of Railways in the United States*. Washington, D.C.: Government Printing Office, 1893.

————. *Statistics of Railways in the United States*. Washington, D.C.: Government Printing Office, 1894.

————. *Statistics of Railways in the United States*. Washington, D.C.: Government Printing Office, 1895.

————. *Statistics of Railways in the United States*. Washington, D.C.: Government Printing Office, 1896.

————. *Statistics of Railways in the United States*. Washington, D.C.: Government Printing Office, 1897.

————. *Statistics of Railways in the United States*. Washington, D.C.: Government Printing Office, 1898.

————. *Statistics of Railways in the United States*. Washington, D.C.: Government Printing Office, 1899.

————. *Statistics of Railways in the United States*. Washington: Government Printing Office, 1900.

National Board of Health. *Annual Report of the National Board of Health, 1879*. Washington, D.C.: Government Printing Office, 1879.

Railroad Commission of Georgia. *The Twenty-First Report of the Railroad Commission of Georgia, from October 15, 1892 to October 15, 1893*. Atlanta: Office of Railroad Commission of Georgia, 1893.

————. *Twenty-Third Report of the Railroad Commission of Georgia, from October 15, 1894 to October 15, 1895*. Atlanta: Office of Railroad Commission of Georgia, 1895.

————. *Twenty-Fourth Report of the Railroad Commission of Georgia, from October 15, 1895 to October 15, 1896*. Atlanta: Office of Railroad Commission of Georgia, 1896.

Report of the Mississippi State Board of Health, for the Years 1878–'79. Jackson, Miss.: Board of Health of Mississippi, 1879.

Report of the State Board of Health for 1892, in Message of Francis P. Fleming Governor of Florida, to the Legislature, Regular Session of 1891. Tallahassee, Fla.: Times-Union, Legislative Printer, 1891.

BOOKS AND PAMPHLETS

Adams, Charles, ed. *Report of the Jacksonville Auxiliary Sanitation Association, of Jacksonville, Florida; Covering the Work of the Association during the Yellow Fever Epidemic, 1888*. Jacksonville, Fla.: Times-Union Print, 1889.

Agee, G. W. *Rube Burrow, King of Outlaws, and His Band of Train Robbers: An Accurate and Faithful History of their Exploits and Adventures*. Chicago: Henneberry, 1890.

Along the Gulf: An Entertaining Story of an Outing among the Beautiful Resorts on the Mississippi Sound from New Orleans, La., to Mobile, Ala. Being a Complete Description of

the Advantages Which May Be Enjoyed during a Vacation Spent among the Delightful
Seaside Towns of the Mexican Gulf. William E. Myers, Publisher, 1894.

Andrews, Sidney. *The South since the War: As Shown by Fourteen Weeks of Travel and
Observation in Georgia and the Carolinas.* Boston: Ticknor and Fields, 1866.

*Annual Report of the President and Directors of the Louisville and Nashville Railroad
Company: To the Stockholders, for the Fiscal Year Commencing on the July 1, 1883 and
Ending on the June 30, 1884.* Louisville, Ky.: Louisville & Nashville Railroad, 1880.

Bruce, Thomas. *Southwest Virginia and Shenandoah Valley, An Inquiry into the Causes of the
Rapid Growth and Wonderful Development of Southwest Virginia and Shenandoah Valley,
with a History of the Norfolk and Western and Shenandoah Valley Railroads, and Sketches
of the Principal Cities and Towns Instrumental in the Progress of These Sections.* Richmond,
Va.: J. L. Hill, 1891.

Campbell, Reau. *Winter Cities in Summer Lands: A Tour through Florida and the Winter
Resorts of the South.* Cincinnati, Ohio: Cincinnati, New Orleans & Texas Pacific
Railway, 1885.

*The Cape Fear and Yadkin Valley Railway, from Mt Airy at the Base of the Blue Ridge to
Wilmington, NC: Its Origin, Construction, Connections and Extensions.* Philadelphia:
Allen, Lane & Scott Printers, 1889.

Carmer, Carl. *Stars Fell on Alabama.* New York: Quinn & Boden, 1934.

Cowan, John F. *A New Invasion of the South, Being a Narrative of the Expedition of the
Seventy-First Infantry, National Guard through the Southern States, to New Orleans:
February 24–March 7, 1881.* New York: Board of Officers Seventy-First Infantry, 1881.

Daniels, Josephus. *Editor in Politics.* Chapel Hill: University of North Carolina Press, 1941.

Davis, Jefferson. *The Rise and Fall of the Confederate Government Volume One of Two.*
Project Gutenberg Ebook, 2006.

Dromgoole, John Parham. *Dr. Dromgoole's Yellow Fever Heroes, Honors and Horrors of 1878:
A List of over Ten Thousand Victims, Martyr Death-Roll of Volunteer Physicians, Nurses,
Etc.* Louisville, Ky.: J. P. Morton, 1879.

Edmonds, Richard H. *The South's Redemption: From Poverty to Prosperity.* Baltimore:
Manufacturers' Record, 1890.

*Eighteenth Annual Report of the President and Board of Managers, to the Stockholders of the
Vicksburg and Meridian Railroad Company, for the Fiscal Year, Ending February 28, 1879.*
Vicksburg, Miss.: Times and Republican Book and Job Printing Establishment, 1879.

The Epidemic of 1878, in Mississippi: Report of the Yellow Fever Relief Work through J.L. Power.
Jackson, Miss.: Clarion Steam, 1879.

Faulkner, William. *Go Down, Moses.* New York: Vintage, 1973.

———. *The Unvanquished.* New York: Vintage, 1966.

Field, Henry M. *Blood Is Thicker than Water: A Few Days among our Southern Brethren.*
New York: G. Munro, 1886.

———. *Bright Skies and Dark Shadows.* New York: Charles Scribner's Sons, 1890.

*Fiftieth Report of the President and Directors of the Central Rail Road and Banking Company
of Georgia to the Stockholders.* Savannah, Ga.: Geo. N. Nichols' Steam Presses, 1885.

*Fifty-Sixth Report of the President and Directors of the Central Rail Road and Banking
Company of Georgia, to the Stockholders.* Savannah, Ga.: Geo. N. Nichols' Steam Presses,
1891.

Gordon, John B. *Reminiscences of the Civil War.* New York: C. Scribner's Sons, 1903.

Green, Lorenzo and Woodson, Carter G. *The Negro Wage Earner.* Washington, D.C.: Association for the Study of Negro Life and History, 1930.

Hardy, Lady Duffus. *Down South.* London: Chapman and Hall, 1883.

Harley, Rev. Thomas. *Southward Ho! Notes of a Tour to and through the State of Georgia in the Winter 1885–6.* London: Chapman and Hall, 1886.

Harris, Nathaniel E. *Autobiography: The Story of an Old Man's Life with Reminiscences of Seventy-Five Years.* Macon, Ga.: J. W. Burke, 1925.

Harrison, Fairfax. *The History of the Legal Development of the Southern Railway.* Washington, D.C., 1901.

Hillyard, M. B. *The New South: A Description of the Southern States, Noting Each State Separately, and Giving Their Distinctive Features and Most Salient Characteristics.* Baltimore: Manufacturers' Record, 1887.

Illinois Central Railroad. *The Great South.* St. Louis, Mo., 1889.

Illustrated Guide Book of the Western North Carolina Railroad. Salisbury, N.C.: Passenger Department, Western North Carolina Railroad, 1882.

Ingersoll, Ernest. *To the Shenandoah and Beyond: The Chronicle of a Leisurely Journey through the Uplands of Virginia and Tennessee.* New York: Leve & Alden, 1885.

Johnson, James Weldon. *Along This Way: The Autobiography of James Weldon Johnson.* New York: Viking, 1961.

Keating, J. M. *A History of the Yellow Fever: The Yellow Fever Epidemic of 1878, in Memphis Tenn. Embracing a Complete List of the Dead, the Names of the Doctors and Nurses Employed, Names of All Who Contributed Money or Means, and the Names and History of the Howards, Together with Other Data, and Lists of the Data Elsewhere.* Memphis, Tenn.: Printed for the Howard Association, 1879.

Kelley, William D. *The Old South and the New: A Series of Letters.* New York: G. P. Putnam & Sons, 1888.

Kennaway, John H. *On Sherman's Track; or, the South after the War.* London: Seeley, Jackson and Halliday, 1867.

King, Edward. *The Great South; A Record of Journeys in Louisiana, Texas, the Indian Territory, Missouri, Arkansas, Mississippi, Alabama, Georgia, Florida, South Carolina, North Carolina, Kentucky, Tennessee, Virginia, West Virginia, and Maryland.* Hartford, Conn.: American Pub., 1875.

Lawson, W. B. *Jesse James, Rube Burrows & Co.: A Thrilling Story of Missouri.* New York: Street & Smith, 1894.

———. *The Last of the Burrows Gang; or, Joe Jackson's Last Leap.* New York: Street & Smith, 1894.

McClure, A. K. *The South: Its Industrial, Financial and Political Condition.* Philadelphia: J. B. Lippincott Company, 1886.

McCombs, W. F. *The Stone Creek Wreck: A Modern Will-O'-the-Wisp.* London: F. Tennyson Neely, 1898.

Mullen, John F. C. *The Dream of "Ellen N," an Illustrated Descriptive and Historic Narrative of Southern Travels Issued under the Auspices of the Louisville and Nashville Railroad Passenger Department.* Cincinnati: John F. C. Mullen, 1886.

Nitze, H. B. C. *Report of the Mineral Resources along the Route of the Roanoke & Southern Railroad Made by H.B.C. Nitze, E.M. of Baltimore Maryland*. Salem, Va.: Press Electric Print, 1890.

Norris, Frank. *The Octopus: A Story of California*. New York: Doubleday, 1901.

Official Catalogue of the World's Industrial and Cotton Centennial Exposition: Held under the Joint Auspices: The United States of America, the National Cotton Planters' Association, and the City of New Orleans, during the Period from the 16th of December 1884, to the 31st of May, 1885, at New Orleans, Louisiana. New Orleans: J. S. Rivers, 1885.

Our Great All Around Tour for the Winter of '84–'85: To or from Balmy Florida and the Grand Exposition at New Orleans via the Piedmont Air Line and the Atlantic Coast Line with a Trip to Fertile Texas and Picturesque Mexico. Issued by the Passenger Departments of Richmond & Danville Railroad, Piedmont Air Line and Atlantic Coast Line. New York: Levi & Alden Printing Company, 1884.

Perkins, Daniel W. *Practical Common Sense Guide Book through the World's Industrial and Cotton Centennial Exposition at New Orleans*. Harrisburg, Pa.: Lane S. Hart, 1885.

Poor, H. V. *Manual of the Railroads of the United States for 1877–1878, Showing Their Mileage, Stocks, Bonds, Cost, Traffic, Earnings, Expenses and Organizations: With a Sketch of Their Rise, Progress, Influence Etc*. New York: H. V. & H. W. Poor, 1877.

Powell, J. C. *The American Siberia or Fourteen Years' Experience in a Southern Convict Camp*. Oakland, Ca.: H. J. Smith, 1891.

Proceedings of the Annual Meeting of Stockholders of the Cape Fear and Yadkin Valley Railway Company, Fayetteville, April 5, 1883. Fayetteville, N.C.: J. E. Garrett, Book and Job Printers, 1883.

Presbrey, Frank. *The Southland, An Exposition of the Present Resources and Development of the South*. Washington, D.C.: Southern Railway Co., 1898.

Ralph, Julian. *Dixie or Southern Scenes and Sketches*. New York: Harper & Brothers, 1896.

Raymond's Vacation Excursions. *A Twenty Days' Tour through the New South, Leaving Boston Monday, December 1, 1890*. Boston: W. Raymond, 1890.

Reid, Whitelaw. *After the War: A Southern Tour; May 1, 1865 to May 1, 1866*. London: Moore, Wilstach and Baldwin, 1866.

Reports of the General Manager of the Georgia Railroad from April 1st, 1881 to June 30th 1892. Augusta, Ga.: Richards & Shaver, Printers, 1893.

Sala, George Augustus. *America Revisited: From the Bay of New York to the Gulf of Mexico and from Lake Michigan to the Pacific*. London: Vizetezzi, 1883.

State Democratic Executive Committee of North Carolina. *The Democratic Hand Book: 1898*. Raleigh, N.C.: Edwards & Broughton, 1898.

Stimson, A. L. *History of the Express Business; Including the Origin of the Railway System in America, and the Relation of Both to the Increase of New Settlements and the Prosperity of Cities in the United States*. New York: Baker and Godwin, 1881.

Stout, F. E. *Rube Burrow; or, Life, Exploits and Death of the Bold Train Robber*. Aberdeen, Miss.: Henneberry, 1890.

Trowbridge, J. T. *A Picture of the Devastated States; and the Work of Restoration: 1865–1866*. Hartford, Conn.: L. Stebbins, 1868.

Twenty-Second Annual Report of the President, Vice-President and Directors of the Mississippi and Tennessee Railroad Company to the Stockholders Embracing the Reports of the Treasurer and Superintendent for the Fiscal Year Ending September 30, 1878. Memphis, Tenn., 1878.

The Visitors Guide to the World's Exposition: Compact, Accurate, Comprehensive, December 16th, 1884 to May 31st 1885. New Orleans: Theo Pohlman, 1884.

Visitors' Guide to the World's Industrial and Cotton Centennial Exposition, and New Orleans Commencing Dec. 16, 1884, and Ending May 31, 1885. Louisville, Ky.: Courier-Journal Job Printing, 1884.

Ward, William. *Rube Burrow of Sunny Alabama: The True Story of the Prince of Train Robbers.* Cleveland, Ohio: Arthur Westbrook, 1900.

Warner, Charles Dudley. *Studies in the South and West with Comments on Canada.* New York: Harper & Brothers, 1889.

Wells, Ida B. *Crusade for Justice: The Autobiography of Ida B. Wells.* Chicago: University of Chicago Press, 1970.

The World's Exposition Catalogue and Guide, a Complete Catalogue of Exhibits & Exhibitors, an Accurate & Comprehensive Guide. New Orleans: Crescent News Company, 1885.

The World's Industrial and Cotton Centennial Exposition New Orleans: Opens Dec. 1st, 1884. Continues Six Months, Compiled by Miss Lydia Strawn. Chicago: Illinois Central Railroad, 1884.

Zacharie, James S. *New Orleans Guide: With Descriptions of the Routes to New Orleans, Sights of the City Arranged Alphabetically, and Other Information Useful to Travelers.* New Orleans: New Orleans News Co., 1885.

Secondary Sources

Adams, Sean Patrick. "Soulless Monsters and Iron Horses: The Civil War, Institutional Change, and American Capitalism." In *Capitalism Takes Command: The Social Transformation of Nineteenth-Century America,* edited by Michael Zakim and Gary Kornblith, 249–77. Chicago: University of Chicago Press, 2012.

Agnew, Jean-Christophe. *Worlds Apart: The Market and the Theater in Anglo-American Thought, 1550–1750.* Cambridge: Cambridge University Press, 1996.

Aldrich, Mark. *Death Rode the Rails: American Railroad Accidents and Safety, 1828–1965.* Baltimore: Johns Hopkins University Press, 2006.

Alvarez, Eugene. *Travel in Antebellum Southern Railroads, 1828–1860.* University: University of Alabama Press, 1974.

Appleby, Joyce. *The Relentless Revolution: A History of Capitalism.* New York: W. W. Norton, 2010.

Arnesen, Eric. *Brotherhoods of Color: Black Railroad Workers and the Struggle for Equality.* Cambridge, Mass.: Harvard University Press, 2001.

———. *Waterfront Workers of New Orleans: Race, Class, and Politics; 1863–1923.* Champaign: University of Illinois Press, 1994.

Ayers, Edward L. *The Promise of the New South: Life after Reconstruction.* New York: Oxford University Press, 1992.

————. *Vengeance and Justice: Crime and Punishment in the 19th-Century South.* New York: Oxford University Press, 1984.

Baker, Eirlys. "'A Sneaky, Cowardly Enemy': Tampa's Yellow Fever Epidemic of 1887–88." *Tampa Bay History* 8 (Fall–Winter 1985): 18.

Baptist, Edward. *The Half Has Never Been Told: Slavery and the Making of American Capitalism.* New York: Basic Books, 2014.

————. "Toxic Debt, Liar Loans, Collateralized and Securitized Human Beings, and the Panic of 1837." In *Capitalism Takes Command: The Social Transformation of Nineteenth-Century America,* edited by Michael Zakim and Gary Kornblith, 69–92. Chicago: Chicago University Press, 2012.

Barnes, L. Diane, Brian Schoen, and Frank Towers, eds. *The Old South's Modern Worlds: Slavery, Region, and Nation in the Age of Progress.* New York: Oxford University Press, 2011.

Bates, Beth Tompkins. *Pullman Porters and the Rise of Protest Politics in Black America, 1925–1945.* Chapel Hill: University of North Carolina Press, 2001.

Beckert, Sven. *Empire of Cotton: A Global History.* New York: Vintage, 2014.

————. *The Monied Metropolis: New York City and the Consolidation of the American Bourgeoisie, 1850–1896.* Cambridge: Cambridge University Press, 2001.

Beckert, Sven, and Christine Desan, eds. *American Capitalism: New Histories.* New York: Columbia University Press, 2018.

Beckert, Sven, and Seth Rockman, eds. *Slavery's Capitalism: A New History of American Economic Development.* Philadelphia: University of Pennsylvania Press, 2016.

Beeby, James A. *Revolt of the Tar Heels: The North Carolina Populist Movement, 1890–1901.* Oxford: University Press of Mississippi, 2008.

Beezley, Paul Richard. "Exhibiting Visions of a New South: Mississippi and the World's Fairs, 1884–1904." PhD diss., University of Mississippi, 1999.

Benjamin, Walter. *The Arcades Project.* Cambridge, Mass.: Belknap Press, 1999.

Berk, Gerald. *Alternative Tracks: The Constitution of American Industrial Order, 1865–1917.* Baltimore: Johns Hopkins University Press, 1994.

Berry, Steven. *All That Makes a Man: Love and Ambition in the Civil War South.* Cambridge: Oxford University Press, 2003.

————, ed. *Weirding the War: Stories from the Civil War's Ragged Edges.* Athens: University of Georgia Press, 2011.

Billings Jr., Dwight B. *Planters and the Making of a "New South": Class, Politics, and Development in North Carolina, 1865–1900.* Chapel Hill: University of North Carolina Press, 1979.

Blake, Nelson Morehouse. *William Mahone of Virginia: Soldier and Political Insurgent.* Richmond, Va.: Garrett & Massie, 1935.

Blight, David. *Race and Reunion: The Civil War in American Memory.* Cambridge, Mass.: Belknap Press, 2001.

Bloom, Khaled J. *The Mississippi Valley's Great Yellow Fever Epidemic of 1878.* Baton Rouge: Louisiana State University Press, 1993.

Blum, Edward J. *Reforging the White Republic: Race, Religion and American Nationalism, 1865–1898.* Baton Rouge: Louisiana State University Press, 2005.

Brown, Cecil Kenneth. *A State Movement in Railroad Development: North Carolina's First Effort to Establish an East and West Railroad.* Chapel Hill: University of North Carolina Press, 1928.

Bruce, Robert V. *1877: Year of Violence*. Chicago: Ivan R. Dee, 1989.

Brundage, W. Fitzhugh. *Lynching in the New South: Georgia and Virginia, 1880–1930*. Urbana: University of Illinois Press, 1993.

Bruton, Peter William. "The National Board of Health." PhD diss., University of Maryland, 1974.

Camp, Stephanie. *Closer to Freedom: Enslaved Women and Resistance in the Plantation South*. Chapel Hill: University of North Carolina Press, 2004.

Campbell, E. G. *The Reorganization of the American Railroad System, 1893–1900*. New York: Columbia University Press, 1938.

Cardon, Nathan. "The South's 'New Negroes' and African American Visions of Progress at the Atlanta and Nashville International Expositions, 1895–1897." *Journal of Southern History* 80 (May 2014): 287–326.

Carlton, David. *Mill and Town in South Carolina, 1880–1920*. Baton Rouge: Louisiana State University Press, 1982.

Carlton, David L., and Peter A. Coclanis. *The South, the Nation, and the World: Perspectives on Southern Economic Development*. Charlottesville: University of Virginia Press, 2003.

Cash, Johnny. *Johnny Cash—Ridin' the Rails: The Great American Train Story*. Directed by Nicholas Webster, DVD, 2005.

Chandler, Alfred D. *The Visible Hand: The Managerial Revolution in American Business*. Cambridge, Mass.: Belknap Press, 1977.

Churella, Albert J. *The Pennsylvania Railroad: Volume 1, Building an Empire, 1846–1917*. Philadelphia: University of Pennsylvania Press, 2013.

Clark, A. Kim. *The Redemptive Work: Railway and Nation in Ecuador, 1895–1930*. Wilmington, Del.: Rowman & Littlefield, 1998.

Clark Jr., John E. *Railroads in the Civil War: The Impact of Management on Victory and Defeat*. Baton Rouge: Louisiana State University Press, 2002.

Clark, Thomas D. *A Pioneer Southern Railroad from New Orleans to Cairo*. Chapel Hill: University of North Carolina Press, 1936.

———, ed. *Travels in the New South: A Bibliography*. Norman: University of Oklahoma Press, 1962.

Cohen, Norm. *Long Steel Rail: The Railroad in American Folksong*. Urbana: University of Illinois Press, 1981.

Cohen, William. *At Freedom's Edge: Black Mobility and the Southern White Quest for Racial Control, 1861–1915*. Baton Rouge: Louisiana State University Press, 1991.

Corliss, Carlton J. *The Main Line of Mid-America: The Story of the Illinois Central*. New York: Creative Age Press, 1950.

Cox, Karen L. *Dreaming of Dixie: How the South Was Created in American Popular Culture*. Chapel Hill: University of North Carolina Press, 2011.

Craig, Lee. *Josephus Daniels: His Life and Times*. Chapel Hill: University of North Carolina Press, 2013.

Cronon, William. *Changes in the Land: Indians, Colonists, and the Ecology of New England*. New York: Hill and Wang, 1983.

———. *Nature's Metropolis: Chicago and the Great West*. New York: W. W. Norton, 1992.

Davis, Burke. *The Southern Railway: Road of the Innovators*. Chapel Hill: University of North Carolina Press, 1985.

Davis, T. Frederick. *History of Jacksonville, Florida and Vicinity: 1513 to 1924.* Gainesville: University Press of Florida, 1964.

Decosta-Willis, Miriam, ed. *The Memphis Diary of Ida B. Wells: An Intimate Portrait of the Activist as a Young Woman.* Boston: Beacon, 1995.

Delfino, Susanna, Michele Gillespie, and Louis M. Kyriakoudes, eds. *Southern Society and Its Transformations, 1790–1860.* Columbia: University of Missouri Press, 2011.

Dinerstein, Joel. *Swinging the Machine: Modernity, Technology and African American Culture between the World Wars.* Amherst: University of Massachusetts Press, 2003.

Doster, James F. *Railroads in Alabama Politics, 1875–1914.* Tuscaloosa: University of Alabama Press, 1957.

Downey, Tom. *Planting a Capitalist South: Masters, Merchants, and Manufacturers in the Southern Interior, 1790–1860.* Baton Rouge: Louisiana State University Press, 2006.

Downs, Gregory P. *After Appomattox: Military Occupation and the Ends of War.* Cambridge, Mass.: Harvard University Press, 2015.

Downs, Jim. *Sick from Freedom: African-American Illness and Suffering during the Civil War and Reconstruction.* New York: Oxford University Press, 2012.

Du Bois, W. E. B. *Darkwater: Voices from within the Veil.* New York: Dover Publications, 2003.

Duffy, John. *Sword of Pestilence: The New Orleans Yellow Fever Epidemic of 1853.* Baton Rouge: Louisiana State University Press, 1966.

Earle, Steve, and the Del McCoury Band. "Texas Eagle." *The Mountain.* E-Squared, 1999.

Eckert, Ralph Lowell. *John Brown Gordon: Soldier, Southerner, American.* Baton Rouge: Louisiana State University Press, 1989.

Ellis, John H. *Yellow Fever and Public Health in the South.* Lexington: University Press of Kentucky, 1992.

Espinosa, Mariola. *Epidemic Invasions: Yellow Fever and the Limits of Cuban Independence.* Chicago: University of Chicago Press, 2009.

Faust, Drew Gilpin. *This Republic of Suffering: Death and the American Civil War.* New York: Vintage, 2008.

Fenn, Elizabeth A. *Pox Americana: The Great Smallpox Epidemic of 1775–82.* New York: Hill and Wang, 2001.

Ferguson, Charles. *The Inside Job.* DVD. Directed by Charles Ferguson, Sony Pictures, 2010.

Filene, Benjamin. *Romancing the Folk: Public Memory and American Roots Music.* Chapel Hill: University of North Carolina Press, 2000.

Fogel, Robert William. *Railroads and American Economic Growth: Essays in Econometric History.* Baltimore: Johns Hopkins University Press, 1964.

Ford Jr., Lacy K. *Origins of Southern Radicalism: The South Carolina Upcountry 1800–1860.* New York: Oxford University Press, 1988.

Foster, Gaines M. *Ghosts of the Confederacy: Defeat, the Lost Cause, and the Emergence of the New South, 1865 to 1913.* New York: Oxford University Press, 1987.

Freedman, Alisa. *Tokyo in Transit: Japanese Culture on the Rails and Road.* Stanford, Calif.: Stanford University Press, 2011.

Gallamore, Robert, and John R. Meyer. *American Railroads: Decline and Renaissance in the Twentieth Century.* Cambridge, Mass.: Harvard University Press, 2015.

Gaston, Paul. *The New South Creed: A Study in Southern Mythmaking*. Baton Rouge: Louisiana State University Press, 1970.

Gates, Paul Wallace. *The Illinois Central Railroad and Its Colonization Work*. Cambridge, Mass.: Harvard University Press, 1934.

Giggie, John M. *After Redemption: Jim Crow and the Transformation of African-American Religion in the Delta*. New York: Oxford University Press, 2008.

Gilmore, Glenda. *Gender and Jim Crow: Women and the Politics of White Supremacy in North Carolina, 1896–1920*. Chapel Hill: University of North Carolina Press, 1996.

Goodwyn, Lawrence. *The Populist Moment: A Short History of the Agrarian Revolt in America*. New York: Oxford University Press, 1978.

Grant, H. Roger. *Rails through the Wiregrass: A History of the Georgia & Florida Railroad*. DeKalb: Northern Illinois University Press, 2006.

Hahn, Steven. *A Nation under Our Feet: Black Political Struggles in the Rural South from Slavery to the Great Migration*. Cambridge, Mass.: Belknap Press, 2003.

———. *The Roots of Southern Populism: Yeoman Farmers and the Transformation of the Georgia Upcountry, 1850–1890*. New York: Oxford University Press, 1983.

Hale, Grace Elizabeth. *Making Whiteness: The Culture of Segregation in the South, 1890–1940*. New York: Vintage, 1998.

Hall, Jacquelyn Dowd. *Like a Family: The Making of a Southern Cotton Mill World*. Chapel Hill: University of North Carolina Press, 1987.

Hamilton, Shane. *Trucking Country: The Road to America's Wal-Mart Economy*. Princeton, N.J.: Princeton University Press, 2008.

Harvey, Donald Clive. "The World's Industrial and Cotton Centennial Exposition." Master's thesis, Tulane University, 1964.

Haskell, Thomas, and Richard F. Teichgraeber III, eds. *The Culture of the Market: Historical Essays*. Cambridge: Cambridge University Press, 1993.

Headrick, Daniel. *Tools of Empire: Technology and European Imperialism in the Nineteenth Century*. New York: Oxford University Press, 1981.

Hildreth, Charles. "Railroads out of Pensacola, 1833–1883." *Florida Historical Quarterly* 37, nos. 3–4 (January–April 1959): 397–417.

Hobsbawm, Eric. *Bandits*. New York: Delacorte Press, 1969.

———. *Primitive Rebels: Studies in Archaic Forms of Social Movement in the 19th and 20th Centuries*. New York: W. W. Norton, 1959.

Huffard Jr., R. Scott. "Ghosts, Wreckers and Rotten Ties: The 1891 Train Wreck at Bostian's Bridge." *Southern Cultures* 20 (Summer 2014): 25–39.

———. "Infected Rails: Yellow Fever and Southern Railroads." *Journal of Southern History* 79, no. 1 (February 2013): 79–112.

Humphreys, Margaret. *Yellow Fever and the South*. Baltimore: Johns Hopkins University Press, 1992.

Inscoe, John C. *Writing through the Self: Explorations in Southern Autobiography*. Athens: University of Georgia Press, 2011.

Johnson, Walter. *River of Dark Dreams: Slavery and Empire in the Cotton Kingdom*. Cambridge, Mass.: Belknap Press, 2013.

———. *Soul by Soul: Life inside the Antebellum Slave Market*. Cambridge, Mass.: Harvard University Press, 1999.

Jones, Loval. *Minstrel of the Appalachians: The Story of Bascom Lamar Lunsford*. Lexington: University Press of Kentucky, 1985.

Jones, William P. *The Tribe of Black Ulysses: African American Lumber Workers in the Jim Crow South*. Urbana: University of Illinois Press, 2005.

Kantrowitz, Steven. *Ben Tillman and the Reconstruction of White Supremacy*. Chapel Hill: University of North Carolina Press, 2000.

Kelley, Blair L. M. *Right to Ride: Streetcar Boycotts and African American Citizenship in the Era of Plessy V. Ferguson*. Chapel Hill: University of North Carolina Press, 2010.

Kelman, Ari. *A River and Its City: The Nature of Landscape in New Orleans*. Berkeley: University of California Press, 2006.

Kirby, Jack Temple. *Mockingbird Song: Ecological Landscapes of the South*. Chapel Hill: University of North Carolina Press, 2006.

Klein, Maury. "Competition and Regulation: The Railroad Model." *Business History Review* 64 (Summer 1990): 311–25.

———. *The Great Richmond Terminal: A Study in Businessmen and Business Strategy*. Charlottesville: University Press of Virginia, 1970.

———. *History of the Louisville & Nashville Railroad*. New York: Macmillan, 1972.

Kornweibel, Theodore. *Railroads in the African American Experience: A Photographic Journey*. Baltimore: Johns Hopkins University Press, 2010.

Kvach, John. *DeBow's Review: The Antebellum Vision of a New South*. Lexington: University Press of Kentucky, 2013.

Lears, Jackson. *Rebirth of a Nation: The Making of Modern America, 1877–1920*. New York: Harper, 2009.

LeFlouria, Talitha L. *Chained in Silence: Black Women and Convict Labor in the New South*. Chapel Hill: University of North Carolina Press, 2015.

Letwin, Daniel. *The Challenge of Interracial Unionism: Alabama Coal Miners, 1878–1921*. Chapel Hill: University of North Carolina Press, 1998.

Levy, Jonathan. *Freaks of Fortune: The Emerging World of Capitalism and Risk in America*. Cambridge, Mass.: Harvard University Press, 2012.

Lichtenstein, Alex. *Twice the Work of Free Labor: The Political Economy of Convict Labor in the New South*. New York: Verso, 1996.

Linebaugh, Peter, and Marcus Rediker. *The Many-Headed Hydra: Sailors, Slaves, Commoners, and the Hidden History of the Revolutionary Atlantic*. Boston: Beacon, 2000.

Link, William A. *Atlanta: Cradle of the New South; Race and Remembering in the Civil War's Aftermath*. Chapel Hill: University of North Carolina Press, 2013.

———. *Roots of Secession: Slavery and Politics in Antebellum Virginia*. Chapel Hill: University of North Carolina Press, 1999.

Lyle, Katie Letcher. *Scalded to Death by the Steam: The True Stories of Railroad Disasters and the Songs That Were Written about Them*. Chapel Hill: Algonquin Books, 1991.

Majewski, John. *A House Dividing: Economic Development in Pennsylvania and Virginia before the Civil War*. Cambridge: Cambridge University Press, 2000.

———. *Modernizing a Slave Economy: The Economic Vision of the Confederate Nation*. Chapel Hill: University of North Carolina Press, 2009.

Marler, Scott P. *The Merchants' Capital: New Orleans and the Political Economy of the Nineteenth-Century South*. Cambridge: Cambridge University Press, 2013.

Marrs, Aaron. *Railroads in the Old South: Pursuing Progress in a Slave Society*. Baltimore: Johns Hopkins University Press, 2009.

Martin, Albro. *Railroads Triumphant: The Growth Rejection and Rebirth of a Vital American Force*. New York: Oxford University Press, 1992.

Marx, Karl. *Capital: Volume 1: A Critique of Political Economy*. Translated by Ben Fowkes. New York: Penguin Classics, 1990.

Marx, Leo. *The Machine in the Garden: Technology and the Pastoral Ideal in America*. New York: Oxford University Press, 1964.

Massey, Larry L. *The Life and Crimes of Railroad Bill, Legendary African American Desperado*. Gainesville: University Press of Florida, 2015.

Matthews, Burgin. "'Looking for Railroad Bill': On the Trail of an Alabama Badman." *Southern Cultures* 9 (Fall 2003): 66–88.

Matthews, Michael. *The Civilizing Machine: A Cultural History of Mexican Railroads*. Lincoln: University of Nebraska Press, 2014.

McKinney, Gordon B. "Zeb Vance and the Construction of the Western North Carolina Railroad." *Appalachian Journal* 29 (2001): 58–67.

McLaurin, Melton. *The Knights of Labor in the South*. Westport, Conn.: Praeger, 1978.

McNally, David. *Monsters of the Market: Zombies, Vampires, and Global Capitalism*. Chicago: Haymarket, 2011.

McNeill, J. R. *Mosquito Empires: Ecology and War in the Greater Caribbean, 1620–1914*. Cambridge: Cambridge University Press, 2010.

Millichap, Joseph R. *Dixie Limited: Railroads, Culture, and the Southern Renaissance*. Lexington: University Press of Kentucky, 2002.

Mitchell, Broadus. *The Rise of Cotton Mills in the South, with a New Introduction by David L. Carlton*. Columbia: University of South Carolina Press, 2001.

Moreton, Bethany. *To Serve God and Wal-Mart: The Making of Christian Free Enterprise*. Cambridge, Mass.: Harvard University Press, 2009.

Nash, Roderick Frazier. *Wilderness and the American Mind*, 4th ed. New Haven, Conn.: Yale University Press, 2001.

Nelson, Megan Kate. *Ruin Nation: Destruction and the American Civil War*. Athens: University of Georgia Press, 2012.

Nelson, Scott Reynolds. *Iron Confederacies: Southern Railways, Klan Violence, and Reconstruction*. Chapel Hill: University of North Carolina Press, 1999.

———. *A Nation of Deadbeats: An Uncommon History of America's Financial Disasters*. New York: Knopf, 2012.

———. *Steel Drivin' Man: The Untold Story of an American Legend*. New York: Oxford University Press, 2006.

Nixon, Raymond B. *Henry Grady: Spokesman of the New South*. New York: Knopf, 1943.

Noe, Kenneth W. *Southwest Virginia's Railroad: Modernization and the Sectional Crisis*. Urbana: University of Illinois Press, 1994.

Nuwer, Deanne Stephens. *Plague among the Magnolias: The 1878 Yellow Fever Epidemic in Mississippi*. Tuscaloosa: University of Alabama Press, 2009.

O'Donovan, Susan Eva. *Becoming Free in the Cotton South*. Cambridge, Mass.: Harvard University Press, 2007.

Odum, Howard W. "Folk-Song and Folk-Poetry as Found in the Secular Songs of the Southern Negroes." *Journal of American Folklore* 24 (July–Sept 1911): 289–93.

———. *The Negro and His Songs: A Study of Typical Negro Songs in the South.* Chapel Hill: University of North Carolina Press, 1925.

———. *Negro Workaday Songs.* Chapel Hill: University of North Carolina Press, 1926.

———. *Rainbow Round My Shoulder: The Blue Trail of Black Ulysses.* Bloomington: Indiana University Press, 1972.

Oldfield, John. "State Politics, Railroads, and Civil Rights in South Carolina, 1883–89." *American Nineteenth Century History* 5 (Summer 2004): 71–91.

Orsi, Richard J. *Sunset Limited: The Southern Pacific Railroad and the Development of the American West, 1850–1930.* Berkeley: University of California Press, 2007.

Ortiz, Paul. *Emancipation Betrayed: The Hidden History of Black Organizing and White Violence in Florida from Reconstruction to the Bloody Election of 1920.* Berkeley: University of California Press, 2005.

Osnos, Evan. "Letter from China, Boss Rail: The Disaster That Exposed the Underside of the Boom." *New Yorker,* October 22, 2012.

Osterhammel, Jürgen. *The Transformation of the World: A Global History of the Nineteenth Century.* Princeton, N.J.: Princeton University Press, 2014.

Outland, Robert B. *Tapping the Pines: The Naval Stores Industry in the American South.* Baton Rouge: Louisiana State University Press, 2004.

Overton, Richard C. *Burlington Route: A History of the Burlington Lines.* New York: Knopf, 1965.

Payne, Matthew J. *Stalin's Railroad: Turksib and the Building of Socialism.* Pittsburgh: University of Pittsburgh Press, 2001.

Penick, James. "Railroad Bill." *Gulf Coast Historical Review* 10 (Fall 1994): 85–92.

Piketty, Thomas. *Capital in the Twenty-First Century.* Cambridge, Mass.: Harvard University Press, 2014.

Polenberg, Richard. *Hear My Sad Story: The True Tales That Inspired "Stagolee," "John Henry," and Other Traditional American Folk Songs.* Ithaca, N.Y.: Cornell University Press, 2015.

Postel, Charles. *The Populist Vision.* New York: Oxford University Press, 2007.

Prince, K. Stephen. *Stories of the South: Race and the Reconstruction of Southern Identity.* Chapel Hill: University of North Carolina Press, 2014.

Pryor, Elizabeth Stordeur. *Colored Travelers: Mobility and the Fight for Citizenship before the Civil War.* Chapel Hill: University of North Carolina Press, 2016.

Puffert, Douglas J. *Tracks across Continents, Paths through History: The Economic Dynamics of Standardization in Railway Gauge.* Chicago: University of Chicago Press, 2009.

Randall, Adrian. *Before the Luddites: Custom, Community and Machinery in the English Woolen Industry, 1776–1809.* Cambridge: Cambridge University Press, 1991.

Rabinowitz, Howard N. *Race Relations in the Urban South, 1865–1900.* New York: Oxford University Press, 1978.

Reddy, William M. *The Rise of Market Culture: The Textile Trade and French Society, 1750–1900.* Cambridge: Cambridge University Press, 1984.

R.E.M. "Driver 8." *Fables of the Reconstruction.* I.R.S. Records/Capital, 1985.

Richards, Thomas. *The Commodity Culture of Victorian England: Advertising and Spectacle, 1851–1914*. Stanford, Calif.: Stanford University Press, 1990.

Richter, Amy G. *Home on the Rails: Women, the Railroad and the Rise of Public Domesticity*. Chapel Hill: University of North Carolina Press, 2005.

Rogers Jr., William Warren. "Rube Burrow, 'King of Outlaws,' and His Florida Adventures." *Florida Historical Quarterly* 59 (October 1980): 182–98.

———. "Violence and Outlawry in the New South: Rube Burrow's Train Robbing Days in Alabama, Mississippi, and Florida." MA Thesis, Auburn University, 1979.

Rosenberg, Charles E. *The Cholera Years: The United States in 1832, 1849, and 1866*. Chicago: University of Chicago Press, 1962.

Rothman, Joshua. *Flush Times and Fever Dreams: A Story of Capitalism and Slavery in the Age of Jackson*. Athens: University Press of Georgia, 2012.

Rydell, Robert W. *All the World's a Fair: Visions of Empire at American International Expositions, 1876–1916*. Chicago: University of Chicago Press, 1984.

Saler, Michael. "Modernity and Enchantment: A Historiographic Review." *American Historical Review* 111 (June 2006): 692–716.

Schivelbusch, Wolfgang. *The Culture of Defeat: On National Trauma, Mourning, and Recovery*. New York: Metropolitan, 2001.

———. *The Railway Journey: Trains and Travel in the 19th Century*. New York: Urizen Books, 1979.

Scranton, Phillip, and Patrick Fridenson. *Reimagining Business History*. Baltimore: Johns Hopkins University Press, 2013.

Shapiro, Karin A. *New South Rebellion: The Battle against Convict Labor in the Tennessee Coalfields, 1871–1896*. Chapel Hill: University of North Carolina Press, 1998.

Shaw, Barton C. *The Wool-Hat Boys: Georgia's Populist Party*. Baton Rouge: Louisiana State University Press, 1984.

Smith, Mark M. *Mastered by the Clock: Time, Slavery, and Freedom in the American South*. Chapel Hill: University of North Carolina Press, 1997.

Stiles, T. J. *Jesse James: Last Rebel of the Civil War*. New York: Vintage, 2002.

Stilgoe, John R. *Metropolitan Corridors: Railroads and the American Scene*. New Haven, Conn.: Yale University Press, 1983.

———. *Train Time: Railroads and the Imminent Reshaping of the United States Landscape*. Charlottesville: University of Virginia Press, 2007.

Stover, John F. *The Railroads of the South, 1865–1900: A Study in Finance and Control*. Chapel Hill: University of North Carolina Press, 1955.

Stowell, David Omar. *Streets, Railroads, and the Great Strike of 1877*. Chicago: University of Chicago Press, 1999.

Summers, Mark W. "Iron Confederacies: Southern Railways, Klan Violence, and Reconstruction." *Journal of Southern History* 66 (November 2000): 891–92.

———. *Railroads, Reconstruction, and the Gospel of Prosperity: Aid under the Radical Republicans, 1865–1877*. Princeton, N.J.: Princeton University Press, 1984.

Thomas, William G. *The Iron Way: Railroads, the Civil War, and the Making of Modern America*. New Haven, Conn.: Yale University Press, 2011.

———. *Lawyering for the Railroad: Business, Law and Power in the New South*. Baton Rouge: Louisiana State University Press, 1999.

————. "'Swerve Me?': The South, Railroads, and the Rush to Modernity." In *The Old South's Modern Worlds: Slavery, Region, and Nation in the Age of Progress*, edited by L. Diane Barnes, Brian Schoen, and Frank Towers, 166–88. New York: Oxford University Press, 2011.

Toews, John E., ed. *The Communist Manifesto by Karl Marx and Frederick Engels with Related Documents*. New York: Bedford/St. Martin's, 1999.

Trelease, Allen W. *The North Carolina Railroad, 1849–1871, and the Modernization of North Carolina*. Chapel Hill: University of North Carolina Press, 1991.

Turner III, Frederick William. "Badmen, Black and White: The Continuity of American Folk Traditions." PhD diss., University of Pennsylvania, 1965.

Turner, Gregg M. *A Journey into Florida Railroad History*. Gainesville: University Press of Florida, 2008.

Tye, Larry. *Rising from the Rails: Pullman Porters and the Making of the Black Middle Class*. New York: Macmillan, 2004.

Usselman, Steven W. *Regulating Railroad Innovation: Business, Technology, and Politics in America, 1840–1920*. Cambridge: Cambridge University Press, 2002.

Weber, Eugen. *Peasants into Frenchmen: The Modernization of Rural France, 1870–1914*. Stanford, Calif.: Stanford University Press, 1976.

Weiner, Jonathan M. *Social Origins of the New South: Alabama, 1860–1885*. Baton Rouge: Louisiana State University, 1978.

Welch, Gillian. "Down along the Dixie Line." *The Harrow & the Harvest*. CD, Acony. 2011.

Welkie, Barbara Young. *Recasting American Liberty: Gender, Race, Law, and the Railroad Revolution, 1865–1920*. Cambridge: Cambridge University Press, 2001.

White, Richard. *Railroaded: The Transcontinentals and the Making of Modern America*. New York: W. W. Norton, 2011.

————. "Utopian Capitalism." In *American Capitalism: New Histories*, edited by Sven Beckert and Christine Desan, 119–39. New York: Columbia University Press, 2018.

Wiebe, Robert. *Search for Order, 1877–1920*. New York: Hill and Wang, 1966.

Williams, Rosalind. *Dream Worlds: Mass Consumption in Late Nineteenth-Century France*. Berkeley: University of California Press, 1982.

Williamson, Edward C. *Florida Politics in the Gilded Age, 1877–1893*. Gainesville: University Press of Florida, 1976.

Willis, John C. *Forgotten Time: The Yazoo-Mississippi Delta after the Civil War*. Charlottesville: University Press of Virginia, 2000.

Wolmar, Christian. *Blood, Iron, and Gold: How the Railroads Transformed the World*. New York: Atlantic Books, 2010.

Wood, Amy Louise. *Lynching and Spectacle: Witnessing Racial Violence in America, 1890–1940*. Chapel Hill: University of North Carolina Press, 2009.

Woodman, Harold. *King Cotton and His Retainers: Financing and Marketing the Cotton Crop of the South, 1800–1925*. Columbia: University of South Carolina Press, 1990.

Woodward, C. Vann. *Origins of the New South, 1877–1913*. Baton Rouge: Louisiana State University Press, 1951.

————. *The Strange Career of Jim Crow*. Oxford: Oxford University Press, 1974.

————. *Tom Watson: Agrarian Rebel*. New York: Oxford University Press, 1963.

Wright, Gavin. *Old South, New South: Revolutions in the Southern Economy since the Civil War*. New York: Basic Books, 1986.

Zakim, Michael. "Importing the Crystal Palace." In *American Capitalism: New Histories*, edited by Sven Beckert and Christine Desan, 337–60. New York: Columbia University Press, 2018.

Zakim, Michael, and Gary Kornblith, eds. *Capitalism Takes Command: The Social Transformation of Nineteenth-Century America*. Chicago: Chicago University Press, 2012.

Zoellner, Tom. *Train: Riding the Rails That Created the Modern World*. New York: Penguin Books, 2014.

Index

Made in the USA
Middletown, DE
21 March 2020

86998981R00194